# PULITZER'S SCHOOL

# PULITZER'S SCHOOL

Columbia University's School of Journalism, 1903–2003

JAMES BOYLAN

*Columbia University Press*
*New York*

Columbia University Press
*Publishers Since 1893*
New York    Chichester, West Sussex

Copyright © 2003 James Boylan
Library of Congress Cataloging-in-Publication Data
Boylan, James R.
Pulitzer's School : Columbia University's School of Journalism,
1903–2003 / James Boylan.
p.    cm.
Includes bibliographical references and index.
ISBN 0–231–13090–2 (cloth)
1. Columbia University. Graduate School of Journalism—History.
I. Title.
PN4791.C7B69    2003
070.4'071'17471—dc21
2003043479

Columbia University Press books are printed on permanent
and durable acid-free paper.
Printed in the United States of America
c 10 9 8 7 6 5 4 3 2 1

# CONTENTS

## PREFACE

IN 1954, my teacher, colleague, and friend Richard Terrill Baker completed a history of Columbia University's Graduate School of Journalism that was published as part of a series commissioned for the university's bicentennial—the only history of the school before this one. Baker's narrative passed deftly and swiftly (in only 129 pages) through the incubation and first four decades of the life of the Pulitzer School. His account was polished and politic, omitting many rough spots. Moreover, he covered only half of a history that has now stretched to a century. Nor of course did he cover the rest of his own career at the school, during which he served as acting dean and as administrator of the Pulitzer Prizes.[1]

In 1997, the school's dean, Tom Goldstein, asked me to write a new history. I was to be compensated with a fixed sum, and earnings from the book, if any, were to go to the school.

Dean Goldstein offered me the freedom to present my findings as an independent historian. Of course, being independent did not mean being detached or unopinionated. I had worked at the school for twenty-two years (1957–1979), witnessed some of what I describe, and knew—and still know—

many who are part of the narrative. I also bore the burden of believing that I remembered firsthand some portions of what I was to write about. But as one historian has remarked: "Memory scoffs at chronology; our memories mix like pennies in a jar." So I have tried to discipline memory by drawing on contemporary sources—school and university records, documents that I have saved or acquired, and, where necessary, parts of my own journal that help establish detail, date, or sequence.[2]

I have tried to frame a central narrative of the school's life—occurrences, circumstances, and conflicts within what often seemed a suffocatingly small community that changed or affirmed its character. Larger issues have been at stake as well, not least of them the survival of Pulitzer's vision—and I have tried to illuminate them.

The result is neither commemorative nor encyclopedic, and will surely disappoint those looking for courtesy listings in the index. I suspect, moreover, that nearly every reader familiar with the school and its occupants will quarrel with at least parts of it. Inevitably, some details will be wrong, and I take responsibility for them, and for the more general conclusions drawn.

Besides those listed in the essay on sources, I offer my gratitude, for assistance and encouragement, to those who were my classmates, students, and colleagues in my years at the school. More specifically, I thank Jonnet Abeles, Marvin Barrett, Jonathan Beard, Katherine Beeby, Andrew Cooper, Gloria Cooper, Susan Currell, W. Phillips Davison, John Henry, Penn Kimball (for reading the entire manuscript), Spencer Klaw, Kathleen S. Lundeen, Kent MacDougall, Mel Mencher, Cormac O'Malley, Lawrence Pinkham, Jackson Rodgers and Condon Rodgers, Bernard Roshco, and Jon Swan. Thanks also to William B. Strachan, president and director of Columbia University Press during the book's gestation, and the two perceptive, anonymous reviewers he enlisted. For their valuable aid along the road to publication, I thank Suzanne Ryan, John Michel, William Meyers, and Leslie Kriesel. Most of all, I thank Betsy Wade, fellow graduate, editor, adviser, and spouse.

*James Boylan*
*June 2003*

# PULITZER'S SCHOOL

## INTRODUCTION

A HUNDRED YEARS AGO, a successful, neurasthenic newspaper publisher, Joseph Pulitzer, and an autocratic Ivy League president, Nicholas Murray Butler, signed what amounted to a treaty between two contentious parties: in return for a contribution of two million dollars, Columbia University in the City of New York consented to permit the teaching of journalism on its premises.

On both sides, it was a unique and daring bargain. Until that time, instruction in journalism had been confined largely to bucolic state universities, often as a vocational elective offered by English departments; no elite university had dared to teach journalism as a discipline. Nor had any publisher braved the ridicule he might attract by urging the removal of the journalist's apprenticeship from newspaper offices to an effete academic setting.

Even after the agreement was made, Pulitzer was so hesitant about his commitment that only his death, eight years later, permitted Columbia to carry out its side of the bargain. He had good reason to hesitate. The years since have been a continual test of Pulitzer's faith that a university education could help create journalists of skill, intellect, and public-spiritedness—and of Butler's hope that a school of journalism would do Columbia more good than harm.

The fledgling institution at first was referred to as the "Pulitzer school." But that usage faded, and Columbia resisted suggestions that either the school or its building be officially named for the donor. Moreover, Pulitzer's gift, so large for its time, was attenuated by the university's investment policies and came to represent only a fraction of the support required to keep the school running. So it gradually became known as the Columbia School of Journalism and, ultimately, the Columbia University Graduate School of Journalism. Pulitzer's name lives on primarily in the prizes in journalism, arts, and letters that he endowed simultaneously with the school. To many the school is known, if at all, only as the place where the Pulitzer Prizes are distributed.

Yet the school has been a visible presence in the world's most visible journalism community. It has been seen as a metaphor—or an epithet—for journalism education. It has been honored as the bearer of the gold standard in its field and condemned as a sham; it has been valued as an incubator of journalists who have risen to the top of their profession, and discounted as a holding tank for the mediocre. It has been seen as a standard setter and ethicist-in-chief; it has been condemned as a citadel of the establishment. Whatever the truth of these evaluations—and all have probably been true at one time or another—the debate over its merits and shortcomings has been strong, sometimes vehement, even into the twenty-first century. As the school has pushed along through the decades, something important has always seemed, at least, to be at stake—and always in doubt.

More than sentiment is involved in returning to the beginning and again calling it "Pulitzer's school." His fierce assertion that journalists must be not merely operatives but practitioners in the public interest provides an initial standard for measuring not only the school but the journalism into which it has sent its graduates.

CHAPTER 1

# "I Have Selected Columbia"

THE COLUMBIA UNIVERSITY School of Journalism was conceived at Chat-wold, a sizable "cottage" at Bar Harbor, Maine, in August 1902. The idea em-anated from the indefatigable mind of Joseph Pulitzer, who was momentarily at rest on the Maine coast. He was fifty-five years old, but had been leading the life of an ancient but wealthy wanderer since the failure of his sight twelve years before. Tormented by noise, even the sounds of eating, he traveled compulsively along a circuit from Manhattan to the Georgia Sea Islands to Europe to Maine in search of quiet and health. Even so, he remained intent on supervising and bedeviling his newspapers—the *World*, which he had made New York's most important daily; the *Evening World*, its sometimes roguish sibling; and his first major property, the *St. Louis Post-Dispatch*. Through a cadre of male secretaries, he unremittingly drove their editors and managers by telegram and letter and summons.[1]

But in 1902, he seemed also to be searching for a legacy, and for respect. The Spanish-American War of 1898, with its morally reckless yellow jour-nalism, had darkened the reputation of the *World*, which had thrown itself into frenzied competition with William Randolph Hearst's *Journal*. Pulitzer suffered the ignominy of having his own name twinned with that of Hearst, whom he regarded as frivolous and unscrupulous. Although Pulitzer had never avoided vigorous sensationalism—and indeed was an apologist for it, arguing that scandal and sentimentality were necessary to attract readers to serious matters—he had been appalled by the excesses of wartime journalism: immense headlines, frantic replating of editions, and extravagant expenditures, which, for the first time since he acquired the *World* in 1883, had forced him to dip into capital. Four years later, he had long since recovered his financial losses, but inevitably considered his personal reputation clouded.[2]

In what he called "a rough memorandum," Pulitzer sought to associate his name with something better:

> Here is the germ of an idea which requires careful formulation to become useful, effective and legally binding. It is dictated roughly without having been previously discussed with anybody.
>
> I mean to enlarge the provision already made for a Chair to a School or Department of Journalism in Columbia College.
>
> My idea is to recognize that journalism is, or ought to be, one of the great and intellectual professions; to encourage, elevate and educate in a practical way the present and, still more, future members of that profession, exactly as if it were the profession of law or medicine. . . .
>
> To differentiate between Journalism as an intellectual profession and as a business must be a fundamental object.
>
> My point of view is that a great newspaper must be a public institution for the public good, although incidentally and inevitably it cannot help also being a business. But so is the Church, so are Statesmanship, Art and Literature—the element of business is involved in them all. . . .
>
> I have selected Columbia because it is located in New York, because it is centrally located and accessible to all students, journalists, reporters, lecturers, and the leading editors. . . .
>
> Why not teach in it things which every right minded journalist must aspire to know, an easy opportunity of acquiring which would raise professional tone and pride? Why not teach, for instance, politics, literature, government, constitutional principles and traditions (especially American), history, political economy; also the history and the power of public opinion and public service, illustrated by concrete examples, showing the mission, duty and opportunity of the Press as a moral teacher?

Besides this, teach if possible the practical side—news gathering, news editing, news writing, style, composition, accuracy, everything, even to the makeup of a newspaper. It all could be taught.

Incidentally, I strongly wish the College to pay from the large income I am providing a sum of _____ [left blank] in annual prizes to particular journalists or writers for various accomplishments, achievements and forms of excellence. . . .

While I am primarily anxious to do something for the profession, I cannot help thinking that there is no profession in which every student of the United States is more directly interested, or which represents for good or for evil the moral force and the moral sense of the nation.

Although later versions were more polished, these thoughts contained the essentials—a school of journalism, based at Columbia, and an annual array of awards for journalists.

But the rest of the memorandum, addressed to his lawyers, was interlaced with doubts and challenges. Where could the school go if Columbia refused? Would not the school need an "Advisory Board" to supply the professional expertise lacking in Columbia's faculty? Would Columbia cede him the authority to pick the board's members? How could the board be assured adequate powers? Should the school be set up as a separate corporation? Should the money be held by an outside entity? Was the gift he had in mind too large? Would not its recipient suffer a "temptation to divert it"?[3]

These were not idle questions. Their resolution kept the plan from being realized for a decade, and until Pulitzer was no longer present to indulge his doubts. Yet it is possible to look back and see that the plan that Pulitzer sketched was ultimately carried out largely as he envisioned it.

CHAPTER 2

# Schools for Journalists?

THE IDEA OF a college course, or a professorship, or a school of journalism—as opposed to the specific idea of a Columbia University School of Journalism—hardly originated with Pulitzer. It had been lingering around the edges of the journalistic workplace for much of the nineteenth century, closely linked to the notion that journalism was, or ought to be, or might become a profession, however that term might be understood.

Once city newspapers began to add reporters to their staffs in the 1840s, proprietors maintained an oversupply of cheap and dispensable help—not usually, as legend has it, working-class stalwarts who made their way up from the printer's case, but more often castoffs from more respectable callings who, as Henry Adams remarked, were "fit for nothing else." One critic of the 1860s sniffed that "the New York reporter is understood to be a person who never writes English, who never ceases to carry the odor of bad liquor, and is never known to have a clean shirt."[1]

Paradoxically, the very proprietors who saw to it that journalists remained grubby became those who called most loudly for respectability. As early as 1842, the *United States Magazine and Democratic Review* declared that journalism was "a distinct and lofty profession"—a foreshadowing of Pulitzer's words sixty years later. In the 1870s, Whitelaw Reid, successor to Horace Greeley at the *New York Tribune*, declared: "Our greatest newspapers are carried on rigorously upon the idea that journalism is a profession." James Parton, the leading commentator on the journalism of that era, saw such declarations as self-serving. Of American newspapers, he wrote: "The nauseating trail of fifteen dollars a week is seen all over them." Only the *Times* of London, he asserted, treated its staff "with justice and consideration." He concluded that if journalism was a profession, it was a profession only in proprietors' self-deluding dreams.[2]

It occurred to Reid and others that the route to professionalism lay through the campus—either by attracting the college-educated to journalism or by making the college the site of professional preparation. As early as 1872, Reid set forth specifications for a "School of Journalism, to be appended to the regular college course, as one of the additional features of university instruction, like the School of Mines, or Medicine, or Law." Specifically, he wanted a school for editors, who would be trained in history, law, economics, logic, the arts, science, literature, and modern languages, including proper English. This formulation—that a school of journalism should offer not only writing and editing skills but an acquaintance with the full range of public concerns—eventually engaged Pulitzer as well.[3]

Reid added, correctly: "No separate school is likely now, or soon, to be founded for such a course." But the very notion set off an energetic debate. Much of the discussion centered on a diversionary issue: Could journalism be taught at all—or, rather, could it be taught by any means but by working at a newspaper? Frederic Hudson, historian and former managing editor of the *New York Herald*, had no doubt: "The only place where one can learn to be a journalist is in a great newspaper office." Horace White of the *Chicago Tribune* conceded flippantly that a school of journalism was possible, "just as a swimming school is possible." A similar comment appeared in Pulitzer's *Post-Dispatch*, to the effect that a professorship of journalism was like "a professorship of matrimony, it being one of those things of which nothing can be learned by those who have never tried it."[4]

David G. Croly, an editor on the *New York Graphic*, raised a second issue—that the schools would be too precious for practical journalism: "The danger . . . will be in putting them in charge of broken-down parsons, or 'brilliant' newspaper leader-writers—persons whose heads are filled with all sorts of high notions and fine spun theories which would shiver like glass at the first rude contact with the realities of competitive journalism." However,

Croly's spouse, Jennie C. Croly, also a journalist (she wrote under the name of "Jennie June"), liked the idea of a school because she thought it would help women, who were then and for years to come excluded from newsroom apprenticeships. Both Crolys proved correct to a degree.[5]

The underlying question was less whether journalism could be taught—clearly, it could be taught in one fashion or another—than whether journalism should join the march toward respectability of other emerging professions, such as teaching, by finding a place in the university. That place gradually and sporadically began to open up in the last two decades of the nineteenth century. The college-educated, and now not always the failures, turned increasingly to journalism. By 1900, according to one tabulation, nearly 60 percent of the leading newspaper editors were college men (still all men, of course).[6]

Given the partiality that most people demonstrate for the education that they chose for themselves, newspapers run by college men became less likely to laugh at the idea of college training for journalists. The clearest support came in 1888 from Eugene M. Camp, editor of the Philadelphia *Times*. Speaking at the first reunion of the alumni of the University of Pennsylvania's Wharton School, Camp said that journalists could be made, and that university instruction was a way of making them. The business school briefly offered such instruction five years later.[7]

By the time Camp made his proposal, Joseph Pulitzer had been proprietor of the *World* for five years and, his reputation enhanced by financial success and such promotional coups as his campaign to install the Statue of Liberty, had become a prominent national figure. He let himself be depicted as at least a mild proponent of journalism schooling by permitting Camp to quote him as saying: "I have thought seriously upon this subject, and think well of the idea." Pulitzer, a Hungarian immigrant whose learning was self-acquired, may have felt the tug of respectability and status that a college education might bestow on his calling. But not until he had struck up an acquaintance with Columbia College did he become an advocate.[8]

The Columbia that Joseph Pulitzer encountered in the late 1880s was a college transforming itself into a university. Founded in 1754 as King's College, as late as the 1870s it remained tiny and confined to an undistinguished cluster of buildings in mid-Manhattan. But expansion began under Frederick A. P. Barnard, who was named president in 1865. He made plans to add at least a dozen affiliated schools and raise an endowment. Seeking scholarly standing, Barnard recruited the historian and political scientist John W. Burgess, who led the effort to make Columbia a full-scale graduate institution. Barnard died in 1889—Columbia's new women's college was named in his honor—and in 1890, the trustees selected a fellow trustee, Seth Low, to take his place.[9]

Low, a wealthy former mayor of Brooklyn (then still a separate city), accelerated the pace of change. Most dramatically, he led Columbia to acquire the abandoned site of the Bloomingdale Insane Asylum on Morningside Heights in upper Manhattan, lying between Harlem and the Hudson River. The preeminent architectural firm of McKim, Mead & White created a formal design in Italian Renaissance style, in contrast with the Gothic of other Eastern campuses. Hoping that his example would attract money, Low provided a million dollars to construct the central building, an immense domed library named for his merchant father. The expansion of its schools and resources meant that Columbia was being reborn as a modern university, a peer of the other new universities—Cornell in upstate New York, the University of Chicago, and Stanford in California.[10]

Low visualized an urban institution based on what the historian Thomas Bender has called "a fruitful tension" between academic disciplines and a diverse civic culture. In his inaugural address, Low asserted that "the city may be made to a considerable extent, a part of the university," and decreed that many lectures and events would be open to all New Yorkers. The name he proclaimed for the new institution was not happenstance: "Columbia University in the City of New York."[11]

Because Columbia lacked one dominant patron, such as Chicago's Rockefeller or Stanford's railroad magnate Leland Stanford, Low scoured the city for funds to build the Morningside Heights campus. Eventually he cast his eye on Pulitzer, whose contact with Columbia had begun almost simultaneously with Low's installation, when he established a handful of scholarships for boys from New York public schools. Pulitzer directed that recipients should be prepared for college at Horace Mann, the experimental school operated by Columbia's new Teachers College.[12]

In 1892, Low and Pulitzer conferred at Baden Baden, one of Pulitzer's European rest stops. One immediate result was Pulitzer's contribution of $100,000 on May 10, 1893, the tenth anniversary of his acquisition of the *World*, to endow his scholarships at Horace Mann. The meeting at Baden Baden also triggered Pulitzer's first serious proposals on journalism instruction. Two of his secretaries—these were not stenographers, but men on whom he relied for intellectual and administrative support—were set to drafting memorandums. Walter Allen proposed a lectureship in journalism; E. O. Chamberlain a chair of journalism, tied to internships at New York newspapers.[13]

Pulitzer's thinking—and its limits—at this point may best be measured in the Allen memorandum:

> In an age when Universities are recognizing music, architecture, engineering and the mechanic arts as well as the humanities within their province they are not wise to continue regarding journalism as a Pariah in the castes of scholarship.
>
> A school of journalism such as some persons have proposed is a vain scheme. There is no special knowledge needed by a journalist, not now taught in the larger Universities of this country that can be well acquired otherwise than in a newspaper office or by doing newspaper work.
>
> A professor of journalism would be almost as useless as a school. . . .
>
> A lectureship on journalism is a different thing altogether. It would do what a lectureship on poetry or preaching or oratory as an art would do: acquaint the hearers with the history and the peculiar nature and requirements of this kind of literary occupation.

Allen proposed a roster of lecturers drawn from the era's most respectable editors: Charles A. Dana of the *Sun*, Edwin L. Godkin of *The Nation*, Whitelaw Reid of the *Tribune*, Henry Watterson of the Louisville *Courier-Journal*, Joseph Medill of the *Chicago Tribune*. Many of these names were ultimately to reappear as Pulitzer's nominees for his school of journalism's advisory board. Pulitzer approved a trial period for the lectureship, and Columbia's trustees accepted $3,000 to start it, but there is no evidence that the plan was carried out, and Pulitzer took inaction as rejection.[14]

Pulitzer and Low might have seemed natural allies, being near contemporaries, fellow admirers of the diversity of New York, and compatible in political outlook and public spirit. But their negotiations never moved far. Low continued to cultivate Pulitzer, using the fundraiser's classic method of asking for modest help in hopes of a later windfall. In 1895, just before the cornerstone was laid for Low Library, he engaged Pulitzer in an exchange about giving a building. Pulitzer said that he was eager to support Columbia and might be interested in a theater or a gymnasium. But a few months later, Pulitzer offered what became his customary excuse when cornered—the state of his health.[15]

Pulitzer made one more effort to interest Low in the journalism lectureship. In 1901, he had William H. Merrill, chief editorial writer of the *World*, paraphrase his thoughts:

Mr. P. . . . suggested his former idea of a school or Lectureship on Journalism—the entire details to be ordered by the Trustees & Faculty. He
thinks that a methodical and progressive course of Lectures on this subject
for the increasing number of young men who desire to enter journalism
would serve a high public end.— But if this is still open to objection, can
you suggest any other fund that will appeal to his mind & heart? He
would like to give you $100,000. I suggested a chair on American Histo-
ry & Literature (if you have it not already). The idea seemed to strike him
favorably. Or is there another building for some intellectual purpose of
the University that you would like? It seems a pity not to give such an im-
pulse an opening.[16]

There is no record that Low responded affirmatively, and that failed initiative was all but the end of the Pulitzer-Low dialogue. In 1897, Low ran for
mayor of the new five-borough New York City on an anti-Tammany ticket;
he lost. In 1901, he tried again with the support of, among others, Pulitzer
and the *World*, and won. He remained a Columbia trustee, but of course left
the Columbia presidency. It is not clear whether Low's own resistance or his
unwillingness to thrust journalism upon reluctant trustees, as Pulitzer suspected, quashed the opportunity for a collaboration. In any case, Pulitzer
was left to deal with Low's somewhat less compatible successor.[17]

# CHAPTER 3

# "Dealing with a Wild Man"

WHEN COLUMBIA'S TRUSTEES named Nicholas Murray Butler to succeed Seth Low, they could not have realized that they were naming a president for life. Just two days short of forty when he was installed on April 19, 1902, Butler had more than four decades of service left in him. His was already a Columbian career: he remained close to the college after his undergraduate days and had been instrumental in both the founding of Teachers College and the acquisition of the Morningside Heights campus. If Low ran the university like an urban reform politician, which he was, Butler's approach was more corporate. He was an imperious chief executive and an ardent self-publicist. Like Low, he believed in an expanding university, but he saw it less as an institution at the service of the city than as a training ground for America's elite.[1]

Butler had been in office only a few months when Pulitzer dictated the Chatwold memorandum, in which he became an outright advocate of a full-scale, endowed school of journalism. He turned his outline over to his closest confidant, Dr. George W. Hosmer, a physician twenty years Pulitzer's senior and his "chief secretary." Hosmer made the initial contact with Butler; and the response was encouraging enough to lead Pulitzer to change his will in the fall of 1902 to provide money to Columbia to start the journalism school, even if he should die (as he constantly suggested he might) before the plan was complete.[2]

Late in 1902, as Pulitzer and his entourage rode the train to his winter refuge at Jekyll Island, Georgia, he had Hosmer hand the proposal to Don C. Seitz, then the top executive at the *World*. While Seitz was still glancing at it, Pulitzer groped his way down the car to his side, and challenged him: "You don't think much of it." Seitz said that he did not. Pulitzer asked what he should do. "Endow the *World*," Seitz replied. They argued on the way south, but Pulitzer made it clear that he was determined to found a school, whatever became of the *World*.[3]

The plan, as drafted by Hosmer—accompanied by a persuasive essay, "The Making of a Journalist: Why a Technical and Professional School is Needed"—was submitted formally on March 24, 1903, not only to Butler but, surprisingly, to Charles W. Eliot, president of Harvard. Pulitzer's bid to Harvard may have been strategic, to keep Columbia on its toes. Eliot took three weeks to reply, but he wrote a full and influential essay on a journalism curriculum, later used as the basis of the program at the University of Missouri. But by the time Pulitzer received Eliot's plan, he had affirmed his commitment to Columbia.[4]

Butler moved forward swiftly. Identifying Pulitzer only as "the gentleman who proposes to give the funds for the establishment of a school of journalism," he went before the trustee committee on education three days after receiving the Pulitzer proposal. Nine days later, he presented the plan to the trustees and urged acceptance of the gift: a million dollars—half of it for a new building, and the establishment of a four-year course in journalism leading to a bachelor of science degree, starting in September 1904, only eighteen months away. A second million was to become available after three years of successful operation and would be used partly to establish prizes in journalism and the arts.[5]

Then the negotiations began to sour. The education committee attached three changes to the draft agreement: that the building be less expensive than Pulitzer had specified; that it not bear his name, despite his request; and that the provisions for the advisory board and the curriculum be struck, leaving control in the hands of the university. This last deletion also removed Pulitzer's favorite provision—the acceptance of special students who lacked formal credentials.[6]

Pulitzer was offended. Columbia's insistence on what Hosmer (speaking for Pulitzer) called its "privileges and powers and dignities" impinged on

Pulitzer's own imperiousness. Hosmer, as directed, wrote to insist on three provisions—the admission of special students ("Mr. Pulitzer could not have been admitted"), an advisory board, and the full expenditure for the proposed building that he had specified. Clearly using Pulitzer's own phrasing, Hosmer warned that Pulitzer might abandon the project: "No one can be surprised, I think, if a man inclined to do so much to give effect to a grand scheme, to put on foot on a good working basis, an institution destined to be of great value to the American people should feel disappointed and chagrined to find himself stayed and prevented at every point by objections that are illiberal, if not trivial and frivolous."[7]

But after soothing letters from Butler, Hosmer reported, "Mr. Pulitzer is in a more receptive frame of mind." There followed an exchange of documents between the trustees' education committee and the Pulitzer legal team. Pulitzer approved the main points of the agreement, and left for a summer in Europe.[8]

Early in July, Bradford Merrill, financial manager of the *World*, received a long letter from Pulitzer, summering at Etretat on the English Channel, over Hosmer's signature. Enclosed was a final draft of the agreement, and Merrill was instructed to deliver it to Columbia for signature. The letter evinced Pulitzer's continuing distrust: "You will be very careful before delivering the check and agreement in comparing the latter with the one Columbia is to execute." Two weeks passed, and the trustees signed the agreement, backdating it—a requested courtesy—to April 10, Pulitzer's fifty-sixth birthday.[9]

The form at least of a school of journalism was now in place. The text of the agreement, fewer than a thousand words, showed that Pulitzer had won his points. The university agreed to spend $500,000 on the new building, agreed to the admission of suitable candidates without college credentials, and agreed to "be influenced by the advice and conclusions of an Advisory Board . . . appointed by the University upon the nomination of the Donor." The board was to continue for at least twenty years. Not least: "This building shall bear the name of the Donor after his death." The agreement also stipulated a tablet to be placed in the building to the memory of Pulitzer's daughter Lucille, who had died at Chatwold in 1897.[10]

Curiously, the agreement appeared to increase Pulitzer's apprehension. Hosmer had already relayed Pulitzer's instructions about the tone of the initial public announcement: "He wishes you scrupulously to avoid conveying the impression that the school is the *World*'s scheme; or that the *World* is to run it; or will have anything to do with it. The endowment once made it is out of his hands. . . . He has put the responsibility in the hands of the University and the Advisory Board." But he contradicted himself in the same letter; he could not keep his hands off. He fussed over the membership of the advisory board, insisting that three members were indispensable: Whitelaw Reid of the *Tribune*, St. Clair McKelway of the *Brooklyn Daily Eagle*, and Charles Emory Smith of the Philadelphia *Press*. He was momentarily so intent on those three that he said that if they declined he would consider dropping the whole plan for the time being or—and these were prophetic words—"during my life." He went on for paragraphs, juggling other names and newspapers.[11]

Although Pulitzer assumed that the agreement would be announced promptly, Butler urged delay, warning that he and several trustees believed that "a certain portion of the newspaper press of the country is likely to be antagonistic, or at least cynical, toward the proposal." Before the end of July, even so, there was agreement that an announcement could be made as soon as the advisory board was named.[12]

Then, almost as if he wished to torpedo the whole scheme, Pulitzer made a demand he knew to be outrageous. He insisted that the presidents of Harvard and Cornell, Charles W. Eliot and Andrew D. White, be added to the advisory board. There was no explanation, just the demand. Not surprisingly, Butler declined. On August 11, Pulitzer cabled: "Understand jealousy. Telegraph Butler my insistence. Unalterable. Final." Butler restrained himself in corresponding with Pulitzer, but let loose in letters to associates: "[Pulitzer's] idea is to advertise himself by dragging Eliot & White into it, &, incidentally to give Columbia their 'support.' I prefer Columbia to support itself. . . . P. is evidently a hard task-master & those who work for him are terribly afraid of him, & don't understand why we are not."[13]

Like a runaway carriage, the first announcement of the school of journalism careered toward release. Pulitzer wanted the *World* to publish the story on Friday, August 14, with the names of the advisory board, including Eliot and White, even though Columbia had not agreed to appoint them. Trying to catch up, Butler released an announcement, and commented to George L. Rives, chairman of the trustees: "We are certainly dealing with a wild man." Pulitzer's feelings toward Butler were no gentler. He wrote to Whitelaw Reid: "Dr. Butler is very weak and, I fear, totally unaware of his weakness, totally unaware of the great need he has for advice."[14]

Still, out of the discord came an overwhelmingly respectful reception for the school-to-be. The papers of Sunday, August 16, carried long and detailed stories. Seitz was able to send to Pulitzer, still grumbling from afar, "bales of clippings" to soothe him.[15]

Pulitzer was not to be soothed. At the end of September, he wrote a long, unhappy letter to Butler, still harping on the advisory board. He warned Butler not to commit himself to plans for the new building. Butler promised that no further steps would be taken, but he went ahead with planning and hoped for better relations. He had McKim, Mead & White, the campus architects, obtain estimates for the building, which came in as low as $340,000. He commissioned Franklin Matthews of the *Sun* (recommended by President White of Cornell) to draft a plan for the school.[16]

On November 17, 1903, the University Council, Columbia's academic governing body, adopted a "Report on the Organization and the Academic Relations of the Proposed School of Journalism." It posited the creation of a faculty of journalism under a dean, a four-year undergraduate curriculum, a two-year professional curriculum for those qualified, and "practice-work in reporting and in editorial writing." The report was signed by distinguished scholars from the humanities, among them John W. Burgess, Brander Matthews, and George Rice Carpenter, as well as Franklin Henry Giddings, who was engaged in the parallel enterprise of starting Columbia's School of Social Work. For the first time, academic Columbia had committed itself to teaching journalism. But Butler recognized that the situation remained volatile. In December, he responded to a teaching application by saying that the school was in an "inchoate" condition.[17]

In January 1904, George L. Rives, the trustees' chairman, took over the Pulitzer assignment from Butler. He was a distinguished senior lawyer who had done work on occasion for Pulitzer, and the tone of their correspondence was friendly. After meeting Pulitzer in Manhattan, Rives submitted to him a further draft agreement aimed at assuaging Pulitzer's anxieties. He also proposed that Pulitzer permit the laying of his building's cornerstone during Columbia's 150th anniversary, in 1904. Pulitzer went off to Jekyll Island and soon wrote back: "My mind is unchanged, and the state of my health, and the necessity for me to avoid vexations and disappointments, compels me to adhere to my objection. I see before me only a choice of evils; postponement is the smaller of these." He made a new demand: that he or the advisory board, rather than the university, should have veto power over appointments to the journalism faculty. He added, somewhat quizzically: "And by the way I wish you would say to President Butler that no matter what has happened there is no personal consideration whatever; no predilection that will stand in the way of my agreement to any idea that may insure the success of the School."[18]

Seizing on this little encouragement, Rives traveled to Jekyll Island, and he offered a supplementary agreement giving Pulitzer and the advisory board their veto. Pulitzer was again elusive: "Though I started with a strong desire to act upon your idea of making the laying of the cornerstone on the date of the University anniversary—and should like to do it—I dare not. The worry [over the advisory board], the state of my health, the knowledge of my temperament and the unfortunate difference with Dr. Butler . . . compel me, although with great reluctance and unwillingness, to adhere to the conclusions conveyed to you in New York to postpone the execution of the plan till after my death in order to save myself vexation and disappointment." Again—after his death.[19]

Pulitzer ultimately returned to the city and signed the supplementary agreement. There was also language assuring the donor that he could set his own pace—"free to defer action on his part and so postpone for the present and possibly until after his death the establishment of the School of Journalism." The agreement contained a shadow advisory board, to be named in case of Pulitzer's death; in fact, six of the seven named eventually served. A will dated April 1904, prepared with Rives's advice, unequivocally affirmed Pulitzer's support of the school, specified nine categories for the prizes to be given in his name, and set up what later became known as the Pulitzer Traveling Scholarships, for graduating students in journalism, art, and architecture.[20]

If Pulitzer seemed frantically vacillating in dealing with Columbia, he never wavered in his determination that a school of journalism should ultimately come into being. And once he had committed the first half of the endowment to Columbia, he defended the enterprise fiercely. In 1904, he began to assemble his personal brief for the school. The opportunity was presented with the appearance of an article by Horace White, now of the *Evening Post*, who had challenged the proposal in the January 1904 *North American Review*. White's criticism was not unfriendly, but he was fixed in his belief that a university could or should teach nothing about the skills needed by journalists. The techniques of journalism, he asserted, included a "nose for news" (unteachable), shorthand, typewriting, and proofreading: "Columbia would no more think of embracing these things in her curriculum than she would of establishing a chair of head-lines, a chair of interviews, or a chair of 'scoops'." Nonetheless, he conceded, Pulitzer's school might draw to Columbia a number of students wanting to be journalists, and they would receive a good education there.[21]

When George Harvey, editor of the *North American Review* (for which Pulitzer had written a previous article, on politics), invited Pulitzer to reply, he responded not only to White but also to "all other criticisms and misgivings." He wrote (dictated): "If my comment upon these criticisms shall seem to be diffuse and perhaps repetitious, my apology is that—alas!—I am compelled to write by voice, not by pen, and to revise the proofs by ear, not by eye—a somewhat difficult task." He also aimed to persuade skeptics within the gates, such as Seitz and other staff members at the *World*, and even his spouse, to whom he wrote, after finishing the article: "I am sorry you are still unconvinced, but as you will live long enough and much longer, I hope, you may be converted by results. Now I have really taken a lot of trouble with this pamphlet. . . . Whether the thing is a success or not, I don't believe I have ever done anything that will give the children and their children, I hope, a better name, and that withal is something."[22]

Forty pages long and the lead article of the May 1904 *North American Review*, "The College of Journalism" was discursive but still rang with Pulitzer's intensity, sweep, and acumen; the school's historian, Richard Baker, called it Pulitzer's "magnum opus." Pulitzer used criticisms such as White's to shape his own argument. But he may also have been paying tribute to Whitelaw Reid, who more than thirty years before had projected a school of journalism much like the one that Pulitzer now wanted to bring into being. There is nothing in the article attributed to Reid's 1872 lecture, but the similarities suggest that Pulitzer knew it well.[23]

Pulitzer devoted most of his argument to defining what a college of journalism, as he chose to call it, should teach—and should not teach. Most emphatically, he insisted that the teaching should not be commercial or merely technical:

> This is not university work. It needs no endowment. It is the idea of work
> for the community, not commerce, not for one's self, but primarily for the
> public, that needs to be taught. The School of Journalism is to be, in my
> conception, not only not commercial, but anti-commercial.

He added that he had never spent an hour in any publication (business) office, even of the newspapers he owned (not adding, as his collected papers show, that he received a constant stream of business reports). Even so, he made the point at length—that the school "must mark the distinction between real journalists and men who do a kind of newspaper work that requires neither culture nor conviction, but merely business training."[24]

He went on to describe the nature of the school's instruction, and the scope was immense: writing of "Gallic lucidity and precision," law, ethics, literature, history, sociology, economics, statistics, modern languages, science—all these adapted to the requirements of journalism; and the principles and history of journalism itself, aimed at developing those qualities that Horace White insisted were inborn.[25]

At the end, Pulitzer made his most powerful argument. He wrote that the primary goal of his plan was neither solely to help young journalists nor to make journalism a better profession, although he confessed that both would give him satisfaction:

> In all my planning the chief end I had in view was the welfare of the Republic. It will be the object of the college to make better journalists, who will make better newspapers, which will better serve the public. It will impart knowledge—not for its own sake, but to be used for the public service. It will try to develop character, but even that will be only a means to the one supreme end—the public good.

He asked how the Republic would be faring seventy years thence (the year, as it turned out, of President Nixon's resignation): "Shall we preserve the government of the Constitution, the equality of all citizens before the law and the purity of justice—or shall we have the government of either money or the mob?" Tacitly rebutting the growing swarm of critics of the era who depicted the press as venal and craven, he insisted that "the press is the only great organized force which is actively and as a body upholding the standard of civic righteousness. . . . The press alone makes the public interests its own."[26]

His last paragraph contained the words by which he is most frequently remembered, and which have come to be adopted as the foundation statement of the School of Journalism:

> Our Republic and its press will rise or fall together. An able, disinterested, public-spirited press, with trained intelligence to know the right and courage to do it, can preserve that public virtue without which popular government is a sham and a mockery. A cynical, mercenary, demagogic, press will produce in time a people as base as itself. The power to mould the future of the Republic will be in the hands of the journalists of future generations.

The final words are commonly omitted:

> This is why I urge my colleagues to aid the important experiment which I have ventured to endow. Upon their generous aid and cooperation the ultimate success of the project must depend.[27]

Pulitzer's essay, although not aimed directly at the campus, made his case with the academic, as well as the professional, community. Butler wrote to Pulitzer that he had distributed copies of the article to the university faculty. The university also republished the article, lightly revised, as a small book, *The School of Journalism in Columbia University*.[28]

Again, the response was favorable. But if Butler hoped that Pulitzer could now be encouraged to proceed, he faced another disappointment. In February 1905, Pulitzer made public the decision he had implied repeatedly in private. From Jekyll Island, Bradford Merrill issued an authorized statement: "[Pulitzer's] present determination is that the active establishment of the School of Journalism shall be postponed until his death." Merrill added, no doubt closely echoing Pulitzer's own words: "The things that interest him interest him intensely, excessively, and from the results of this habit of mind—from possible interference that this fault of temperament might lead to—he is anxious the faculty shall be absolutely free." Merrill concluded: "To avoid all uncertainties or misconception, I may add that the endowment of the college is absolutely irrevocable, and its establishment beyond a shadow of a doubt."[29]

Pulitzer had transformed the birth of the school of journalism into a death watch.

# CHAPTER 4

# "A Posthumous Affair"

WHAT NICHOLAS MURRAY BUTLER truly thought during those years while he waited to take possession of the Pulitzer endowment he kept to himself. In dealing with Joseph Pulitzer, he was all patience, setting aside their disagreements, encouraging the donor to move forward, but careful to demand nothing. A curiously respectful relationship developed between the two. Butler's cordiality extended to Pulitzer's family. Pulitzer's wife, Kate, asked Butler to recommend a new personal secretary for her husband; Ralph, Pulitzer's eldest son, cultivated social relations with him.[1]

For two years after the senior Pulitzer decided that the school must wait until he died, plans lay dormant. Then, apparently troubled, Pulitzer reopened the matter in 1907, with a letter hand-delivered to Butler by a secretary sent all the way from Karlsbad Spa, in Bohemia. Pulitzer opened on a note of self-pity: "I feel like apologizing, like Charles the second," he wrote, paraphrasing Macaulay, "for the unconscionable time I am in dying, so far as you and the University and the School of Journalism are concerned."[2]

He asked the university to provide a detailed plan for the school; in particular, he wanted it to find the "one *chief* man" to head it. "The selection of the right man for this position is much more important than any theory or system; success will depend upon him, upon his experience and fitness, his ideas, ideals and moral perceptions. . . . I may add that I have tried very hard myself but have never been able to find an editor really representing my own ideal." Then, a tease: "If the plan submitted to me is satisfactory I shall release the restraint and let you go ahead." Specifically, he hinted that he might authorize an announcement on May 10, 1908, the twenty-fifth anniversary of his acquisition of the *World*.[3]

Butler responded by launching overlapping searches—for a journalist to write a master plan for the school, and for another, who might be the same person, to be its "executive head or dean." He consulted Chester S. Lord of the *Sun*, who, after reading Pulitzer's memo, commented: "The only man who has ever occurred to me for this position is Talcott Williams, and while I do not know enough about him to form a judgment, I should think him very promising if he could be induced to take the position." In fact, Butler had already discussed Williams with George Rives, the chairman of the trustees.[4]

But the promising flurry of activity died away, and when the twenty-fifth anniversary arrived, Butler had to content himself with accepting Ralph Pulitzer's invitation to attend the celebration in the *World* building downtown. But something important had happened, nonetheless: the name of Talcott Williams had been linked with the plans for the school.

Williams was a senior statesman of the press, fifty-nine years old in 1908, two years younger than Pulitzer. Born in the Middle East of missionary parents, he had a strong preaching streak. He was the nominal editor of the Philadelphia *Press*, but spent much of his time on good causes—election reform, municipal politics, settlement houses, missionary enterprises, going about the country giving speeches and collecting honorary degrees. In fact, those who mentioned him usually knew little about him beyond his air of reputability.[5]

Butler returned to biding his time, gently nudging Pulitzer on occasion. He forwarded an article about the creation of a chair of journalism at the University of Washington, and in mid-1908 sent the first bulletin of the University of Missouri School of Journalism, which had seized the honor of being the nation's first while Pulitzer hesitated.[6]

There was another stir in August 1910. It began when John L. Heaton of the *World* editorial page wrote to Frederick P. Keppel, dean of Columbia College, saying that Pulitzer had assigned him to prepare a plan for the school within three months. Heaton wrote: "It is fair to assume from my instructions that Mr. Pulitzer is now in the mood to proceed with the School without waiting to make it a posthumous affair." At the same time, Rives, chairman of the trustees, met Pulitzer in Newport for a consultation.[7]

Afterward, Butler wrote to Rives wearily: "What Mr. Pulitzer said to you at Newport is almost verbatim what he sent a man all the way from Karlsbad to say to me in June 1907. I did at that time everything which he suggested or desired, but nothing came of it. . . . It would really be a most desirable thing if he would let us go ahead in the near future; several of the Western institutions, acting on the hint given by Pulitzer's gift, have started schools of Journalism, but they are all very poor affairs and only serve to emphasize the necessity for such a school as we should be able to organize."[8]

Exchanges continued, Pulitzer asserting his willingness to go ahead if the right men were found. He now envisioned a double leadership—one chief for the practical side, one for the "strictly editorial, political, ethical, intellectual side." Butler threw in the name of Talcott Williams again, and Pulitzer responded that "somehow I have a very good opinion of Mr Talcott Williams although I am not aware of having read anything he has written and think his school, training and bent doubtful,—very doubtful if he is on the Philadelphia Press,—a thick and thin partisan paper."[9]

On October 10, 1911, Pulitzer wrote Butler, not unflatteringly and as a friend: "I am delighted at the growth of Columbia and hope you will not be too modest about your own share in the work should a gentleman representing the World, and engaged in preparing a story, call on you. I need hardly tell you that I am very much interested in Columbia and wish to God you could find me the right Dean for the School of Journalism."[10]

A week later, Pulitzer sailed from New York on his yacht, the *Liberty*, for a coastal cruise to the south. (The hard-driven secretaries who sailed with him referred to the vessel as the *Liberty, Ha! Ha!*) He took to his bed on the second day out, and the *Liberty* put in at Charleston, South Carolina, for medical assistance. A few days later, Kate Pulitzer was summoned from New York. Pulitzer was listening to the reading of a biography when he said in one of the languages of his childhood, "Leise, ganz leise, ganz leise"—"Softly, quite softly, quite softly"—his warning to a reader that he was falling asleep. These were his final words.[11]

CHAPTER 5

# "We Will Start Right Away"

COLUMBIA MOVED with alacrity—even unseemly haste—after Pulitzer's death on October 29, 1911. Even before the body could be returned to New York, an unidentified Columbia official told the *Sun*: "Mr. Pulitzer's death not only makes this money available, but we are obligated to use it. We will start right away." Officially, President Butler held his tongue out of respect, but a few days after the funeral he spent an evening with the trustees' chairman, George Rives, and they decided to move ahead swiftly. They wanted the school to begin operation on July 1, 1912, so as to close its three-year probation period promptly and to make Pulitzer's second million dollars available on July 1, 1915. The school was to open for students in September 1912.[1]

It was a challenging task—to create and open to students a full-fledged school of journalism in ten months. The project had to encompass, at a minimum, a scheme of governance established according to the Pulitzer agreement; a four-year curriculum leading to a bachelor's degree; a director found and set in place; a teaching faculty hired, borrowed, or stolen; and, not least, students. The raw materials were a hodgepodge—Pulitzer's desires as expressed in his 1904 article, his will and its revisions, the plans written by his subordinates and by various Columbia committees over the long incubation, and a field of study that was, academically speaking, in its infancy, with only the Missouri school in operation, and a scattering of courses and lectureships and sprouting departments elsewhere. Walter B. Pitkin, destined to be one of the founding teachers, called the obligation "Pulitzer's implied program of a school which trained the young in the duty and art of omniscience."[2]

The university had already sited the journalism building. In 1910, the trustees' committee on buildings and grounds had agreed that the structure should be at the southeast corner of Broadway and 116th Street, on the western edge of the campus. Earlier proposed sites had been given away during the long wait. The architects required little time for design because the building was to be a near replica of Hamilton Hall, which sat in a comparable position on the east side of the campus. Ground was broken in December 1911.[3]

Again, as during the false dawn eight years before, Butler convened a committee of academics and administrators to write a plan for the school. The blueprint adopted on December 12, 1911, was the work of a subcommittee that included Ashley H. Thorndike and William P. Trent of the English department, and Munroe Smith and Charles A. Beard of political science. Besides sketching out a curriculum, the subcommittee apparently originated the idea of offering graduates an unusual and distinctive bachelor of letters degree, rather than the bachelor of science Butler had proposed earlier. They were, truly, among the founders of the school.[4]

Beard also submitted an enthusiastic scheme for a floor in the new journalism building to be devoted to the raw materials of history, politics, and economics: "We are all agreed that the central work in the new school of Journalism is to be made up of instruction in these great subjects." The floor would contain a Bureau of Information—a reference library of current materials, scholarly, journalistic, and governmental. "It is our ideal in this new laboratory work in history and politics to inspire our students to care about the government of their country and its relation with other countries, to show them how to get accurate information on the living issues about us, and to train them in ideals of efficiency. . . . I believe that the new school of Journalism now affords an opportunity to develop what we may call applied Politics—an opportunity of which we should make the most."[5]

On January 16, 1912, the advisory board that Pulitzer had fought for had its first meeting, in Low Memorial Library. The core of its membership was still as Pulitzer had specified in the 1904 supplementary agreement: Whitelaw Reid, briefly taking leave from his post as ambassador in London, became chairman; and St. Clair McKelway of the *Brooklyn Daily Eagle* was vice-chairman. Melville E. Stone of the Associated Press also attended, as did Samuel Bowles of the *Springfield Republican*, and representatives from Pulitzer's *World* and *Post-Dispatch*, and two other New York newspapers, the *Times* and the *Sun*.

The board listened to a presentation by Thorndike, one of the authors of the Columbia proposal. The board did not much like the proposed "Bachelor of Letters" degree; why not "Bachelor of Journalism?" It preferred that women not be admitted. It thought that the school might take over the Columbia College newspaper, the *Spectator* (a bad idea that was a long time in dying), but eventually leaned toward a laboratory publication. Newspaper articles about the meeting were brief and neutral, but McKelway was quoted as saying that "the plan as outlined has too much of Columbia and too little of journalism."[6]

The next meeting, on February 16, was crucial; it was to determine the leadership of the new school. In January, Butler had written to John W. Cunliffe asking him to become director. Cunliffe had only secondary credentials in journalism. Born in England, he had long ago worked on provincial English papers and on the Montreal *Gazette*. But he was primarily a literary scholar; years before, he had lectured in English at Columbia, and now he headed the English department at the University of Wisconsin. He hardly seemed the "right Dean" that Pulitzer had called for in his last letter to Butler, but he was the first applicant, having written to Butler months after the 1903 agreement. Earlier in the month, Butler had had the trustees appoint him a professor of English and director of the school, contingent upon his "acceptability"—to the advisory board, presumably.[7]

Butler's strategy was obscure. When he presented Cunliffe to the advisory board, he may simply have been carrying out an obligation, or he may have been trying to install a candidate of little standing among journalists who would be obligated primarily to Columbia and Butler personally rather than to the board. In his memoir, Walter B. Pitkin suggested another theory—that Cunliffe was in fact the candidate of the critic Brander Matthews and the English department. Or, finally, as Baker suggests in his history, Butler may have offered Cunliffe as a straw candidate, knowing that the board would find him unacceptable and would name a director of its own choosing, thus ensuring an amicable beginning.[8]

What actually happened was clear enough. The board was chilly toward Cunliffe, and McKelway proposed Talcott Williams. Cunliffe was called in and given a polite explanation, and the board resolved that it wanted Cunliffe to teach at the school (he became associate director), but it wanted as director "some man who had more varied experience in the practical work of journalism in the United States." The unargumentative Cunliffe accepted the decision gracefully. Nor did Butler seem displeased by the naming of Williams.[9]

Butler wrote to Williams the next day, reporting the unanimous vote and flattering him: "It was felt by every member of the Advisory Board that your long and distinguished journalistic experience, your wide scholarship, your high character, and your unfailing good citizenship, had combined to elect you, as the Calvinists might say, for this important position . . . we all feel that the post named is as conspicuous as it is novel, and that to be the organizer and director of this first great university school of journalism would be a fitting crown to the career of any man who had served journalism so long and so faithfully as you have." He asked for a decision in nine days.[10]

The letter went astray, and a second copy had to be delivered by hand six days later. Williams wrote back to say that he knew, of course, about the offer, and had concluded from the delay that some "bar" to his appointment had arisen. Now he demurred: "Your offer, call rather, would have taken me from any task in my calling ten years ago, but it cuts too deep and changes too much for me to decide by Thursday"—that is, in three days. But he did accept, within a week. The question is why. Pitkin later wrote that he believed that Williams's age, lack of stamina, and temperament were bound to make the job torture, but as the son of missionaries Williams could not shirk duty.[11]

Williams's appointment generated a wave of newspaper articles, many accompanied by a picture of the elderly gentleman in academic robes, with his drooping white mustache, a photograph taken while he was posing for an oil portrait. At the end of February, Williams met with Butler and afterward typed a four-page letter that introduced Butler, and Columbia, to his sonorous nineteenth-century prose. He promised to run a demanding school: "the student must feel the arduous, unremitting daily pressure of the newspaper office or he will not be ready for it, when it comes, and grow soft, instead of being annealed and tempered by his study for his calling." The school, he promised as he held forth, would be no place for misfits of the sort that had populated journalism for so many years: "The trifler & the man who wants the social advantages of university life, while avoiding its burdens . . . , the man who looks on journalism as a province in Bohemia, and, worst of all, for the man unfit or uncertain, particularly uncertain, who knocks daily at the door of a newspaper because the apparently irregular life of journalism deceives him to believe that he can pick up a living there when he is unwilling or unable to acquire or to bear the yoke of more organized callings in the professions or business." He predicted, accurately, that not all who enrolled would survive.[12]

Williams's appointment was confirmed too late for him to attend the organizing meeting of the administrative board. The administrative board—not to be confused with the advisory board, which was the panel of outside visitors—comprised friendly academics from other departments assigned to serve as a governing body for the school, since no faculty of journalism existed, or would exist, it turned out, for nearly two decades. On the board, Butler placed, besides himself, Trent, Thorndike, Beard, College Dean Frederick P. Keppel, the economist Henry R. Seager, and James T. Shotwell of the history department. Cunliffe, and Williams, when he arrived, completed the membership.[13]

Even as the administrative board was polishing its plans, the issue of the admission of women, to which the advisory board had been opposed, surfaced in the newspapers. In the *Times*, a Dr. A. L. Jones, identified as chairman of Columbia's committee on admissions, was quoted as saying that the administrative and advisory boards had decided that "girls are not allowed in the new school," because Columbia College was not coeducational and because Pulitzer's will made no requirement as to women. Nor, Dr. Jones added, could women students even attend journalism classes, although most classes in the university were already open to students at Barnard, Columbia's college for women. Dean Virginia Gildersleeve of Barnard, the article reported, was not pleased with the exclusion.[14]

Williams, who as it happened opposed suffrage for women, came down firmly for equal educational access. On April 23, 1912, he announced that supposed opposition by the administrative and advisory boards had dissolved, and that women would be able to study journalism. In fact, he had threatened to decline his new post if they could not. Pending completion of the journalism building, women students would study at Barnard, then shift to professional training in the school for two years, becoming in effect Columbia College's first female undergraduates.[15]

The school's elements were set in order swiftly, and an opening for September 1912 no longer seemed precipitous. On April 16, the University Council, the campus academic governing body, approved a four-year curriculum. The first year—informally called the "College" year—resembled a standard bachelor of arts course, except that, as the *Columbia University Quarterly* explained, "each subject is taught with reference to the needs of journalism," as Pulitzer had proposed. For example: "The French and German is to be read in the daily newspapers of the two countries. The course in science is to be a survey of the present condition of science intended to give the reporter the knowledge he will need to work up a scientific subject. . . . American politics are to be studied in the newspapers of the period." Students were to take a single course in journalism in the second year, two in the third year, and four in the fourth, including history of journalism and law of libel. The aim was to provide "a sound general education" and "specialized technical training" in the same four years usually required for general education alone. The curriculum appeared to have ingeniously bridged the gap between the liberal and practical arts and, equally important, to have invested the scholarly resources of the university in the success of the school.[16]

The prospectus published in *Columbia University Quarterly* promised that the advanced journalism course would be offered jointly by staff members from New York morning newspapers (who would be free during the day) and by at least one full-time teacher "fresh from the practice of his calling." The school hired that teacher in May—Robert Emmet MacAlarney, city editor of the *Evening Mail*, the first in what became the school's long succession of demanding practitioner-instructors. But he was not scornful, as the stereotype might have suggested, of college education; a graduate of Dickinson College in Pennsylvania, he had also done graduate work at Harvard. He was just short of forty. Another early recruit was Edwin E. Slosson, a versatile chemist who had become literary editor of the weekly *Independent*, assigned to present a course in science tailored to journalism students.[17]

MacAlarney was soon joined by Franklin Matthews, night city editor of the *Times* and a veteran, earlier, of Talcott Williams's paper, the Philadelphia *Press*; Matthews had prepared one of the many plans for starting up the school while Pulitzer wavered. His nickname, for reasons not explained, was "Boss." Another addition was Gerhard R. Lomer, who was to write one of the first journalism textbooks. Nineteen other teachers were borrowed from Columbia faculty, many distinguished names among them. The most significant loan was Walter B. Pitkin of philosophy, whose association with the school was to last more than thirty years.[18]

The school's first announcement was issued in May 1912. Students were offered not only the bachelor of letters but the option of working simultaneously for a bachelor of arts or bachelor of science degree, with the B.Lit. degree completed in a fifth year. Students who already held a bachelor's degree would be admitted to complete the journalism degree in a single year. The single-year institution that the school ultimately became was foreshadowed in its beginnings.[19]

Besides describing the entrance examinations, the bulletin estimated costs—eighty-five dollars for a term's tuition, five hundred dollars or so for everything else, including room and board—and provided the times and places of classes, which were to be scattered for the first year through seven campus buildings and offered Monday through Saturday.

Throughout the spring and summer, Williams spread the word about the school. He visited the four-year-old school of journalism at the University of Missouri and no doubt conferred with its dean, Walter Williams (no relation); spoke in St. Louis; and went on to Richmond, Indiana, where a recent graduate of Earlham College, Carl W. Ackerman, heard him and decided to attend Columbia. Ackerman was not the first enrollee, however; that honor belonged to Charles Harold Waterbury, a Columbia junior who remained a year, did not receive a degree, and eventually became a manufacturer of dental supplies.[20]

In June, Williams attended a preliminary meeting in Chicago of an organization that became the American Conference of Teachers of Journalism and then the Association for Education in Journalism. Later in the year, he and Cunliffe attended the ACTJ founding meeting, and Williams chaired the committee to create a permanent organization. At this conference, Williams must have been made aware of the wave of journalism instruction sweeping through the country's universities, especially the public universities. Williams was placed on the executive committee and plans were made for the group to meet at Columbia in 1914. The initial indication was that Columbia would play a cooperative and helpful role in the development of journalism education. But that promise was to be carried out only sporadically.[21]

In the spring, Williams churned out, in his characteristically diffuse style, an article of more than five thousand words, explaining the school for the *Columbia University Quarterly*. Much of it may have made readers' heads spin, particularly when he compared social processes to "yards of flourishing, smooth-rolling well-fed intestine." But he noted: "It is the first school of journalism to use a great city as its laboratory for technical training," and this assertion survived, in many forms, as a maxim for the school.[22]

The cornerstone for the journalism building was laid on July 2, 1912, by Pulitzer's widow. Director Williams spoke—"briefly," one account claimed. A box was placed in the stone, with issues of the newspapers represented on the advisory board, a copy of Pulitzer's article on the school, extracts from Pulitzer's will, and the 1912–1913 announcement of the school.[23]

By the end of August, preparations were all but complete. In ten months, Columbia had assembled a school, an advisory board of visitors, a supervisory board, and a teaching staff. A school of journalism was about to be launched, but no one could be sure that it would float.

# CHAPTER 6

# A Building Called "Journalism"

ON SEPTEMBER 30, 1912, Columbia University opened its new school of journalism, just 337 days after the death of its progenitor and patron, Joseph Pulitzer. Even before the director, Talcott Williams, gave his ornate opening address under the dome of Earl Hall, the new journalism students caught the IRT subway to go downtown and cover New York City.[1]

They instantly became the butt of good-natured hazing. One student went to Democratic Party national headquarters, under instructions to learn how "Jack" Hammond, the publicity chief, contrived "to get tainted news into the papers." Leading the victim on, Hammond said: "We retire into that rear room there and hold a few whispered conversations. Then I give every reporter $10. There are twelve of them, and it costs us $120 a day." He pulled out a wad of soiled bills and said he would get them changed because reporters did not like dirty money. The student departed, with thanks, and his supposed gullibility was exposed in the *Tribune* the next day.[2]

On the second day, a reporter for the *Evening Post* was admitted to the classrooms of the school's first journalism instructor, Robert Emmet MacAlarney, to observe a session with advanced students. After starting the story with the requisite joshing, the reporter offered a not-unfriendly view of the proceedings:

The first class in reporting met this morning for business in the lecture room on the top floor of Kent Hall, which is really the Law School building, but which must serve as a city room until they get the new Pulitzer building finished. There were about twenty cub students in the class, and two of them were women. Professor MacAlarney handed out assignments before dismissing the class and hurrying over to the next city room, in the Philosophy building, where the senior cubs were mobilizing. One student was to "cover" Democratic headquarters, another was to cover Republican headquarters, a third was to get a talk with some prominent Socialist on the Lawrence strike, a fourth was to nose around in the Bull Moose headquarters, and so on.

As for the young women in the front row, they were to go together to the Charity Organization Society and do a bit of slumming in the tenements, so that they would be able to put the sob-sister flavor into their "stuff" when, in days to come, the city editor sent them out on a good heartthrob story. You know, coldest day in winter and all that.

And so to the senior class in journalism 43–4, "practice in editing and rewriting copy; lectures on differences in styles of presentation and theories of headlines. Tu., Th., and S., at 10, and S. at 11." There were no young women in this class, but there was one Chinese student, H. K. Tong, in the fifteen who aspired to be college-made reporters. As this class had to meet in the hall that is dedicated to philosophy, the familiar handsomely carved mahogany writing desks and gold-filled typewriters of a regular newspaper office were not in evidence. However, with the first zip of the ten o'clock gong, every one of the fifteen students had a batch of copy in his hand and he had just fifteen minutes to whip it into shape, put a head on it, and catch an edition. . . .

Also he had to slug it. Did the senior class in Journalism 42–4 look up in surprise when Professor MacAlarney told them to slug all stories? Not a bit of it. They had already learned that much journalism, anyway. Every journalist knows what a slug is, as well as newspaper men. . . .

During the fifteen-minute period before going to press, the students bent to their copy with a will and soft pencils, like regular fabulous-salaried copy-readers. They had copy that had been turned out by the junior class in journalism, which had been scouring the city yesterday for news. It wasn't first-class copy to handle and put a double-decker head on, but all of it began half-way down the page, and none of it was written on both sides of the sheet, and so, when the senior class had slugged it up in the corner, it took on the looks of real copy.

"Copy boy," called the professor at the stroke of 10:15, and every journalist passed up his magnum opus and saw it tossed unceremoniously in a heap on the professor-city-editor's desk. The results of the quarter-hour of toil and labor included:

BOY WENT FISHING: IS DROWNED.

$193,000,000 TO MELT NORTH POLE ICE.

AGED ORGAN GRINDER DIES IN STREET.

It took the rest of the hour to explain what was the matter with the heads.[3]

Having no doubt seen the newspapers, President Butler sent a note to Director Williams on October 2, sharply suggesting that he clamp down on publicity "concerning the daily work of the School of Journalism." But the pattern of that daily work, built around the practices of the industry, was set and was to continue, with variations, for the rest of the century.[4]

Columbia, and Talcott Williams and Robert E. MacAlarney, and their associates, had pulled it off. A journalism school was open and functioning. Students were fanning out through New York City, were being taught newspaper work by those who practiced it, and were getting an undergraduate education as well. Moreover, from the first instant, the school seemed to have an identity and vitality of its own.

Who turned up for that opening week? Director Williams noted that "nearly half the entering class of the school is composed of those who have already spent from one to four years on newspapers in various parts of the country." He added: "In more than one case men engaged in exhausting night work in New York offices are using their scanty leisure to take the courses of the school. They will get six years, or more if necessary, to take their degree."[5]

A roster compiled on the first day of classes listed ninety names, which, with dropouts and latecomers, shook down to seventy-nine enrolled. A dozen were women, all but two of them Barnard students. There were two dozen of the nonmatriculated students on whose admission Pulitzer had insisted. Only a minority of the total enrollment came from New York City; many more were from cities in the Northeast, South, and Midwest. There was a considerable age range: the youngest listed was Maxwell M. Geffen of New York City, 16; the oldest was 27-year-old John B. Penniston, already a degree holder from the rival school in Missouri. Fewer than a third of the enrollees were destined to earn degrees.[6]

The advanced students were plunged by MacAlarney into the city's news maelstrom. A week into the term, he asked for passes to put Carl Ackerman and Geddes Smith on the press ship when President Taft, as part of his unsuccessful reelection campaign, was reviewing the fleet in New York harbor. Later in the week, students were sent to the sensational murder trial of Charles Becker, the rogue police officer who had ordered the execution of an uncooperative gambler. Director Williams boasted afterward: "Half the class were in the courtroom when the verdict came in at midnight and came to the University and wrote their stories. . . . How seven got in with an official admission for only two and the courtroom vigilantly 'tiled,' I did not ask, but every newspaper man knows, and knows, too, that this is part of the 'School of the reporter.' To go where you are not wanted, and get what is wanted, these are the first and second commandments of the newspaper decalogue." The exploit drew sniffish comment from editorialists, who deemed it inappropriate for a school that was trying to make gentlemen of journalists.[7]

Williams went on: "These men in the fourth year have seen the election returns come in inside of a newspaper office. They have covered every national party headquarters, they have been for a week or a fortnight at every city department, police headquarters and the ship news. They have done investigations like the sessions of the Committee of the Board of Aldermen, police trials and the Goode inquiry. . . . They saw the Women's Suffrage night procession and wrote it up that night. They saw the Horse Show day by day and again measured what they did as beginners against the work of older men." On top of this, the fourth-year class wrote art and drama criticism, and editorials.

By midyear, the intense common experience had knit the seniors into a club called "The Staff"—thirteen students and an honorary member, MacAlarney. The Staff's first dinner was organized to say good-bye to Hollington K. Tong, whose notable exploit had been to serve as an undercover waiter in a downtown cocaine den. Now he was returning to China to find a spot on the *Peking Daily*. That he and Carl Ackerman spent a semester together was to prove significant for the school thirty years later.[8]

Throughout the year, the student body trudged to Earl Hall for weekly guest lectures. One guest was the founder's son Ralph Pulitzer: FATHER HATED INACCURACIES, HE TELLS STUDENTS OF THE SCHOOL OF JOURNALISM, read the headline. The same gathering also was a memorial to Whitelaw Reid, who had died a day before, and Williams paid tribute to Reid's role in engendering the idea of a school of journalism forty years before. In January, Williams found himself defending the guest lectures to President Butler, who grumpily observed that he found such occasions "almost valueless for instructional purposes."[9]

Nor was Butler sympathetic when Williams complained of the teachers' reading load—for Gerhard Lomer, with four freshman and sophomore writing sections, 50,000 words a week; for John Cunliffe, 30,000; and for Walter Pitkin, who initiated the complaint, 108,000 a week.[10]

More ominously, Butler reported his concern that the next year's budget was projected at $55,000, up nearly 70 percent from the first year, while the income from the "Journalism Fund"—he as he called the Pulitzer endowment—was only $41,500. Butler made clear that the school must derive all of its support from the endowment income, and that the university intended to contribute nothing further, although it retained the tuition and fees paid by journalism students.[11]

The school's first participation in a Columbia commencement came on June 4, 1913, when nine fourth-year students received the B.Lit. degree. One, Carl W. Ackerman, was destined to be the first dean of the school after a career as a foreign correspondent. Leon Fraser became prominent in international law and finance before his suicide in 1945. Edward F. Mason settled into a career of journalism teaching. William D. Conklin became a small-town publisher. Geddes Smith worked for the *Survey* magazine. Sara Addington, nonmatriculated and not a degree recipient, took up fiction, and Laurence H. Sloan, another nonrecipient, helped found Sigma Delta Chi, the national journalism fraternity.[12]

The director's first annual report, issued some months later, expressed satisfaction with the year, despite the dropout rate of 47 percent, which included more than half of the nonmatriculated students. The chief cause, Williams wrote, was a failure to meet the foreign-language requirement, a demonstrated ability to read a newspaper in French or German.[13]

Early in 1913, while the new building was being completed, Columbia carried out, after its fashion, its agreement to name the structure for its donor. On January 27, 1913, Butler received from the relevant committee a "MEMORANDUM In Regard to Inscription in the Journalism *Building*." The committee noted that the agreement dated April 10, 1903, "provides that the building shall bear the name of the donor after his death and shall have erected within it a tablet inscribed to the memory of 'my daughter Lucille.'"

Then it proposed: "In compliance with the foregoing requirement it is suggested that an inscription in bronze letters be inlaid in the floor of the vestibule of the Journalism Building." The inscription was to read:

SCHOOL OF JOURNALISM

ERECTED AND ENDOWED BY

JOSEPH PULITZER

IN MEMORY OF HIS DAUGHTER

LUCILLE

MDCCCCXII

The memorandum concluded: "RESOLVED, that the foregoing form of inscription be approved and that the architects be requested to prepare and submit a drawing of the same."[14]

There seem to have been no demurrals to this action, which (from the perspective of ninety years) appears *not* to name the building for the donor at all. Yet no objections are on record from members of the Pulitzer family, from Pulitzer's associates who helped in the negotiations, or from the advisory board, the director, or the faculty. Perhaps they all accepted Columbia's claim that the floor tablet carried out the agreement. But the result was that neither the building nor the school itself, except informally, was to bear Pulitzer's name. In May 1913, the trustees notified the architect that the word "JOURNALISM" was to be carved above the main entrance. It was done.[15]

The circumstance might hardly be worth noting were it not for Columbia's shifting policies in naming new buildings on its Morningside Heights campus. The earliest ones, erected under the Seth Low administration, almost always bore the names of major donors—Schermerhorn, Fayerweather, Havemeyer, as well as Milbank and Brinckerhoff across the street at Barnard. But the rules became fluid under Butler. Some of the new buildings bore the name of such donors as Hartley, Avery, and Furnald. However, the building given by Adolph Lewisohn was initially called "School of Mines" and only decades later given his name. Similarly, four years after the construction of the journalism building, the Barnard building donated by the financier Jacob Schiff became "Students' Building" (later, Barnard Hall), and subsequent efforts by the Schiff family to change it were unavailing. In his history of the architecture of Morningside Heights, Andrew S. Dolkart notes that Schiff's gift is commemorated only in a "marble tablet set into the floor of the lobby"—a recognition that bears an odd, perhaps not coincidental, resemblance to the Pulitzer tablet in the journalism building.[16]

Dolkart relates the reluctance to name buildings for Lewisohn and Schiff directly to the anti-Semitic views of Butler and the trustees, one of whom noted that he believed Columbia had to deal with the "Hebrew question" and rid itself of its reputation as a "Jew college." Granted, Pulitzer's identity as a Jew had been considerably blurred. Although his Hungarian parents were both Jewish—as has been reestablished in recent research—he was not religious beyond an affiliation of convenience with the Episcopal church, in which he was married. Moreover, the sporadic attacks on him—"Joey the Jew" or "Jewseph Pulitzer"—when he first came to New York had subsided or gone underground.[17]

Columbia's dealings concerning Pulitzer, external and internal, are free of any references to him as a Jew, yet it hardly seems possible that Butler and his trustees—hypersensitive as they were to the supposed encroachments of Jewishness—would be unaware of that identity. The pertinent questions remain: Was the relegation of Pulitzer's name to a tablet in the lobby a slight? If so, was he slighted because he was a Jew or because he was one of the creators of yellow journalism? Or was he slighted at all? The civility of Butler's late correspondence with Pulitzer would suggest not; but Butler's policies toward non-Jewish donors leave doubts.

By September 1913, the building's finishing touches were being added. As requested by Pulitzer, sculptured medallions in light blue were mounted on the walls of the lobby to honor six historically notable journalists, three of them English: Defoe, novelist-journalist; Addison of *The Tatler* and *The Spectator*; Delane of the *Times* of London; and three Americans: Franklin, Greeley, and Isaiah Thomas, revolutionary patriot editor and historian of printing. To the right was a replica of Rodin's bust of Pulitzer, executed the year before Pulitzer died. At the last minute, a trustees' committee inspected the vestibule and was alarmed by a scattering of "small female figures" in the ornamentation. W. M. Kendall of McKim, Mead & White stubbornly defended the decor, but for once the determination of the client overcame the will of the architect and the figures were removed.[18]

The next summer, a statue of Jefferson by Ordway Partridge, for which Pulitzer had provided $25,000 in his will, was mounted in front of the journalism building. However, Pulitzer had wanted a statue of Jefferson in a prominent public place, and an inside corner of the Columbia campus was not necessarily what he had had in mind. But his son Ralph, as a trustee of the will, concurred in the choice. The statue, an ambivalent symbol considering Jefferson's mixed attitudes toward the press, was unveiled in June 1914.[19]

In June 1913, Gregory T. Humes, a *World* reporter, was mortally injured in a Connecticut train wreck, and with his all-but-dying words he instructed somebody to alert his editor. His colleagues at the *World* asked if they could install a memorial plaque in the school vestibule. Williams liked the idea, and wrote to Butler: "I feel myself that nothing better could happen to the School of Journalism than to have the calling begin to look on the hall of the building as in a way a Westminster Abbey for the profession—its visible center and hearthstone." Butler, no sentimentalist, turned the request aside; he feared "a tendency to turn the buildings of Columbia University into a Columbarium." The Humes plaque was installed at the *World*, and remained there until the paper closed in February 1931, then was moved to the school, and little noted thereafter, except when a writer in 1935 wrote that the "dusty plaque" symbolized the romanticism that employers used to exploit working reporters.[20]

The new building, with five working floors measuring 208 by 55 feet, had no difficulty accommodating the 129 students who registered in the fall of 1913. On the entrance floor were offices for the director and associate director, an auditorium, and a large typewriter room. Between the directors' offices was stored the morgue—the collection of clippings that Talcott Williams had started in the 1870s, numbering by 1913 more than 400,000 items. Continuously augmented for the next forty years, it came to contain possibly four million pieces, the older portions becoming increasingly fragile. In 1954, Richard T. Baker asserted that "this morgue will be written down as one of the most enduring contributions Columbia ever made to the communications profession." In the 1970s, after microfilming of the collection was found to be cumbersome, expensive, and inconvenient, the morgue was consigned to scrap-paper dealers.[21]

On the next floor, there was an ambitious library and reading room, designed along the lines that Charles Beard had recommended, stocked with government and organizational documents, reference indexes, and current files of a hundred newspapers. The mezzanine above the library contained a city room for fourth-year students, equipped with desks, typewriters, a telephone, and a semicircular copy desk. A time-locking copy box was set up to enforce deadlines.[22]

The university was quick to occupy the building's excess space. The university bookstore moved into the basement, and an Institute of Arts and Sciences and the departments of music and anthropology occupied upper floors. Accounting got space for a while. Later, anthropology and Arts and Sciences moved out, and the Columbia University Press moved in. The music department was still there nearly fifty years later.[23]

All told, the building had a seating capacity of 2,200 students. The total cost, after finishing, was a little more than the $500,000 that Pulitzer had designated for it. The faculty and students moved in on September 13, 1913, and on October 28 the advisory board inspected the building and accepted it. The effects of moving in were immediate. As the director put it, in his decorous way: "The sense of corporate union and professional enthusiasm which existed in the first year of the School, though its members were scattered through a number of buildings, has been greatly quickened by a daily contact, which brings the whole School in mutual touch."[24]

# CHAPTER 7

# "What Journalism Will Do to Columbia"

THE DOMINANT FIGURES of those early years were the director, Talcott Williams, senior journalism instructor Robert E. MacAlarney, and Walter B. Pitkin, the philosopher-journalist. Williams instantly became the stuff of student folklore—too eccentric and wispy to be taken entirely seriously but too powerful to disregard. He was known for a literally encyclopedic mind—that is, for having absorbed the contents of whole encyclopedias, quoting entries on whatever occasion. In his affectionate portrait of Williams, whom he called the Walrus, Pitkin remarked: "The Walrus had a mind of absolutely no depth. But what gorgeous expanses it possessed!" His nickname, "Talkalot Williams," was often invoked, particularly when his introductions of speakers left them severely short of time.[1]

He was notorious for not remembering the names of students, for greeting them with inexplicable injunctions ("Young man, save your money!"), and for extemporaneous speeches, such as a lecture he gave to a student on Greek orators while they rode the subway. Assuming the role of resident puritan, he deplored what women students wore as scandalous and snooped about the building for immoral activity; the women responded by sending mysterious perfumed notes. He was frequently absent, and always in demand as an out-of-town speaker or committee member or trustee—owing to that same air of good repute that had brought him the job as director.[2]

And yet he was serious. Behind his ornate prose lay a determination that the school should make such demands on its students that only the deserving would survive. As early as the second year, there was those who muttered that keeping up meant seceding from the joys of life. Moreover, when the time came to deal with dissent, he proved to be unforgiving.

But given the occasion, he could inspire. Ahmed Emin Yalman, a Turkish Ph.D. candidate, turned up at the school in 1912, and he became, once Williams realized that they were both born in Turkey, Williams's ward. The next summer, Williams planned a nationwide itinerary for him, and when Yalman left for Turkey in 1914, he found a letter from Williams in the cabin: "Devote yourself to the cause of advancement of Turkey, our common country of birth." Yalman became an advocate of press freedom in his native land and survived a murder attempt and a prison term.[3]

MacAlarney's reputation was more straightforward. Young, buoyant, and challenging, he lacked the vein of cruelty often associated with city editors. The heart of his instruction came on Mondays, the day devoted entirely to the work toward which all the school's training and learning pointed—production of the *Blot*, the dummied simulation of a New York afternoon newspaper, run by MacAlarney and student editors. At dawn, a student was already down at the harbor to board incoming ships; others fanned out to city hall, police headquarters, criminal courts. By midday, copy was reaching the student copy desk, and by midafternoon the dummy *Blot* was done.

Not always content with mere reality, MacAlarney sometimes introduced "pressure tests"—a called-in (and fake) subway crash; an imagined crisis in Europe. Such exercises, MacAlarney maintained, trained a journalist "to exhaust a situation for possibilities so that when the real test comes he is not found wanting." His examinations were laced with "as if" situations: the collapse of a reviewing stand; a murder at the St. Regis.[4]

As a top-grade talent, MacAlarney was still on his way up, and at the end of 1913 he was named city editor of the *Tribune*—news first revealed in the *Blot*. It appeared at first that he might have to resign, which would have been a major loss to the school. In the end, he left his associate professorship and became a part-timer, while Franklin Matthews stepped up to the position of associate professor.[5]

For his part, Pitkin was assigned to teach omniscience. "I was supposed to cover the history of philosophy, modern psychology, a dash of anthropology (say about one generation of it), the world's great ethical systems (by special request of Pulitzer), and an outline of logic which, if it accomplished nothing more, would at least aid the young reporter to smell a *non sequitur* in the cross-examination of a witness at a murder trial." He failed, of course, but he enjoyed the challenge.[6]

The second senior class, that of 1914, comprised twenty-eight students, eight of them promoted from within the school and twenty admitted with bachelor's degrees. Of the twenty-eight, only ten received journalism degrees, although the school's overall departure rate declined to 34 percent. In his second annual report, Williams again showed his tough side:

> This large proportion of those who failed to complete the year was principally due to lack in writing. . . . The incapacity to write with vigor and effect should not and does not exclude a man from acquiring a college degree; but a school of journalism can no more give a man its degree than a law school can present for the degree of B.LL. a man who lacks the "legal mind." This limitation is not always recognized by law schools, and it is not easy to refuse the degree of a school of journalism to a painstaking, industrious man. Life would be easier for all if dull men were never ambitious and able men never lacked industry and ambition, but it is the duty of a professional school to be as rigorous in its tests as professional life.[7]

His biographer recalls an example of Williams's punitive way of deciding students' destinies; he confided to her that in 1914 he had failed the best writer in a class because he had misspelled a word: "If he hadn't been the best I should not have done it; it was a lesson he'll never forget." His biographer added: "I'm sure the *student* never did forget—or forgive."[8]

Yet at times the director seemed equally disappointed in himself. In 1914, he wrote to a relative, "My second year is almost over. It has not, for many reasons been quite the joy of the first. The boys are not so able in the class. I have not done the work quite so well and my critical instinct is always at work over the result of my labors. I have never had so much praise, appreciation & consideration. It comes in many forms and is all dear; but I am just now overworked and my errors and mistakes are always before me. . . . I am too tired to reach decisions & the daily routine of my life which I once held so secure is now broken in by a great flood of demands of many sorts and many orders."[9]

Among the ten who succeeded in graduating in 1914 were twenty-year-old Lester Markel, destined to become a major and much feared editor at the

*Times*; Burnett O. McAnney, already acclaimed a hero for rescuing a six-year-old girl as she was being swept down the Hudson, who went on to a career in New York newspapers; and the first two women to receive degrees, C. Claudia Moritz and Grace A. Owen.[10]

In the fall of 1914, the journalism students, or "scribes," as they were sometimes called in the campus daily, set about to inform Columbia that they saw themselves as a breed apart. They first discarded the tradition of hazing freshmen. Instead of following the college's tradition of abusing the incoming class, Journalism '17 threw a party for Journalism '18. Columbia College undergraduates did not like what they saw of Journalism's blossoming nonconformity, and floated a proposal that all class organizations be merged, to wipe out Journalism's identity. Nonsense, Journalism replied; as a professional school, it needed to maintain its separation. The proposal died. Journalism students concentrated on Journalism-only activities—class dinners, the new clubroom on the seventh floor with its own Victrola, and a Pulitzer Press Club.[11]

Student activism took a new turn in January 1915 with the formation of the Too-Much-Work movement, an effort to fight back against the director's policy of making the school's burdens all but unbearable. Earlier in the year, Pitkin had reported to Williams that the quality of writing was dropping because both students and instructors were being stretched to the limit—in particular because writing courses at the school were not merely canned exercises but involved active research and reporting. In the two previous years, Pitkin noted, "The students have not complained, but they have said freely that they could scarcely hold the pace."

The resistance was led by the sophomore class of 1917; the committee included M. Lincoln Schuster, seventeen years old, who was said to have been the only journalism student ever to turn up in knickerbockers. Williams responded by suggesting that the remedy would be to extend the course of study to a fifth year—not necessarily what the committee wanted to hear. Yet Williams conceded at the end of the year that overwork had led to four instances of illness.[12]

Williams reported a lower rate of attrition—only 18 percent—in the 1914–15 year, partly because a greater proportion of students had reached the upper classes after one year or two of preparation at the school. But he still felt a need to defend the earlier academic devastation. In his report he asserted that rigorous schools always started with high rates of failure. Nor, he added, did newspaper work always provide the material incentive to stay in school; cub reporters, he noted, still received the same starting pay of fifteen dollars a week that predominated forty years before. In 1915, the graduating class was still a slender company of but sixteen, hardly of a size to revolutionize American journalism. Moreover, among them a number immediately moved on to advertising and the newly attractive field of public relations. One became an employee of Ivy Lee, one of the progenitors of "p.r."[13]

In the spring of 1915, the school approached the end of its probationary period. The Pulitzer agreement and the will had specified that the second million dollars of his endowment would become available after three years of successful operation. His executors had to determine whether to release the money or, given the remote chance of an adverse decision, to send it to Harvard to set up a similar school.

So far as Columbia was concerned, there was no doubt about the outcome. His eye on the second million, Butler solicited material from Williams about the school's increasing enrollment and its placement record. On May 24, 1915, Butler and four other members of the advisory board, headed by Ralph Pulitzer, toured the school with Williams and Cunliffe as guides. Then they adjourned to the trustees' room in Low Library and adopted a resolution of approval: "Having before them the record of the organization and work of the School for three years beginning May 6, 1912 [the date of the trustee action officially opening the school], supplemented by their personal knowledge and inspection, the Advisory Board of the School of Journalism makes formal record of the fact that, in its judgment, for three years the School of Journalism has been and now is in successful operation." On June 22, the trustees of the Pulitzer estate concurred.

At the same time, Butler offered a Plan of Award—drafted largely by Frank Diehl Fackenthal, secretary of the university—for what were to become known as the Pulitzer Prizes. The ultimate authority in the granting of the awards, the plan made clear, must be the trustees of Columbia University, but nothing in the plan suggested that they could alter or veto prizes. Initially, the plan envisioned that nominations in journalism would come from the school's advisory board and that the American Academy of Arts and Letters would provide the arts nominations. No particular role was assigned to the advisory board, but the board insisted on an empowering clause in the plan, giving it "authority and control" over procedures for nomination and selection. Not only did the board come to exert that authority, but awarding the prizes eventually became the board's sole task. For students, the most important result of that day's work was the authorization of the three Pulitzer Traveling Scholarships of $1,500 each for travel in Europe. Because the first Pulitzer Prizes were postponed to 1917, the traveling scholarships also had to wait.[14]

Even before the remaining endowment became available in May 1916, Butler began to take a tougher attitude toward the school. He wrote to Williams early in 1916: "It is plain that the income from the fund given by Mr. Pulitzer for the endowment of this School will not be sufficient to maintain it and to permit its expansion along existing lines. The Committee [on Education] have instructed me to make a careful study of the question as to how far expense can be saved by amalgamating with the work of the College the instruction of Journalism students in such subjects as History, Economics, French, German and English." That is, he wanted to economize by ending much of the liberal arts instruction that had been tailored for journalism students.[15]

Responding, Williams wrote to Dean Keppel of the college maintaining his (and Pulitzer's) position that journalism instruction and liberal arts instruction should be interwoven from the beginning: "The experience of the past three years has deepened the conviction of a lifetime spent in the newspaper office that the work of training the writer must begin as soon as he leaves the High School, and that a man who is expecting to write ought, from the start, to be asked to write more, to do the work more carefully and to accompany it by study directed to the content upon which he writes." [16]

By the time Williams wrote, his position had been undercut. The administrative board, the campuswide faculty committee that supervised the school, supported amalgamation. Moreover, it agreed with Butler that the Pulitzer funds could cover no more than three years of instruction. The trustees approved the change, and in his 1916 report Williams went along and proclaimed the opposite of what he had said only months before: "Too early a demand for professional study backed by professional zeal has its cost." He announced that starting in 1918 the school would offer a three-year course, preceded by two required years of college: "Such a plan, with the line sharply drawn between college and professional work, is far superior to the various methods of study for the work of the newspaper elsewhere pursued." The experiment that had just been declared a great success—an undergraduate liberal arts curriculum designed for journalists—had actually been adjudged not a success at all, but an unbearable burden.[17]

The journalism school's class of 1916 slipped away before the turbulence of war enveloped the campus. In his annual report that summer, Talcott Williams noted that the class included the first students who had attended the school for four years. (Moreover, they were all but the last, because the school was about to move to the new policy of admitting only in the junior year.) A few became eminent. Maxwell M. Geffen, who married his classmate Pauline Felix, became a business-magazine magnate and a notable supporter of the school. The redoubtable Otto D. Tolischus was a mainstay of the *Times* as a foreign correspondent and editorial writer for almost fifty years. He won a Pulitzer Prize after the Nazis expelled him from Germany in 1940; he was later imprisoned by the Japanese, and released in a prisoner exchange.[18]

But long before Journalism '16 departed, the school's momentum had passed to the class of 1917, the first to spend four years in the journalism building. A college instructor quoted in the *Christian Science Monitor* was referring to the energy of '17 when he said that it was no longer a question of what Columbia University would do with the school of journalism: "It is rather a question of what the school of journalism will do to Columbia University." Journalism students, the paper reported, were "permeating every phase of university life." One member of the class, James W. Danahy, headed the university debating team; four journalism students were on the board of the campus newspaper, the *Spectator*; and a journalism student, Morrie Ryskind, was the managing editor of the humor magazine, the *Jester*. The class trait was enthusiasm: eighty-seven students entered the contest for a $50 prize offered by Arthur Brisbane of the *American* for the best editorial on the theme of "habit." Max Schuster won.[19]

Fifty years later, Schuster remembered the time as "an adventure unparalleled." He savored particularly the life-changing opportunities the school gave him to study with Columbia's academic giants—the iconoclastic constitutional scholar Charles Beard, the intellectual historian James Harvey Robinson, the philosopher John Dewey. He also remembered fondly his journalism teachers: Williams, who taught him the Dewey Decimal System; Matthews, MacAlarney, Cunliffe. He remembered Pitkin as stirring. "Our class," he recalled, "was lucky beyond words to be at Morningside."[20]

But the world and campus politics became increasingly ominous. During the spring of 1916, a new magazine, *Challenge*, appeared on the campus, its masthead including many journalism students—Ryskind, Schuster, Marshall Beuick, James Marshall (later to be a big-league lawyer), and the brothers Fred and Albert Seadler (whose ubiquitous presence led Talcott Williams for a time to call almost every student "Mr. Seadler"). The magazine was socialist in orientation—the somewhat dilute, optimistic, pacifistic socialism of that era. As M. R. Werner of the class of 1918 wrote later: "In the School, if you weren't a Socialist, you were practically a crew man"— that is, the type later known as a "jock." The Intercollegiate Socialist Society selected the school as a friendly site for its December 1916 meeting, and at one time or another almost every major socialist in the New York region appeared there.[21]

Ryskind, not having enough on his plate editing the *Jester* and *Challenge* and supplying items to Franklin P. Adams's famous "Conning Tower" column in the *World*, decided to run for the Board of Student Representatives, a body elected by all undergraduates but composed historically of fraternity men. The votes were counted, and Ryskind and his journalism classmate Danahy were winners. But the incumbent chair of the board literally stopped the presses of the *Spectator* and pulled the story; the results were canceled. The sitting board raised two objections: that women journalism students had voted (with President Butler's approval); and that, as the *Tribune* put it: "It is against precedent for a Hebrew to be there"—meaning Ryskind. There was a second ballot, with the journalism students backing their candidates, but they lost, and a protest to a faculty committee on student organizations failed. But this exacerbated another Columbia College grudge against Journalism—not only too independent, but too Jewish.[22]

The fall of 1916 went smoothly enough until mid-December, when the *Spectator*, and then the downtown papers, reported that the fourth-year journalism class had gone on strike. The grievances of the previous year's Too-Much-Work committee had remained unresolved. This time the crisis started when the class was directed to read and prepare a scenario from Thackeray's novel *Pendennis* in forty-eight hours, and was simultaneously ordered to write a history of journalism in Philadelphia, although only two relevant books were available in the library for thirty-two students.[23]

Talcott Williams's biographer was sympathetic to the students: "You know about TW's lack of memory for faces; he had another blind side,—it never dawned on him that others were as busy as he. Every secretary that worked for him before he came to New York collapsed. He was a tyrant in getting work out of people." Williams left town for a meeting of the Amherst College trustees, directing that his secretary distribute two quizzes in his absence. The class, thinking the tests were punishment, walked out. When he came back, Williams explained that he had meant no punishment, and the protest subsided.[24]

But the incident was not trifling. Its significance could be seen in the fact that, as Williams's biographer notes, "the man was breaking." She saw him afterward: "Sitting in his office, his back to the campus, shoulders pitifully humped, he turned to the window and thought out loud, 'Trouble, trouble.' . . . The strike hurt TW more than it hurt his boys." He had turned sixty-seven the summer before, and an old sixty-seven at that.[25]

CHAPTER 8

## "If Sedition Is to Be Excluded"

FROM ITS BEGINNING IN 1914, Talcott Williams was obsessed with the European war. It was only days old when he wrote to a relative: "I cannot keep the war out of my mind," and added, with prescience shared by few, that "the contest is certain to be a long war." Days later, he wrote to President Butler, who had been in Europe: "You return to a country sobered and more serious than in any previous war." Moreover, he added, the country had made up its mind: "In every man's thought is the prospect of our own responsibility and peril if Germany should win." In public appearances, he immediately stood on the side of what was called "preparedness."[1]

Even before American entry into the Great War raised the price of dissent, Nicholas Murray Butler had earned a reputation as an uncertain friend of academic freedom. The Columbia community was roiled in 1911 by the abrupt sacking of Joel E. Spingarn, professor of comparative literature and an early supporter of the National Association for the Advancement of Colored People, who had dared to challenge the dismissal of a colleague. In 1916, Charles A. Beard was criticized, primarily by the trustees, for a false newspaper report that he had exclaimed, "To hell with the flag!" at a public meeting.[2]

When the Columbia campus divided in the fevered weeks before the declaration of war in April 1917, there was little doubt that Williams would align the school with Butler and against dissent, and that dissenters among the students would feel betrayed. The historian Richard Baker scoffs mildly at what happened that spring: "The years have tended to romanticize this era in the student life of the School of Journalism." But at the time the protest had real enough consequences in the lives of individual students, much as was the case with the Vietnam draft resisters fifty years later.[3]

Early in 1917, several antiwar organizations consolidated into an Emergency Peace Federation and called a Washington rally for February 12. Lured by an activist Columbia literature teacher, Henry Wadsworth Longfellow Dana (who was dismissed later in the year), a delegation from the school— James Danahy, Albert Seadler, Morrie Ryskind, George Sokolsky, M. R. Werner, Lowell Pratt, and others—took a chartered train to Washington and earnestly spoke out against war to members of Congress, mostly to deaf ears. They got in to see Joseph P. Tumulty, President Wilson's secretary, who treated them courteously. They were undercut the next day, when Butler telegraphed the president, assuring him that the university stood unanimously ready to support military intervention.[4]

The clash of opinions produced casualties. The first was Ryskind, who intemperately compared Butler in the February issue of the *Jester* to Czar Nicholas and declared that other campus figures, including Williams, were scarcely better. Most of his *Jester* editorial board demanded his resignation; his journalism schoolmates S. M. Herzig and Robert A. Simon stood by him. The stacked student board likewise voted against him. He refused to resign, and the matter was appealed to the secretary of the university, Frank D. Fackenthal, who oversaw student organizations; Ryskind was removed. On April 7, Williams expelled him: "Mr. Ryskind has been dismissed for a breach of discipline in editing the February issue of the Jester." But he hardly left in disgrace. The class elected him its permanent vice-president and voted him its second favorite poet, after Kipling.[5]

The class was disappointed at losing Ryskind, but its president, George A. Hough, said that there would be no open protest, and there was not—perhaps because the student body had its collective eye on the next controversy. It involved George Sokolsky, who had burst into the newspapers in his first year at the school, when he testified on behalf of two members of the radical Industrial Workers of the World who had been beaten by the police in Union Square. Sokolsky was the stereotypical embodiment of a radical—bushy hair, intellectual mien, voluble speech. He was a pacifist and socialist, needless to say—even "a dangerous Red."[6]

By 1917 he had already been under the scrutiny not only of Williams but of President Butler. On March 2, 1917, Butler sent a carefully masked letter to Williams: "During the past two or three days renewed statements have been made to me of the inappropriateness, to say the least, of longer retaining Mr. Sokolsky upon the rolls of the University." Williams replied: "No clearer ground for dismissal of a student can be found than the conscious commission of a flagrantly ungentlemanly or vulgar act." He added, in longhand: "I have the evidence which justifies the immediate expulsion of George S. Sokolsky."[7]

Word got out to the *Sun*, which ran a headline casting the matter in parody of the Russian revolution: DUMA AT PULITZER SCHOOL IN REVOLT. There was a rumor that Williams would order Sokolsky from his classroom, having warned him to quit or be expelled. Anticipating the action, the entire class pledged to strike against "autocratic unfairness." At the same time, the class appeared mystified as to why Williams was so intent on punishing Sokolsky. A few thought it was because he had joined the peace train to Washington, but otherwise they knew of "no moral reproach [Williams] could cast upon the young man."[8]

Williams finessed the protest. He was smiling and affable when he met the class: "Amenities dripped like honey from an overstocked comb," wrote the *Sun* reporter. Nor did the director hesitate, when he called the roll, at the name, "Sokolsky, George," who was present. He glided seamlessly into a lecture on one of his favorite topics, journalism in Philadelphia. DUMA AT PULITZER SCHOOL IN A DAZE was the headline.[9]

What happened after that remains a little mysterious. Sokolsky was listed as attending the annual school dinner on April 19, and as late as May 15, near the end of the academic year, was routinely noted in the faculty minutes as being excused from classes to serve on a prison reform committee. Williams had neatly avoided a blowup over the matter. In the 1930s, Dean Carl W. Ackerman referred to Sokolsky's ultimate departure as a "withdrawal." In any case, Sokolsky did not receive a degree.[10]

But what was the "flagrantly ungentlemanly or vulgar act" to which Williams referred? The historian Richard Baker believed he knew. He wrote to a colleague in 1968:

Let me recall the case of George Sokolsky, class of 1917. The file shows a letter from Butler to T. Williams, calling the eminent director's attention to the fact that Butler's spies have learned of Sok[olsky]'s co-habiting with a member of the opposite sex in a nearby apartment, and would T. W. please put an end to the situation. Later, in another letter, Butler had learned that the situation ["]to which I called your attention in my earlier letter["] still persisted. That was when Sok got booted, and ever after explained that his rupture was due to political causes. He was a socialist and a pacifist, plus adulterer, but I as supreme historian [Baker was joking, presumably] know that the boot was applied for co-habitation. How times do change.

Probably true enough—that Sokolsky had made himself vulnerable with a violation of conventional morals, and had handed Butler and Williams the means to rid themselves of a political irritant and to silence him as well; if he had protested, they could have made seamy revelations that would have undercut his stance as a martyr. Not considering him disgraced, the class voted him the member most likely to become famous.[11]

The disappointment centered on Williams. Given his proclivity for sexual snooping, Williams no doubt took a keen interest in Sokolsky's private behavior. An unidentified member of the class of 1917 wrote afterward: "The point is that Talcott had been out in the world and was supposed to be a courageous editor. For him therefore to come out for God, for Country and for Butler was a greater disappointment than if a routine cloistered dean who had worked up from a fellowship had done the same thing."[12]

There was still another case, involving the school indirectly. Leon Fraser of the class of 1913 had gone on to earn a Ph.D. and had become an instructor in politics at Columbia College. In 1916, he commented critically on the opening of the military training camp at Plattsburgh, New York, and was called on to explain himself to a committee of trustees. A year later, his department was warned not to reappoint Fraser because he was not acceptable to one of the trustees, and he was not rehired.[13]

After the declaration of war against Germany on April 6, the school was swept into the tide of exhilarating urgency that enveloped country and campus. Even before the declaration, Walter Pitkin turned manic. In February, he ignored his chain of command and wrote to President Butler proposing that the school of journalism suspend its regular business and turn itself into a bureau for "civic education"—that is, for propaganda promoting the war.

By the end of March, he was writing on a red letterhead—"Division of Intelligence and Publicity / Columbia University"—urging Butler to find $250,000 for his work.[14]

On April 11, the school's committee on instruction met and adopted resolutions that permitted the school to "provide instruction needed in the present national emergency"—that is, to cancel classes. Two dozen third- and fourth-year students went to work for Pitkin, including three who were sent to Washington as student correspondents. Forty-five other students were given exemptions, many signing up for training in the Officers' Reserve Corps; others joined the ambulance corps and the Naval Reserve. All were given credit for the full session. The year was in tatters, but the *Spectator* found the school's mobilization admirable: "Journalism seems to be meeting the emergency nobly."[15]

Before the year ended, the air went out of Pitkin's balloon. He was bombarding Butler with plans for a series of "Columbia War Papers," the publication of each to be supported by a major advertiser. Late in May, Butler shut him down: "It will be necessary for us to discontinue any but formal activity of our Division of Publicity, because I have found it impracticable to secure more than a very limited financial support." Pitkin was already in Washington with a new letterhead—"The New Republic News Service"—and then still another, the "Council of National Defense."[16]

At the end of the year, the first Pulitzer Prizes were awarded and the first Pulitzer Traveling Scholars were named, almost unnoticed. In journalism, the juries—formed from the journalism teaching staff—awarded only two prizes, having received no nominations in several categories. An editorial-writing prize went to the *Tribune* for a jingoistic anti-German essay; Herbert Bayard Swope of the *World* won in reporting for his dispatches from Germany. The literary prizes, nominated by the American Academy of Arts and Letters, were lame: no prizes in drama or fiction, a history award to a book written by the French ambassador, and a biography of Julia Ward Howe by her daughters. Although later the traveling scholarships usually went to members of the graduating class, three earlier graduates won in 1917: Geddes Smith, 1913; David S. Levy, 1914; and Otto D. Tolischus, 1916. The recipients' travel was to be postponed until after the war, and they never collected the awards.[17]

The anger at Germans, pacifists, and socialists that led to harsh suppression of dissent nationwide was echoed at Columbia, and Williams played a supporting role. In the spring of 1917, Williams forwarded to Butler a list of persons who attended a meeting on May 8 at the headquarters of the Columbia branch of the Anti-Militarism League, an anti-draft group. A few days later, Butler wrote to Williams: "The newspaper[s?] contain a circumstantial report to the effect that certain students of the University, headed by Mr. Danahy, who is registered in the School of Journalism, have organized or are organizing resistance to the operation of the laws of the U.S. relating to the Army. If on inquiry you find this to be true, kindly report the facts to me as I am entirely unwilling to have any person who is in open resistance to the laws of his country remain a registered student in this University or be recommended for a degree."[18]

Indeed, James Danahy, the champion debater and defeated student board candidate, was registered in the school, and he was, as Williams confirmed, president of the Collegiate Anti-Militarism League. Danahy insisted that his members had resolved to obey the law and continue to hold their own opinions. But independent opinions were not welcome; in fact, Butler had officially banned them.[19]

Williams left town late in May 1917 to collect three honorary degrees. When he returned, he found a letter from Butler, enclosing a letter from Danahy, who bitterly quoted Butler back to himself: "The enclosed remarks about giving 'complete liberty of assembly, of speech and of publication to all members of the University who, in lawful ways, might wish to influence and guide public policy,' probably sound 'high and noble' to outsiders and alumni, but those of us who remember [he listed several incidents] and the . . . rah-rah patriotism meeting which threw me out of a University building, think differently on the matter. These are all matters of the past, but when I remember them, and the infamous treatment I received a year ago from the Committee on Student Activities in the student-board affair, and the fact there was talk up to the last minute of withholding my degree, I am overcome by certain emotions which are best left unsaid." Butler furiously called the letter "impertinent and essentially untruthful" and added that Columbia had made a mistake in letting Danahy get away with a degree.[20]

To placate Butler, Williams replied that he had told Danahy he could never give him a reference, and blamed the troubles on "disloyal" professors such as Dana. He added, "If the School of Journalism has been more before the public, it is because a man who can write, and knows how to get what he writes printed will accomplish more." As propitiation he added: "I enclose a list which may be useful if sedition is to be excluded from the University"—attendees at "The First American Conference for Democracy and Terms of Peace" at the Garden Theater in New York on May 31. Butler by now had a full head of steam, complaining to Williams of a lack of patriotism in the university: "We propose to clear the skirts of Columbia University of any suspicion of complicity, direct or indirect, in what is to all intents and purposes treason."[21]

The political juice seemed to drain from the school after the class of 1917 dispersed. Elsewhere on the campus, President Butler completed his purge by engineering the dismissal of Professor Dana and a psychology professor, James McKeen Cattell, who had criticized Butler relentlessly. Charles Beard, who was on the school's administrative board and taught a course in politics for journalism students, left soon after—not, he explained, out of pique but out of loss of confidence in the future of the university.[22]

The school suffered a loss closer to home in November 1917 when Professor Franklin Matthews, who had been the workhorse of the newsroom, died at the age of sixty-one. He was remembered affectionately, and eventually a reporting award was named for him and a plaque put up in the senior city room. The school scrambled to cover Matthews's responsibilities. Even before a search began for a replacement, Pitkin bypassed Williams again and wrote to Butler urging the appointment of a younger man because of "the importance of getting men on our faculty who have a future instead of a past." Nonetheless, the next professor of journalism was a mature notable, Roscoe C. E. Brown, former editorial writer and managing editor of the *Tribune*.[23]

In fact, during the two war years, the school scarcely needed to expand its faculty. The number of male students fell precipitously; Director Williams was annoyed by the sound of knitting needles in his class—no doubt women working on warm garments for soldiers. In 1918–19, the enrollment dropped to only forty-seven from a prewar maximum of 172, and the graduating class of 1918 numbered nineteen, with eight men (among them Henry Beetle Hough, who became the famed editor of the *Vineyard Gazette*). Three graduates of the school died in France—William Stewart Lahey, class of 1914; Meyer Cohn, class of 1915; and Lee West Sellers, class of 1917.[24]

Although a few men returned for the second semester after the war ended in November 1918, the class of 1919 had but twenty graduates, ten of them men. (One of the women was Elizabeth Wilson Bowie, who became Henry Beetle Hough's wife and partner.) The school was at a low ebb as it ended its first epoch, with a new director, a new curriculum, and a new relationship with the university in prospect.[25]

# CHAPTER 9

# Red Apple and Maraschino Cherry

THE SPRING OF 1919 brought the last days of the Talcott Williams era as the director reached the age of seventy. The announcement of his retirement, a few days before commencement, brought warm praise. Looking back, Williams said that the school's first achievement had been to demonstrate that education for journalism was not, as practiced in so many other institutions, a collection of writing courses growing out of the English department. He claimed to have pursued Pulitzer's vision that the "one chief work of such a school is to require training in the fundamental studies of the journalist's future labors—political economy, political science, history and like fields of knowledge"—in short, that journalism education was a full education in public affairs.[1]

Yet, as he left, the school was on the verge of diminishing that goal, no longer attempting to fit a full liberal-arts education to the requirements of journalism. The change had initially been announced in 1917 as a "five year course"—two years in Columbia College, then three years of professional training in the school of journalism, leading to both A.B. and B.Lit. degrees. The five-year course faded before it took full effect, and the school never developed a third professional year. The B.Lit. became a two-year course requiring two years of previous undergraduate study. There remained an option of going on to a one-year master of science, comprising mostly electives.[2]

One effect of this change, which began to be phased in during the fall of 1919, was the disappearance of the senior professors from other departments who in earlier years had come to the school to teach. The outsiders were no longer listed in the 1918–19 announcement, and only two courses, in law and statistics, were taught by members of other faculties. Later, what had been a general course in elements of law became a more utilitarian, and narrower, offering in libel law, presented by Henry Woodward Sackett, counsel for the *Tribune*.[3]

The entire upper-level curriculum became more technical, less general. Although students could still opt for courses taught in other divisions, the wide-ranging contact of journalism students with scholars from other faculties was gone. In the redrafted curriculum, Columbia journalism undergraduates had available professional courses amounting to more than a third to a half of the roughly 120 points needed for graduation. This was substantially higher than the 25 percent that later came to be the ceiling, to protect the liberal arts, in accredited undergraduate programs.[4]

Another sign of separation of school from campus could be seen in the new composition of the administrative board—the multidepartmental faculty body that had overseen the school through its early years. In 1919–20, the board became, except for courtesy seats occupied by President Butler and Dean Hawkes of the college, an all-journalism body—a de facto faculty of journalism, although it was not to be given that title for another decade.[5]

Directorship of the school was handed, on Williams's retirement, to John W. Cunliffe, who had been waiting reticently in the wings since 1912. He seemed no better suited to the post than before. He never taught a real journalism course; his courses, listed under journalism numbers, were confined to modern European drama, fiction, and poetry. John Hohenberg, class of 1927, who as a teacher became an apostle of the intensely practical, paradoxically recalled that Cunliffe's courses, unpopular with newsroom-minded students, were his most important as a student.[6]

After a year as acting director, Cunliffe was given the full title with unanimous support from the advisory board, apparently lobbied by Butler. Cunliffe wrote to the president: "I have been, of course, aware of the difficulties of the situation, and I am exceedingly grateful to you personally for the way in which they have been overcome." He was clearly alluding to the advisory board's doubts about naming a nonjournalist. Cunliffe seemed destined, by character and succession, to be a caretaker.[7]

There was apprehension in the faculty over Cunliffe's promotion. Pitkin recalled that a faction of alumni and professors were certain that the school would "bog down and end up as an annex of the English Department." Another faction, according to Pitkin, argued that the "manifest destiny" of the school was the humble one of turning out "able young reporters, craftsmen of a skill below a cabinet-maker and above a plumber." As for maintaining a genuinely professional school, patterned after law or medicine, the rebuttal was: "Only two professions pay the youngest members best and the oldest least."[8]

(In fact, it seems that one student sought to practice both. In *A House Is Not a Home*, the best-seller published in 1953, Polly Adler tells of one employee in her brothel, whom she calls "Fran," who was studying journalism at Columbia. Fran did not smoke, drink, or stay out late, so as to be alert for her studies in the morning. "She was the delight of my patrons for some time," Adler wrote, and added that Fran went on to become a novelist. The context suggests a relatively long term of employment, which would place Fran in the undergraduate era, probably in the 1920s. Dean Carl W. Ackerman is said—by a staff member who was working at the school in 1953–54—to have called for relevant student records when the book appeared; it is not known whether he identified Fran.)[9]

In the fall of 1919, enrollment rebounded to more than a hundred, and the school needed more faculty and more typewriters. Charles P. Cooper, another practitioner over fifty and assistant night city editor at the *Times*, was named an associate professor. He was destined for an important role as a successor to MacAlarney and Matthews, dominating the school's newsrooms for years with his foghorn voice. He also served as a real-world counterbalance to Cunliffe's academicism. "Coop"—as he was called, not to his face—initiated the custom of awarding an imaginary big red apple, which was actually a series of red X's scrawled on copy in wax pencil, for the week's outstanding work. Alas, literalists turned his imaginary apple into a metal plaque given to a "best reporter" in the class, stripping it of its charm.[10]

Recent graduates were recruited to teach. The first was Carl Dickey of the *Times*, class of 1915, who had covered the fighting on the Mexican border in 1916 and had sailed on an armed American liner during the period of unrestricted submarine warfare. In 1920, four more alumni became "assistants" in journalism—George A. Hough, Merryle S. Rukeyser, and Alan Temple of the class of 1917, and David S. Levy, 1915. The school also hired its first woman teacher, or rather borrowed her. An assistant professor of English at Barnard College, Clare M. Howard became adviser to women journalism students in 1917 and was given teaching chores starting in 1920.[11]

The school announcement for 1920–21 listed only four full-time journalism teachers: Cunliffe, Roscoe C. E. Brown, Walter B. Pitkin, and Charles P. Cooper. They were outnumbered by a dozen assistants or associates. This "downtown" majority—part-time practitioner-teachers from New York newspapers—became an enduring characteristic of the teaching staff, the rationale being the downtowners' contact with the current journalism, the underlying reason being their availability for low pay.

Early in the Cunliffe administration, the school began a practice that tacitly undermined one of Joseph Pulitzer's contentions, that university training would be more thorough than instruction picked up on the job. Echoing a practice from wartime, when students were exempted from classes for training or special projects, the school began to release students for paid work. The releases began on a small scale, probably on the initiative of Cooper, and the exemptions increased through the 1920s. They were not entirely the equivalent of what came to be known, in imitation of medical practice, as internships; the exempted students reported regularly to Cooper, but there was no burden on the employer to provide systematic training.

No general faculty resolution appears to have sanctioned this policy. Instead, there were individual motions such as the following: "On motion Samuel N. Kirkland was excused from attendance at recitation in Journalism 41 and Journalism 43, on the recommendation of Professor Cooper, on account of his professional work for the Wall Street Journal, which Professor Cooper regards as equivalent to class exercise, subject to monthly reports which satisfy Professor Cooper that Mr. Kirkland is properly pursuing the work of the course." Years later, the practice of permitting exemptions for part-time work was finally acknowledged in the school announcement as "a valuable supplement to the School curriculum" that "often opens the way to a full-time professional post"—that is, as an employment rather than an educational strategy.[12]

In 1920, graduates of the school coalesced into an alumni organization. The preliminary step was a Friday noon luncheon club; then came a weekly Tuesday night dinner at Keene's Chop House on 44th Street. As might have been anticipated, members of the class of 1917 were the moving spirits—among them James Danahy (now at Hearst's *American*), Maria Sermolino of the brand-new *Daily News*, and Palmer Smith and George Hough of the *World*. On May 22, 1920, the Columbia University School of Journalism

Alumni Association was founded at the seventh annual all-school dinner. The president was Edwin N. Lewis, 1915, a public-relations practitioner; M. Lincoln Schuster, 1917, then laboring for the Motor Accessories Manufacturing Association but soon to become a notable book publisher, was elected secretary and treasurer. The alumni distributed the first issue of *Clean Copy*, a magazine to be published quarterly.[13]

*Clean Copy* contained a "job census." Of 172 alumni (that is, those who held degrees or had attended the school for three or four years), 133 responded. Of these, thirty-seven were on newspapers and a dozen on magazines. But already there were enough in publicity and advertising—forty-one—to feed the school's underground reputation as a pipeline out of journalism to bigger money. This hunch was confirmed, backhandedly, in the protective subheadline the *World* put on a story about the next year's list: "Directory Refutes the Charge that Graduates Do Not Engage in Newspaper Work."[14]

The school entered its tenth year of operation in the fall of 1921. Director Cunliffe made a point of announcing at the start of the year that less than a quarter of the enrollment of the school now came from New York City. This coincided with a reduction across the campus in the enrollment of New York City students. The favored interpretation was, of course, that the school, and the university, were becoming national institutions and drawing their students from a greater pool.[15]

Or, another perspective: President Butler had been concerned that Jews constituted two of five public high school graduates in New York City. Without acknowledging that he was doing so, he reversed the old policy of favoring New York applicants (implicitly contradicting the spirit of Joseph Pulitzer's first benefaction to Columbia, his scholarships for New York public school students). Instead, Columbia favored students from outside the city, and the percentage of Jews in the campus student body dropped from 40 percent to 22 percent by 1921. The historian Thomas Bender has commented: "What is finally most disturbing about all of this is that Columbia's bigoted irresponsibility was a significant factor in Butler's successful effort to consolidate Columbia's position as a national elite institution." There is no indication that the school joined consciously in this restrictive policy, but it implemented it nonetheless.[16]

This 1921–22 year included the seventy-fifth anniversary of Pulitzer's birth, April 10, 1922. A laurel wreath was placed beneath his bust in the lobby. Talcott Williams emerged to lecture on the origins of the school. The only challenging note, it seemed, came from Herbert Bayard Swope, ebullient executive editor of the *World* and honorary member of the class of 1917. Why,

Swope asked, should not the school of journalism bear the name of Joseph Pulitzer? The reply came from President Butler himself, who responded that such a change would add no distinction to the institution, and indeed might handicap it—just how, he did not specify. He added that the proper title was the one he said it already bore: "The School of Journalism, endowed by Joseph Pulitzer."[17]

The school's official observance of its tenth anniversary coincided with the graduation of the tenth class in May 1923. The ceremonies started with the unveiling of a smallish bust of Talcott Williams in the school's vestibule; facing Rodin's Pulitzer, it seemed outmatched. Then there was a dinner for 300 at the Hotel Commodore, with Ralph Pulitzer, chairman of the advisory board, presiding. A retrospective yearbook containing pictures of past and present faculty and current students, prepared by the classes of 1923 and 1924, was distributed. It was the first of a series called *The Columbia Journalist*.[18]

In his annual report that fall, Cunliffe summed up what he believed to be the school's achievements to that point. The basic statistics were: 277 B.Lit. degrees awarded—187 to men, 90 to women. He praised the women students for their determination to escape the seraglio of women's pages. In fact, the alumni association had just elected its first woman president, Clara Sharp Hough, class of 1918. Cunliffe contended that the institution had overcome skepticism, "at least modifying the opinions of two extremists, the college professor and the newspaper man." He recalled for an interviewer that Charles Beard had told him that the original scheme for the school had "included all that he would want his children to know in the way of a general education; that, were his children old enough, he would send them to the school whether or not they intended to study journalism." In fact, Beard's daughter Miriam, when she reached college age, came to the school in 1921. But Cunliffe failed to note the irony—that much of the general-education component that Beard praised had been stripped away, and perhaps with it some of the mind-stretching demands it made on students. For her part, Miriam Beard left after a year.[19]

That the school was entering the intellectual doldrums was later alleged by a jaundiced observer, A. J. Liebling, who arrived fresh from being dismissed by Dartmouth. His Columbia instructors, he found, were preaching conformity to the writing standards of the "especially tasteless *Times* of 1923, a political hermaphrodite capable of intercourse with conservatives of both parties at the same time." Nonetheless, he remained for his second year, thanks to Cooper, whom he rather liked for his mastery of profanity and expectoration. Cooper offered to give Liebling a permanent assignment at police headquarters as an understudy to Max Fischel of the *Evening World*. (Liebling evidently had no inkling that this kind of farming-out had been going on for years.) Liebling loved it, but commented on his departure: "As a maraschino cherry on the sundae of academic absurdity, the degree was entitled Bachelor of Literature [actually, Letters], although what literature had to do with rewriting the *Times* paragraphs I never found out."[20]

Yet the school continued to turn out journalists, and to set unshaped students on the path to careers. Herbert Brucker arrived in the class of 1924 innocent of any previous contact with journalism, even service on a high school or campus newspaper, but he ultimately became president of the American Society of Newspaper Editors. Brucker recalled: "Out of it all, and out of the endlessly repeated drill of writing, writing, and writing, always subject to detailed and expert revision, one somehow acquired a whiff of that breadth and understanding, that discipline in finding words to fit the facts and the thoughts they are to convey, that form the bedrock of journalism."[21]

Nor was the roster of graduates of those Cunliffe years insubstantial. Martene Windsor Corum (1921) became the sports writer Bill Corum. Harold G. Borland (1923) became Hal Borland, nature author and editorial writer. Robert Garst (1924) and Theodore M. Bernstein (1925) became desk mainstays at the *Times* and long-time teachers at the school. So did the feature writer Allan Keller (1926) and Jacob Hohenberg (1927), who, as John Hohenberg, was a pioneer United Nations correspondent and later a professor at the school.[22]

One hope was lost. Katherine Ewing MacMahon, a cousin of Adlai E. Stevenson, vice president under Cleveland, was a Phi Beta Kappa graduate of the University of Chicago. She earned her B.Lit. at the school of journalism in a year and won a Pulitzer Traveling Scholarship, which she used for study at the University of London. On her return, she taught journalism courses at Mount Holyoke College and reported for the *Christian Science Monitor*. The school hired her as an instructor in the fall of 1922, and she was named to the committee on instruction—the most important faculty body—the following spring. Half a year later, she died. Her shocked colleagues adopted a resolution praising her as a student, as a teacher, and as an adviser: "Her example was a source of strength and encouragement to the oldest as well as the youngest of us." Her estate returned the $1,500 she received for her traveling scholarship to be used as a scholarship and financial aid fund. It is still awarded. Her loss had incalculable effects—not only on the impact that a tenured woman might have had on her colleagues but on the attitudes in the school toward women students.[23]

In April 1927, Talcott Williams spoke at founder's day—the annual com-
memoration of Joseph Pulitzer's birth—and remarked that he still prided
himself on insisting that women be admitted to the school. It was all but a
farewell appearance. The following January 24, he died at his home on West
117th Street, seventy-eight years old. The service in St. Paul's Chapel on the
campus amounted to the school's first state funeral. There were twenty honorary pallbearers, mostly drawn from the advisory board and the faculty,
and ten graduate pallbearers, including James W. Danahy, class of 1917, his
wartime anger at Williams and Columbia long cooled.[24]

Robert E. MacAlarney wrote a tribute in the *World* to Williams's basic
kindness: "Had there been a chair of the human equation at the university . . .
Talcott Williams could have filled it superbly." At the same time, he recalled
the bafflement of arrivals expecting to receive "so many spoonfuls of tangible newspaper training per diem." Instead, they found "they were supposed
to accumulate and then arrange a background of focused culture without
which there can be no truly great journalists." This, MacAlarney insisted,
was the core of the Pulitzer heritage, but he seemed oblivious to the diminu-
tions of recent years.[25]

Two weeks after Williams's death, Director Cunliffe returned to the
school after a seven-month medical absence in Florida. Two years later, just
before his sixty-fifth birthday, Cunliffe received from Butler a letter reminding him pointedly that he was now entitled to retire. Cunliffe responded that
he had no interest in doing so, probably thinking that he would serve until
he was seventy, as Williams had. But during the spring of 1930, he was
nudged by Frank D. Fackenthal, secretary of the university, who reminded
him that he was entitled to a pension of $4,000 a year. He no doubt under-
stood by then that his successor was in the wings.[26]

CHAPTER 10

# The First Dean

AS HE NEARED THE END of his time as director, John W. Cunliffe could reflect that in a few obvious ways the school of journalism had prospered.
Graduating classes had grown larger, peaking at seventy-four in 1929. In addition, a dozen or so graduate students were enrolled in the master of science
program, an add-on retained offhandedly since the Talcott Williams era.

A study of graduates requested by the advisory board was published in
1926, midway in Cunliffe's term. Two-thirds of the 437 graduates responded to a questionnaire about their working lives. More than half were in core
journalism jobs, editing or reporting; these were young alumni, of course,
and it was yet to be determined whether they could afford to remain in journalism. A second study, conducted by Walter Pitkin and published in 1931,
asserted that many of the best graduates were getting out of the business—a
finding that produced, Pitkin recalled, "deep pain followed by deeper silence" in newspaper offices, which were by then tightening wages in the
Great Depression.[1]

Butler brought Cunliffe's successor onto the scene in 1930. In June, President Butler wrote Cunliffe to say that he was sorry that he had been unable

to reach him and in the meantime had made Carl W. Ackerman, class of 1913, an associate in journalism, at no salary, to help with fundraising. Cunliffe raised no objection; how could he object to one of the school's best known and most loyal graduates? By January 1931, Butler was able to send Ackerman a coded note saying that "our friend" would cooperate "in carrying out the plan which I have in mind"—that is, Cunliffe had been persuaded to retire and concur in Ackerman's appointment as director. Butler assured Ackerman, moreover, that he would not be director long, but would become the school's first dean, at $9,000 a year.[2]

Ackerman was a natural choice; as early as 1919, in fact, Talcott Williams had thought of him as a successor. He was young, just forty—Butler's age when he became president nearly thirty years before. A member of the first graduating class, Ackerman had remained actively interested in the school and its alumni association while engaged in an enterprising career as a correspondent. He covered the White House and was later a war correspondent in London and Berlin. In 1918, the *Times* sent him across the Pacific and on to Ekaterinburg, Siberia, to investigate the execution of the czar and his family. After the war, as bureau chief for the Philadelphia *Public Ledger*, he was a go-between in the Anglo-Irish peace negotiations of 1920 and 1921. After 1921, he turned to public relations for major corporations such as Remington Rand and Eastman Kodak (he wrote a biography of George Eastman), and had just taken a new job as assistant to the president of General Motors.[3]

Butler found that both the advisory board and the alumni association wanted Ackerman. So did the younger Joseph Pulitzer and his brother Ralph, initially. But a week after his initial letter of approval, Ralph Pulitzer sent a telegram: "If after thoroughly combing the field there are no other nominations I would gladly approve the nominee named in your letter of January thirty first although I wish we might find a man who is not a publicity director stop most publicity directors are concerned primarily with adulterating the news columns and with distorting and misrepresenting facts solely in the interest of the corporation they represent and often with little or no regard for the public interest." It was obvious that he had discussed the matter with someone; with whom became obvious when he recommended consideration of Herbert Bayard Swope, the flamboyant former executive editor of the *World*. Butler dismissed Swope: "The brilliant and attractive gentleman whom you mention could not, I feel sure, ever be turned into an academic person, even if all the universities in the country were to unite their efforts upon him." And defended Ackerman: "He is the outstanding alumnus of the School . . . his present work in charge of public relations for the

General Motors Company has given him a number of important contacts that I feel sure will redound to the advantage of the School." On March 3, 1931, Butler announced Ackerman's appointment.[4]

It was a watershed time, not only for the school but also for New York journalism: only five days before Ackerman's appointment, the *World* printed its final issue, and it became irrevocably clear that the school and its prizes, not the newspaper, would be Pulitzer's enduring legacy in New York. Although Pulitzer had tried to provide for the *World*'s perpetuation in his will, the paper had been losing circulation and money for at least three years, with a culminating loss of $1.7 million in 1930. It had let its stars go—not only Swope but also the columnist Heywood Broun—and it had dismissed a hundred employees, many of whom had served under the senior Pulitzer. In January 1931, the Pulitzer brothers agreed to sell the newspaper to the Scripps-Howard chain, and obtained court permission to disregard their father's will. The sale was completed, despite frantic efforts by the employees to buy the newspaper. The flagship morning *World* vanished; the *Evening World* survived humbly as part of the nameplate of the *World-Telegram*.[5]

For the school, the *World* had served as a somewhat distant godparent. Although Ralph Pulitzer and John Langdon Heaton of the *World* had served on the advisory board from the beginning, and Ralph Pulitzer and *World* editors were often guest speakers, the newspaper had supplied no full-time teachers to the school, and the *Times* overtook the *World* in hiring graduates. Yet the *World* remained a potent symbol, and in the months after the closing, Ralph Pulitzer tried to create a kind of shrine to the newspaper by giving the school the *World*'s Great War service plaque and its three Pulitzer Prize public-service medals.[6]

One of Ackerman's old foreign-correspondent colleagues, Stephen Bonsal, tied the coincidence together in a congratulatory letter to Ackerman: "It is a tremendous opportunity and your success which is assured will reconcile the late Joseph Pulitzer, if any thing can, to the death of what was His World in every sense of the word." Ackerman was less sentimental than Bonsal. He wrote to Roy Howard, the purchaser and Ackerman's one-time employer at United Press, addressing him as "Dear Teacher" and praising him for "the masterful way in which you handled the consolidation of the World newspapers with The Telegram."[7]

Although such school veterans as Robert MacAlarney—who had taught him—welcomed Ackerman, he was not unanimously cheered. The graduating class described the change as a "shock," because Cunliffe had "endeared himself to the student body with his lectures and his friendly counsel." The campus *Spectator* reprinted a strikingly bitter editorial that it attributed to the trade magazine *Editor & Publisher*, although it sounded more like Swope:

> Mr. Ackerman is said to be the personal choice of President Nicholas Murray Butler, who continues persistent in an effort to dignify the free publicity racket in this country. . . . A clique among the alumni have also been working for the appointment of Mr. Ackerman for some time. Other members of the association have protested bitterly on the ground that Mr. Ackerman does not typify the liberal spirit of Joseph Pulitzer. . . . Talcott Williams was ideal as representing Pulitzer journalistic practice. Prof. John W. Cunliffe, director since 1919, was at best a routine professor of English literature. Now a director comes straight from a corporation publicity job! We can think of a score of distinguished editorial men, who have never compromised ethics, and were available for the post.[8]

Butler disregarded the fuss. He prompted university governance to restructure the school, in effect to take it finally out of probationary status after twenty years. Ackerman was given the title of dean. The administrative board—the faculty group that oversaw the school—disbanded; the self-governing Faculty of Journalism was created, and waited expectantly for its new leader.[9]

After he arrived in the fall of 1931, Ackerman held his peace for a time, but when he spoke out he was almost wrathful. His first target was the hodge-podge master's program. Its requirements, beyond the need to earn thirty points, were largely determined by individual students and their advisers, although all were required to take Pitkin's course called "The Psychology of News and Popular Reading" and write an article or articles totaling 15,000 words. Condemning "the superficiality of the courses and the routine instruction and supervision by the staff," the new dean said that the graduate program should be revised, and a month later that it should be abolished.[10]

That step was included in a package of curriculum reforms that Ackerman presented to the president in his first major policy letter, early in 1932. Essentially, he sought to rehabilitate the five-year program that had been announced but not implemented under Talcott Williams: students would arrive having completed at least three years of college and would study two years for the B.Lit. At the same time, he wanted to abolish the point system for courses and place all work on a unified pass-fail basis. Most important, he advocated putting the school into a full work-simulation, or industrial, mode: "That the course be organized on a time basis, i.e., eight hours of work per day for five days each week during the academic year." He made a gesture toward restoring ties with the rest of the university by proposing that students be assigned to take "regular university classes in government, economics, business, music, philosophy, law, history, typography, stenography, magazine writing and editing and other subjects as a reporter would be given assignments by his city editor." But that part was never fully implemented. Students were to work their forty-hour weeks largely inside the building.[11]

Butler urged Ackerman to prepare his proposals for submission to university governance. At the same time he urged the abandonment of the B.Lit. degree, which he professed to have disliked from the beginning: "Since the training for journalism rests upon an ordered and scientifically planned foundation, why not assimilate this professional degree to those established elsewhere in the University and give the degree of Bachelor of Science in Journalism rather than that of Bachelor of Letters. This would, I think, give the journalistic training a better academic status before the world than is possible by the use of an unusual and odd degree."[12]

Ackerman incorporated the B.S. degree in his proposal and circulated his reformed curriculum on campus and off. Most of the responses were favorable. Dean Herbert E. Hawkes of Columbia College was concerned about the "working day" requirement. Ralph Pulitzer grumbled: "I think my father would turn in his grave if heard journalism described as a science," but subsided after Ackerman forwarded Butler's double-talking claim that "science" referred to the method of studying of the field, not its substance. The written responses Ackerman received from the faculty were supportive, although F. Fraser Bond, class of 1921, who had joined the faculty during the Cunliffe years, wrote that he wished the proposal had had faculty input. The University Council approved the changes promptly.[13]

The new program was made public at the start of April 1932, to the accompaniment of the greatest surge of favorable publicity since the school's opening. The reaction must have gladdened Ackerman, whose arrival had been greeted with such doubts. Notably, the American Society of Newspaper Editors adopted a resolution with the most enthusiastic words the organization had ever offered on journalism education:

> The projected changes at the Pulitzer School will come about as near to receiving one hundred per cent approval from the editors of the United States as any move that has ever been made in the field of journalism. For one thing, the new set-up at Columbia will eliminate even more drastically the drones and the unfit. . . . Many schools of journalism have

yielded to the temptation to go in for numbers whereas the newspaper whom they served would always have preferred to receive a few really superior newspaper men than a great quantity of indifferent ones. Your committee expresses in the most emphatic terms its hearty approval of the action of Columbia.[14]

Later, an acute comment on the new deanship came from Stanley Walker of the *Herald Tribune* in his book, *City Editor*. The changes, he wrote, placed "Ackerman himself in a position of virtual complete control of the school, with as much power to fire or promote as any managing editor." The dean, wrote Walker, could "bounce a man because he didn't like his pompadour, or his peculiar hang-dog look, or merely felt . . . that he would never make good newspaper material." But Walker did not view this power as a drawback, merely an academic emulation of what news executives—including Walker himself—did all the time. It accurately predicted the autocratic nature of Ackerman's deanship.[15]

Ackerman underlined his intentions in another interview with *Editor & Publisher*. He harshly disavowed the general-education concept that had ruled the school's earliest years: "The Pulitzer agreement requires us to train students for the profession of journalism. . . . We are not giving a substitute college education, nor running a girls' finishing school." Indeed, women were to be a target of what he saw as necessary strictures on enrollment: "I know of no newspaper or press association with even 25 per cent of its editorial staff made up of women. . . . I think the school should not encourage women to believe that there will be unlimited opportunities when we know the opportunities are limited."[16]

Ackerman's first staff recruit at the school was thirty-two-year-old Herbert Brucker, class of 1924. Brucker, who had worked briefly on the *World* and was working as an editor at *Review of Reviews*, had written to Ackerman to ask to interview the new dean. Ackerman apparently liked his interviewer, because he appointed Brucker assistant to the dean at a hundred dollars a week, with a secretary at thirty dollars.[17]

Brucker was handed a variety of jobs; one of the stickiest was to chair a committee investigating the campus newspaper, the *Spectator*, in the wake of the expulsion of its editor, Reed Harris, for attacking football and the management of the dining halls. Ackerman had distinct views on how to solve the *Spectator* problem for good: enlarge it from a college to a campuswide newspaper, merge it with the *Barnard Bulletin* and the comparable Teachers College publication, and put the whole thing under the supervision of the school of journalism. He stood before a meeting of Columbia College alumni, accused the *Spectator* of "inaccurate, irresponsible reporting," and volunteered the school's help in setting matters straight. The newspaper stirred up opposition to the plan; it never took effect, although Ackerman raised it again from time to time.[18]

Brucker also was given charge of an Ackerman brain child: a publication to be called the *Independent Journal*, after the New York newspaper that had first published *The Federalist* in 1787 and 1788. Ackerman scraped up a gift of $2,000, and a first experimental issue, elegantly designed in the general shape and size of its forebear, appeared in April 1933. Its statement of intent quoted Joseph Pulitzer II as saying that newspapers should be "forever intent upon exploring the truth which underlies any report of surface fact." The first issue published a list of the names of all the Columbia faculty and staff holding government appointments under Franklin D. Roosevelt—the newly minted "brains trust."[19]

Ackerman meanwhile tried to bring his faculty up to the demands of his new working-day curriculum. He had inherited half a dozen professors: Director Emeritus Cunliffe, carrying on as a teacher of fiction, poetry, and drama; Roscoe C. E. Brown, offering the practices and lore of editorial pages; Walter B. Pitkin, popular and erratic, author of a book a year, and about to dominate best-seller lists with *Life Begins at Forty*; Charles P. Cooper, the newsroom boss; Allen Sinclair Will, who had been referred to by A. J. Liebling as "a dull, handsome old man whose reputation was principally based on a two-volume biography of a Baltimore cardinal"; and F. Fraser Bond, a junior professor who retained a job at the *Times*.

This core was augmented by eleven associates and lecturers, of which the most notable were the critic Joseph Wood Krutch; the young deskmen Robert E. Garst and Theodore M. Bernstein of the *Times*; Harold Livingston Cross, counsel for the *Herald Tribune*, who had succeeded his colleague Henry Woodward Sackett as the libel-law teacher; and Elmer Davis, historian of the *Times* and freelance writer and novelist, later head of the wartime Office of War Information.[20]

As a group, the full-time teachers were elderly—three of them had graduated from college in the nineteenth century—and were not a good match for the youngish new dean. Ackerman held his peace until the first year of the new curriculum was nearly completed. Then he reported to Butler, centering his criticism on Pitkin, whose new feature-writing course had foundered and been divided among four other instructors. But his grievance against Pitkin was more general: "Due to the fact that Professor Pitkin has been accustomed to devoting a large part of his time to his outside interests, it has been difficult to obtain that measure of his time which I think we ought to expect from a man in his professorial position."[21]

He also grumbled about Professor Will, who was giving two days a week to Rutgers University and collecting supplementary pay there of $5,000 a year. Will resolved the problem by dying in 1934. Ackerman also wanted to shake up the part-time teachers. He terminated the critic Joseph Wood Krutch and Merryl Stanley Rukeyser, the financial writer. He recruited four alumni—Joseph L. Jones (1922), Lester Markel (1914), Carl C. Dickey (1915), and Max Schuster (1917)—to teach without pay. Having set his house in order for the time being, Ackerman turned his attention to the larger world.[22]

CHAPTER 11
_____

# "Ackerman Hails Stand of Press"

IN ITS FIRST TWENTY YEARS, the school of journalism rarely became involved in politics—that is, politics in the general sense of taking positions of public concern, such as debates over the sins and virtues of journalism or controversies over the rights and obligations of the press in society. In general, the school justified A. J. Liebling's charge that its attitude toward the newspaper business was one of passive collaboration. Such comment as was made reflexively defended the established press, as when, at the 1921 annual dinner, Director Cunliffe and Professor Emeritus Williams decried the charges of press corruption in the muckraker Upton Sinclair's polemic, *The Brass Check* (titled for a token used in a house of prostitution). Cunliffe made the feeble claim that "the proportion of honorable men engaged in newspaper work is as great as in any other profession"; Williams trivialized Sinclair by accusing him of believing that "something is wrong with the world which failed to appreciate him adequately." The quietude was reflected in the curriculum, which by the 1930s contained no courses investigating the place of journalism in society, nor even the former instruction in history and ethics.[1]

Dean Ackerman moved from occasional to persistent defense of the establishment. Perhaps because his credentials as a journalist had been challenged when he was appointed, he set about to position himself as one of the stoutest advocates of the press. In 1932, he was featured in a promotional advertisement for the trade journal *Editor & Publisher*, in which he stated: "I am tired of hearing the press criticized by business men, bankers, advertisers and educators." At the meeting the following spring of the American Society of Newspaper Editors, he listed and rebutted nineteen current criticisms of the press.[2]

The arrival of Franklin D. Roosevelt's New Deal in March 1933 presented Ackerman with an opportunity to play a more prominent role. Emergency legislation was rushed through Congress in Roosevelt's first hundred days, seeking to lift the country out of nearly four years of depression. One such enactment created the National Recovery Administration, aimed at enlisting industries to write codes that would increase employment and govern working conditions. While individual industries prepared codes, the NRA's chief, Hugh S. Johnson, launched his saturation publicity campaign under the NRA's Blue Eagle symbol.[3]

Ackerman saw his opening when the American Newspaper Publishers Association warned newspapers not to cooperate with a government-sanctioned code, even one aimed solely at business practices, "because giving the power to license gives the power to control, and such power completely abridges the freedom of the press." The publishers were particularly wary of the NRA because it sanctioned the right of editorial employees to form a union and threatened to invoke child-labor restrictions on the use of underage newspaper deliverers. Nonetheless, after intense negotiations the publishers wrote a preliminary code, but one containing a proviso that nothing in it would "waive any constitutional rights . . . that might restrict or interfere with the constitutional guaranty of the freedom of the press."[4]

On the day that the publishers submitted their code, Ackerman, just returned from a 3,000-mile automobile trip, fell into stride with the publishers' rhetoric. He was disturbed; he had found the country in an "unhealthy state of mind," under a "government today by emotion rather than government by public opinion." All the more important, he asserted, that the newspaper code should contain a provision "which places the government on record that it still recognizes the constitutional right of the freedom of the press."[5]

Although the issue might have appeared moot, Ackerman was merely gathering momentum. In his annual report early in September 1933, Ackerman brushed past discussion of the school of journalism in favor of a full-scale summary of the controversy with the NRA and the struggle to write into the news-paper code a guarantee of freedom of the press. He concluded: "With the Roosevelt administration in a position to control the radio; with an almost equal power over the motion pictures, and with public emotion stimulated to such a tense state that public meetings must of necessity reflect the spirit as well as the letter of inspired governmental propaganda, the only possibility of the United States escaping a dictatorship was inherent in the fight of the profession of journalism for public recognition of the freedom of the press." The *Times* echoed him in its headline: DICTATORSHIP SEEN AVERTED BY PRESS.[6]

He followed up by enlisting the school's new *Independent Journal*. Early in October, he received a printed copy of the proposed newspaper code, and read on the cover a standard NRA note that the code had not yet been approved. Ackerman persuaded himself to conclude that the note meant that the freedom-of-the-press proviso had thus not been approved, and he printed in the *Journal* a warning that freedom of the press therefore hung "in balance." He released the statement to the major wire services and it appeared throughout the country. In his column, Heywood Broun called the statement an "assortment of delicatessen," and added: "He set his pupils a very bad example. . . . He put everything in his article except evidence." The subsequent issue of the *Independent Journal* courteously carried the observations of Professor Lindsay Rogers of Columbia, a deputy administrator at NRA, who scoffed at Ackerman's alarm. Newspapers, Rogers sensibly maintained, remained under the protection, as always, of the Supreme Court.[7]

His criticism of the case brought Ackerman into friendly relations with Robert R. McCormick, editor and publisher of the *Chicago Tribune* and, as chairman of the ANPA Freedom of the Press Committee, a pugnacious advocate of press rights. McCormick made an appearance at the school, and in exchange Ackerman was invited to give an address to the Commercial Club of Chicago. He did not disappoint; what he said gained headlines across the country, not least from the *Tribune*. Pointedly seeming to absolve Roosevelt personally of desiring "to create a Fascist government in the United States," he saw the danger of fascism in the New Deal nonetheless and praised the "heroic editorial struggle" of newspapers to resist the tide. This was raw meat to the newspapers. But Lindsay Rogers wrote to Howard Davis, business manager of the *Herald Tribune* and ANPA president, "Ackerman must have a warm personal friend on your copy desk. Otherwise I cannot see why the Herald Tribune publishes such tripe."[8]

Eventually, the code reached the president's desk for final approval, and FDR signed; but he could not resist sticking a harpoon in the publishers (and, by association, Ackerman): "Of course . . . nobody waives any constitutional rights by assenting to a Code. The recitation of the freedom of the press clause in the Code has no more place here than would the recitation of the whole Constitution or of the Ten Commandments. The freedom guaranteed by the Constitution is freedom of expression and that will be scrupulously respected—but it is not freedom to work children, or do business in a fire trap or violate the laws against obscenity, libel and lewdness." Roosevelt already sensed that he was at war with the publishers. [9]

In February 1934, John Stewart Bryan, editor and publisher of the *Richmond News Leader*, wrote to the Pulitzer Prize jury to nominate Howard Davis and the *Herald Tribune* for the public service prize for defending freedom of the press. Robert R. McCormick supported the idea. Ackerman initially appeared to favor the award although, when he wrote to Butler, he hinted that he, rather than Davis, had carried the torch: "My own statements have been so widely supported editorially that I have a large clipping book of cuttings which were sent to me voluntarily, as we do not subscribe to a clipping service." Butler sensibly recommended that the matter be dropped. Julian Harris, a member of the advisory board, commented mordantly that such self-laudation by the publishers "might give rise to Homeric laughter among the newspaper workers of America." Ackerman ultimately collected a portion of the credit when the report of the freedom of the press committee of the American Society of Newspaper Editors incorporated his entire account of the NRA controversy.[10]

Ackerman fired a final salvo in August 1934, long after the code had been approved and was living out its short and ineffectual life. Hugh Johnson attacked the press in no uncertain terms: "I have seen news garbled, suppressed and colored and I have seen able young men prostituting their talents in libelous and misleading stories pandered as news at the behest of opinionated bosses." Ackerman replied in an address to the California Newspaper Publishers Association; Johnson, he charged, still wanted "to control the press and suppress public opinion," but now wanted to achieve that end "by criticizing the press over the radio, in the hope and with the expectation that he can undermine public confidence in news and substitute government opinion for public opinion." Hitler, he asserted, used similar tactics before he suppressed the German press.[11]

He had made his mark with the press lords. If there was a flaw in his strategy, it was in the particular alliances he had made. He had won the good opinion of the likes of Hearst and McCormick, but the *Times* and the *St. Louis Post-Dispatch*, the two newspapers closest to the school, had been skeptics on the NRA issue, and had disregarded his efforts. And it must have been clear to him that despite a screen of nonpartisanship he had placed himself on the side of the newspapers that were soon to become the New Deal's bitterest enemies.[12]

Nine months later, the Supreme Court declared the National Recovery Act unconstitutional, but not on First Amendment grounds. Nonetheless, two days later Ackerman called attention for a final time to the newspaper code issue, by sending congratulations to eight national and state publishers' associations. ACKERMAN HAILS STAND OF PRESS IN N.R.A. FIGHT was the headline in the *Herald Tribune*. He was still a master of public relations, whose best client was himself.[13]

# CHAPTER 12

# The Graduate School

LATE IN 1934, Dean Ackerman turned his attention from national politics back to the school of journalism, and prepared what proved to be his most durable reform. This was no ordinary juggling of courses and requirements; the dean proposed to change the school of journalism into an entirely graduate institution, the first of its kind in the United States, as had been proposed by the American Society of Newspaper Editors more than a decade before, to encourage "educational standards . . . on a par with those maintained at the best schools of law or medicine."[1]

The school's historian, Richard T. Baker, saw the conversion to a graduate program as a matter of "inexorable logic." From the first, the school had offered quasi-graduate work—one- or two-year degree programs for students already holding undergraduate degrees. Ackerman himself had earned a one-year degree, in 1913. In the class of 1934, thirty-one of the thirty-four graduates had earlier degrees, and thirty-six of forty-four in the class of 1935. It could be said that they were studying for a graduate degree but receiving only another undergraduate degree, a bachelor of science.[2]

The new plan, approved by the faculty on November 7, 1934, was to require an undergraduate degree for admission and, in effect, to shift the fourth and fifth undergraduate years required for the bachelor of science into fifth and sixth years leading to a new graduate degree. As proposed, the first graduate year combined professional courses in the school with graduate courses elsewhere in the university, emphasizing the public disciplines—law, economics, history, sociology, government. In the second year, students who elected to remain in residence could enroll in a seminar and pursue an individual or group research project, while winners of the Pulitzer Traveling Scholarships and others would have the further option of pursuing study abroad. There was a third choice, that the student could opt out of study and get a job—that is, earn academic credit for employment in a field of journalism approved by the dean, a further evolution of the class-release system of the 1920s.

The arguments the dean and faculty offered for moving entirely to a two-year graduate level emphasized that journalists needed not only professional training but knowledge of other relevant subjects studied at the graduate level: "Journalism needs to prepare for a philosophical approach to public problems through the time-tested channels of academic research." In addition, the proposal suggested, the school needed graduate students to meet the growing demand for research on journalism—for example, on the relations between news organizations and government, the issue that had so vexed Ackerman during his NRA campaign.[3]

The proposal was almost vehement in claiming the right of the journalism school to award for the first time a master of *arts* degree:

When the Faculty of Journalism recommended changes in the curriculum in February 1932, discontinuing courses leading to the Master of Science degree, it recognized a definite break in the trend of education in journalism. It recognized that the degree "Master of Science in Journalism" was a title or label wholly out of place in the profession: first, because journalism is not a science; secondly, because the courses of study are not scientifically organized; and thirdly, because no man or woman is a "master of the science of journalism" until he has had many years of practical experience.

Even an experienced journalist would hesitate to claim that he was a master of the science of journalism and the phrase has excited ridicule in the profession of journalism. Furthermore, until education in journalism is more advanced than it is today, until there is a greater accumulation of professional experience based upon education in journalism the degree offered by a School of Journalism should be academic rather than professional.

The faculty further argued the equivalency of the proposed Master of Arts in Journalism, in academic quality and requirements, with other Columbia master's programs. Loosely structured though it was, this proposal appeared to be an equivalent, transferred to a graduate level, of Joseph Pulitzer's desire to combine "technical" and general education.

But in December 1934, the proposal returned from the University Council shorn of its substance. The committee on instruction of the combined graduate faculties had approved a graduate school but had unanimously denied the authority to offer a master of arts degree. Butler, who was fixed on attaching the "science" degree to journalism, won his point again, for good. Worse, the second year, more venturesome academically, was stripped from the proposal, perhaps for reasons of economy, and the school was empowered to offer only a single year leading to the master of science. Professional training, now concentrated in a single year, was bound to squeeze out general education; as Baker noted, critics called the new program merely a fifth undergraduate year, much like the year Ackerman had spent at the school in 1912–13. Nonetheless, the faculty acquiesced; the University Council created the graduate school in February 1935, and the trustees approved it the next month.[4]

The new curriculum's most enthusiastic booster on the faculty was one of Ackerman's most distinguished recruits, Douglas Southall Freeman, sometimes called the "flying professor." Freeman, editor of the *Richmond News Leader*, commuted weekly from Virginia to Columbia. He was the author of an ambitious biography of Robert E. Lee, which won him a 1935 Pulitzer Prize. He wrote to the dean, "I am all keyed up over our new program and I am confirmed in my belief that you have launched a movement which in its beneficent influence on American journalism, finds no counterpart this side of the date the Associated Press was organized."[5]

Many of the other reactions when the graduate school was formally announced in March 1935 were equally enthusiastic. It was blithely asserted that journalism was now elevated at Columbia to equal standing with the schools of law and medicine. Sevellon Brown, editor of the *Providence Journal*, whose son was already enrolled at the school, welcomed the narrowed curriculum: "I know the tussle you have had with the Board of Trustees and I am happy to learn from your announcement that all non-professional graduate courses are to be taken 'upon the advice of the Dean.' If a full year on a forty-hour basis gives you time enough with graduate material, you should be sending us even better men than you have in the past."[6]

There was one annoying dissent. In its inimitably terse way, the *Daily News* commented: "We see by the papers that the Pulitzer School of Journalism at Columbia University is going to curtail its course to one year. We consider that a step in the right direction, but believe that course is still one year too long." Ackerman and a long roster of students wrote protests to the paper, but the publisher, Joseph Medill Patterson, stood his ground, saying that he, as one of the founders of the Medill School of Journalism at Northwestern University, had been much disappointed in it and thought Columbia was no better. Nor would he accept Ackerman's invitation to visit the school.[7]

The first bulletin of the newly renamed Graduate School of Journalism offered a leaden statement of its goals that was light years from Pulitzer's invocation of the public interest:

> The School believes that the success of journalism as a business depends upon its progress as a profession. Therefore it endeavors to develop a limited number of men and women who will have the ability to advance in their profession, and to improve that profession.
>
> The transition from the educational mass-production policies of the nineteen twenties to the policy of individual instruction and development will provide the student with the background and proficiency necessary for advancement in the profession; it will enable him to prepare himself for a selective market, and reveal and make realizable the social, economic, and political ideals of journalism and the responsibilities of the profession in a republic.[8]

The reference to "educational mass-production policies" reflected not only Ackerman's view of what he regarded as the school's lax undergraduate days but a national situation to which he was to devote part of his annual report in 1935. Evidently distressed by the quality of many of the applications for admission to the new graduate school, he charged that overenrollment had degraded the value of the college degree. It seemed that the goal of the school of journalism was to find and educate a well-qualified elite for an ill-paid profession.[9]

The bulletin also made explicit the new policy toward women applicants: "Women of superior ability will be admitted to the School in numbers proportionate to the opportunities which shall develop for them in the future in professional work." The underlying assumption, of course, was that there

would be few future opportunities for women as journalists; hence, few women admitted. Similarly, the announcement said that no creative writers—
"those who are primarily interested in the novel, short story, photoplay or
similar specialized fields"—need apply.[10]

What survived the reconfiguration was the school's basic method of instruction—hands-on, intensive, copious production. Douglas Southall Freeman's opinion after a semester remained favorable: "Our new curriculum
has, in my judgment, entirely vindicated itself. A few of our students have
overworked themselves because they have attempted too much for the [Na-
tional] Youth Administration [a New Deal agency offering part-time jobs to
college students]. The others have worked hard but not, I take it, too hard."
He added an eternal refrain: "They require more facility in writing decent
English and more practice in news-stories that are carefully corrected for
their information."[11]

Once in place, the M.S. curriculum seemed set in stone. Its basics—the
emphasis on simulation of newspaper work, the forty-hour week (which of
course students found ways to nibble at), the single year of instruction—endured and endured, even after the end of Ackerman's long term as dean. It
had obvious drawbacks: it did not truly simulate on-the-job conditions because students taking various courses were in effect apprentices on several
jobs at once; it led to further isolation of journalism students because there
was little or no place in their schedules for courses elsewhere in the university. Because there was no overlap from one graduating class to the next,
members of a given class knew only their own classmates and lacked the invaluable advice and lore of predecessors.

However, the first class of the graduate era, entering in the fall of 1935,
was greeted by a splendid new newsroom, up one floor from the lobby of the
building; there were individual desks with typewriters, horseshoe copy
desks, and three Teletypes. The yearbook of the previous year's class (the
last to study for an undergraduate degree), which witnessed the dedication
ceremonies, called the high-ceilinged, high-windowed room "palatial." Professor Charles P. Cooper was a little sad at leaving the shabby, scarred old
senior newsroom upstairs, which for him exuded "the atmosphere and the
feeling [of] the famous news rooms of Park Row."[12]

But the new newsroom meant that the graduate classes of the next two
decades worked, studied, and all but lived together in that one capacious
room. Not surprisingly, these cohorts of sixty or so developed an intense co-
hesiveness that remained with them ever after.

# CHAPTER 13

# Speaking to Cabots

BEFORE THE GRADUATE SCHOOL had finished its first year, Carl W. Ackerman was drawn to a new opportunity, and distraction. In February 1936, Joseph L. Jones, class of 1922 and foreign editor of the United Press wire service, brought together Ackerman and John Moors Cabot, a Department of State career officer and a son of Godfrey Lowell Cabot, a Massachusetts carbon-black and natural-gas manufacturer of substantial wealth. The younger Cabot, who had served primarily in Latin America, was intent on establishing prizes for journalism in that region to honor his mother, Maria Moors Cabot, who died in 1934.[1]

Ackerman was at that juncture on the rebound from a disappointment. Lucius W. Nieman, publisher of the *Milwaukee Journal*, had come to Columbia in 1935 with a plan to support journalism education. President Butler, snatching the offer from Ackerman's grasp, had insisted that Nieman instead fund a new center for the arts. As a result, Columbia got nothing, and when Nieman died his widow established in his memory the Nieman Foundation for Journalism at Harvard, which has offered prestigious mid-career fellowships to journalists for more than sixty years.[2]

At first, the Cabots seemed to be offering nothing on a grand scale—only $4,500 to start the awards program. However, Ackerman persisted hopefully, and persuaded the Cabots to finance a trip to Latin America. He sailed in June 1937, in pursuit of what he called a "'journalistic' Good Neighbor policy," adapting Franklin Roosevelt's slogan. His eagerness to deal with the Cabots had no doubt been whetted by the news a few days before he left that the father (despite his undeserved skinflint reputation) had given $600,000 to Harvard for a Maria Moors Cabot Foundation for Botanical Research. Why not Columbia?[3]

The trip expanded Ackerman's horizons. As he wrote to the younger Cabot in September 1937, he was deeply concerned over what he had observed of the penetration of the South American press by Nazism and Fascism, and used the term "Black Plague" as a theme for his annual report. It caught the eye of the White House, which had the report distributed in the State Department and to United States embassies in Latin America. Ackerman now saw the need for a much expanded Cabot program, a kind of Nobel Prize for the hemisphere. He drafted a proposal that defined the prizes as rewarding not only good journalism but pro-democratic politics. Responding, John Cabot warned Ackerman not to become entangled with political goals; in the many drafts and revisions that followed, Ackerman eventually agreed to concentrate on journalism alone. By March 1938 John Cabot and the dean had reached a full agreement.[4]

Perhaps wary of having another project taken away, Ackerman unveiled the plan to President Butler belatedly. Butler chose to grumble about the proposed award of gold medals: "I notice that the sales lists of various auction houses are filled with medals of a generation or so ago which have been absolutely forgotten or overlooked." Ackerman insisted that the medals would be greatly esteemed in Latin America, and Butler gave way: "If people prefer medals, it is not for me to prevent them from getting them." But the president continued to drag his feet, even after the elder Cabot offered further evidence of his philanthropic scope by giving $647,000 to the Massachusetts Institute of Technology.[5]

Ackerman sent a final draft of the award agreement to The Hague, where John Cabot was stationed and his father was visiting. The father wrote back to insist that State Department approval must be assured, or he would withdraw. Ackerman asked his commuting professor, Douglas Southall Freeman, who had good connections, to sound out the department. Late in August, George S. Messersmith, head of cultural relations, assured Freeman that the department had no reservations, given the understanding that the awards would have entirely private sponsorship. With this green light, the dean traveled to Godfrey Lowell Cabot's home in Beverly, Massachusetts, and they signed the agreement on August 29, 1938. Butler, still reluctant, did not entirely give way until Ackerman all but waved the check at him: "Cash on the barrel-head convinced him," the dean remarked years later.[6]

Despite the stated intentions of Ackerman and the Cabots, the prizes were destined to be continually entangled in politics. When Ackerman set out to collect information on possible medalists, he went first to Washington to consult with the State Department's new Division of Cultural Relations. He was authorized to speak with the desk officer for each country, and used the information to build files on Latin American journalists—the type of information, of course, that had been compiled by those more concerned with foreign policy than with journalism. Nor did those being scrutinized know. As the historian of the Cabot prizes, Ackerman's grandson, wrote: "Information obtained from United States officials in Latin America came from a covert source. It was not likely that anyone would suspect that Columbia received any aid from the State Department in gathering information about newspapermen." Although it was understood that no government official could propose a candidate for an award, more than one came near the edge.[7]

In July 1939, Ackerman submitted the first Cabot nominations to Butler. He had made the choices himself, with advice from colleagues. The nominees comprised a newspaper each in Argentina, Chile, and Peru, with owners or top editors as medal recipients, and the United Press Buenos Aires bureau and its head, James I. Miller, who had pioneered in the distribution of news in Latin America. Columbia's trustees approved the choices and, as opposed to their later behavior in respect to the Pulitzer Prizes, never turned down a nominee. However, there were hitches, and two award-winners dropped out because they could not be present, as specified in the agreement.[8]

Eventually, the first two winners, Dr. José Santos Gollan of La Prensa (Buenos Aires) and Dr. Luis Miro Quesada of El Comercio (Lima), arrived in New York for a lavish round of fetes. They were welcomed to New York by the mayor, Fiorello La Guardia. The next day, there were elaborate ceremonies under the great dome of Columbia's Low Library. Then the medalists went to Washington and to luncheons at the Pan American Union and the National Press Club, a meeting with Secretary of State Cordell Hull, and attendance at one of Franklin D. Roosevelt's famous press conferences. They topped off the weekend by attending the Army-Navy football game in Annapolis—all of this financed, of course, by the Cabots. The press reaction, on both continents, was fulsome.[9]

In 1941, the behind-the-scenes influence of the State Department created a public crisis for the new prizes. John Cabot had urged that nominees be considered on the basis of the quality of their journalism, not on their attitudes toward the United States. Nor were State Department officials supposed to make nominations. Still, in 1940, Spruille Braden, ambassador to Colombia, tried to push a prize for a friendly newspaper there. And George S. Messersmith, now ambassador to Cuba, nominated and supported one José Ignacio Rivero, editor and publisher of *Diario de la Marina* (Havana). Ackerman responded with extraordinary alacrity to the nomination, adding *Diario* to the list of honorees a month after he submitted the rest of the list.[10]

Rivero attracted this attention because he had recently become friendly toward the United States when, as Messersmith put it to Ackerman, "it was personally, politically, and professionally difficult [for him] to do so." The problem was that Rivero was until that point a supporter of Generalissimo Francisco Franco, who became dictator of Spain when the Spanish Civil War ended in 1939, and of the related Falangist movement in Cuba. However, in State Department eyes, being pro-Washington trumped being friendly with Franco.[11]

Rivero and the other medalists appeared in New York in October 1941. His presence was immediately seized upon by New York's liberal-left daily, *PM*, and there were rumbles as well from Havana—not only from *Hoy*, the Communist daily, but from a group of leftist scholars. The New York–based United American Spanish Aid Committee, formed to support the Loyalist side in the Spanish Civil War, wrote a letter of complaint to President Butler and picketed the convocation at Low Library. Ulric Bell of Fight for Freedom, an anti-Nazi organization, wrote to Secretary of State Hull and demanded Rivero's expulsion.[12]

None of this stir affected the ceremonies directly. Rivero received his medal and spoke, emphasizing his anticommunist credentials. Afterward, Ackerman held a news conference and said that he was aware of Rivero's record and regarded it as "water over the dam." But not all the water was over the dam. Before the banquet scheduled at the Waldorf-Astoria the day after the ceremony, Ackerman, as he recalled, received regrets from every Jew who had been invited. Further, the *Christian Science Monitor* published an editorial so stinging that Godfrey Lowell Cabot asked Ackerman and Messersmith to respond. Erwin D. Canham, the editor, while conceding that their additional information might have led to different phrasing, stood by the editorial. (The following year, the *Monitor* itself received a mollifying Cabot Prize.)[13]

Even as this crisis was developing, the elder Cabot ensured the continuance of the prizes by donating nearly $280,000 as an endowment—40 shares of his company's stock with a book value of $6,885.56 each—and prohibiting Columbia to sell the stock during Godfrey Lowell Cabot's lifetime. The stock did well, and while it did not fulfill Ackerman's hope of creating an endowment on the scale of Pulitzer's, the annual income grew from $8,000 to nearly $25,000 over the next twenty years, and proved immensely useful to the school. Once it was clear that the prize ceremonies alone could not use up the annual income, Ackerman's successor reached an agreement with the Cabots that permitted diversion of the surplus to other purposes.[14]

Partly to forestall diplomatic difficulties during World War II, Ackerman laid out an "unwritten agreement"—that is, a policy stated only in correspondence—that there would be consultation with the State Department before making final selections "so as not to interfere with United States foreign policy." He added that he and the Cabots would nonetheless reserve "complete freedom of choice." Godfrey Lowell Cabot, perhaps having in mind the dispute over Rivero, added a codicil: that the State Department should never be permitted to suggest a candidate, a rule that subsequently was sometimes skirted.[15]

Certainly, it did not avoid disputes over the political background of award winners. In 1944, *PM* charged that a 1943 medalist, Rodrigo de Llano of the Mexican daily *Excelsior*, had been associated with fascism and anti-Semitism. John Cabot dismissed the accusations by asserting that the information was incorrect, having come from Communist agents in Costa Rica. But a year later, Cabot found himself on the other side of the pale. Now chargé d'affaires in Buenos Aires, Cabot favored a prize for a socialist daily there that had covered the beginnings of Peronism. Ackerman, shy now of controversy, turned him down.[16]

In the years after the war, the scope of the Cabot prizes expanded. Once confined to major city newspapers in the Western Hemisphere, they came to include regional papers, magazines, radio, and ultimately television. Once given only to owners and top managers, they went as well to working correspondents, starting in 1948 with Crede Calhoun, Panama correspondent of the *Times*. Their scope expanded with the inclusion of Canada and such international organizations as the Pan American Union. By the time of Ackerman's retirement in 1956, only three countries—Haiti, Nicaragua, and the Dominican Republic—had failed to produce medalists.[17]

But the old political battle lines remained in place after the war. As late as 1955, two winners were criticized for undemocratic connections. It was charged that *Clarin*, Robert Jorge Noble's newspaper in Buenos Aires, was under the control of the Peron dictatorship. Pedro G. Beltran, owner of *La Prensa* and *Ultima Hora* in Lima, was, like Noble, the target of an attack that appeared in *La Bohemia* (Havana) charging that prizes had been awarded to "Nazi-Falangist reactionaries." Nor was Ackerman himself spared. But putting the best gloss on it he argued, in Noble's case, that Argentines should not be subject to "cultural isolation" and in any case such criticisms showed that the awards were drawing serious attention.[18]

On his retirement, Ackerman handed over the awards, with their dubious political reputation and their cooptation by the State Department still intact. The new custodian was Edward W. Barrett, himself a department veteran.

CHAPTER 14

# "My Dear Dean"

IT WAS A MARK of Dean Carl W. Ackerman's deanship that he never remained focused long on the main business of the school—education—and earned the reputation among students of being remote from its daily work. The record of his term shows a continual restlessness, a casting-about for new enterprises. To be sure, most administrators look for ways to expand or enhance their domains, but Ackerman was an acute case. Only two years into his tenure, he all but forgot the school while he sought to lead the newspaper publishers' fight against the National Recovery Administration. Even when he had completed what proved to be the most enduring change in the school's configuration, the conversion to a single-year graduate curriculum, he did not tarry to monitor the new program but began almost at once to look about for something new.

His activities suggested that he was looking for a way to supersede the narrow focus of a small school of journalism. His 1936 annual report recommended the creation on the Columbia campus of a research center, based at the school, for analysis of the press, radio, and public opinion. Then he moved on to a larger study in which he called for the creation of a four-year school of communication, with instruction drawn from relevant faculties and partly housed in the school of journalism. The idea did not gain the favor of President Butler, but it had indirectly beneficial results for the school in the creation of courses in radio news and public opinion analysis, under notable instructors, such as Paul W. White, a founder of CBS News, and Dr. George Gallup and Elmo Roper, who popularized public-opinion polling.[1]

Ackerman's annual report late in 1937 was indicative of a further broadening of his agenda. He devoted part of it to a surprising warning, populist in tone, that American newspaper publishers should confine themselves to the business side and place control of their papers in the hands of strengthened professional staffs: "The newspaper in the United States is a public institution. It must be the instrument of the mass and not of the few."[2]

Ackerman's lecture to publishers earned important readers, among them Henry Luce, a founder and chief of the multimagazine publishing concern Time Inc. In August 1938, Ackerman reported to the university administration that he and Herbert Brucker, his chief aide, had had conversations with Luce about a national study of the press. Butler evidently checked out the idea with Arthur Hays Sulzberger, publisher of the *Times*, and urged Ackerman to hold off. A few days later, Ackerman sent Butler a telegram: "Have notified Time Magazine cannot undertake study. Will send you complete report."[3]

But Ackerman was not content, especially after he received a letter from Sulzberger about the publisher's fear "with respect to a general survey of the press at this time." Ackerman, responding, demanded to know why Sulzberger would consider such a study "dangerous," and added that the failure to undertake it would be a sign that Columbia had been intimidated. A month later, Ackerman reported to President Butler that he had heard that two other institutions had offered to serve as a base for the study. He added: "It appears . . . that the conservative publishers: McCormick, Gannett, Knowland, Sulzberger and others are not really opposed to a study of the press if they can control the questions and the final report. The situation is causing me considerable anxiety because the great majority of newspaper editors and publishers who were willing to cooperate with us are inclined to think that our abandonment of a study of the press was due to pressure from a few powerful newspapers."[4]

But he could do nothing further. Luce's study went to the University of Chicago, whence it was issued in 1947 as the report of the Commission on Freedom of the Press, generally known as the Hutchins Commission, after the chancellor of that university. Ackerman must later have reflected bitterly, not only on another serious loss equivalent to that of losing the Nieman program, but on the paradox that the same publishers he had defended so stoutly against the NRA had prevented him from heading what might well have been the Ackerman Commission.[5]

Ackerman's failure to tend his own garden resulted in an internal crisis in the fall of 1939. On October 2, he drafted a confidential memorandum for Butler, of which, he said, no copy would be kept in the school files. "This Memorandum," he wrote, "is submitted with a deep feeling of disappointment and injury." The subject was, of all people, the straight-shooter Herbert Brucker, whom he had hired as his assistant at the start of his tenure, and who now had the additional title of associate professor and was the author of a well-received book, *The Changing American Newspaper.* "Some time last Spring I began to notice a disposition on his part not to carry out the assignments I turned over to him. . . . Each time that I have delegated matters to him he has either delayed in making a report or he has not submitted a report or he has acted without advising me of his decision or action." Brucker, he complained, was processing applications for admission tardily, was not helping on the planning for the Cabot Prizes, and, worst, may have been stimulating a whispering campaign about the dean's remoteness from the student body.[6]

Evidently this draft was not sent on to Butler, but in December 1939 Ackerman submitted to the president a "special report in regard to present conditions in the Graduate School of Journalism." He began: "The functioning of the Faculty of Journalism has not been satisfactory for some time." He started with his chronic problem, the school's senior faculty member, Walter B. Pitkin. While conceding that Pitkin was an "inspiring lecturer," the dean complained that he was working only one day a week and frequently missed classes. Earlier, a note from a school bulletin board found its way into Ackerman's files: "Prof. (Speed) Pitkin is ill and will not be able to meet his classes until the book is finished."[7]

In truth, Pitkin was bored. In his memoir he wrote that he had long since come to view the school as "a land of pedestrians, of faithful plodders, of obedient pupils, of youths with scant imagination." Further, he viewed the institution itself as drifting and chaotic. Difficulties arose, he wrote, when student malcontents rebelled or subverted the curriculum by cheating—usually plagiarism; tempestuous faculty meetings to decide what to do led nowhere.[8]

Ackerman saved his main indictment for Brucker: "From May to November 1939 he adopted a policy of passive resistance to administrative assignments which was very close to an academic sit-down strike." There was a buried clue in the narrative: that Brucker's lapses dated from the time he became a member of the universitywide committee to prepare for the visit in June 1939 of King George VI and Queen Elizabeth, an appointment that was certainly an item of presidential patronage. President Butler, it appeared, was acquainted with Brucker and had offered him the use of the president's box at a Columbia football game. He may even have consulted Brucker before replying to Ackerman's complaint. Details aside, Brucker could be seen as a man who wanted to stop being a permanent assistant and flunky.[9]

Butler's reply constituted a stern review of the conduct of Ackerman's entire administration:

My dear Dean:

Following our conversation of Tuesday, I have reread and reflected upon your letter of December 10 and the report which accompanies it.

The impression produced upon me may perhaps be best summarized in these few paragraphs:

1. You have been giving too much time to the external relationships of the School of Journalism and not enough to its intensive administration. The external relations have now been most successfully established and the School is both influential and everywhere highly appreciated. My first suggestion is that you should devote yourself intensively hereafter to the work of the School, to the immediate personal oversight of the Faculty and students and to dealing directly with the internal problems which day by day are an essential part of the work of any school or faculty in Columbia University.

2. So long as the School remains of its present size or nearly so, I think you should dispense with the service of an associate or assistant dean and should keep the administrative work entirely in your own hands, simply with such secretarial assistance as circumstances might require.

3. Professor Brucker, being relieved of administrative work, should be assigned full academic service as a member of the Faculty in whatever special field he is most competent and in which he is most interested.

4. Professor Pitkin should be asked to accept full academic service, and if his health will not permit him to do so, he should share in making plans for his early retirement from active service, as otherwise the Faculty must be crippled in its constitution and work.

5. The program of study should be overhauled in some such way as you suggest, and particularly it should be enlarged by University courses now given in history, in polities, in economics, in international relations and in modern languages, so as to broaden and deepen the

equipment of the students of the School when they are graduated and enter upon their professional work.

6. At least three or four University professors related to the subjects I have just mentioned should be added to the Faculty of Journalism in order to emphasize its University relationships and influence.

7. The Faculty of Journalism should meet, as do other faculties, at regular intervals, for the careful discussion and settlement of academic problems. Doubtless you can follow the example of Dean Hawkes [of Columbia College] and have many of these problems threshed out in advance by informal gatherings at the Faculty Club, so that when the Faculty actually assembles formally it will have nothing to do but record officially the conclusions which have been arrived at after weeks and perhaps months of careful study and discussion.

8. Some of the salaries which the University is paying are too large for the amount of service rendered. This whole aspect of the matter should be carefully examined and readjusted in accordance with the principles of our general University policies.

The type of student that the School is attracting seems to me to be excellent, and we owe it to them and to the profession which they have chosen to do our best for them and to make them feel that they are not only students of Journalism but are in active fellowship with the entire University family and its influences.

Whatever I can do to help the work of the School will always be done gladly.

Faithfully yours,
Nicholas Murray Butler[10]

The letter provides a startlingly direct view of the president's concerns over the school and its dean; after all, Butler had been there at the creation. Ackerman, knowing that his deanship might be at stake, responded: "You will recall that in 1932 there was a somewhat similar situation. Now, as then, there is not the slightest doubt in my mind in regard to policies and program of action. I had complete confidence seven years ago in my ability to steer this School through a period of transition. I have the same confidence today. I have called a Faculty conference for tomorrow. Similar meetings will be held monthly in the future."[11]

Brucker, permanently released from the dean's office, became a full-time professor. He was soon back on good terms with Ackerman, and the dean even recommended him for an extra raise—to the then-substantial salary of

$6,500—in 1942 to keep him. But that fall, Brucker took leave to serve with the Office of War Information and did not return. He became associate editor of the *Hartford Courant* in 1944 and spent the rest of his career there.[12]

Ackerman proved himself unable to carry out the rest of the president's recommendations. He did not immediately succeed in retiring or reforming Pitkin, who continued to teach to the extent that his health and book commitments allowed. The prescription of study elsewhere on the campus for journalism students fell by the wayside. Nor were professors from other faculties added to the Faculty of Journalism. Nor, finally, did the faculty become a full partner in running the school.

Moreover, Ackerman continued to find diversions. He joined an old ally from his fight against the NRA, Elisha Hanson, counsel of the American Newspaper Publishers Association, in opposing the application of federal minimum-wage legislation to journalists. The publishers feared that the law would compel them to pay overtime; they would be excused if journalists could be classified as "professionals." Ackerman provided a deposition in a court action and even sought to append the deposition to his annual report. And he was sympathetic when Hanson wrote a bitter letter to Arthur Hays Sulzberger, publisher of the *Times*, because an editorial had opposed the exemption. We must "do everything we can," Ackerman wrote to Hanson, "to protect the press from damage to the press by a Fifth Columnist in our own ranks." In the end, the newspaper publishers did not receive their exemption, although some continued to contest the issue into the 1980s.[13]

As of 1940, the school's faculty included the emeritus director, John W. Cunliffe; Brucker; the will-o'-the-wisp Pitkin; the commuting Freeman; Henry F. Pringle, distinguished Washington writer and biographer; the part-time editing instructors Robert Garst and Theodore M. Bernstein of the *Times*; and the veteran libel-law teacher, Harold L. Cross, on whom Ackerman increasingly relied for counsel. Cunliffe, of whom Ackerman complained that "he delays procedure at faculty meetings by his long discourses and he is indiscreet in his conferences with students," was induced to retire.[14]

The stentor of the newsroom, Charles P. Cooper, seventy-four years old, also retired after two decades at the school. Before Cooper left in the spring of 1940, Ackerman had already recruited a new maestro of the typewriters. In December 1939, on his way to Mexico on Cabot business, the dean detoured through St. Louis and talked with Roscoe B. Ellard of the other pioneering journalism school, at the University of Missouri. Ackerman wrote back to the university's second-in-command, Frank D. Fackenthal, "The interview exceeded my high expectations."[15]

At the age of forty-five, Ellard had worked for the *Chicago Daily News*; had been director of the journalism program at Washington and Lee University in Virginia; had returned to his alma mater, Missouri, where he supervised graduate students and lectured on history and ethics; and was the co-author of a textbook, *Pictorial Journalism*. Despite his relatively slender experience he had a formidable presence that all but reeked of long years in the business. Mort Stern of the class of 1949 remembered his first glimpse of the man: "He was pacing up and down in front of the students, punctuating his anecdote with great sweeping gestures of his arm, his fingers extended like a baseball pitcher's. Finally he came to the end of his story with a chuckle and a stuttered punch line that had his audience straining forward in suspense and excitement." On some occasions, that stuttered word would be, roguishly, "Birdsh-sh-sh-sh-ot!"[16]

The dean made up his mind at once; Ellard should be appointed. Ellard arrived at the school for the spring 1940 semester. Ackerman believed that he had neatly solved the problems of replacing Cooper, covering for Pitkin, and placing the burdens of education on a deputy. But it was not long before he found that he had simply bought himself another problem.[17]

# CHAPTER 15

# Outpost in Chungking

THE CLASS OF 1941 was the last, for four years, to complete its year at the school in peacetime. By the time the class of 1942 graduated, the United States had been at war nearly six months. Yet the war brought nothing like the upheavals of 1917. Nicholas Murray Butler, approaching eighty, could no longer be the scourge of the disloyal, nor did he need to be. The last prewar classes at the school were distinguished less by politics than an anxious competitiveness, as exemplified by Marguerite Higgins, who talked herself into the class of 1942 at the last minute and then grabbed off the coveted position of *Herald Tribune* campus correspondent. The nearest thing to disruption in the period was the memorable alumni "open house" of January 1941, which turned into a brawl after the dean went home. University security complained: "On the east stairway between the 500 and 600 floors the wall was stained from beer having been thrown against it, also the stairway was used as a toilet." Replying, the dean blandly suggested the presence of outsiders.[1]

After Pearl Harbor, Dean Ackerman yielded classroom space to Navy trainees (those later depicted in the opening sections of Herman Wouk's *The*

*Caine Mutiny*). Anticipating faculty losses, he called back the school's first newsroom mentor, Robert MacAlarney, now seventy. Two other mature figures were added in 1943: Thomas R. Ybarra, a 1905 Harvard graduate, foreign correspondent, and magazine editor; and William O. Trapp, who had worked for Talcott Williams's Philadelphia *Press*. Trapp was hired to teach libel law when Harold L. Cross went to China, and stayed on to become a retirement problem. Walter B. Pitkin finally retired in 1943, having served thirty years; he was heard from again in 1950 when an aide to Dwight Eisenhower, then university president, complained to Ackerman that Pitkin was writing letters to the general on Columbia letterhead urging a blitzkrieg in Korea. He died in 1953.[2]

Eleanor Carroll, class of 1920, an adviser to women students since 1936, was raised to full-time status because, as the dean correctly anticipated, the barriers to women enrollees would be lowered during the war. In fact, the undersized class of 1943, which entered in fall 1942, was the first in the school's history with a female majority. A year later, women occupied 75 percent of the seats.[3]

The four classes admitted in wartime, 1943 through 1946, were drawn from a diminished pool of applicants—only ninety-three one year—and were considered by the school administrators to be anomalous because of the number of women and thus inferior to the classes that preceded and followed them. Many of the women who graduated in those years were fated to drop out of journalism as they faced an unfriendly postwar job market and a cultural environment pressing them back toward domesticity. Even so, these classes produced pioneers who made their way into journalism before journalism was necessarily ready for them—among them Kathleen Teltsch, 1944, *Times* bureau chief at the United Nations; Alice Weel, 1944, of CBS News; Edith Efron, 1945, of *Look* magazine and later a media critic; and Judith Crist, 1945, *Herald Tribune* reporter and film critic, who eventually served a record of forty-plus years as an adjunct teacher at the school.[4]

Predictably, Ackerman was not content to keep the home fires burning. A year after Pearl Harbor, he found a wartime mission for the school. Hollington K. Tong, who had been Ackerman's journalism classmate for a semester in 1912, came to the United States late in 1942 in his capacity as vice minister of information for the Chinese Nationalist government—and as press officer, mightily abetted by Henry R. Luce and his *Time* and *Life* magazines, for the extended tour of Madame Chiang Kai-shek, the formidable American-educated wife of China's leader, Generalissimo Chiang Kai-shek. Before leaving China, Tong had convinced Madame Chiang that China might benefit—

and Americans might be impressed—by having a school where students could be trained for journalism in the American style.[5]

Tong sought out Ackerman. The dean drafted a proposal that the school of journalism, responding to Tong's invitation, would sponsor a branch in Chungking, the wartime capital of China, far inland and presumably beyond the range of the Japanese invaders. Even in the early draft, the proposed institution did not sound precisely like a *journalism* school. It would be designed to "instruct Chinese journalists to prepare them during the war period for services to the government in Chinese embassies and legations throughout the world, to the ministers of state, the commanding generals in the field, and also prepare men to establish, publish and edit daily newspapers in the provinces." The memo added: "A friend, who insists on anonymity, will deposit a sum of $30,000 annually with the Treasurer of Columbia University for the duration of the war and possibly thereafter."[6]

Ackerman chose not to put on paper the identity of the "friend." He initially expected that the State Department's Division of Cultural Relations, with which he had consulted on the Cabot Prizes, would finance the project, but the department declined. Ackerman turned to the Office of Strategic Services, the wartime intelligence agency under Major General William Donovan. Ackerman had a contact there—Brigadier General Bonner F. Fellers, an undergraduate classmate from Earlham College in Indiana. In Ackerman's papers, a single handwritten message from Fellers, from February 18, 1943, seems to refer to the China plan: "The telegram & letter are in Donovan's hands & no one else is in on the idea."[7]

Evidently, approval arrived promptly, because a month later Ackerman was able to lay before President Butler Tong's formal invitation, anointed with "the approval of Madame Chiang Kai-shek." On March 29, 1943, Ackerman forwarded to the president a check—not for $30,000 but for $50,000—drawn on Bankers Trust, donor not identified and not to be revealed publicly. Butler congratulated him.[8]

Ackerman tapped crusty Harold L. Cross, the school's libel instructor and general counsel to the *Herald Tribune*, to be the dean in Chungking. Cross in turn recruited three teachers, all recent graduates: Anthony F. J. Dralle and Floyd D. Rodgers, Jr., class of 1936, and Richard T. Baker, a Pulitzer traveling scholar from the class of 1937. He also helped to recruit four others for a separate State Department cultural program attaching advisers to Chinese information agencies: George H. Grim, Jr., class of 1934, of radio station WCCO, Minneapolis; Frank T. Buchner, class of 1935; Floyd Taylor, a former editor of the Columbia *Spectator*, later on the *New York World-Telegram*; and George Alexanderson, a photographer.[9]

After rounds of consultations in Washington and a whirl of obtaining travel permissions, documents, and inoculations, the three teachers and Cross were ready to go in July 1943, only to hear from Tong that the whole thing was off, allegedly because of the high cost of living in Chungking. Ackerman shrewdly offered as a subsidy $25,000 of the anonymous donor's money, and the project regained momentum. The quartet left by train from Washington on July 19. Two months later, after traveling 15,000 miles via unconvoyed Liberty ship on the Pacific and Indian oceans, by train across India, and by plane over the Himalayan Hump, they arrived in Chungking—at least three of them did; Dralle was left behind temporarily in Calcutta with dengue fever.[10]

They had scarcely had time to drop their bags at their quarters in the press hostel before they were at work. Thirty-five English-speaking students had been chosen from two hundred applicants. The Chinese Post-Graduate School of Journalism opened with long formal ceremonies on October 11, the same day that Dean Ackerman disclosed the project to American papers. The new teachers and their students faced spartan conditions in a swollen, primitive, disease-ridden city that, as Cross wrote, was considered "the most *depressing* capital in the world." The school occupied a single unheated, and uncooled, classroom in a rebuilt structure adorned with the shell casings of two Japanese bombs. As contrasted with the comparative comfort of the press hostel, the students lived in mud-and-bamboo bunkhouses infested with rats.[11]

Nonetheless, the school functioned from the start. The heterogeneous teaching staff proved adaptable and tenacious, compensating for what Cross noted as their lack of "big two-fisted" newspaper experience. Baker, an Iowan with a divinity degree who had been working for *World Outlook*, a Methodist magazine, seemed, like Talcott Williams, to have missionary genes and formed close bonds with the students. Rodgers was a radio journalist from Columbia, South Carolina, who (according to an associate) presented himself as a "lazy hill-billy type and most of the time conceals the fact that he is very intelligent." Dralle, who had been an editor in upstate New York, was a patient if gloomy teacher, but his health was shaky; after he recovered from dengue fever he was laid low by gastroenteritis. For his part, Cross did his share of the teaching and worked hard at the official and social obligations of his job, but became increasingly brittle and impatient.[12]

Superficially, the school appeared to be a miniature, in an exotic setting, of its parent on the Columbia campus. The faculty taught without interfer-

ence a near-replica of the Columbia one-year curriculum, based on the practices and premises of an uncensored press. Cross asserted the virtues of press
freedom, American and English style, and the others told students how to
gather and write news according to American standards and eventually sent
them out to practice what they had learned.[13]

And yet the school was vulnerable. Only after their arrival did the Americans discover that the Ministry of Information with which Tong was affiliated was not a government bureau but a subsidiary of the Kuomintang, the
only legal political party in Chiang Kai-shek's China. This affiliation laid the
teaching staff open to criticism, in particular from American correspondents,
who were increasingly at odds with the ministry's restrictions. Moreover, the
faculty lived with the unspoken understanding that in most instances they
were not training journalists at all, but, as Cross wrote, "bigger and better
propagandists for the Kuomintang." And they knew or guessed that students
were being trained for possible wartime assignments devised by the OSS.[14]

A high point of the first year was an audience with Chiang Kai-shek on
January 17, 1944. Cross recorded the occasion: "While we were all standing
there [in a long narrow room heated by a stove] wondering and indeed inquiring just what to do 'in the presence' the Generalissimo suddenly appeared. He was dressed simply but effectively in a fatigue uniform of an officer of the Chinese Army. . . . We were presented to him one by one, Dr.
Tong doing the presenting. As befits my years and position I was presented
first. . . . I said [the students] were eager, earnest industrious and at the end
of the School would become good journalists by standards to be applied in
China. I was too honest and too little of the diplomat to be able to leave out
those last seven words."[15]

The school encountered "the standards to be applied in China" when it
undertook to publish a laboratory newspaper, the *Chungking Reporter*. After
prolonged consultation with Tong, the first dummy issue was produced near
the end of January 1944. "Dr. Tong rather liked it," Cross reported. In the
meantime, students were being sent out on a mission to teach government
officials how to talk to reporters, with gradual success. The problems of actually publishing were overcome one by one: English-language type was
flown in over the Hump and set by hand by compositors who knew no English; the ministry of information provided a flatbed press, operated manual-
ly. The design made it look—unsurprisingly, given Cross's affiliation—like
the *Herald Tribune*.[16]

But the real obstacles were substantive. Cross complained to his wife:
"All copy has to be submitted to Dr. Tong himself for censorship, for he is

very tender about the fact that this paper will come out in his own department, which is the propaganda, publicity and censorship Ministry of the Kuomintang." Yet he felt a small sense of triumph when the February 10 issue was printed: "Even now its appearance, in my opinion and that of most people here, is better than that of any other paper printed in China in English." The issue of March 9 was offered for general sale. But there was continuing trouble with Tong, especially after Cross slipped and permitted several uncensored articles to appear.[17]

The difficulties came to a head in April. Students covered a report by a Nationalist mission recently returned from England. Long after the stories had cleared the censor, the student editor-in-chief was summoned to Tong's office and told to alter one story and kill another. Informed that the pages in question had been printed, Tong ordered the printed copies destroyed. The sensitive point, evidently, was the quotation marks the story had placed around a reference to "a 'strong' China"; Tong believed that such a reference would make Madame Chiang unhappy.[18]

Rodgers, referring to himself in the third person in a letter to his wife, recounted the aftermath: "Rodgers, Baker and Dralle quit work on the paper. We told Cross the story and decided on a show-down as to whether it was a student paper or a Ministry of Information paper. . . . We insisted that [Tong] go before the class next morning and make a public explanation and apology. . . . Cross backed his junior partners with gusto and finesse. . . . We're willing to abide by the censorship laws, but we are not willing to have our authority overruled, our judgments reversed and stories already passed by the censor arbitrarily killed because they might hurt someone's feelings. We refused to be pure propagandists for the Kuomintang. Tong cringed and fidgeted."

Many of the students resented the faculty position. Rodgers wondered whether they were "reactionary, have had such a dose of fascism we can't dent 'em." More likely, they disliked seeing the Americans humble Tong, the representative of their own people.[19]

Baker in particular suffered a loss of standing; Rodgers suspected he had it coming because of too-cozy relationships with students: "He mothered and coddled them until they began to take over his room. At all hours of the day and night, the students wandered in. They drank his tea and ate his cakes, interrupted him when he was at work, barged in calmly when it was plain that he was entertaining visitors. They woke him up early, kept him up late. Nothing was sacred to them. They read his letters over his shoulder, perused his grade book on the desk. If he happened to be bathing or shaving, dressing or undressing . . . it made no difference." But one morning a student slipped into his room unbidden before Baker got up. Baker exploded, and word went around the school that he was no longer a friend.[20]

But the students were far from irredeemable. They gradually made up with the faculty and began themselves to enjoy the thrill of beating the censor. They scored an exclusive on a noxious new statute—dubbed a "thought-control" law—designed to silence Chinese students studying abroad. The story passed the censor via an old stratagem—placing the important material far down in the story. Once out, the story caught the attention of the foreign correspondents, who spread word to the United States. Similarly, a student reporter found out about a restrictive new press code and showed a small item about it to a sleepy censor at 4 A.M. Again, the word spread.[21]

Meanwhile, tension was growing between Chungking and New York. Cross was aggrieved, first, that as "casual civilians" he and the teaching staff had been denied the State Department mail pouch, and, second, that in response to his regular reports he had not received a letter from Ackerman in months. "I do not understand why he does not write unless he is peeved because I have reported to him some of the facts of life which can not be made to disappear simply by waving a wand of rosy optimism produced by the comforts and lack of understanding at 116th and Broadway." In April 1944, Cross received a cable from Ackerman declaring, on Joseph Pulitzer's ninety-seventh birthday, that the *Chungking Reporter* was the greatest achievement ever in journalism teaching. Cross commented to his wife: "I hope that [Pulitzer's] rest was not disturbed by what was being said in his name concerning a heavily censored newspaper which, try as we will, depicts a state of affairs far removed from grim reality." Ever since he arrived, Cross had been counting down the days until his departure at the end of the academic year, and he unhesitatingly spurned Tong's entreaties to stay on.[22]

Student morale deteriorated as the year neared its end. Part of the problem was uncertainty. Students wanted to be given summer reporting jobs before returning in September for their graduation; almost universally, they wanted to study in America the next year. Moreover, there was trouble because they had not been paid their stipend, the "rice allowance." Suddenly, the students disappeared from their classes, although they denied that they were on strike, and Tong threatened at first to close the school; as Rodgers wrote, "The whole American faculty [was] ready to pack their bags."[23]

Cross sought a meeting with the American ambassador, Clarence E. Gauss, to clarify the American government's attitude toward the school.

Gauss praised Cross for insisting on academic freedom; he said he liked the *Chungking Reporter*; he predicted a "liberal, democratic China" after the war. Rodgers wrote home that Cross had "earned respect for the School in both Chinese and foreign circles here . . . he has pulled no punches on freedom of speech and freedom of the press . . . he has seen to it that our teaching has not been interfered with. . . . We'll miss Cross when he goes." In addition, Cross had intervened to see that the American correspondents were represented when the Nationalist government ultimately, and reluctantly, permitted press travel to the Communist-held areas to the north.[24]

The rice allowance was paid, the school closed for the summer, and Cross went home. Baker left Chungking for Kunming, to the southwest, to report for church publications; Rodgers also traveled, contracted typhus in Chengtu, almost died, and recovered. In August, reinforcements arrived—two new teachers and a new dean, with cash in hand for a second year.[25]

# CHAPTER 16

# "Sweat and Tears"

THE RETURN OF Harold L. Cross to New York produced rumbles heard as far away as Chungking, as the now former dean of the China school vented his feelings and views. Ackerman was perturbed when he heard Cross declaim that the relationship of the school with the Chinese government was corrupt because the Nationalist government was fascist and hostile to freedom of the press and of education. But Ackerman discounted Cross: "As Professor Cross is a lawyer and not a journalist; as he is a New England puritan rather than a realist; as he has never been in China before and has no knowledge or experience in international affairs it was evident that he had built up a defense in anticipation of attack either at home or by someone in Chungking." Cross gave a "finger-waggling" lecture to Ackerman at a faculty meeting, insisting that the school was a failure and that the three members of the carryover faculty agreed with him.[1]

Ackerman wrote to Cross's successor: "I have heard that Baker, Dralle and Rodgers have similar sentiments. If so I think they should be brought back to New York as soon as we can replace them with men who will be loyal to you and to our mission." But word of an armistice soon arrived in China—"another communique, from Supreme Educational Command Headquarters on Morningside Heights," as Rodgers put it. "Was to the effect that the storm had blown over, the weather cleared, forget the flurry." In fact, Cross continued teaching at Columbia for five years more before going on to lead a distinguished campaign for the American Society of Newspaper Editors (ASNE) to open government records, which led the FBI to initiate an investigative file on him.[2]

Ackerman must already have been aware that the new dean in Chungking was hardly more of a Chiang enthusiast than Cross. In April 1944, knowing Cross was bent on leaving, Ackerman had tapped Rodney Gilbert, a member of the *Herald Tribune* editorial staff who had lived in China for seventeen years before the war and spoke two Chinese dialects. He was no doubt more qualified as a China expert than Cross, but he had only a tepid interest in the Chungking school. He really hoped that he would do intelligence work, and corresponded with Brigadier General John Magruder, deputy director for intelligence at OSS, to whom he exclaimed that he was not "at all enthusiastic about going to China to fret over a school to train little apologists for big Kuomintang highbinders"—using an old term for Chinese gangsters. Irritated by travel red tape and a long ocean trip, he was testy when he arrived in Chungking in August 1944.[3]

Two new faculty members arrived in Chungking at roughly the same time as Gilbert. Both were Columbia journalism graduates: Steffan Andrews was from the class of 1940; Robert V. Ackerman, the dean's only child, graduated in 1941 and had been working as an assistant editor at the Louisville *Courier-Journal*. Neither made a good impression. Young Ackerman noted Andrews's unpopularity in a letter to his father, while Robert Ackerman himself suffered from colleagues' suspicion of nepotism.[4]

The school's second year opened with the graduation of the previous year's class, held in an auditorium at a national government building. Rodgers recounted: "A few minutes of waiting and Generalissimo Chiang Kai-shek, clad in a plain brown Hung San uniform, entered from a door at the front of our room to the right. He took from Tong a booklet containing all the students' names and started down the rows to speak to each one of them. . . . China's president stood in front of the first student . . . looked in the book and called a name. It was the wrong name. The Gissimo turned angrily back . . . and after a few heated word[s] in an undertone wheeled and strode to the table at the front of the room. There he glowered at us all for a moment. Then, his anger apparently subsiding, he launched into what seemed to be a very eloquent eight or ten minutes talk. He spoke of truth, of good morals, of speed and accuracy in reporting. At the end of his talk he bowed to the students." That night, the graduating class had a farewell party before starting their first jobs—a six-month term each at the Ministry of Information.[5]

As the second year began, Baker emerged as a leader. Gilbert appraised him in a way that foreshadowed his later career at Columbia: "Baker is the man who organized the curriculum and attends to all the detail. He is a good teacher and he likes teaching. He assumes leadership and is conceded the right to do so as a matter of course. . . . He is not very well liked. He is too much the prim, precise, intolerant Methodist parson. He is also at times extremely self-centered and thoughtlessly rude. He could not run the school; but anyone who tried to run it another year without him is going to discover that he has been the most important man in the school."[6]

During the fall, Ackerman sent a query asking whether, if funding were available, the faculty would remain for a third year. Rather surprisingly, all three of the veterans said that they would, subject to spousal approval and a month's home leave the next summer.[7]

Although the school functioned without crises during the fall of 1944, there was an immediate threat to its continuance—the Japanese. In December 1944, Japan's final offensive was pushing south toward Indo-China and west toward Chungking. In Washington, Ackerman picked up word that if the government abandoned Chungking, it would move to Tibet and the school would have to close. Rodgers wrote home that when the Japanese reached Kweiyang, less than two hundred miles away, the teachers would pack. "Chungking seems literally to be the end of the road . . . at least insofar as our School is concerned. There are no plans to snake it farther into the hinterland and set up shop, say, on the edge of Tibet." But the offensive was blunted, and the school remained.[8]

Back in New York, Ackerman was trying to line up an installment of $50,000 for the third year, but was encountering obstacles. Early in October 1944, an auditor sent by the OSS conduit, one Charles J. Lennihan, Jr., spent three days in Ackerman's office examining records. Ackerman complained in a letter to Lennihan that he typed from his home in Lambertville, New Jersey: "Your representative made certain statements to me from time to time indicating beyond doubt that they were primarily interested in finding out whether I had personally received any money and if so for what purpose. When it became clear to me that my own honesty and integrity were involved I refused to obtain from the bursar's office my personal vouchers for their examination" because, he wrote, he wanted to conceal the names of the government officials with whom he had consulted. He added: "It has been my policy (as a newspaper man) for thirty years never to reveal confidential information or sources of information. This is the keystone of sound journalism and I would rather lose $2,000 (although I can ill afford to do so) than I would violate the confidential relationships which I have with you or with anyone in or outside of the government."[9]

A day later, he wrote himself a memorandum summarizing a telephone conversation with Norwood Allman, head of the OSS Far East division. He complained to Allman that Lennihan had failed to complete payments due to operate the school, and demanded to know whether General Donovan would stick with the school: "Time has come when either OSS makes good its promises upon which Gilbert and I have made commitments or we will have to withdraw School staff and close by Jan. in which case the OSS will have to assume complete responsibility for the consequences. . . . Mr. Lennihan and his auditor have been questioning my honesty and integrity and I do not intend any longer to submit to their third degree measures."[10]

A week later, Allman called to say that Lennihan had been instructed to pay up. Ackerman drove in from New Jersey and found his tormentor at the Hotel Drake, and they arranged for delivery of the second-year check for $50,000. But Lennihan continued to delay funding for the third year, and in fact did not release the money until May 1945.[11]

In January 1945, Ackerman left the United States as a member of a delegation dispatched by the American Society of Newspaper Editors to promote the incorporation of American ideas of freedom of the press into postwar peace agreements. His tourmates were Wilbur Forrest of the *Herald Tribune*, ASNE president-elect, and Ralph McGill of the *Atlanta Constitution*, who chaired the ASNE freedom of information committee. They worked their way eastward, through Britain, France, Italy, Greece, Egypt, Turkey, the Soviet Union, and, finally, China.[12]

The party arrived by air in Chungking on March 28, 1945, and was greeted by the entire faculty, including Ackerman's son. "I was so emotionally moved," Ackerman wrote to his wife, "that I had difficulty introducing my colleagues." On the next day, Ackerman, Forrest, and McGill met the students of the school, and were later wined and dined by Tong and Dean Gilbert. Discord struck on April 1. McGill, who had been drinking continually during the trip, was evidently drunk during a lunch with the students and twice shouted "Liar!" while Ackerman was speaking.[13]

McGill was still belligerent, although semicomatose, when the three Americans paid their official call on Chiang Kai-shek. The Atlantan, Ackerman wrote his wife, "was intoxicated and slumped on the sofa, half of the time with his eyes closed, mumbling incoherent words." McGill roused himself to ask a belligerent question about the Chinese Communists. Ackerman was highly impressed by the generalissimo—McGill later recalled that the dean compared Chiang to a god—but burning with anger at McGill. Back at the hotel, Ackerman announced that he was resigning from the mission. Forrest and McGill departed without Ackerman, but not before McGill made the rounds one last time. The official newsletter wrote, euphemistically: "Late in the night the sincere and courageous Mr. McGill called upon us again, to say good-bye and to have some more 'kan pei's [bottoms up's]."[14]

The next day, Ackerman wrote to the president of the ASNE submitting his resignation, complaining that McGill's conduct had been "a disgrace to journalism." He added that he did not intend to go public with the matter. After a week of getting reacquainted with his son and discussing the future of the school with Tong, he flew out to Calcutta, caught up briefly with Forrest and McGill in Australia, then flew to the Philippines at the invitation of his college classmate, Brigadier General Bonner Fellers, now on General MacArthur's staff. He stayed in Manila, all but destroyed when it was recaptured, and broadcast an appeal to Japanese journalists for reconciliation after the war. He had an audience with MacArthur, paused in San Francisco at the start of the conference that created the United Nations, and finally arrived back at the school.[15]

Early in the morning of April 13, 1945, Rodgers was awakened by a press hostel neighbor who said that there was a rumor that President Roosevelt was dead. Rodgers turned on the radio and picked up a shortwave broadcast from San Francisco that confirmed the report. He hurried to Gilbert's room and shouted, "Roosevelt is dead!" Gilbert, true to his Republican credentials, replied "Thank God!" and rolled over. But he soon stirred; the school set about producing an extra of the *Chungking Reporter* and had it on the street by two in the afternoon. The next day, the faculty attended a memorial service, one feature of which was a eulogy written for Chiang by, of course, Gilbert.[16]

Ackerman was reunited with Forrest and McGill for a meeting at the White House with the new president, Harry S. Truman, and *Editor & Publisher* devoted a whole issue to the team's report, most of it written by McGill. Years later, McGill became convinced, unsurprisingly, that Ackerman was blocking his road to a Pulitzer Prize, and in fact not until after Ackerman's retirement did a more sober McGill win one.[17]

By the time the school finished its second academic year, there were gathering doubts about its future. Gilbert terminated his Columbia appointment and left Chungking on an assignment for the OSS. Baker, Dralle, and Rodgers saw him in Kunming on their way home for what they believed would be a month's leave. They had left their possessions in Chungking, and were reassured when Gilbert told them that a third year was on track. But Baker, back in New York, warned Ackerman, in a confidential memorandum on August 9, that the school had made enemies. He believed that General George Olmsted, who among other duties oversaw American civilian activities in the China theater, had decided that the school was worthless. He attributed that attitude to the influence of Theodore H. White, senior *Time* correspondent in Chungking, now in rebellion against Luce's pro-Chiang editorial policy. Baker observed: "White is sharply antagonistic to Dr. Tong's Department, even though he began his service in China in Dr. Tong's employ [a prewar job with the ministry]. Perhaps conscientiously he feels that it is a mistake to have American money and support being poured into a Chinese propaganda ministry, and that our presence there is something akin to treason."[18]

While conceding the possibility that the school might already be doomed, Baker—now its acting head—made the case nonetheless for continuing it:

We have tried to train journalists in American newspaper methods, we have tried to instill a few ideals of press freedom, we have tried to provide a foundation upon which smoother military and public relations liaison in Chungking could be maintained. All these things we have done with considerable success. That is our apologia pro sua vita. We stand on the record. . . .

More immediately, however, there are perils in abandoning the project at this time. We are committed to the Chinese, Columbia is committed. She will find it hard to back out now, without revealing the reason. And the reason, once revealed, undercuts much of the good fruits of the school. We do not wish to reveal our true backing, it seems to me.

But on August 23, 1945, eight days after V-J Day, Ackerman received a cable from Gilbert saying that "the earlier than expected peace" necessitated indefinite suspension of the school.[19]

Baker later received from Gilbert a frank, angry letter confirming that politics, not the outbreak of peace, had terminated the school. Gilbert had been stunned to hear, near the end of July, that Tong had received a cable from Ackerman saying that return transportation back to China for the faculty had been refused and that the school would have to be turned over to the Chinese. Gilbert was baffled and furious. The school could continue, it seemed, only if Chiang Kai-shek himself demanded it, but Tong would not ask this; he had himself lost influence and was being eased out. But Gilbert had no idea that Ackerman would go public with his announcement: "Just to assert his stinking authority first and get a few lines of publicity!" The school was dead, of a thousand cuts.[20]

There were loose ends. Ackerman arranged to refund $50,000 to the OSS, and three years later he sent in his own check for $13,921.10 to settle the expenditures that the accountants had disputed. Although the dean let the university know that the government had been the source of the school's funding, he did not specify the OSS. In fact, there was every effort to keep that aspect a secret. Baker was alarmed when he heard that President Truman was shutting down the OSS, and sent a memorandum to Ackerman saying that he wanted "to remind you of the way our school helped promote the U.S. Military mission in China." He added: "I do not anticipate that the backing of our school will be publicly aired, but I do want to place before you our conviction that it would be a mistake to allow such news into the public domain. It might wreck Dr. Tong's standing with his own government and people." It was years, in fact, before any of the China faculty talked openly about the OSS support, and some of them remained secretive to the end.[21]

Ackerman let the three senior teachers write the official report on the Chungking school, a vivid exposition that claimed that the students had become imbued with the spirit of free journalism. In a postscript, Ackerman added a Churchillian note: "We backed this enterprise through sweat and tears."[22]

Ackerman added that Columbia was prepared to welcome students from the Chinese school, and eventually ten of them graduated, the first two being Peng Jui-fu and Wellington Lee, both of whom became residents of the United States. A few, Baker commented coyly in his 1954 history, "chose to work out their careers behind the red silk curtain."[23]

Was the Chinese school anything more than an oddity, a wartime diversion? At the least, it was an object lesson in the complications that arise when a school dedicated to free journalism uses secret government financing to create an institution under the wing of a foreign propaganda agency. It was constantly under pressure and under surveillance—and yet it seems to have done the nonpolitical side of its work well.

The subsequent Communist government also employed Americans, starting in 1979, to teach American methods of journalism to Chinese students. This time, although there was no Columbia sponsorship, Columbia journalism graduates were prominent among the teachers. Baker's classmate James Aronson was the first.[24]

CHAPTER 17

# Postwar Ventures

LESS THAN TWO WEEKS after the death of President Roosevelt on April 12, 1945, the much longer administration of Nicholas Murray Butler also came to an end. Butler agreed, at the trustees' request, to resign as president of Columbia University after forty-four years. Ackerman heard about the resignation while he was in the Far East and wrote to his wife: "That was a development I never expected," although he could hardly have escaped knowing that it was inevitable. That fall, the provost, Frank D. Fackenthal, to whom Butler had been gradually relinquishing his duties for the previous eight years, was named acting president, and a search for a new president was begun.[1]

For the school of journalism, the months after World War II brought the loss of two of the last links with its earliest days. Robert MacAlarney, having come back to teach at the school during the war, died in November 1945. Five months later, John W. Cunliffe, the quiet literary scholar who headed the school in the 1920s, died after reaching his eighties. In addition, the school was now missing several prewar faculty members, notably Herbert Brucker, now editor of the *Hartford Courant*; Henry F. Pringle, recipient of a Guggenheim Fellowship; and Douglas Southall Freeman, who resigned in 1941, perhaps after catching wind of Butler's complaint that he was paid too much.[2]

Freeman in particular had left his mark, not least because his teaching inspired the school's next enterprise. Sevellon Brown, editor of the *Providence Journal*, sent two sons to the school, and his paper was staffed with a veritable regiment of Columbia graduates. Visiting in 1935, while the elder son, Sevellon, Jr., was attending the school's first all-graduate year, he heard Freeman lecture in a course that among other things taught students how to read newspapers critically, and was captivated by Freeman's wisdom and acuity. Why should not journalists in general have access to such teachers?[3]

In a lecture at the school in 1940 (while his younger son, Barry, was in attendance), Brown proposed an institute providing short-term seminars for working journalists, which would draw on the scholarly resources of the university and at the same time provide advanced technical instruction. He nursed the idea along until the end of the war and, a week after V-J Day, wrote to Ackerman, promising that the *Journal* would make the initial contribution of $10,000 to start up the new institute.[4]

Ackerman seized on the idea, seeing in it an opportunity to enhance the work and influence of the school. There was one irritating, if temporary, opponent. Joseph Pulitzer II, head of the school's advisory board, did not like the idea: "I simply cannot bring myself to believe that a month's seminar in New York to study European reconstruction or any other subject would do the working newspaperman much good." Ackerman was furious; he commented to Fackenthal, "It is quite evident from Mr. Pulitzer's letter that he does not have the slightest interest in this school. His letter indicates further what I have known for some time that some members of the Advisory Board are interested in other universities and that those interests cannot be reconciled with our desire for support and cooperation of the Board members. Personally, I am glad Mr. Pulitzer has taken this position because it will clarify some of our problems."[5]

Ackerman was not deterred, however, and before long Pulitzer fell into line (although relations between him and the dean remained cool). Just as he had focused his energies on the Chungking school during the war, Ackerman now bent every effort to bring the new institute into being. By January 1946, newspapers had contributed $114,000 to the new American Press Institute. Ackerman gloated: "This is the first time since Joseph Pulitzer endowed our school that we have received financial support from the newspaper industry."

Ackerman submitted the API plans formally to the university and gave the faculty an opportunity to rubber-stamp the proposal.[6]

The first hint of conflict came as early as the organizing conference in February 1946 at the Waldorf-Astoria. An advisory committee (later advisory board) was selected from among the attendees, twenty-one high-ranking newspaper editors; Sevellon Brown was the single overlap with the school's advisory board. The discussions were joined not only by Ackerman but by Floyd Taylor, an experienced newspaperman who had served as a State Department adviser to the Ministry of Information during the school's Chungking ventures; on his return he had become an editorial writer for the *Herald Tribune* and a member of the school faculty. Now bearing the title of associate dean, he was to be named the first director of the American Press Institute.

A statement of purpose—"to contribute to the improvement of American newspapers"—was adopted and rough details of the program worked out. A key document was the statement signed by Ackerman and Brown:

> For administrative purposes, the Institute will be an affiliate of the Graduate School of Journalism at Columbia, of which Mr. Taylor has been named associate dean, but will conduct its seminars without relation to the School's curriculum. The Institute will have quarters on the ground floor of the Journalism Building at Columbia.

Indeed, Ackerman had given away to the institute all of the ground floor that was not taken up by the university bookstore, leaving the school hidden upstairs like a poor relation. He even moved his own office.[7]

But there was more mischief hidden in the joint statement. Ackerman's view was embodied in the words "an affiliate of the Graduate School of Journalism," while the position of API's founders was reflected in the assertion that API would "conduct its seminars without relation to the School's curriculum." The dean saw the institute as a subordinate branch of the school; the institute personnel saw it from the beginning as an independent organization that happened to be based on the campus. Fackenthal warned of possible conflict "with a group of this kind from outside the University," but nothing was done to head it off.[8]

The first seminar, a gathering of twenty-five managing editors and news editors, met for three weeks starting at the end of September 1946. The pace was frantic, with forty-eight guest speakers. The folkways were established in the first session: Participants, all male, stayed in a campus dormitory; attendance at all sessions was mandatory; wives were left at home. No women professionals were invited until the third year, when an all-woman seminar of newspaper librarians convened.[9]

As the year went on, the seminars remained hard-working and the content was increasingly technical-industrial. For example, the second seminar was devoted to the quality of photographic reproduction in newspapers. There was only a hint of Brown's Freeman-inspired vision of a decade before; journalism faculty members were not invited, and scholars from elsewhere on campus rarely appeared. However, API staff taught part-time in the journalism school.[10]

One of the discussion leaders in an early seminar was J. Montgomery Curtis, city editor of the *Buffalo Evening News*. When Claude A. Jagger, API's associate director, resigned after a few months on the job, Curtis was named as his replacement. Blunt, outspoken, combative, and tall, he immediately became a dominant figure at API—so much so that he, rather than Ackerman or Brown or Taylor, was later considered API's creator, or at least the architect of its success. Curtis was a protégé of the editor of the *Evening News*, A. H. Kirchhofer, a member of API's founding group, and like Sevellon Brown an exemplar of the clean, sober, and earnest journalism that was the foundation of API's teaching.[11]

An initial crisis in API's relations with the school arose in August 1947, when Sevellon Brown proposed that the institute be organized as a separate corporation, with only a "formal affiliation" with the university. Ackerman supported the proposal warily, thinking that it might help fund-raising with publishers who had affiliations with other universities. But he warned stiffly: "The American Press Institute is now and must remain affiliated with the Graduate School of Journalism and with Columbia University." API's advisory committee, he declared, was a university body "functioning through me as Dean." Evidently API was not yet ready for a confrontation, and Ackerman advised university counsel a few months later that the matter of incorporation was "dormant."[12]

The truce was broken three years later, after both sides had accumulated further grievances. API's administrators were convinced that mid-career seminar participants had a strong aversion to the notion that they were in any sense attending a journalism school, and felt that the only remedy was disaffiliation. For this and perhaps other reasons, both support and enrollment were down, so much so that Director Taylor, uneasy with the fund-raising aspect of his job, was ready to leave for a State Department position. Still, he was effective enough, obtaining Rockefeller Foundation support for German and Japanese editors to come to Columbia for seminars—for retraining in the ways of the free (American) press.[13]

For his part, Ackerman was aggrieved that API had failed to pay its overhead or its share of employee benefits. He complained that Taylor, Curtis, and a new associate director, Walter Everett, class of 1933, of the *Providence Journal*, were better paid than journalism faculty. And he felt the sting of ingratitude: not only had his fund-raising efforts benefited API but API "was assigned the best space in the Pulitzer Building on my recommendation." He drew his line: "I cannot voluntarily agree to separation." Once again there was no showdown; Ackerman sat down with the API advisory board in April 1951, and the session was, as he reported to Low Library, "a love feast."[14]

But there was a turn for the worse later in the year, with the sudden death of the soft-spoken, respected Floyd Taylor. Curtis succeeded him, and he was bolstered by the arrival of rough-hewn Ben Reese, newly retired as managing editor of the *St. Louis Post-Dispatch*, as co-chair of the API advisory board. Reese was brought in, apparently, to relieve Curtis of the burden of dealing with the dean and the university. Curtis initially resented Reese, but they became allies against the common adversary, the school of journalism. They won at least a token victory when the newly named president of Columbia University, Grayson L. Kirk, let them bypass the dean and deal directly with Low Library.[15]

This measure eased tensions somewhat, but did not prevent the jostling that occurred when two worthy but incompatible enterprises occupied the same building. The institute's historians, sympathetic to API, nonetheless found irony in the situation because "after all, it was on Sevellon Brown's request to Dean Ackerman and Ackerman's endorsement that API found its first home at Columbia."[16]

The American Press Institute was scarcely started when Ackerman sailed for Venezuela, in May 1947, to undertake yet another venture, organizing a new school of journalism. At the end of the war, the school had received a flurry of offers to establish branches overseas along the lines of the Chinese school; Japan, Egypt, eighteen countries altogether expressed interest. One plan for Czechoslovakia bore the promise of such bountiful financing that Ackerman contemplated a leave of five years to live in Prague. But of all the proposals, only one—the Venezuela proposal—took shape.[17]

To an extent, creating the school presented problems similar to those of the Chungking branch. Again there was an underwriter demanding anonymity—

not a government agency but the oil industry of Venezuela, headed by Creole Petroleum, a subsidiary of the Rockefellers' Standard Oil. Ackerman's contact in Caracas was Everett A. Bauman, a 1941 graduate of the school heading public relations for Creole, who wrote to the dean, "It is the desire of the Industry to be kept completely out of the picture." The financing remained a secret.[18]

Ackerman's trip to Caracas, the first of three, was in response to an invitation from the Universidad Central de Venezuela and the Venezuelan ministry of education. After appropriate planning, the university's governing council, with Ackerman in attendance, authorized what the dean called the "Plan Ackerman." When the dean returned to New York he recruited, to be Columbia's man in Caracas, John Foster, Jr., a forty-one-year-old Spanish-speaking Arizonan with a background in financial and aviation journalism, and most recently executive editor of *Aviation Week*. Later Ackerman sent Myrick Land, class of 1946 and winner of a Pulitzer Traveling Scholarship, to assist Foster. They were not to run the school, as in Chungking, but to advise.[19]

There was a hitch when Creole hesitated and Ackerman threatened to terminate the project, but the oil money came through, and by the end of September 1947, Ackerman was back in Caracas. He petitioned and received from the ministry of education an appropriation (also secret) matching the oil money. On October 24, President Romulo Betancourt opened the Escuela Nacional de Periodismo.[20]

Correspondence after the dean's return hints at continual political trouble—much of it attributed to Communists. When Ackerman forwarded Foster's appointment as associate professor to the provost, he added: "I think Mr. Foster has the ability and personality to handle the difficult situation in Caracas." A few weeks later he wrote to Bauman: "Foster has not only stood up very well under all of the punishment of problems and uncertainties but I think he is a stronger and better man for us because of these experiences."[21]

Then the Venezuelan director of the school was refused a United States visa because of alleged left-wing affiliations. Ackerman complained vigorously to the attorney general, Tom Clark, that the regulations imperiled his agreement with the Universidad Central, which specified that fifteen Venezuelan journalists would come to Columbia for an API seminar. To all such requests, Ackerman wrote, "we shall have to reply that so long as academic freedom is under the control of the Department of Justice we will have to decline to assist them." Clark responded by telegram denying all, but the Venezuelan director was still refused his visit.[22]

There was a headache of a different kind when Foster's young assistant, Myrick Land, caused a stir by writing articles for the North American Newspaper Alliance syndicate on the decline of Franklin Roosevelt's Good Neighbor policy and on the popularity in South America of the left-wing Progressive presidential candidate Henry A. Wallace. Bauman urged Land to stop, then reported him to the dean, who cabled a rebuke and recalled him. Because of the turbulent situation—there had been a student strike—Foster too soon returned.[23]

Ackerman went again to Caracas late in the summer of 1948. He felt that he was treated coolly by the administration of the new president, Romulo Gallegos, and all but decided that Columbia's relationship with the school might have to be terminated. But in November, Gallegos was overthrown by a military junta, and the dean patched together a new agreement with the generals. A new director was installed and was faced with what Bauman called "a systematic Communist attempt to wreck the University school . . . and win back control of any instruction that is given to newspapermen or newspapermen-to-be."[24]

By this time the American advisers were gone, but the school continued, surviving difficulties imposed from the right as well as the left. It almost withered away during the dictatorship in the 1950s of Marcos Perez Jimenez, but recovered when Venezuela became a stable democracy. In 1970, it was renamed, in the style of many North American universities, the Escuela de Comunicación Social, and taught not only journalism but public relations and broadcasting, and all the other subsidiary specialties of such academic empires. It survived through the rest of the century, but in 2001, its Web site did not mention either its initial North American guidance or its support from the oil industry.[25]

CHAPTER 18

# The Dean and the Prizes

IN THEIR EARLY YEARS, the Pulitzer Prizes remained small and simple—and somewhat subsidiary to the school of journalism, as Pulitzer had intended. In the time of Directors Williams and Cunliffe, the American Academy of Arts and Letters named the nonjournalism jurors—that is, the specialists assigned to make recommendations to the advisory board—but President Butler soon covertly assigned that role to himself. The school's teaching staff served as jurors for the journalism prizes, customarily making their recommendations as part of routine business at faculty meetings. Nominations were few and haphazard, and jurors so often failed to recommend awards that the advisory board had to remind them that of course the prizes were there to be given. As late as 1920, the prizes remained so little known that Eugene O'Neill, notified that he had won the drama award for *Beyond the Horizon*, said that he had never heard of the Pulitzer Prize.[1]

Eventually controversies, mostly on the literary side, led at least to notoriety. Sinclair Lewis came in second twice in the early 1920s; *Main Street* lost out to Edith Wharton's *The Age of Innocence*, and *Babbitt* to Willa Cather's *One of Ours*. He was still simmering when he was awarded the 1926 prize for *Arrow-*

*smith*, and wrote a famous letter refusing the prize and urging other novelists to do likewise; moreover, he returned his check for $1,000 to Columbia.[2]

The journalism side produced no comparable disputes. There was mild grumbling—"Pulitzer Prizes for Pulitzer Papers"—when the *World* won medals for meritorious public service in 1922 and 1924. But the complaints were subdued because the prizes were so clearly earned—the first for an exposé of the Ku Klux Klan, the second for stories on the peonage system in Florida prison camps. Indifference, it turned out, was the worst enemy of the journalism prizes, and in 1925, the board created the post of executive secretary to stir up interest and increase the number of nominations. Not much was done; in 1929, Ralph Pulitzer, chairing the advisory board, wrote to President Butler: "We are in grave danger, as I see it, of having these prizes fail of their usefulness through the apathy, indifference and carelessness of newspapermen busy with their daily work."[3]

The situation did not begin to mend until Carl W. Ackerman's appointment as dean in 1931. Years later, Ackerman recalled that Butler had recruited him in part "because of the many difficult diplomatic questions involved in the relationship of the University to the Advisory Board"—questions that remained unresolved nearly thirty years after Butler and Joseph Pulitzer contested them in the gestation period. From the beginning, under Butler's guidance, Ackerman upheld, as he wrote later, "the superior authority of the University in my relations with advisory boards, especially at times when board members exercised pressure to dictate policies. . . . I was frequently criticized and condemned by board members but I maintained that the prestige and responsibility of the University should not be bartered for newspaper friendships."[4]

By the time Ackerman took office, the advisory board had abjured any direct authority over the school, and had made its sole business the recommendation of the prizes to the trustees; for their part, the trustees merely gave formal approval. Neither of the school's early directors had a place at the table with the advisory board, but Ackerman got himself elected the board's secretary in 1933 and, as the historian of the prizes writes, "took control of the journalism awards, and retained it for twenty years."[5]

That control did not extend, except in indirect ways, to picking winners. Instead, Ackerman tinkered with the language of the plan of award and, when appropriate, supported the addition of new prizes, such as the splitting of the correspondence prize into national and international reporting, and the addition of a photography award. Starting in 1938, there were sometimes "Special Citations" for otherwise uncategorizable honorees. The dean phased out the participation of the American Society of Newspaper Editors on the journalism juries, and returned to the practice of selecting jurors from the faculty. Students were enlisted as well to read and summarize nominations. And despite lagging attendance by advisory board members, he continued to stage the annual black-tie dinners at which the prizes were announced—distressing Joseph Pulitzer II, whose afternoon *Post-Dispatch* was always beaten on the story by his morning competitor.[6]

The prizes of that era were considered tame, even timid. The public-service medals seemed always to go to exposés of local corruption, rather than stories of national importance. Nor were the writing prizes much stronger; the columnist Heywood Broun commented on the 1935 reporting prize given to William H. Taylor of the *Herald Tribune*: "Surely it is not unfair to say that in a year of prodigious economic ferment and strife the American press stands convicted as incompetent if it is really true that the most distinguished reporting during the year was a series of pieces on the international yacht races." Broun's observation was on target: few prizes during the Great Depression went to journalists chronicling the country's distress, reflecting to a degree the phobic reaction of publishers to publicizing bad times. In that same year, 1935, a jury and the board disregarded Lillian Hellman's *The Children's Hour* because of its rumored lesbianism in favor of, oddly, *The Old Maid* by Zoë Akins.[7]

Even so, there were repeated disputes, especially over the novel award, with a climax reached in 1941, when the jurors passed over Ernest Hemingway's novel about the Spanish civil war, *For Whom the Bell Tolls*, and recommended two frontier novels. Fearing another embarrassment, the advisory board revolted and voted the award to Hemingway. But President Butler, who considered the book offensive, rose in wrath; Arthur Krock of the *Times*, then a junior member of the board, recalled Butler as declaring: "I hope you will reconsider before you ask the university to be associated with an award for a work of this nature." (His reference was apparently to the sexual, rather than political, content.) When the board resisted, he said that he would refuse to submit the recommendation to the trustees. The board backed down, but refused to vote any award, and nobody—the president, the board, the jurors—was pleased. Strangely, considering the more recent alacrity of the press in exposing such internal disputes, almost nothing about the controversy got into the newspapers.[8]

During World War II, an incident took place that became notorious in alumni folklore as representative of Columbia's bureaucracy. In 1943, Ira Wolfert of the class of 1930, writing for the North American Newspaper Alliance syndicate, won a prize for his coverage of the fifth battle of the Solomon Islands. When he received his check, he found that it was a few dollars short of the stipulated $1,000 because, the bursar notified him, he still owed a small amount on his tuition from thirteen years before. As the story is usually told, the faceless bursar takes the rap; but John Hohenberg, historian of the prizes, reveals that the initiative came from Dean Ackerman, who must have stumbled on the shortfall in doing research on Wolfert.[9]

Almost as soon as World War II ended, the board was beset with a flurry of proposals for expansion into other fields—radio, television, film. W. R. Mathews, a board member, pushed hard for a film prize, partly on the ground that it would help the school expand its curriculum, but Joseph Pulitzer II opposed it, and his view prevailed. In addition, program developers wanted to exploit the prizes commercially—for example, by dramatizing material from the journalism prizes on the radio. As dean and secretary—that is, managing executive—of the advisory board, Ackerman assumed that he alone should deal with such initiatives. But the discussion of the right to use the Pulitzer name inspired a contest for dominance between the dean and Joseph Pulitzer II, who had headed the board since the death of his brother Ralph in 1939.[10]

The disagreement started with a small matter, the assumption by Joseph Pulitzer II that he could veto the use of the term "Pulitzer Prizes" on a commercial radio program. But it became more serious, even fundamental, with the apparent willingness of university counsel to defer to Pulitzer's judgments, based on the "continued supervision" assigned to the Pulitzer family in the agreements of 1903 and 1904 that created the school of journalism. Writing to the university counsel, Ackerman warned that if such a power were recognized in prize deliberations, a good part of the advisory board would resign.

Getting down to cases, Ackerman wrote: "In light of my experience with the Advisory Board, I do not think that the University should be in a position of conceding a veto power to Mr. Pulitzer. . . . I do not think that he is entitled to the authority to consent or approve the use of the phrase 'Pulitzer Prizes' in a radio program, or in any other manner that the University might deem to be in the best interests of the University, subject to the consent or approval of the Advisory Board."[11]

Apparently university counsel encouraged the dean to take charge, because at a meeting of a board committee studying changes in the prizes, Ackerman discussed an offer for a radio program that would dramatize Pulitzer Prize stories, with the board retaining the power to approve scripts and the university receiving $50,000 a year. Early in 1947, he wrote to Fackenthal, the acting president: "Another agent has 'phoned from Hollywood asking whether Vandy [his wife] and I would prefer a cottage or an apartment. Fortunately I have a sister in L.A. to protect us. However, this is the third cash offer for 'Pulitzer Prizes.' As long as we have this kind of bidding I think I should see what can actually be worked out to our advantage." Ackerman indeed went to Hollywood, in part to discuss a Pulitzer Prize in film with industry leaders (who were cool to the idea) and in part to sign an agreement with Famous Artists Corporation, authorizing a weekly half-hour radio program dramatizing the prizes.[12]

Even as Ackerman opened the way to commercialization, it became apparent that the prizes were suffering a crisis. Procedurally, the jury system was not functioning well, from the point of view of both the advisory board and jurors. Ackerman commented: "We are blistered every year by disappointed jurors," who complained that the board never read the raw materials they submitted. By board policy, the identities and recommendations of juries remained secret, except when an outraged juror spoke to the press. For their part, board members complained about jury recommendations, especially the nominations for the journalism prizes, which were again being handled by designees of the American Society of Newspaper Editors.[13]

There was a more serious complaint—that board members either maneuvered to win prizes for their own organizations or engaged in vote-swapping. Ackerman reminded Joseph Pulitzer II that six of the nine journalism prizes in 1947 had gone to newspapers represented on the board. Pulitzer had already declined to broaden the pool of possible prizewinners when the board rejected a proposal to split the public-service award into divisions for larger and smaller papers.[14]

Ackerman summarized the problem to Fackenthal at the end of the year: "Last year the published criticism of the Pulitzer Prizes which I have expected for some time injured the reputation of the University. There are two basic reasons for this: one, the policy of the Advisory Board of voting prizes around the table, is not a matter I can control . . . we must recognize that there is also an evil in the lack on our part of literally searching the country for nominations."[15]

As prize-giving time approached in 1948, there was a new flurry of criticism. The critic taken most seriously was the respected Carroll Binder, foreign editor of the *Chicago Daily News*. He disclosed a long-term boycott of the prizes by the United Press, one of the country's three leading wire services, which began when the advisory board overrode a jury recommendation of a prize to UP for reporting of the war in Ethiopia. (The boycott did not end until 1954, when the prizes were under new management.) A board member, Arthur Krock, wrote directly to Binder to rebut his charges of favoritism; for example, he asserted, he had nominated the war reporter Homer Bigart of the *Times*'s rival, the *Herald Tribune*, for his 1946 prize.[16]

Even so, in 1948, the journalism prizes favored three papers represented at the table, not the least of them Pulitzer's *Post-Dispatch*. Again, the public-service medal was scarcely unmerited; the *Post-Dispatch* had done a major investigation following the Centralia, Illinois, coal-mine disaster. The board believed itself to be in a no-win position; it could avoid accusations by ignoring nominations from organizations represented on the board, but it would commit an injustice if it thus had to pass over an otherwise deserving nominee.[17]

By 1949, Ackerman was aware that the prizes also faced a structural crisis. Costs of the program, while modest, were eating into the Pulitzer endowment. The dean's effort to raise funds led to another disagreement with Joseph Pulitzer II, who informed him, in Ackerman's words, that "no members of the Pulitzer family are interested in contributing to the School or to the Prize fund." Ackerman retaliated by warning him that another donor, rather than the first Joseph Pulitzer, might eventually have his name associated with the school.[18]

The board was restive. Ackerman warned the provost, Grayson Kirk, early in 1950: "There is further evidence that a storm is brewing in several newspaper offices as well as in the Advisory Board." Evidently the board as a whole shared the younger Pulitzer's distaste for supporting the school, or admitting any association with the school, much as the board of the American Press Institute had kept its distance. Its executive committee recommended that the school have a separate board. Ackerman even hinted that, despite the provision of Pulitzer's will, the solution might be the severance of the prizes from the school.[19]

Complete severance did not take place, but the board nonetheless was relieved from thinking that monitoring the school might again become part of its burdens. By a resolution of April 18, 1950, the board changed its name to the Advisory Board on the Pulitzer Prizes, and defined its function as "the control of the annual selection of the winners of the Pulitzer prizes, and of the jurors who screen the material, and of the form in which the public announcements are made." The trustees later ratified the action.[20]

The action could be said to have ended the first phase of the school's history, when its structure was more or less what its founder-donor had envisioned. Pulitzer had insisted on an advisory board because he believed that those who taught journalism needed the counsel of senior figures in the field. Their job of prize-giving was secondary. Almost from the beginning, the board largely disregarded its primary duty and eventually dealt solely with the prizes. The name change merely recognized reality.

This turning point could also have provided an opportunity for reform. In particular, the accusations of self-dealing could have been tempered if the procedures had become more open—in particular, if the jury choices were revealed. But Ackerman, supported by Joseph Pulitzer II, stood firmly against disclosure: "I shall never agree to any arrangement whereby *any* publicity of the recommendation of the juries is authorized or left to the discretion of the juries themselves." Suggesting that there were second-place choices, he appeared to believe, would dilute the authority of the prizes. For the most part, secrecy remained in place for two decades more.[21]

Ackerman continued to act as marketing agent for the prizes. Only a month after the severance resolution, the dean told the board that his negotiations with the entertainment industry had resulted in a proposal to present Pulitzer Prize plays on television under the sponsorship of the Schlitz Brewing Company. The beer company would contribute $50,000 each to the school and to the prize fund. The board favored the proposal, with a few reservations, 11–1.[22]

Thus it came about that a one-hour version of the 1937 drama prize winner, the Kaufman-Hart comedy *You Can't Take It With You*, was broadcast on ABC on October 6, 1950, and other plays followed. The program ran until June 29, 1951, and reappeared for a time early in 1952. The only noisy complaint came from the Women's Christian Temperance Union, which called the program "a scheme of education for alcoholism which uses American classics as springboards for beer promotion." Such criticism was brushed off by Columbia's president, Dwight Eisenhower, who remarked: "If Tiffany's had made a grant of this kind, everybody would be in favor of it and nothing would be said. But frankly, I prefer beer to diamonds."[23]

Ackerman wasted no time in utilizing the money that became available to the school. He acquired television sets for the full-time faculty, so that they could watch the program. But for students, the chief change was the replacement of the wooden desks that had been installed in the new newsroom in 1935. Ackerman noted: "The desks are so worn and battered that students are repeatedly losing typewriters, purses and anything else they leave in the desks because the locks do not hold or are easily broken." When the class of 1952 arrived, it found the newsroom stocked with all-steel desks, but with no plaque to thank Schlitz.[24]

CHAPTER 19

# "Training Ground"

IN HIS REPORT in mid-1946, Dean Ackerman disclosed that the school of journalism had reached a tipping point. That is, its new identity as a graduate school was now dominant: with the class of 1947, M.S. graduates would outnumber the 747 who earned the old B.Lit. The graduate school had awarded as many degrees in eleven years as had the old undergraduate school in twenty-plus. The new program had proved itself efficient—fewer dropouts, fewer failures, and with its one-year limit a minimal drain on the university's resources.[1]

In 1946, with the return of World War II veterans, applications soared to a record of more than four hundred for the school's sixty-five places. However, not every applicant received equal consideration on credentials alone. As Ackerman explained, in the interest of creating a nationwide student body, no more than two applicants would be admitted from any given undergraduate institution—an exception made in this one year for seven graduates of the Chungking school. This policy, he said, was justified by the need to keep a surplus of New Yorkers from being dumped on the tight New York job market. Although the policy may have sounded as if it promoted diversity, it still echoed Nicholas Murray Butler's fear of overloading the university with graduates of New York City high schools—that is, Jews. In the class of 1947, only eight graduates from New York City institutions made the cut; two were from Columbia College and one from Barnard.[2]

Given the high selectivity (not to mention the restored male majority), it is not surprising that in faculty folk memory '47 came to rank with the legendary '17. Many in the class became well-known practitioners—Joseph Durso (New York University), a *Times* sports columnist; Reuven Frank (College of the City of New York), who headed NBC News; Gerald Green (Columbia College), NBC producer and novelist; Irving R. Levine (Brown University), NBC correspondent; Warren Weaver, Jr. (Amherst College), a political writer for the *Times*; and Gabe Pressman (New York University), the most enduring reporter on New York local television. The class of 1947 did not emulate '17 in dominating the school's alumni organization; that was left to the extraordinarily well-organized class of 1952.[3]

Fittingly, this premier class of 1947 graduated in the year when the school observed the centennial of Pulitzer's birth. In the school's early days and into the 1920s, students marked the founder's birthday, April 10, by placing a wreath of roses or laurel on the bust in the lobby, but the custom fell into disuse in the less sentimental Ackerman years. The dean decided to stage an elaborate public tribute in 1947. He got in touch with Charles G. Ross, President Truman's press secretary and a veteran of Pulitzer's *Post-Dispatch*; Ross passed him on to Postmaster General Robert E. Hannegan, who assented to Ackerman's proposal of a commemorative stamp. It was executed with the dean's guidance—a reproduction of the John Singer Sargent portrait of Pulitzer; on the opposite side, a depiction of the Statue of Liberty, for the erection of which Pulitzer conducted his most famous promotional campaign; and the quotation: "Our Republic and its press will rise or fall together."[4]

The stamp was a huge success. The New York postmaster informed the dean that the booths set up in Low Library for the April 10 ceremony sold 18,433 stamps. Across the nation, post offices sold 6.4 million, a record. A few years later, Ackerman recalled that the stamp sold more than the combined first-day sales of stamps featuring Franklin Roosevelt, Thomas A. Edison, or Will Rogers, and eventually more than Columbia's own 1954 bicentennial stamp, for that matter.[5]

Did the Pulitzer name have a forgotten magic? Was it the prizes, which were by this time much better known than the school? Or was Pulitzer remembered vaguely as a kind of American hero? Ackerman did not try to explain the phenomenon. But the *Times*, in a warm editorial, noted: "He helped give our press two things on which it still builds a growing influence: mass circulation and a rugged independence of political or any other outside control." It added: "The traditions he established remain a living force. The Pulitzer School of Journalism each year turns out future editors to hand those traditions on."[6]

Coincidentally, days before the Pulitzer birthday observance, the Commission on Freedom of the Press (the Hutchins Commission, which Ackerman had momentarily had a chance to sponsor) issued its report—a critique deploring the state of the press and calling for reforms, all of which the press initially rejected. The report also had a few words on schools of journalism:

> [Professional] ideals and attitudes in the professions of law, medicine, and divinity are cultivated by the professional schools of those disciplines. They act as independent centers of criticism. . . . The schools of journalism have not yet accepted this obligation. With few exceptions they fall short of professional standards. Most of them devote themselves to vocational training, and even here they are not so effective as they should be. The kind of training a journalist needs most today is not training in the tricks and machinery of the trade. If he is to be a competent judge of public affairs, he needs the broadest and most liberal education. The schools of journalism as a whole have not yet successfully worked out the method by which their students may acquire this education.

In its recommendations for action, the commission also wrote: "It is important that students who enter schools of journalism should not be deprived of liberal education because they have made up their minds that they want to work on the press. . . . It is therefore imperative that [the schools] associate themselves as closely as possible with other departments and schools of their universities." It was Pulitzer's idea restated, but with a broad hint that it was nowhere practiced, perhaps not even at Columbia, nor was there any response from the school. The suggestion that a journalism school could serve as a center of criticism as well as training eventually took root at Columbia, but long after Ackerman's time.[7]

In the postwar years, Ackerman concentrated on reconfiguring the school's administration and augmenting the faculty. He envisioned the new American Press Institute on the ground floor as a coequal branch with the school of journalism, each branch run by an associate dean, leaving Ackerman free to conduct other enterprises. The associate dean and director of

API was Floyd Taylor, who, with the API board, sought to distance API from the school.

The other associate deanship proved a problem as well. As head of instruction, Ackerman proposed Roscoe Ellard. In his seven years at the school, Ellard had had a patchy career. In his first three years, Ellard won the dean's confidence, notably in creating a program of field trips that sent out Columbia students to staff a suburban newspaper—the Port Chester *Item* was the first—and publish it for a day. In the second year of the program, students put out eight newspapers, one with a sports page staffed entirely by women.[8]

In March 1943, Ackerman made his first attempt to nominate Ellard to be associate dean. What the dean had in mind was clear in his letter to President Butler: "By education and experience Professor Ellard is eminently qualified to take full charge of education for the profession of journalism in this School under my direction." With the distracting Chungking enterprise looming, Ackerman expected once more to remove himself from the day-to-day operations. Less than two months later, Ackerman was obliged to ask the president to halt the process. Among Ellard's new duties was to assist the advisory board. Scarcely had he met the board than he crossed the formidable Arthur Krock over what Ackerman called an "assumption of board prerogatives." A statement (of which Ellard had no doubt been the source) had been published in St. Louis saying that Ellard had claimed to be "well known for his connection with the Pulitzer Prize Committee." Ackerman withdrew the nomination.[9]

By the end of the war, Ellard had restored his standing with Ackerman and was awarded his associate deanship. In his 1946 report, the dean wrote hopefully: "Professor Ellard's plans for the year 1946–1947 will set a new standard in the application of newspaper knowledge to the classroom." But early in 1947, Ellard went AWOL for a week on private business in Chicago, and left his secretary to introduce a distinguished guest, the columnist Marquis Childs. The dean forced him to resign from the associate deanship, and Ellard did so in a manner that verged on insubordination.[10]

Ellard stayed on as a professor, but he was progressively surrounded by a new postwar faculty. Initially, the school gained permanent faculty members from its two overseas enterprises. John Foster, Jr., after weathering the difficulties of counseling the new journalism school in Caracas, joined the home faculty as a professor in the fall of 1948. A dapper, affable man, he undertook the task of acquainting the school with mid-twentieth-century technology. He introduced students to such new printing techniques as offset lithography;

and with Elliott A. Crooks (class of 1928) of Hogan Laboratories, he super-vised a modest facsimile newspaper that students transmitted to New York State's agricultural fair. In the early 1950s, he assembled the school's first ven-ture into television journalism, a program called "News-O-Rama," which ap-peared on a local channel.[11]

Another newcomer was Richard T. Baker, who had led the Chungking school through its last difficult months. After the war, he completed a book about Methodism in China, *Ten Thousand Years*, and returned to the Far East to gather material for *Darkness of the Sun*, on religion in Japan. He was nom-inated by the dean in 1947 to be an associate professor. There was an unusu-al addition by Ackerman to his nomination letter: "[Baker] is coming with the understanding that this is a full time job and a life-time career, if he can give us satisfactory service."[12]

Baker was an odd sort for the school of journalism. He had no mainstream newspaper experience and was educated as much for the divine as the pro-fane profession. In the roles he filled, he more exemplified the gentlemanly, scholarly tradition of John W. Cunliffe and Douglas Southall Freeman, whom he admired, than the rough-hewn drill instructors of the newsroom. Yet Ackerman could not have spoken of a lifelong commitment for a man in his mid-thirties had he not envisioned Baker as a future leader, perhaps a dean. His confidence was reflected in his entrusting to Baker the history of the school to be written for the Columbia bicentennial.

John Hohenberg, the next major addition, was an alumnus of the school (1927) who had made a name for himself in New York afternoon journalism. Most recently he had pioneered as United Nations correspondent for the *Post-Home News*, where, according to the dean, he had been "receiving one of the highest reportorial salaries in New York, $12,500 annually." He took a pay cut of $5,000 and became a professor at the school in 1950. His ap-pointment, incidentally, was one of the first at the school that was subjected to the scrutiny of a campus-wide "ad hoc" committee—which approved it. He became known at once for his headlong, impatient teaching style, which earned him the nickname "Hoppy" (for the Hollywood cowboy Hopalong Cassidy). But there was genuine excitement for the students he shepherded out to the temporary United Nations headquarters at Lake Success on Long Island and later to the permanent headquarters in Manhattan.[13]

Thus, at the start of the 1950s, the full-time faculty numbered four—Roscoe Ellard and the newcomers Foster, Baker, and Hohenberg. Named head of instruction in 1949, Ellard stood first among equals, reputedly cast-ing a triple vote in the twice-a-year student rankings. There was a temporary fifth teacher, the dean's son, Robert, who had served at the Chungking School. The annual bulletin always listed the adjuncts so as to suggest that about thirty teachers were on hand, but several of those with professorial titles were American Press Institute staff members who did little teaching; the rest were part-time downtowners—a majority of them from the *Times*— who had stocked the school almost from its beginning.[14]

The school was to be subjected in 1948 to the scrutiny of the American Council on Education for Journalism, the new national accrediting body. As he awaited the council's visit, Ackerman was not at ease with the state of the school. He wrote to the acting president at the end of 1947:

> The time has passed when we could assert that New York City is the best newspaper laboratory in the world and expect that assumption of supremacy to take the place of our own laboratory deficiencies. . . . I have endeavored for 16 years to limit my recommendations not only to absolute necessities but also to the prevailing University financial situation. This cannot be done for the next academic year. We cannot escape or ignore the findings of the Council for Education in Journalism. We cannot escape or ignore the criticism of the Pulitzer Prizes. We cannot escape or ignore the developments in radio, television and facsimile in newspaper offices.[15]

The school won its accreditation. Still, it remained a shabby, under-equipped place, although these conditions did little to dampen the robust *esprit* of each year's class. And certainly the school provided no worse than the daily squalor of hundreds of newspaper offices across the country. As measured in the declining enrollment at journalism schools, journalism in the postwar decade offered neither the money nor the prestige to attract the brightest of returning veterans. The school's historian, Baker, conceded that journalism still paid "a young man's salary" and many could not afford to remain.[16]

The ethos of the school could be read, sometimes between the lines, in the final chapter of Baker's 1954 history, where he assembled a composite of "The Columbia Journalist." The school's isolation was reflected in his statement that it was "somewhat of a community to itself." Its apologia for nonintellectualism and inattention to ethics and history was contained in the observation:

> The practitioner is Columbia's real contribution to journalism, more than the thinker and speculator. The Columbia journalist has plunged into his job without too much assessing what the finer philosophical meanings of

that job are. Each class of sixty-five since 1935 has presented half a dozen Phi Beta Kappas, but there is no particular premium at the School of Journalism upon straight-A records. Experience has shown that the conventional grading tradition of undergraduate colleges frequently produces a B-level graduate who makes a better journalist than a student whose record is heavily freighted with A's.

After noting the high percentage of graduates who had entered journalism, Baker concluded: "The School . . . thinks of itself as a training ground and is proud of the efficiency of the returns on its investment of time and money."[17]

As to whether the school had contributed to Pulitzer's prime objective—the education of journalists who would play a critical role in the American democracy—Baker remained silent, either because he took the conclusion for granted or he had not found it relevant.

CHAPTER 20

# "The Pulitzer Mandate"

CARL ACKERMAN completed his twentieth year as dean in 1951. He had come to Columbia as a protégé of Nicholas Murray Butler, to whom he was unfailingly loyal, even as Butler's powers declined. When Butler retired in 1945, the atmosphere remained comfortable; Frank D. Fackenthal, the acting president, was an old friend who had been involved with the Pulitzer Prizes from the start. Despite his age—he was in his sixties—Fackenthal was Ackerman's personal favorite to succeed Butler. Publicly, Ackerman maintained that he wanted no role in making the selection.[1]

Ackerman must have sensed that his familiar old Columbia was about to vanish when he was asked what he thought of General of the Army Dwight D. Eisenhower, commander of the victorious allied armies in Europe. Ackerman replied that he ranked Eisenhower's character below that of General George C. Marshall, soon to be secretary of state and author of the Marshall Plan. Eisenhower, now serving as Army chief of staff, had already been asked about the Columbia presidency and had replied noncommittally.[2]

The search limped along for more than a year until in June 1947 the trustees agreed to make a firm offer to Eisenhower. The general met on short notice with a small group of trustees, deans, and administrators. Ackerman was unimpressed and noted that the audience greeted in silence Eisenhower's remark that he had a choice of leading the Boy Scouts of America or Columbia, and chose—almost by happenstance, it seemed—the latter. The dean confessed himself disappointed.[3]

Released from active service at the Pentagon, Eisenhower arrived on the campus in May 1948 and was installed in the fall. Ackerman was gingerly in his approach to the new president and his phalanx of military-style aides. For several months, business between them was routine. But the dean hit a snag when he tried to draft Eisenhower to participate in the annual Maria Moors Cabot awards. Afterward, he wrote himself a memorandum on "the education of a dean": "I have learned that the most energy, the most patience and the greatest concentration of skill and will power have to be concentrated on the inside, behind the scenes, especially with superiors or men who think they are superior." The general declined to attend the dinner honoring the medalists, cursed when he found that he would have to attend the convocation and luncheon the next day, and was the picture of gloom throughout.[4]

Yet Eisenhower was not utterly indifferent to the school. He called on Ackerman to present the president of Venezuela, Romulo Gallegos, for an honorary degree. He agreed readily enough to meet with the American Press Institute board, and gave Ackerman a suggestion, which he accepted, that the dean distribute to the Columbia trustees a hundred letters praising API. He congratulated the dean on the year's grants and gifts, and even invited him for lunch at the president's house.[5]

But the general was to be a fleeting presence on the campus. He was away on leave on military business for most of 1949. Early in 1951, he departed for good to command the forces of the North Atlantic Treaty Organization. At a farewell in the Faculty Club, he said that he hoped to return to Columbia; Ackerman noted: "Rather perfunctory applause." Eisenhower remained president in name, but in every other sense, Grayson L. Kirk, vice president and provost, succeeded him.[6]

By now, Ackerman knew that he was in his twilight years. Unlike Butler, he could not serve into his eighties; regulations adopted during the Eisenhower presidency made retirement for administrators mandatory at sixty-five. Ackerman would reach that age in 1955. For the most part, he went on as before. He was ever more isolated from the daily operations of the school. The students' sense that they saw him only at the opening tea was not far from the truth. They might have seen him at commencement as well, but the school remained so employment-oriented that any student

with a new job could skip commencement and several final weeks of classes without penalty.[7]

In his latter years, Ackerman became more outspoken, as he demonstrated in a bitter campus dispute during the 1952 presidential campaign, a contest between Governor Adlai E. Stevenson of Illinois and Eisenhower, the
Columbia president-in-name. A "Volunteers for Stevenson" faculty committee raised money for an advertisement in the *Times* designed to show that
Columbia was not unanimously for Eisenhower. Ackerman contributed, in-
tending to have his name at the head of the list. But the acting president,
Kirk, was unhappy about the ad and about the presence there of a ranking
administrator; he asked the committee to remove Ackerman's name.[8]

Ackerman agreed to the deletion, but exploded in a telegram to the *St.
Louis Post-Dispatch*. He charged that he had been urged to remain silent; but,
he declared, "I do not intend to remain silent as long as General Eisenhower is free and unrestricted in his use of the University's name and property
for campaign purposes." Indeed, Eisenhower was using the president's
house at 60 Morningside Drive as his voting residence and office. He added:
"General Eisenhower's supporters at Columbia University have sought by
their use of powerful vehicles of public information to give the impression
that the university community is solidly back of General Eisenhower whereas there is tremendous support for Governor Stevenson." Clearly, Ackerman was more anti-Eisenhower than pro-Stevenson.[9]

The issue, and the controversy over dueling signature advertisements by
Columbia's Stevenson and Eisenhower committees in the *Times*, was
splashed through the papers for several days. The dean's independence even
earned a commendatory editorial in the *Daily Mirror*, which was supporting
Eisenhower. Once the election was over, of course, Eisenhower resigned to
move to the White House. Kirk was named president of Columbia; Ackerman sent him a letter of congratulations on Eisenhower's inaugural day.[10]

It was only a matter of months before Ackerman took another, even more
dramatic stand. Early in 1953, the volatile Senator Joseph R. McCarthy, head
of the Congressional Committee on Government Operations, was launching
almost daily new charges of communist subversion. The new Eisenhower
administration struggled to control the issue by toughening loyalty and security inquiries. It was the high tide of the postwar Red Scare.[11]

In March, Ackerman prepared an article for the monthly *Bulletin* of the
American Society of Newspaper Editors declaring that he was closing the
school's records to government investigators. As a courtesy and a warning,
he told Robert C. Harron, in charge of university publicity, about the arti-

cle. Harron was dismayed and fearful that the story might harm the university, but was rebuffed when he asked Ackerman to withdraw it. Seeking to soften its impact, Harron suggested: "I was wondering last night what you would think of dropping in on J. Edgar Hoover when you are next in Washington to explain the problem to him just as you explained it to me?"[12]

When he wrote to Harron the next day, the dean ignored the hint that he should humble himself before the director of the FBI, and instead made a dramatic statement of conscience:

Dear Bob Harron:

I decided last night not to withdraw the article I wrote for the ASNE Bulletin. However, I will not release the text myself either at the University or personally elsewhere. Release procedure and time will be left entirely to the ASNE.

I appreciate the earnest consideration and the great amount of time you gave the reading and study of the article. I value and respect your judgment as you know, or I would not have sought it in the first place.

However, there are a few controlling factors beyond the content, the timing and the appropriateness of the subject,

The first is that I received last week THE STORY OF THE ST. LOUIS POST-DISPATCH. . . . At the opening of the booklet there is a photograph of Sargent's painting of Joseph Pulitzer and a reproduction of the plaque in the lobby of the POST-DISPATCH Building in St. Louis dated April 10, 1907.

That plaque and the one in the foyer of Journalism Building [the plaque, dedicated on Pulitzer's birthday in 1951, displays the 1904 quotation, "Our Republic and its press will rise or fall together . . . "] have always been something like personal heirlooms because I was a student when the School began, and also because I happen to be the first Dean, and also, perhaps, because I have served a longer period of time than my two predecessors combined, I feel an obligation to the Joseph Pulitzer inheritance, which is probably not shared by others.

Anyway, I remarked to one of my colleagues here yesterday, who also opposed the publication of the article, that I was too close to the Joseph Pulitzer tradition to disregard what I have always considered an obligation, the obligation to support the Pulitzer platform in St. Louis and the platform we have on the wall in the foyer here. However, I added that I could see his point of view as a younger man, and that it was quite evident to me that whoever succeeds me as Dean, now in less than two years, could not possibly have the same feeling of obligation to the Pulitzer tradition.

Now, therefore, inasmuch as I have always considered it my duty to follow the Pulitzer mandate, in so far as possible, I can not conscientiously recall an article which I had written for the ASNE Bulletin which revealed and expressed a conviction.[13]

Fifteen days later, with the release of his ASNE article, the dean was back on page one of the *Times*: "Dean Closes Files to 'Loyalty Hunts' / Ackerman of Columbia Says He Will Not Help Agencies Except on Lawyer's Advice." Quoted in the story, he again invoked Pulitzer, saying that the founder's standard of "drastic independence" was in jeopardy, both on campus and in journalism, because students feared that campus activism and opinions could later be used against them: "If we have reached the stage in our democracy when fear of investigation becomes universal and the loyalty of college students must be investigated we will be erecting an iron curtain of our own." A few days later, Columbia College made it clear that it had no intention of following Ackerman's lead, nor did the rest of the university.[14]

Ackerman gave no clue as to whether a particular instance had spurred him to speak. He may have been aware of the case of James Wechsler of the *Post*, whose left-wing activities as a Columbia College student in the 1930s were under attack by McCarthy. Or he may have regretted his previous cooperation with investigating agencies. Some years before, he had permitted the FBI to obtain the results of the typing test administered to Priscilla Hobson, who studied at the school in 1925–26 and later married Alger Hiss, to help ascertain whether she could have typed secret documents involved in the Hiss case. (At her husband's first trial, the prosecution brought out that she received a B.)[15]

In the immediate context, Ackerman may have appeared to have swung left. But in the context of his past politics, his stand was consistent with antigovernment positions he took against the National Recovery Administration, in complaining about propaganda issuing from Washington during the war, and in challenging the exclusion of a Venezuelan visitor as a subversive. He drew on an older conservatism than the virulent, disruptive variety then holding sway in Washington, and took a stand far different from that of Talcott Williams, who had abetted witch-hunting during the Great War.[16]

This declaration was all but a valedictory, as the reference to his departure made clear. He took the first steps later in the year. He was feeling downcast; the American Press Institute had failed to invite him to the dedication of its Floyd Taylor memorial library, and he recalled that the university had declined to name the school library for Directors Williams or Cunliffe. In a file memorandum typed on Thanksgiving Day 1953, he noted that he and his wife watched Archbishop Fulton J. Sheen's mesmerizing inspirational program, *Life Is Worth Living*, and he was moved to announce to her the next day that he would retire at the pleasure of the trustees. He conferred with Low Library officials and said that he would like to be Dean Emeritus in Residence. They agreed that a new dean should be in place by July 1, 1954, but the process took two years more.[17]

He set about redistributing his responsibilities. He put John Hohenberg forward to administer the Pulitzer Prizes—Hohenberg, he said, "because he has had diplomatic experience at the UN and abroad and possess[es], I think the understanding and finesse to represent the University." The actual transition took place in April 1954, when he invited Hohenberg to attend a meeting of the advisory board and asked him to take minutes. After the meeting, according to Hohenberg, he thrust a pile of documents into Hohenberg's hands without a word and walked away. When Hohenberg went to the next day's meeting he was greeted as "Mr. Secretary," and he remained so for two decades.[18]

As it happened, this was the first meeting of the advisory board in what became known as the World Room, the new incarnation of what had been a ramshackle lounge where earlier classes had operated their cheap-lunch cooperatives. It was so named because it displayed, starting in April 1954, a 90-square-foot stained glass window depicting the Statue of Liberty salvaged from the *World* building, which was being torn down to make way for a new approach to the Brooklyn Bridge. Hohenberg, serving as president of the journalism alumni association, had himself been instrumental in obtaining the window for the school, as had Herbert Bayard Swope, former executive editor of the *World*, and it was Swope who proposed the name for the room. In the end, the window was a gift from New York City. Joseph Pulitzer II spoke at the dedication and the subsequent meeting of the advisory board. It was his last visit; he died on March 30, 1955.[19]

Ackerman planned as well to relieve Ellard of his authority as head of instruction and to place Richard Baker in that position. He wrote to the president: "As far as Professor Ellard is concerned I am not worried because I think I will have that problem under control by proceeding as indicated." The first step was to name Baker secretary of the faculty, and photographs of Baker and Hohenberg appeared in a joint announcement in the *Times* in May 1954.[20]

Ackerman's path to retirement was darkened by the death of his wife in August 1954. He had married Mabel Vander Hoof, known as Vandy, an illustrator and painter, thirty years before. Their only child, Robert, who had taught briefly at the school and in Chungking, died four years later.[21]

In the spring of 1955, the trustees were made aware of Ackerman's coming retirement, but there was no new dean in place and he was forced to serve another year. He handled more or less routine business, receiving several new benefactions—a scholarship given by Maxwell Geffen, class of 1916; a Julius Ochs Adler scholarship, named for the general manager of the *Times*, recently deceased; and a Benjamin Franklin scholarship, given by eleven local newspapers. He added a junior member to the slender full-time faculty—Lawrence D. Pinkham of the class of 1951, who had been working for United Press.[22]

On May 7, 1956, the trustees designated him Dean Emeritus of the Faculty of Journalism and Professor Emeritus of Journalism, and later awarded him a Cabot gold medal, to his surprise. The alumni association paid tribute to him at its annual meeting, and an editorial in the *Herald Tribune* said, "His services will be long remembered." But there was inevitably a touch of pique. Speaking briefly at the Overseas Press Club, he condemned mandatory retirement at 65 as "wasteful."[23]

As Ackerman already knew, his successor had been named and was waiting to take over the office on the fifth floor. Unlike his predecessors, the dean had no taste for lingering at the school or forcing his successors to deal with his increasingly crusty presence. After leaving in midsummer 1956, he reappeared only rarely and reluctantly.

Even so, his imprint remained on the school for decades to come. Like any dean, he handed on a generation of faculty, for better or worse. More important, the pattern of education that he established—the single year of graduate school, the work-simulating five-day week, the continuing extensive use of part-time teachers, and the semi-isolation of the school and its students from the rest of the university—endured like boulders in a stream. Later deans would try to push aside one or another, only to have them remain stubbornly in place. Truly, Carl W. Ackerman was the second founder of Pulitzer's school.

# CHAPTER 21

# From Dropout to Dean

THE MENTIONING OF NAMES for a new dean started more than eighteen months before Carl Ackerman actually left. President Kirk asked for nominations from the Pulitzer Prize and American Press Institute advisory boards, although technically neither body had any role in governing the school. The boards' members offered fifty or so names, some associated with large schools of journalism, but the majority of them well-thought-of newspaper editors. The only person mentioned more than a handful of times—and the nominee whom Kirk may have favored—was J. Montgomery Curtis, director of the American Press Institute. But Curtis made it clear at once that he would stay where he was.[1]

The search took a decisive turn in June 1955 when Turner Catledge, managing editor of the *New York Times* and, as it happened, a member of both the prize board and the API board, wrote to Kirk:

Today I have received this suggestion from a friend whom I had taken into my effort to find a candidate: Edward W. Barrett.

On the face of things Mr. Barrett's would seem to be a formidable name. I am sure you know him. He is a man of pleasing presence; is about

forty-five years old and a graduate of Princeton . . . I also understand that
he is more or less independent financially. My informant believes he inherited some money from his father, whom [sic] I recall was once an owner of one of the Birmingham (Ala.) papers—I believe The News. Mr. Barrett is very much interested in rendering public service and, of course, he
is widely acquainted.

Kirk replied on June 30: "I am tremendously interested in the suggestion
of Ed Barrett for the Deanship of our School of Journalism. I have known
Ed in a casual way for some years and I have come to have a high regard for
his capacity." For all practical purposes, the search was over.[2]

What was formidable about Edward W. Barrett? He had indeed become
widely acquainted, in a career alternating between the public and private sec-
tors. In 1933, after stopping briefly at CBS, he worked his way up at
*Newsweek*, becoming national affairs editor before he left in 1942 to join the
Office of War Information. He rose there as well, to director of overseas operations. He returned to *Newsweek* as editorial director, then was called into
the Truman administration as assistant secretary of state for public affairs—
a position held first by the poet Archibald MacLeish and later by William
Benton. He stayed two years, wrote a book about Cold War psychological
warfare called *Truth Is Our Weapon*, and left after tangling with congressional committees. He returned to New York and formed his own public-
relations firm, which was bought by the giant Hill & Knowlton, then trying
to help the tobacco industry cope with early health warnings. Barrett became
an executive vice-president and worked on the tobacco accounts.[3]

Ackerman was miffed when he heard the identity of his successor, partly
because Barrett was a dropout. The old dean commented to his former associate Herbert Brucker: "The other day I looked up Edward Barrett's file.
You may recall that he was a student here for a few weeks in 1932. Both you
and I tried to make adjustments to keep him here, but he wanted to work full
time at Columbia Broadcasting." Barrett meanwhile had urged, correctly,
that there should be no claim in announcements that he was a bona fide alumnus of the school.[4]

In fact, there were more parallels between Ackerman and Barrett than the
retiring dean would have conceded. At the time of appointment, neither was
an active journalist, and each won the position for presumed public-relations
and administrative skills. Each was relatively young at the start and not in
search of a sinecure. And, much as Ackerman felt he needed to revitalize the

easygoing school of the 1920s, Barrett found a school that he perceived as static and in need of modernization.

Where they differed, as soon became apparent, was in temperament—Ackerman tending to isolate himself and favoring formal communication; Barrett, hands on, with honed political and organizing skills. He established many contacts across the campus, while becoming a powerful presence in the school itself—signaled by his innovation of a year-opening address to the class and his intense involvement in the curriculum.[5]

When Barrett took office in August 1956, it was with a general agenda that he had accepted from Kirk. Kirk felt that Ackerman had "drawn all too little upon the resources of the University for the benefit of his students," and gained Barrett's agreement before the appointment that he would look into broadening the curriculum, perhaps expanding it to a second year.[6]

From the first, Barrett left no doubt that he was committed to change. He requested or raised $50,000 in new money—a portion each for experimental courses, refurbishing, and a new program for foreign students. He also projected a mid-career program in science writing and a workshop in opinion reporting. Not least, he said, the school's quiescent alumni and development programs should be revitalized. At an early faculty meeting, he raised the subject of recruiting African-American students, who had never numbered more than one or two in any preceding classes.[7]

Meanwhile, he began to use his new position to speak out on current issues in journalism, initially deploring the refusal of his old employer, the State Department, to grant visas to permit reporting in Communist China. Later, in speeches and reports, he chided the newspaper business for underpaying the talent that the school was educating, and went on to criticize the performance of journalism in general as not being up to the job in critical times.[8]

He tightened up the slack ways of the late Ackerman years. Gone were the long days when students, after finishing their assignments early, spent afternoons playing bridge. He also ended the practice of excusing students from the final weeks of class to report to new jobs; students were required to attend commencement or place their degrees in jeopardy. But he gave them reason to stick around. For example, he ended his first year with a flair—a student news conference in the World Room with former President Truman, who handled the questions with the aplomb of a Joe DiMaggio taking batting practice. Then there was a jubilant picnic for the class on his ample lawn in suburban Greenwich, Connecticut.[9]

For the school, moving on to Barrett's second year was like shifting from a stately sedan into a speeding sports car. It was a long parade of announcements, almost in the style of Franklin D. Roosevelt's Hundred Days. The new dean knew that newspapers still fed on handouts, and he saw to it that every new step was well publicized.

The first major innovation was a new course, "Basic Issues in the News," set up with a grant of $6,500 from the New York Times Foundation. "BI," as it came to be known, brought senior scholars from other parts of the university back into the curriculum for the first time since the days of Talcott Williams. Each visiting scholar was teamed with a member of the journalism faculty, including the dean, who took to teaching as avidly as Ackerman had avoided it. BI students were obligated to study readings compiled in each of six subjects and, at the end, produce a paper of up to 20,000 words.[10]

At the same time, an International Division was unveiled and placed under the wing of Louis M. Starr, historian and director of Columbia's Oral History Research Office, who as an additional service restored journalism history to the school's curriculum under a grant from the Sevellon Brown Foundation. Six foreign students were already on hand, and the dean won permission to award them a master of science in comparative journalism.[11]

Then came the Opinion Reporting Workshop, headed by Samuel Lubell, a 1933 graduate of the school whose widely read studies, *The Future of American Politics* and *Revolt of the Moderates*, reflected his emphasis on face-to-face encounters with voters; in a few weeks, Lubell's students assembled a report on the off-year elections.[12]

Next was the Advanced Science Writing Program program, funded by initial grants of $70,000 from the Alfred P. Sloan Foundation and $100,000 from the Rockefeller Foundation. It was directed by John Foster. The first six fellows arrived in September 1958, studied at the school and elsewhere at Columbia, went on ambitious field trips, and declared themselves at the end to be overwhelmingly satisfied.[13]

During the same year, Barrett dexterously disposed of a long-standing issue. From time to time George Sokolsky, now a columnist in the Hearst newspapers, had politely raised the question of the B.Lit. degree he was denied in 1917. Sokolsky had long since recanted his youthful socialism—"perhaps it was not too bad that I got most of the poisons out of my mind when I was very young," he told Butler—and made his peace with the university. He had been awarded a University Medal (just short of an honorary degree) and had been Nicholas Murray Butler's dinner guest. Ackerman had regarded him as one of the three "most outstanding" graduates of the school (the other two being Lester Markel of the *Times* and M. Lincoln Schuster of Simon & Schuster).[14]

But the journalism faculty had never acted, for the stated reason that it was reluctant to second-guess its predecessors' actions. The unstated one was that many members disliked Sokolsky's now conservative politics. After winning the half-hearted assent of the faculty, the dean arranged with Kirk to have Sokolsky awarded his degree at a luncheon downtown; further, he advised Robert C. Harron, the university publicist, that it would not be necessary to list Sokolsky in the commencement program. And so it was done, with a certain amount of unnecessary stealth, and evidently without any attention being paid in the newspapers.[15]

Barrett, a believer in ceremonies and special events, ended his second year by creating Journalism Day—in essence, a class day featuring speeches, panels, and the new Columbia Journalism Award, defined as an honor for those not usually on the Pulitzer Prize list, such as publishers. The first was well-timed, the recipient being eighty-five-year-old J. N. Heiskell, whose *Arkansas Gazette* had stood firm against lawlessness during the 1957 integration crisis in Little Rock.[16]

At first, Barrett had little opportunity to recruit new faculty. Ackerman's postwar appointments had set in place five faculty members destined to outlast Barrett's term. Only one, Roscoe Ellard, was ripe for replacement, and in 1958, Barrett began to maneuver, rather coldly, to retire him at sixty-five, as the university regulations permitted. The first problem was to determine just when Ellard would be sixty-five. Barrett discovered that Ellard had fudged his birth date by two years in *Who's Who*, but found the true date on Ellard's retirement-benefits application. Early in 1959, John A. Krout, the vice-president, notified Ellard that he would be named an emeritus professor at the end of June, and on Journalism Day he received an honorary silver plate.[17]

Ellard remained on hand to do a few emeritus chores, such as running the newspaper field trips, but opted out after two years. Even before he left, the trips to small newspapers were being displaced by the more high-powered Field Observation Week, which sent students on short-term internships at major news organizations along the East Coast. Shortened to FOW, the operation inevitably became known to students, despite its success, as "fuck-off week."[18]

With Ellard gone, Barrett had a candidate ready to fill the vacancy. Penn T. Kimball had been around the school for half a year doing odd jobs—helping Barrett teach, doing a study of readers' reactions to the brief 1958 New York newspaper strike, collaborating with Barrett on an article about news coverage of Latin America. At the age of forty-three, Kimball already had enough résumé for a lifetime—Princeton '37; Rhodes Scholar; service with the Marines in World War II; a stint on the innovative New York daily, *PM*; work at *U.S. News*, *Time*, the *New Republic*, the Sunday *Times*, and the last shift at *Collier's* before it closed in 1956; aide to Governor Chester Bowles and Senator William Benton of Connecticut, as well as Governor Averell Harriman of New York; and candidate for a doctorate at Columbia, which he set aside when Barrett nominated him to be a professor. Barrett wondered if Kimball would be a job-hopper, but Kimball was still around to finish his Ph.D. after retirement three decades later.[19]

Kimball, prickly and independent, speeded the change in the metabolism of the school—from the provincial, traditional orientation favored by Ellard to a bent toward national journalism and politics. Other additions soon diluted the Ackerman mix further—William A. Wood, a pioneer in educational television who had overlapped with Barrett at the State Department, took over the school's rudimentary television news and documentary experiments when John Foster became director of the science writing program. James Boylan, class of 1951 and a co-alumnus of Baker's from Cornell College, was put in charge of alumni matters. With the support of newly recruited alumni officers, headed by Herbert Brucker as president, he brought into being an annual alumni Journalism Fund, headed by M. Lincoln Schuster, who had already volunteered much time and energy.[20]

At the end of his third year, Barrett issued an expansive report, which first surveyed critically the state of American journalism, then commented on journalism education, and ultimately reported on the school itself. He listed gifts of $472,712, the largest being the Sloan and Rockefeller grants for the Advanced Science Writing Program, and $120,000 from the Clapp and Poliak Foundation (Saul Poliak was a member of the class of 1926) to support instruction in economic writing.

But at about the same time, he received a foretaste of trouble ahead. When he submitted an ambitious document titled "The Role of a Graduate School of Journalism in Education and Research," the university director of development, Stanley Salmen, remarked, "Your proposal on education and research seems to me impossibly broad for the budget and staff you have." The implication was that Barrett should not seek budget or staff increases.[21]

Barrett was not deterred. As the school approached its fiftieth year of operation, the efflorescence continued. New awards and scholarships were announced frequently, and new faculty appeared. Celebrity guests submitted themselves to student questioning—none more extraordinary than Fidel Castro, in power less than five months. He had touched base in Washington and, in New York, had been persuaded by his public-relations advisers to hold a news conference at the school—and he did, on April 21, 1959, in the American Press Institute conference room. He spoke at great length, bilingually, on his plans and programs for developing Cuba. Years later, Dean Barrett recalled in his oral history: "We had one gala week there when Fidel Castro came up and answered five questions in three hours. Mr. Truman was up two days later and answered 21 questions in 19 minutes."[22]

The class of 1959 had a sideshow in the classmate who became the school's most famous foreign student. Oleg Kalugin was the school's first exchange scholar from the Soviet Union. A callow twenty-four-year-old, Kalugin attracted considerable curiosity among his classmates, but he worked hard enough, was cautiously friendly, and was, as a lark, elected class president; the *Times* thereupon gave him a cheery "man in the news" profile. But there was little lighthearted about his subsequent career, in which he worked as an intelligence operative in Washington and New York, rose to major general in the KGB, then became its outspoken critic. After the termination of the Soviet Union, he landed in Washington where, besides working as a consultant, he became co-inventor of a spy game with William Colby, former director of the CIA. The headline in a 1991 issue of the school's *Alumni Journal* justly lamented: "Oleg, We Hardly Know You."[23]

# CHAPTER 22

# Short-Changed

AN INSTINCTIVE EXPANSIONIST, Barrett soon began to feel cramped, financially and physically. Although he had greatly increased the visibility of the school, on campus and downtown, circumstances conspired to remind him that he was at the head of a tiny segment of a huge university, with only eighty students, less than one percent of the total. Although the small classes were often cited to suggest elite status, the school in fact was small because of limited money, resources, and personnel. In addition, the size of the student body gave the university a rationale for limiting the school's use of space in its building.[1]

As early as 1958, Barrett began to exert pressure on Low Library for elbow room. In 1959, he submitted a bill of particulars to Stanley Salmen, campus director of development, making clear that he wanted the expanding school to have a larger share of space and money:

1. We are getting no credit for the 64% of the Journalism Building that is being used by other divisions of the University, including the A[merican].P[ress].I[nstitute]., which actually pays rent and the store, which should pay rent.

2. We are getting no credit for the Pulitzer money that was provided for the maintenance of the building.

3. We are being charged for an excessive proportion of the library service [that is, for the central library's staffing of the journalism library] and are once more charged here for the space in the Journalism Building that is used by the library.

4. We are given no credit for appreciation in the Pulitzer endowment.[2]

In short, Barrett charged, the university had helped itself to both components of the Pulitzer legacy—the building and the money. The latter was more serious. The endowment remained on Columbia's books at its original pre–World War I valuation while the university treasury soaked up actual appreciation. Barrett wrote to President Kirk in 1960: "The rapidly shrinking usefulness of the Pulitzer endowment for the conduct of the School and the Pulitzer Prizes is alarming." He pointed out that endowment income was paying only 30 percent of the school's costs, as opposed to 70 percent twenty years before, and demanded that the endowment be credited "with such past average appreciation in principal as has taken place . . . adopting a policy under which large special-purpose endowments are credited with their pro-rata share of appreciation in the University's investment pool." He also criticized the low proportion the university had invested in equities in an expanding economy.[3]

By contrast, Barrett noted, the initially smaller endowment for the Cabot prizes, which had been given with a proviso that the university retain the Cabot stock, was full to overflowing, to the point that its income could no longer justifiably be spent entirely for prizes. Barrett noted that "by insisting that the money be left in the stock of the company, in brief, we will have brought this relatively small fund up to the neighborhood of the so-far static Pulitzer endowment." The overflow from the Cabot endowment became, with the permission of the family, a major bounty to the school.[4]

Readjusting the Pulitzer endowment was to be slow work. Initially, the trustees' finance committee granted a modest rise in its valuation, but not nearly enough to reflect the value of 1912 dollars in 1960, and a general review of investment policies was still in the future. In the meantime, the dean often had to deal with what he considered petty thievery, the disappearance of money given to the school into the university's general funds—for example, $2,784.59 donated by the advisory board for an Ackerman portrait, and the entirety of an Adolph S. Ochs fund given to the school by the *Times*'s owning family.[5]

Barrett also set about to recapture the building. But he soon grew impatient with vague promises and postponements and declared to Salmen: "If anyone is really serious about putting off the Department of Music's move and the renovation of the building [until] 1965–66, we are going to have to find another Dean who is willing to sit still until then." Three years later, he was still waiting, and complained to Kirk: "It has been six years since we started seriously trying to recapture more space in what is nominally the Journalism Building . . . the situation has now come pretty close to the point of being intolerable." The renovation did not take place until 1965–1966.[6]

The most discomfiting tenant was the American Press Institute. The institute's director, J. Montgomery Curtis, took a dislike to Barrett from the first—seeing in the new dean a carbon copy of Carl Ackerman, eager to impinge on the API. He warned the dean to stay clear, both in writing and, more rudely, in person. According to API's historians, when Barrett was introduced to Ben Reese, the *Post-Dispatch* veteran who chaired the API advisory board, and he asked what he could do to help, Reese answered, "You can keep your goddamn hands off API." Barrett shrugged and backed away.[7]

API signed a peace treaty of sorts with the trustees on May 6, 1958. It formalized the earlier understanding that API would report to the president, not the dean of journalism; would continue to use space in the journalism building; would pay $5,000 a year overhead to the university; and could terminate the agreement, as could the university, on a year's notice. After that, relations with the school relaxed to the point that seminar attendees were permitted, without fear of contamination, to have a drink with faculty and students, and journalism faculty attended API's Christmas party.[8]

An outside review of Barrett's early efforts took place in the fall of 1960, when the accrediting team from the American Council on Education for Journalism paid its visit. The report, almost entirely favorable, recommended the school for reaccreditation; the few flaws it found gave the dean ammunition to ask for more space, personnel, and funds. The team praised in particular the science-writing program and Basic Issues, although it noted grumbling among students about the latter. It also recommended more monitoring of part-time teachers, but did not suggest how that might be done. The grade overall might have been called a high A-minus.[9]

The following spring, the school made a bow to its past when it dedicated a refurbished World Room to the memory of Herbert Bayard Swope, the *World* correspondent and executive editor who proposed the name for the room when the Liberty window was installed in 1954. The project had attracted contributors, as Barrett noted, ranging from Cardinal Spellman to

Harpo Marx, and the ceremony was attended by, among others, former Postmaster General James A. Farley, the impresario Billy Rose, and the former boxer Gene Tunney. The main speaker was 90-year-old Bernard M. Baruch, who had first met Swope during World War I when the financier was head of the War Industries Board.[10]

New faces continued to appear in the corridors. In 1960, J. Ben Lieberman, a communication theorist and a founder of the small-press movement, came in as a visiting professor to bolster the school's research side, and also took charge of a program in education writing. Robert O. Shipman, class of 1948 and formerly of Penn State, was hired as an assistant dean. A year later, the start of an Advanced International Reporting Program, supported with Ford Foundation funds allotted from a universitywide grant, brought on John Luter, a *Newsweek* editor, as director. The influx of new part-time teachers emphasized the school's special newspaper relationship: George Barrett, Robert S. Crandall, Joseph Paul Durso, Irvin M. Horowitz, Stanley V. Levey, John L. McHale, Guy D. Passant, Robert H. Phelps, and Betsy Wade all came from the *Times*.[11]

There were also new kinds of faces in the classrooms. In its forty-eighth year of operation, the graduate school admitted its first African-American woman of record, who thus constituted a minority within a minority. She was the energetic, resilient Dorothy Butler, from Louisville via Chicago. She did not find an easy path; she was first told to earn more liberal-arts credits and try again. An alumnus assigned to interview her blunderingly commented on her blackness. In the class of 1961, Butler felt she was engaged in stiff competition against more privileged students. She recalled: "My professor, John Hohenberg, looked at me and he said, 'You know, you've got so many handicaps [being a woman and black], you'll probably make it.' He thought that was being positive. . . . We all kind of loved Hohenberg, but nobody gave him high marks for sensitivity." She did make it, and she made close friends, among them Nina Auchincloss Steers, Jacqueline Kennedy's sister-in-law. After graduation, she spent a summer in Africa and returned to start a long career on the *Washington Post*.[12]

The next year's class of 1962 included Patrick J. Buchanan—remembered at the school less because of his long career in politics and political journalism than for his role in a famous Christmas party fistfight. In his memoir, Buchanan offers a full, somewhat self-incriminating account of the clash—which was over a female classmate rather than politics—in a genial and appreciative account of his year at the school. Like many others of little experience, he found the year transforming, an opportunity to pull himself together and learn how to use his resources. He knew where he was heading politically, but he made friends from all parts of the spectrum, including one of the school's stream of Maryknoll priests—this one destined to become foreign minister in Nicaragua's Sandinista government. Interestingly, Buchanan found the teachers at the school similar in dedication to the Jesuits who had taught him at Georgetown University, religiously inculcating the values of the vocation of journalism.[13]

The fall of 1962 saw the arrival of two new professors whose long terms at the school eventually made them the last survivors of the Barrett years. Melvin Mencher, thirty-five years old, had been a Nieman Fellow at Harvard and had covered the hurly-burly of state politics for newspapers in New Mexico and California; this experience may have left him with a jaundiced view of authority. He came to Columbia from the William Allen White School of Journalism at the University of Kansas, where he had raised a storm by backing a student-newspaper investigation of discrimination in campus housing.[14]

The other newcomer was Frederick T. C. Yu, recruited, like Lieberman, to bolster research interests. Born in China, he worked two years for the American Office of War Information—presumably, the origin of his acquaintance with Barrett—before earning his doctorate at Iowa. His most recent job in a largely academic career was at Montana State University, where he was director of research. In his time at the school, he gravitated increasingly toward administration until, at last, he briefly occupied the dean's office.[15]

At the start of 1963, Barrett turned his full attention to the kind of creation of which he was a master—an ambitious and worthy staged event, the observance of the school's fiftieth year of operation. The building was to be given a cleanup. There was a motto, "That the People Shall Know" (apparently coined for the occasion), imprinted on a medallion that was illustrated with an upraised torch. The medallions were to be distributed to distinguished alumni. There would be panels and honorary degrees. Eventually there was a book, edited by the dean and Robert F. Hewes, who had taken over the alumni office in 1960. *Journalists in Action* contained brief reminiscences by sixty-three graduates (of whom four were women). And there was fund-raising.[16]

At the convocation on April 15, a few days after Pulitzer's 116th birthday, three journalists received honorary degrees—James Reston, Washington correspondent of the *Times*; Ralph McGill, publisher of the *Atlanta Constitution* and a legendary conscience of the South, his scrape with Dean Ackerman long superseded; and Herbert Brucker, editor of the *Hartford Courant* and a president of the American Society of Newspaper Editors. Brucker was the only member of the school's faculty ever to be so recognized, although he was honored as well for other aspects of his career. He was the only graduate of the school, to that point, to be a recipient. Arthur Hays Sulzberger, publisher of the *Times*, complained to President Kirk (after prompting, no doubt) about the omission of another graduate, Lester Markel, 1914, the newspaper's long-time Sunday editor. Kirk, in a letter drafted by Barrett, replied mildly that of course Columbia could not have given degrees to two *Times* staffers.[17]

Then began the next round of honors—the presentation of medallions to graduates judged distinguished by a faculty-alumni committee. In Washington, the dean gave three to graduates who were officers of the American Society of Newspaper Editors. On April 22, one was presented to Carl W. Ackerman, who made an exception to his reluctance to visit the school, and one to Joseph Pulitzer, Jr., grandson of the founder; in addition, Dean Barrett, the nongraduate, received one—a purported surprise.

In the end, more than 140 medallions were handed out, to about five percent of the school's graduates. By far the greatest numbers of recipients were reporters, editors, or publishers. Because of their greater seniority, alumni of the undergraduate school (1912–35) received about 60 percent of the medallions, and fourteen went to members of the class of 1917 alone. Women were a tiny minority, a twentieth of the total.[18]

Most of the press response to the observance was dutifully respectful. Only *Newsweek* ventured serious criticism. After quoting one alumnus as saying that "much of the training is superficial, the full-time staff professors are really out of touch with the news business," *Newsweek* added, sweepingly: "Most [alumni] feel that the primary value of Columbia is that it provides entree into professional journalism for its graduates." Finally, the magazine quoted an unidentified faculty member: "We don't teach people how to write, we don't make them into reporters. . . . When a student leaves he has two things: a little control over his work and a lot of momentum. The students deserve the credit for this. Put it this way: we don't hurt them at all." *Newsweek* headed the article: "'We Don't Hurt Them'." (Penn Kimball later admitted to the comment, and it was quoted back at him for years afterward.)[19]

Still, Kimball was close to the mark when he said that the school lent its graduates "momentum." Students invested their energies in the practical work, and dragged their feet at such respect-building add-ons as "Basic Issues in the News" or the history of journalism. In a sense such additions remained decorative; when it went to a single graduate year, the school all but left behind Pulitzer's idea of a general education designed for journalists. Barrett wanted to counter the school's lack of intellectual status while staying within Ackerman's one-year boundaries, but it was hard to cram more into the tight framework.

In fact, aside from routine references, the founder's proposals were all but forgotten in the fifty-year observance. The historian John Tebbel, class of 1937, recalled Pulitzer's plan in an article in the *Saturday Review*, and the dean's fifty-year report recounted the school's founding in a few paragraphs. But there was no measurement of the school against Pulitzer's goals. Had the school indeed, as Pulitzer hoped, served the welfare of the republic? Had it helped to make journalism a "great and intellectual profession?" Those were possibly unanswerable questions, but at this point they were scarcely addressed.[20]

# CHAPTER 23

# "Why a Review?"

EDWARD W. BARRETT, midway in his fourth year as dean, took a chance. Under previous leaders, the school's public stance—that is, its position on controversies affecting journalism—was the one espoused by most journalism schools: far from criticizing the press, they defended it against detractors. By contrast, Barrett from the start presented pointed, if scrupulously balanced and generalized, criticisms of what he believed was a press that clung to its own deficiencies.

About the time that Barrett issued such a critique in his three-year report, an assistant, James Boylan, placed on his desk a memorandum proposing the creation of a regular journal of press criticism, to be called the *Columbia University Journalism Review* (soon slimmed down to *Columbia Journalism Review*). The memo argued that the press would benefit from regular criticism and debate, that no such vehicle existed (the closest approach being *Nieman Reports*, published by Harvard's Nieman Foundation), and that the school was in a position to "establish now a tradition of strong, independent appraisal of journalism." Barrett saw the proposal as building on the new role he was trying to establish for the school.[1]

During the spring, the plan was placed before the full-time faculty. Richard T. Baker, secretary of the faculty, outlined the discussion in a memorandum:

Important that we avoid two precipices on both sides of our proposition. One—we should not become the kind of carping critic that stands outside the house and uses his niggling critical voice against errors and foibles when he really doesn't believe in journalism or mass communications at all (the academic attitude, sometimes). Two—we should not stand so involved within the house that we lose our perspective and judgment completely. Our posture should be that of a friendly critic, a lover's judgment. The press has a tender skin. It will break contact completely with criticism that sounds like the Hutchins report. It will listen to criticism that boils up around the API [American Press Institute] table downstairs. Authors in the journal should be insiders, the best, most thoughtful, fairest minds—enough so that it is always established where we stand. This might be a place where the API and school could speak occasionally with a single voice.

Although there was no formal vote, the consensus was to go ahead. Baker's forecast was close enough, except in one respect: the American Press Institute from the beginning regarded the new publication with fear and loathing, assuring its client newspapers that it had nothing to do with it.[2]

For Boylan, the proposal was in part an application for a new job, and Barrett made him managing editor despite his slender experience—five years on the *Herald Tribune* magazine supplement—and his age, thirty-two. Although Barrett and Boylan initially aimed at a fall 1960 issue, a trial issue did not appear until a year later. Help was recruited within the school: Lois Ireland as production assistant; Ruth Korzenik Franklin, class of 1958, for research; and Richard G. West, former city editor of the *Herald Tribune*, for rewrite. A network of alumni correspondents was recruited across the country.[3]

The "pilot issue"—sixty-four pages, no advertisements—was mailed to a list of 5,000 in September 1961. It was prefaced by a two-page editorial titled, "Why a Review of Journalism?" A portion therefrom was adopted as a motto for the publication:

. . . to assess the performance of journalism in all its forms, to call attention to its shortcomings and strengths, and to help define—or redefine— standards of honest, responsible service . . .

. . . to help stimulate continuing improvement in the profession and to speak out for what is right, fair, and decent.

The editorial was followed by a fourteen-page study of 1960 campaign coverage. From the faculty, Baker, Louis Starr, and Lawrence Pinkham contributed, and A. J. Liebling, class of 1925, who wrote "The Wayward Press" in *The New Yorker*, did a book review.[4]

Within days, despite a scattering of tough-guy reactions (a *Daily News* reporter called the *Review* "parochial, carping, puerile and unforgivably slanted"), a surprisingly favorable surge of comment flowed in. Barrett told *Newsweek* that the *Review*'s chances of starting regular publication were "about 99 per cent." Planning began for a winter issue, later deferred to spring 1962 to leave time to set up a distribution system, initially supervised by Joan Moravek, then Sylvia Orr. Burton Wenk, an art director of great flexibility, arrived an issue later and remained on a freelance basis for more than a decade, and Robert O. Shipman, the assistant dean, filled in as business manager. Two issues later, the dean initiated a page of comment that he wrote for most issues over the next twenty years.[5]

Boylan was eventually assisted by resources within the school. The faculty named a small, friendly committee—Baker, Pinkham, Penn Kimball, and Melvin Mencher—to advise, write, and read submissions. Students and graduates served as editorial assistants, most notably Barbara Neblett Land, class of 1946.[6]

That the *Review* enjoyed a degree of success in its first years owed much not only to its comparative novelty but to the times. With great national questions—an expanding racial crisis, war in Vietnam, cultural-political upheaval—looming, the issue-by-issue agenda often seemed to write itself. Moreover, despite its quarterly frequency, the *Review* had good fortune in presenting fresh issues, and little difficulty stirring up discussion in the press.

It had further good fortune in recruiting writers to illuminate these issues, particularly Ben H. Bagdikian, then Washington correspondent for the *Providence Journal* and already on his way to becoming a leading press critic. Starting in the summer of 1962, he wrote a Washington article for each issue, one of the most important being "Press Independence and the Cuban Crisis" (Winter 1963). Later, he reported abuses by Du Pont ownership of the Wilmington, Delaware, newspapers, a strong push that, despite a blistering response, started the corporation on the road to eventual divestiture. A few years later, Bagdikian was one of the first to warn of the dangers to journalism in conglomerates—the absorption of news media into omnivorous corporations.[7]

For the most part, the press establishment appeared to accept the *Review*, possibly because criticism issuing from Columbia was to be preferred to, say, Liebling's pointed gibes or to unadulterated academicism. And when editors were tossed a bone of praise—such as John Hohenberg's articles listing worthy exhibits in the Pulitzer Prize competition—a national freshet of clippings would issue.[8]

One of the few sweeping challenges to the intentions of the *Review* came in a speech in August 1963, by Wes Gallagher, general manager of the Associated Press, who questioned the whole idea that journalism schools should criticize the press. While not mentioning the *Review*, he complained of "professors . . . who feast on our faults with the avidity and supercilious wisdom of a wise old barn owl pecking the rodents out of a farmer's hayloft." Such criticism, he charged, was driving promising talent away from journalism.[9]

In response, leading figures in schools across the country defended not only the usefulness of criticism but the *Review* and Barrett specifically. (The year before, the Association for Education in Journalism had adopted a resolution commending the school for starting the *Review*.) Eventually, Barrett met with Gallagher to find common ground, but there was none. The dean reported on the matter to the faculty and got firm support, as noted in the minutes of November 7, 1963: "The faculty clearly indicated that there was no reason for the School to change its role as press critic or for the Dean to insist upon anything but the highest standards for the profession."[10]

In mid-1963, the *Review* brushed against an aspect of the dean's past. The magazine received from Arthur E. Rowse of the *Washington Post* a manuscript on the lack of coverage of the emerging issue of tobacco and health. As a public-relations operative at Hill & Knowlton, Barrett had been involved with defending the tobacco industry; however, in 1962, he had given up his consultancy at the firm and sold his stock in it. Even so, he intervened in the editing of the Rowse article, insisting on deletion of all references in the Rowse manuscript that suggested scientific conclusions on tobacco's hazards. Rowse demanded to have his byline removed and wrote a letter, printed in the next issue, that he had been shocked to hear of the dean's tobacco connections. The dean remained convinced that he had acted correctly.[11]

The *Review* sometimes got itself into scraps unwittingly. In 1965, two staff writers from *The New Yorker* offered the *Review* an extended rebuttal to Tom Wolfe's notoriously fanciful articles about the magazine in the *Herald Tribune* Sunday supplement, edited by Clay Felker. The *Review* printed the item, and ran a hot reply from Felker. Wolfe paid back the *Review* later, when he remarked in recounting the dispute in his history of the New Journalism,

"Reading the *Columbia Journalism Review* is like going to a convention of the American Newspaper Publishers Association."[12]

It is doubtful that Barrett could have guessed at the start that so much of his time and effort for the next two decades would be devoted to the *Review*, or that a magazine begun on such a tiny scale—its initial announced circulation was 3,500—would grow, financially speaking, to become a drag on its host institution.[13]

The dean knew of course that the *Review* would always be unprofitable, and before the end of 1961 he began his long, unsuccessful search for an endowment. He was successful, however, in winning a credit line of $30,000 from President Kirk, which was vital to the magazine's first years. Kirk was also steadfast when he began to feel pressure from those who had not taken kindly to criticism. Barrett also tapped part of the overflow from the Cabot prize fund for the *Review*.[14]

In 1963, Louis G. Cowan, the former president of CBS Television, who had been made a scapegoat during the quiz-show scandals, joined the school's staff and served, among other positions, as head of the "publishing [fund-raising] committee." Cowan gave generously to the *Review* and scouted for other help. But not until 1967 did the magazine receive substantial outside support, in the form of a Ford Foundation grant of $195,000 to help make the *Review* "self-sustaining"—a goal never reached.[15]

Despite the attention given to maintaining links between the faculty and the magazine, the *Review* soon began to show the same centripetal tendencies that had affected the school's relations with the API. The gradually expanding *Review* subunit, with its own deadlines and priorities, moved more and more into a separate orbit. Even so, the ties remained intact as long as the editor was a member of the faculty. When Boylan stepped down in 1969, the connection became tenuous.

# CHAPTER 24

# Era of Expansion

As THE YEARS of his deanship passed, Dean Barrett pursued a policy of "more is better." Although there was no single flurry of innovation like that of his first two years, there were continued additions to the school's programs and responsibilities. The underlying premise seemed to be the desire to demonstrate that the more enterprises and responsibilities the school could support, the less likelihood it would be viewed as small, insignificant, and narrowly vocational.

Barrett added new fellowships, new prize-giving programs, and new staff. With foundation money available, expansion hit full stride after 1963. Braced with the kudos for the fiftieth-anniversary observance and warm praise from the president—"your work during these past few years for the School of Journalism has been spectacularly successful"—Barrett may have been forgiven for having at least mild illusions of omnicompetence.[1]

Not surprisingly, he occasionally overreached. In 1963, the year of the strenuous fiftieth-anniversary observances, the National Aeronautics and Space Administration tempted the dean to apply for a three-year grant, worth nearly $400,000, to study how well NASA was disseminating space information—or, as the *Times* headline put it, "NASA Pays to Find Out If It Is Doing Its Job." When the grant was announced, the plan was tripped up by a story in the *Herald Tribune*, written by Stuart Loory, only five years out of the school, raising questions as to whether a journalism school should accept federal funding. Congressional committees also criticized the grant. Barrett, on the defensive, held out for five days, then wrote to NASA, complaining of "glib misrepresentation," and asked to call the whole thing off. The grant went to the University of Chicago.

Although Barrett defended the project in measured terms in the *Bulletin* of the American Society of Newspaper Editors, in campus correspondence he referred to it as a "fiasco." Having worked in government for so many years, the dean may not have been sufficiently sensitive to the possible embarrassment when journalists—even journalism professors—openly accepted government money.[2]

More often, he knew when to resist temptation. About 1959, the public-relations impresario Ben Sonnenberg approached Barrett with an offer of a great deal of money from the publisher S. I. Newhouse—provided that the school be renamed for him. Making nothing public, Barrett consulted with a few members of the faculty and let Sonnenberg know that the name of Newhouse, identified in that era with mediocrity, would be unacceptable at a school even dimly connected with Pulitzer. Newhouse turned to Syracuse University, which not only named its school of communications for him but also placed him on the board of trustees.[3]

Barrett devoted a great deal of time to spreading the influence of the school. He delivered speeches to most of the major press organizations, and saw to it that leading journalists—particularly the Southern moderates who were his natural confreres—were given guest appearances and honors. He also believed that the school's isolation from its counterparts across the country was a weakness, and sought to reverse the faculty's traditional standoffishness. True, in 1952, the school had played host to the annual meeting of the Association for Education in Journalism, and had dazzled the journalism teachers with a reception sponsored by Time Inc. and attended by Henry R. Luce himself. But any good will engendered soon died of neglect.[4]

Starting in 1959, Dean Barrett and small faculty delegations began to attend the annual meetings of the Association for Education in Journalism. The dean initiated luncheons at the conventions with graduates who had gone into teaching, a tradition that continued for years. At the 1963 convention, Barrett was designated president-elect and served as president in 1965, a swift rise to the top. But after he left, the school's involvement declined again; in the rest of the century, no member of the school's faculty was elected to a major post in the AEJ or, as it came to be called, the AEJMC (Association for Education in Journalism and Mass Communication).[5]

Perhaps because he was assuming a new role of speaking for all journalism schools—at least for the elite schools that were accredited—Barrett felt compelled to respond to general criticisms of journalism education. One critic was Lester Markel, class of 1914, who wrote sweepingly in *Harper's* that "large doubts arise as to whether there is any legitimate reason for [journalism schools'] existence," thus rebutting not only Pulitzer but his own choice of education. The dean wrote to Markel that he had found the comments "a bit of a shocker" and hinted that he no longer considered Markel an ally. Markel was bitter about the exchange (and of course even more so when he was passed over for an honorary degree).[6]

A study of journalism schools completed for the Ford Foundation was on a different level. The author was a professor of English at New York University, David Boroff. He commented early in his report: "If journalism schools and departments were to disappear, I do not think this would be a serious blow to American life and culture." But he went on to take journalism schools seriously nonetheless. He deplored the absence from faculties of major figures in American journalism; the go-along, uncritical spirit of most journalism professors; the low status of journalism programs on many campuses; and the effort to boost that status by becoming a branch of the behavioral sciences. Moreover, in the downbeat mode prevalent at that time, he saw journalism losing its attractiveness as a field for young talent. (He died in 1965, just before a rush to journalism schools began.)[7]

On almost all these points, he made Columbia an exception. He had high praise for the mid-career programs in science and international reporting. He called the M.S. program "practical and demanding." He noted the relative weakness of the broadcast curriculum as compared with print, and inevitably added that, despite the Basic Issues course, the school was not taking sufficient advantage of the resources on the campus.[8]

Boroff, preparing a condensation of his report for *Harper's*, corresponded with Barrett late in 1964. The dean stated his concept of the school succinctly: "I should emphasize (though not for quotation) that Columbia Journalism is not involved in the running debate between 'communicology' and 'trade-school' efforts, because it has no faith in either. We are attempting to function neither as an ersatz sociology department nor as an in-plant training program."[9]

The Boroff report persuaded the Ford Foundation that Columbia was its best bet, and in March 1965, the foundation provided a grant of $1.6 million—the largest single amount of money given to the school since its founding. The grant had to be matched, the vehicle being the Half Century Fund, initiated by the dean in 1963 under the chairmanship of Elliott V. Bell, class of 1926, a McGraw-Hill executive. The matching gifts, primarily from news corporations and related foundations, arrived in chunks of $10,000 to $50,000 each, and the goal was reached in 1967. Even the alumni, reputedly impecunious, chipped in more than $78,000. A separate gift of $400,000 came from the Cabot family to endow a professorship honoring the patriarch, Godfrey Lowell Cabot, who had just died at the age of 101.[10]

By the fall of 1965, the influx of new money put the dean in his full expansionist mode. The first chore, he told an interviewer, was to modernize the fifty-two-year-old building now that the music department had at last moved out. The first need was basic: the school's expanding student body was threatening to outgrow the single newsroom that had served since 1935, and the dean wanted to disperse the class into two or three newsrooms. The price would be the loss of the old all-for-one intimacy. Simultaneously, the library was to be expanded and moved into the old newsroom; honoring gifts from his family, it was renamed for Arthur Hays Sulzberger, former publisher of the *Times*.[11]

Additions to the school's programs abounded. The Russell Sage Foundation gave $180,000 for mid-career fellowships for reporting the behavioral sciences. W. Phillips Davison, a veteran of the RAND Corporation, was appointed, half-time, from the sociology department to supervise; he remained more than twenty years. Fred Yu was put in charge of a program of fellowships under a grant of $250,000 from the Carnegie Corporation and jointly administered with Columbia's East Asian Institute, to train correspondents to work in China and Japan.[12]

Meanwhile, two awards programs were acquired. The magazine field lacked any prizes of national stature, the closest thing being the Benjamin Franklin Magazine Awards, administered at the University of Illinois. As early as Barrett's first weeks on campus, there was a proposal that Columbia take over from Illinois. The idea gained impetus with the founding of the American Society of Magazine Editors in 1963; the ASME was eager to have the same home as the Pulitzer Prizes. Promised financing from the Magazine Publishers Association, the ASME and Barrett agreed, in 1965, that the school would administer what were to be called the National Magazine

Awards. They started simply, with a single award to *Look* magazine and praise for three other publications. But, like the Pulitzers, the National Magazine Awards proliferated, and by 2001, presented prizes in seventeen categories. The school decided to play a quiet logistical role in the awards, to the point that in later years stories on the awards did not even mention the Columbia connection.[13]

Even before the magazine awards were in operation, Barrett began negotiations for a still more elaborate prize program in broadcasting. In 1943, Jessie Ball duPont, widow of an entrepreneur-banker based in Jacksonville, Florida, established the Alfred I. duPont Awards Foundation "to stimulate distinguished performance" in radio and television. At first her bank administered the awards, then Washington & Lee University. But the prizes were still overshadowed by the older George Foster Peabody Awards at the University of Georgia. So her representatives came to Dean Barrett, who was connected, through his wife, with Jacksonville's power elite.[14]

To take on the DuPont awards was a substantial new responsibility, and the dean and a small planning committee decided to design a format that would do more than simply hand out trophies for the mantel. They recommended that the awards program be accompanied by an annual survey of the state of broadcasting. In 1967, an agreement was signed with the bank assigning to the school the income from more than $1.5 million in securities. A search was mounted to find a researcher-writer to create the survey and administer the awards, and the nod went to Marvin Barrett (no relation to the dean), a New York writer with strong magazine experience. In the spring of 1968, the Alfred I. duPont–Columbia University Survey of Broadcast Journalism and the Alfred I. duPont–Columbia Awards came into existence.[15]

The first duPont awards and survey of broadcast journalism were made public late in 1969. Silver batons were awarded to six broadcasting organizations and to Dr. Everett B. Parker of the United Church of Christ, a campaigner for public service in broadcasting. But it was Marvin Barrett's first survey, issued as a paperbound book, that caught most of the attention. An introduction signed by the award jurors deplored the state of broadcasting as "a hideous waste of one of the nation's most important resources." The rest of the volume offered a detailed account of the year and its shortcomings. The broadcasting industry was not pleased, nor did it care for the later annual volumes that Marvin Barrett produced through 1981, although they now constitute a valuable history of broadcasting in the 1970s. The annual volumes were ultimately replaced by a day of panels and discussion.[16]

Added to the Pulitzers, these new awards programs made the school the hub of the flourishing field of journalism honors, a veritable prize-giving factory. Combined, the prize programs not only outweighed in the public eye such critical efforts as research studies and the *Columbia Journalism Review*, they tended to put the school itself into the background.

In his eagerness to innovate, Dean Barrett also set aside, without acknowledging or perhaps even realizing that he was doing so, one of Joseph Pulitzer's strongest interdictions: "The School of Journalism is to be, in my conception, not only not commercial, but anti-commercial." The dean expressed the newer prevailing view that it was in the best interest of the press to have business managers trained in journalism, as well as the reverse—to have editors who could find their way around the business side. Those who thought otherwise saw such plans as infecting the whole "church-state" relationship between business and editorial departments. With the business school dean, Courtney C. Brown, Barrett announced a program that would let participants earn two degrees in five semesters—the M.B.A. and the M.S. in journalism. Thus fell that barrier.[17]

CHAPTER 25

# Edging Toward the Abyss

BY THE MID-SIXTIES, the country, and the campus, were falling under the shadow of Vietnam. Almost daily, tiny rallies, visible from the windows of the journalism newsroom, clustered around the sundial on the 116th Street walk. Although there was a teach-in at Columbia earlier in the year, Columbia's troubles are generally dated from the day in May 1965 when police were called to move protesters who had blocked access to a Naval ROTC awards ceremony in Low Library. The protests thereafter were sporadic, but slowly increased in frequency and intensity as a chapter of the activist Students for a Democratic Society came into being and mobilized dissent.[1]

The school of journalism, too, was becoming aware of the war. The *Columbia Journalism Review* turned its attention to Vietnam with an article in 1964 by Malcolm Browne, then of the Associated Press, on his three years in that country. The first of three notable women correspondents from the school, Beverly Deepe (Keever) of *Newsweek*, class of 1958, arrived in Vietnam as early as 1962. Later, Marguerite Higgins, 1942, of the *Herald Tribune*, and a Pulitzer Prize winner in Korea, became a stout defender of the military and a critic of fellow correspondents. Liz Trotta, 1961, of NBC, was the first woman network-television correspondent on the scene.[2]

Two faculty members had been there as well. In the summer of 1964, John Hohenberg was hired by the Council on Foreign Relations to conduct interviews with leaders throughout Asia, including Vietnam. Earlier, W. Phillips Davison had supervised, for the RAND Corporation on behalf of the Pentagon, a "hearts-and-minds" program, interviewing prisoners from the Viet Cong and the North Vietnamese army.[3]

As it happened, the first direct impact of the war on the school was a windfall. In February 1966, the Senate Foreign Relations Committee held hearings on American goals in Vietnam, which were broadcast on television by CBS and NBC. At 10 A.M. on the third day of testimony, February 10, NBC continued its coverage, but CBS offered what became an infamous fifth rerun of an *I Love Lucy* episode. Five days later, Fred W. Friendly, president of CBS News, resigned in protest over the network's decision. "My departure is a matter of conscience," he wrote.[4]

It was certainly the decade's most striking resignation on principle. Among journalists, Friendly was the best-known off-camera presence in television. He had spent sixteen years at CBS, many of them as the partner of the saint of broadcast journalism, Edward R. Murrow, who had died in 1965. Together, Murrow and Friendly had created documentaries credited with helping to end McCarthyism. Friendly made a name for himself as a practitioner of sometimes finicky ethics—for example, his refusal to import canned sound into Korean battlefield scenes. Who would know? "I'd know," he said.[5]

Within days after walking out of CBS, he was paying a call at the school of journalism. He was no stranger; he had made guest appearances and had received the Columbia Journalism Award in 1964. Seven years before, Dean Barrett had looked him over as a possible faculty member. A month after Friendly's resignation, Barrett wrote to President Kirk to report a deal: McGeorge Bundy, head of the Ford Foundation, had already hired Friendly as an adviser on television, and the school intended to name him as its first (and, it turned out, only) Edward R. Murrow professor. Barrett remarked to Kirk, "This whole undertaking is a gamble, but I think we agree that it is a damned good gamble." The school's tenured faculty approved; the appointment was announced by the university on April 6.[6]

From the time he started work at Columbia in mid-1966, Friendly was a visible presence, not only at the school but on the campus, to a degree not matched by any previous faculty appointee. The school had captured a major television practitioner at mid-flight in his career, and under the most dramatic circumstances. Friendly was an outsize personality—large, blunt, urgent, and rough in a manner that sometimes belied his intelligence.

Barrett commented at the time of the appointment: "It will be noted that Mr. Friendly's formal education is considerably more limited than would be normal in a professor." Indeed, Friendly's education had stopped short of a bachelor's degree, but it soon became clear that he had serious intentions of making his mark as a teacher and scholar. Early in the fall of 1966, the dean informed the president: "Fred Friendly is proving to be (1) a dynamic teacher and lecturer, (2) a strong advocate of broad liberal education, (3) a 'de-emphasizer' of techniques and hardware in relation to content."[7]

Friendly devoted himself to his new profession at an unacademic pace. Between his resignation in February and the start of his first teaching semester at Columbia in October, he finished a memoir-disquisition, *Due to Circumstances Beyond Our Control . . .* , which sold well. At the same time, he worked with the Ford Foundation on an ambitious but short-lived plan to use fees earned by communications satellites to finance public television, the term just starting to replace the older "educational television."[8]

His next big idea, which took shape late in 1966, was an attempt to wed his three major interests—public television, Columbia, and the Ford Foundation. The first step was the announcement by the foundation of a $10 million grant for experiments in noncommercial television. Jack Gould of the *Times* broke the story late in December 1966—that the school would be the administrative base for a weekly "University Broadcast Laboratory," a national Sunday-magazine show to review politics, foreign relations, arts and literature, and science. Friendly started to recruit staff, and early in 1967 Av Westin, a CBS News producer, crossed over to become the project's executive director.[9]

A hint of difficulty arose at the Columbia trustees' meeting early in January, when a subcommittee was named to study the proposal. Gould, to whom everybody was leaking, reported that the trustees were unhappy because the proposal had been given wide publicity—mostly via Gould, of course—before they had studied it. At their February meeting the trustees approved the project in principle, and plans went forward to hire staff, create an advisory board from participating universities, and to broadcast public television's first programs in color.[10]

But that was not the trustees' last word. Their subcommittee's counsel drafted a ten-page document restricting the program's subject matter, barring anything that might duplicate commercial network programming and anything that might cause controversy. There was also a ban on any actions that might appear to be raiding the networks' staffs, especially at CBS. Well into March, there was heavy negotiating behind the scenes between the trustees and the school, so strenuous that at one point Dean Barrett resigned and had to be begged by President Kirk to stay.[11]

In the end Barrett concluded that the laboratory could not operate effectively under the trustees' restrictions, and proposed an alternative solution: a new independent corporation with representation on its board from both Columbia and National Educational Television, then the coordinating body for the nonprofit sector. Barrett was to serve as chair of the new editorial policy board; Friendly was to have no direct role. The entire story was of course leaked to Gould and appeared in the *Times* on March 17. The project continued under a new name, Public Broadcast Laboratory, and went on the air in the fall, to mixed reviews. About a year later, after growing tension between Westin and the board, Barrett resigned as its head, and Friendly declined an offer to take charge of the program.[12]

There was fallout, naturally, affecting Friendly less than Barrett. Barrett declared himself to a somber faculty meeting as being thoroughly disaffected with Columbia's trustees—and, he might have added, with the Kirk administration, as he had made clear to the president. Such negativity was unusual for the persistently upbeat dean. Kirk's response was to offer Barrett a slice of power—a vice-presidency that would put him in charge of Columbia's new $200 million fund-raising campaign.[13]

Barrett responded: "I find I just should not and cannot do it and, in fact, must carry through with my earlier plan to step out of the deanship." He listed his complaints—that he disagreed with the "basic outlook" of the trustees and was out of sympathy with the planning for the fund-raising campaign. He had been frustrated, he added, over the University Broadcast Laboratory, the lack of space in the journalism building, and having to deal with the still fractious American Press Institute. He had promised his wife, he said, to ease up after the Half Century Fund reached its goal, and now proposed to resign on June 30, 1967. He did not, but took a leave that fall.[14]

In fact, his relations with the American Press Institute began to improve with the departure of the director, the blustering Monty Curtis, in May 1967. to work for the Knight newspaper chain. (In a marginal note on a clipping of the story, former Dean Ackerman tartly noted the publicity Curtis had engendered for himself: "How can a man personally create an institute founded and flourishing one year before he joined?") Curtis was succeeded by his deputy, Walter B. Everett, a graduate of the school in 1933 and a more diplomatic personality, although API still remained bent on divorce.[15]

When the dean went on leave in 1967, President Kirk was struggling to cure a rapidly weakening university. Much of the $200 million fund drive was aimed at supporting a physical expansion of the campus that was roundly condemned late in 1966 by Ada Louise Huxtable, the *Times* architecture critic. She questioned in particular the plan to build a $9 million gymnasium on leased air rights in the city's Morningside Park, the steep hillside heights that separated the university from Harlem below, and saw the whole scheme as a "planning disaster."[16]

At the end of the 1966–67 academic year, Kirk, only sixteen months from the mandatory retirement age of sixty-five, reorganized the central administration—the new lineup in which Barrett had declined a place. Jacques Barzun, who had served briefly as provost and dean of faculties, resumed his long life of scholarship. David B. Truman, a political scientist and dean of Columbia College, stepped up to become vice president and provost.[17]

No doubt Barrett was relieved not to be involved when the reorganized Kirk administration lent Columbia's name to selling licenses for a new cigarette filter that would presumably make cigarette smoking safe. Groans echoed across campus. On leave in Santa Barbara, Barrett wrote to Kirk and to David Truman: "I have felt for both of you in regard to the cigarette filter business," and added that he too had worked on a cigarette filter. After seven months, the filter deal was abandoned, but not before the matter became, in the words of the post-1968 investigative commission, "a profound embarrassment to the name and reputation of Columbia."[18]

CHAPTER 26

# Fallout

THE COLUMBIA CAMPUS became increasingly roiled as the SDS and its allies found a cornucopia of issues centering on war and race. Twice—once late
in 1966, once early in 1967—demonstrators interfered with CIA recruiters.
The arrival of Marine Corps recruiters in April 1967 attracted not only SDS
demonstrators but an opposition group prepared to defend the Marines with
their fists—"jocks" against "pukes," as the sides called each other. In vain,
the administration promulgated a new set of rules for demonstrations.[1]

The journalism school remained largely unperturbed. The classes of 1967
and 1968 seemed intent on moving ahead with their careers and staying out
of activist politics. Unlike the class of 1917, with a broad curriculum that
thrust it into politics, the graduate classes may have absorbed unconscious-
ly, even too well, the school's newer ideal of the job-oriented neutral—or
neutered—journalist.

At the start of the spring term in 1968, Dean Barrett returned from leave
and Richard T. Baker, who had been standing in for him, left for a sabbatical
on Taiwan, where he would find a scattering of old friends from Chungking
days. It was not long before the temporary lull on the campus was broken.

Toward the end of February, the SDS picketed a visit by representatives of the Dow Chemical Company, manufacturer of napalm. A day later, demonstrators marched from the 116th Street sundial to the excavation for the new gym in Morningside Park; thirteen were arrested. In March came a demonstration against the Institute for Defense Analyses, a military research organization of which Columbia was one of the sponsors. Students marched through Low Library, led by a bullhorn and chanting slogans. At the memorial service in St. Paul's Chapel on April 9, after the assassination of Martin Luther King, Jr., Mark Rudd, the flamboyant emerging leader of SDS, denounced the service as an "obscenity" and led a small walkout.[2]

Against such tactics, the university administration seemed slow and palsied. Attempts to discipline or suspend SDS leaders simply fed the protesters another issue. The campus was ripe for breakdown, and it came on Tuesday, April 23. About five hundred protesters and onlookers gathered at the sundial. After an attempt to enter Low Library was deflected by counterdemonstrators, black students led a march to the gym site. There was a scuffle, and Rudd led the crowd back to the sundial, thence into nearby Hamilton Hall. The upheaval had begun.

After staying overnight in Hamilton, the SDS-led demonstrators were ousted by members of the Student Afro-American Society at dawn, and the building became a black preserve. The SDS group broke into Low Library and occupied the president's office. Two more buildings, Avery and Fayerweather, were soon occupied, and later Mathematics. New groups sprang into existence—a Strike Steering Committee; a Majority Coalition, seeded with athletes; and an Ad Hoc Faculty Group, bent on mediating. As the days passed, the scheduled activities of the distracted university broke down.[3]

Still, neither journalism students nor faculty played a major role during the week of occupation. One journalism student was known with certainty to have sat in with the protesters. Penn Kimball placed himself in the cordon of professors circling Low, aimed at protecting the SDS within from aggression by the Majority Coalition without. Dean Barrett was aggrieved not to have been asked for advice.[4]

Ultimately, the administration ended the occupation in the only way guaranteed to make matters worse, by calling in the New York police to clear the buildings in the early morning hours of April 30. By prearrangement, the protesters in Hamilton Hall left peacefully, but the struggle elsewhere was bloody—nearly seven hundred arrests, with more than a hundred protesters requiring emergency hospital treatment.[5]

The journalism students came to life at last. Meeting on the day after the
police bust, they adopted a resolution condemning the police action, calling
for restructuring of the university and approving a general strike, but promising to continue their presumed work as investigative journalists. A number
of students arranged with the local edition of *Life* magazine to report on the
Columbia crisis (a short-lived experiment); the dean's office approved this
arrangement with the proviso that the students split their fees with the school.
*The New Republic* commented: "When confronted with local action in which
they had a stake they chose to be observers rather than participants."[6]

On the same day, May 1, Lawrence Pinkham resigned from his new position as director of the broadcast program (that is, as an aide to Friendly) because, as he put it: "I cannot in good conscience carry out duties connected
in even a remote way with a University administration whose top officers are
responsible for the calculated brutality wrought by police on our students
last night." One or two other faculty members declared themselves more or
less on strike.[7]

Further turbulence—including a second ferocious police mop-up before
dawn on May 25—and endless meetings disrupted the campus and the
school. At least one journalism student, Ralph Whitehead, concluded that no
more useful work was being done, left early, and never received his degree.
Others huddled with the faculty and produced a proposal echoing the approach of Students for a Restructured University, a group that emerged after May 1. The plan for a restructured school of journalism contained the formulation then in vogue—tripartitism: a committee or committees made up
of faculty, administration, and students. The journalism faculty approved the
proposal unanimously.[8]

But there was a backlash. On John Foster's motion, the faculty voted
10–5 to withhold all year-end awards, such as the Pulitzer Traveling Fellowships, and even discussed withholding degrees because the year's work
had not been completed or graded. The decision was reversed at the last
possible moment, and the class of 1968 went off into the world bearing the
customary honors.[9]

Dean Barrett had never really recommitted himself after his leave; seem-
ingly, he had already half-resigned. On May 11, he typed an unsolicited letter of advice to Kirk and Truman in a detached way that failed to hint at any
future role for himself. He criticized the trustees as "badly out of touch" and
Kirk and Truman as failing to consult the governance bodies on campus that
might have helped in the crisis. He listed several steps he thought the ad-

ministration could take, such as appointing a vice president for student affairs. And he urged them to break off with one Sidney S. Baron, who had
been serving the university unsuccessfully as what would later be called a
"spin doctor."[10]

Just before commencement, Barrett sent a report on the crisis to the
school's graduates. "The faculty and I," he wrote, "believe that there is basis for the faculty-student discontent." Again taking aim at the trustees, he
recommended that university faculty be given as many as eight seats on the
board of trustees, that at least two of the six alumni trustees be under the age
of thirty-five, and that two student trustees be added.[11]

On July 31, Barrett sent Kirk his letter of resignation: "Differences in outlook are just too great," he said. He wrote to Kirk again four days later, saying that he was unable to sit on a decision already made, and that he did not
believe in making idle threats. After notifying the faculty, the dean gave an
aide a cryptic statement to read to inquiring reporters: "I simply find myself
in disagreement with the basic outlook of a majority of those [who] make
university policy. I should add that, while I have real sympathy for many
who seek constructive change, I have no sympathy whatever for the young
SDS group who seek destruction. I hope that I can do all within my power,
from the outside, to assist the university and particularly the Graduate
School of Journalism, of which I am deeply proud." The *Times* placed the
story on page one.[12]

The faculty immediately sent a letter—signed by nine members, not all of
whom had been Barrett's close allies—asking that a way be found to let him
continue. The executive committee of the alumni association urged the
trustees not to accept the resignation. But the story was out. Barrett affirmed
to Kirk on August 15—the day his resignation took effect—that he would
not reconsider. He had served exactly twelve years.[13]

On August 7, an uneasy faculty watched as Barrett turned the chair over
to the new acting dean, Richard Baker, just back from the Far East. Barrett
said that the faculty should put itself on record as expecting to be consulted
about the next dean. The rest was routine.[14]

Later in the month, there was another aftershock: Grayson Kirk, who had
been subject to brutal criticism, resigned as president, less than two months
short of his sixty-fifth birthday. For the time being, the journalism school
with an acting dean would operate in a university with an acting president.[15]

CHAPTER 27

# Desperately Seeking a Dean

THROUGH MOST OF ITS EXISTENCE, the school of journalism had been dean-driven—Williams (as director), Ackerman, and Barrett had been the motors that made the place run. But one effect of recruiting of new teachers during the Barrett years had been to lend the faculty critical mass, to build it into a separate force rather than a mere administrative support team for the crowd of downtown adjuncts. The bulked-up faculty assigned itself the role of guardian of the school's educational standards, and tended increasingly to hold deans at arm's length.

When the full-time faculty gathered on September 16, 1968, a month after Barrett's resignation, eight professors of eleven were present, as well as nine members of the nonprofessorial full-time staff. Baker, as acting dean (the same role he had played in Chungking in 1945), made it clear at once that he would not put a deanly distance between himself and colleagues but would remain essentially a professor among professors. Henceforth faculty meetings would be consultations rather than, as so often with Barrett, briefings.

One action on September 16 that was symptomatic of the faculty's new grasp was to assign Penn Kimball to draft a resolution calling for unprecedented faculty participation in the search for a new dean. Kimball brought in the resolution; it was discussed and amended, and delivered that day to Andrew W. Cordier, the acting president—in the name of the faculty, not the acting dean.[1]

The composition of the meeting that day also reflected not only numbers but the increasing weight of the broadcast side—a not surprising consequence of the presence of Fred Friendly over the previous two years. Friendly had recruited John M. Patterson, a CBS radio specialist who had lost his legs in the Battle of the Bulge in 1945. Thomas R. Bettag, class of 1967, also joined Friendly's teaching staff, as did two members of the class of 1968, Anthony C. Lame and David Kuhn, as one-year teaching assistants. In addition, at Friendly's request, John Schultz, a documentary specialist, was invited to teach for a year. (He stayed for twenty-five.) In October, the school dedicated a new broadcast laboratory named for Edward Klauber, a pioneer of CBS News.[2]

Taking a cue from the recommendation of the Kerner Commission, formed after the urban disorders of 1968, that the news media "make a reality of integration," Friendly had initiated a summer program in broadcast news for minority students. The Ford Foundation underwrote the workshop, and Friendly recruited, to organize or teach, Lawrence Pinkham, Bettag, Gary Gilson of the class of 1961, Howard Weinberg and Pat O'Keefe of 1965, and Greg Jackson, 1966. Twenty students, selected from more than a hundred applicants, attended, with guarantees of future employment from their sponsors, and received certificates after two months of instruction by Friendly, his staff, and celebrity guests. It was deemed enough of a success to continue in 1969 and the years afterward. Expanded from broadcast into print journalism, it eventually had a teaching staff of eighteen for an enrollment of thirty-five, at a cost of almost $12,000 for each student, which was very expensive for that era.[3]

There were other signs at that 1968 meeting of increasing consciousness of the school's need for diversity. At least nine African Americans were enrolled in the incoming class—a new high. Luther P. Jackson, Jr., son of a Virginia historian and the fourth member of the class of 1951 (with Pinkham, Boylan, and Bernard Roshco) to teach at the school, was hired to direct a new Advanced Program in Interracial Reporting. He had experience at the *Newark Evening News* and the *Washington Post*, and had been a Russell Sage Fellow at the school the year before. As the first and for years the only African-American professor at the school, Jackson shouldered burdens that eventually became overwhelming.[4]

The meeting of September 16, 1968, inevitably took place in the shadow of Columbia's ordeal the previous spring. Abiding by the resolution it had adopted in May, the faculty made its bow to participatory democracy by naming five members—Friendly, Hohenberg, Pinkham, Luter, and Patterson—to the school's new tripartite steering committee. The student members were chosen initially by lot, and later elected. The administration members were to be Baker and Christopher G. Trump, class of 1962, assistant to the dean and admissions officer. The steering committee's powers remained undefined.[5]

The rest of the campus was still far from returning to familiar configurations. An entity called the Executive Committee of the Faculty, on which Friendly served as the journalism representative, was shaping university policy. At the start of the academic year, the committee announced that the university had all but conceded the ostensible issues of the spring demonstrations: construction on the gymnasium was stopped, never to be resumed; the university had severed its ties with the Institute for Defense Analyses; and the unenforceable rule against indoor demonstrations was abolished. Only the demand for amnesty for violators of university rules was resisted, and standing disciplinary "tribunals" groped through often futile proceedings.[6]

The Executive Committee of the Faculty busied itself with setting up mechanisms that might have prevented the previous crisis. It approved a recommendation for the creation of a university-wide senate and assembly. It established a Permanent Rule-Making Body on Campus Conduct, to which Kimball was sent as the journalism representative. Sylvana Foa, a student, was elected to another body called the University Committee on Committees. Eventually a campuswide referendum approved the creation of the University Senate; Friendly defeated Pinkham in the contest to become the first senator from journalism.[7]

With the door opened by the faculty, the class of 1969—almost none of whom, of course, had been present the previous spring—began to enter into the spirit of 1968. Before the end of the semester, the student members of the steering committee found a promising target—a new course called "The Role of the Journalist," taught by Louis M. Starr and James Boylan, neither a theatrical lecturer. The subject matter, primarily historical, could easily be declared irrelevant, and was thus declared. Boylan was summoned by the student members to defend the course, agreed to changes, and sought to reconvene the class, but the students had a guest star, Richard Goldstein, class of 1966, of the *Village Voice*, waiting in the wings, and the instructor yielded the classroom. Years later, a member of the class referred to the incident as (see Melville's *Billy Budd*) "the mutiny on the Nore." The class subsequently limped along to the end of the semester, and was not offered again.[8]

In the spring of 1969, there were disruptions on the campus, but Acting President Cordier dealt with them promptly and effectively. The journalism class stuck largely to its own work, except for sporadic participation in school governance. Students made contributions in two matters of importance—a proposed restructuring of the curriculum and the search for a dean. The curriculum proposals, spearheaded by Pinkham, were aimed at breaking up the old Ackerman 9-to-5 work week and introducing breathing space for students and teachers, in particular opening the way for students to take courses in other divisions of the university. There was also a plan for a weekly schoolwide symposium to discuss issues and hear speakers.[9]

The broadcast faculty concluded that the proposal was aimed at limiting its time with students and opposed the plan. Nonetheless, Dean Baker, who had carpentered together the old curriculum every year, adopted many of the changes, and they went into effect in the fall of 1969. Later, under pressure—or so Pinkham believed—Baker backed off from the reforms and let the old work-week training recover its dominance.[10]

The early stages of the search for a dean produced an extraordinary confidential report, "The Deanship of the School of Journalism." The author was a professor of history, Henry F. Graff, who had been assigned by Cordier to sound out sentiment at the school and to serve on the search committee. Graff went beyond his assignment to assess the state of the school, and he made points that may have been obscured in the glitter of the Barrett years. The report was kept secret; the faculty might well have benefited from its cool realism.[11]

Graff recalled the isolation of the school under Dean Ackerman and the consequent weakening of support by the university: "A result was that under Dean Barrett the financing of the School became increasingly a personal task of the Dean . . . The effects are now clearly seen in a faculty that is pieced together on financial arrangements that probably involved too much soft money"—that is, ad hoc and impermanent funding. He noted, too, that most of the faculty had been appointed through personal ties to the two previous deans. Some gave up careers in journalism, he said, before they had made a "significant mark" and had done little since coming to the school. "A place on the faculty, therefore, has tended in too many cases to institutionalize mediocrity and to build deep personal frustration. . . . These frustrations are a powerful element operating in the politics of the School, because the School . . . is the only stage on which many of the members of the faculty can play a role." He contended that too many adjuncts—the downtowners— were carrying too much of the teaching load, that their appointments were made too casually, and that, in the university's eyes, they were merely cheap labor. He added that the secretarial staff was too large, and often idle.

As to the deanship, in his interviews with faculty he found only one off-campus name that engendered enthusiasm—that of Frank Mankiewicz, class of 1948, most recently press secretary to the assassinated Senator Robert F. Kennedy. He noted two undeclared inside candidates. The first was Richard T. Baker, admired by the faculty for his "humanity and grace and patience." On the other hand, unspecified younger faculty, looking for more vigorous leadership, said that they would leave if Baker became dean. (Baker publicly took himself out of consideration before an alumni group: "I know a lot of people have been mentioned but I know one who is not going to be it.") The other candidate was Friendly, whose appointment would signal a strong commitment to broadcast journalism, which would require counterbalancing measures on the print side.[12]

Graff concluded by urging consultation with students and faculty in the selection process. Acting President Cordier followed this advice initially, and authorized the school to form a search committee. Nine members, in-cluding a student and two members of the part-time faculty, one of whom was an alumna, were appointed. The committee was chaired by John Ho-henberg, who had known Cordier as a key United Nations official. When the search committee convened belatedly in April 1969, it had a list of more than fifty names to consider, from a file collected by Baker. At the second meet-ing, the list was reduced to fifteen—all men, six of them graduates of the school—and a member of the committee was assigned to sound out each. Friendly, whose name had been on the list of fifty, withdrew, saying that he would be "the wrong man in the wrong place at the wrong time."[13]

At the fourth meeting, on May 13, it was apparent that Low Library had chosen a front-runner. Four names remained on the list—Mankiewicz, who chose not to run; Ben Bagdikian, the press critic, who was seriously interest-ed but then accepted a new job at the *Washington Post*; and Edwin Diamond of *Newsweek*; the fourth, and the name that always seemed to remain when others fell away, was Elie Abel, class of 1942, a former *Times* reporter and since 1961 a reporter-commentator for NBC News.[14]

The picture remained muddy. On June 3, Hohenberg wrote a long report to Cordier, saying that the committee would approve appointment of any of three candidates: Abel, Diamond, or a late starter, Elmer Lower, who was ready to step down as president of ABC News. Seven of the nine members of the committee approved the report; Boylan declined to sign, as did William A. Glavin, Jr., the student member, believing that the faculty did not know the candidates.[15]

When Hohenberg unveiled the committee report to the faculty that day, there was reluctance to accept it as the end of the process. Friendly and others warned that delay might result in the imposition of an unknown candidate, or the loss of candidates on hand. A group headed by Penn Kimball suggested that none of the candidates would do—that a person unknown, younger, and more vigorous was required. Ultimately, all present, the acting dean excepted, voted on a roster of questions. On the most critical, asking if the search should be continued, the vote was 16–2 in favor. In a straw vote on the candidates, Abel received six votes and Lower one; nine faculty members declined to support any nominee. These results were forwarded to Cordier.[16]

There was no response from the acting president, who became president in fact over the summer, nor was there a response to the faculty's request for a meeting. But there was important back-channel communication undercutting the faculty position. A member of the search committee, Fred Friendly, advised the president in October: "We are beginning to give the impression of an Institution incapable of charting our own course and if we are incapable of passing a unanimous recommendation on to you then you are going to have to make the decision for us." He urged the appointment of Abel.[17]

A few days later, Henry Graff, who had also served on the committee, shrewdly assayed the lack of enthusiasm for Abel: "Some of the lukewarmness results from the awareness that the School is not now in healthy condition and that it increasingly needs a Dean with positive 'take-charge' qualities—and on this count Abel is an unknown quantity." He urged the president to inform the journalism faculty of his intentions: "It could be disastrous for your appointee's chances of success in the post if the dissident members of the Faculty should be presented with a *fait accompli*." But there was to be no warning.[18]

Baker issued a memorandum in November listing several new candidates for dean, mentioned that Elie Abel and the president had had a meeting, and offered to arrange a faculty luncheon with Abel. It did not take place. On November 18, Frederick Yu, the secretary of the faculty, ran a new poll. This one offered more clarity. Of fifteen respondents, twelve favored naming Baker as dean, for a stated term. One wanted to offer the deanship to Abel. Two others had no position. There was a current of sentiment that Baker's service had earned him the recognition, but one faculty member, quoted anonymously, warned that it would be humiliating to Baker to have faculty support, only to be turned down by the president or trustees. In a memorandum to Cordier, Graff, now out of patience, characterized the poll as stalling.[19]

That comment may have settled the matter. On December 17, the faculty was summoned by Cordier to the trustees' room in Low Library. The president opened the meeting by talking at length about everything but the deanship. Then he announced that he had decided to name Elie Abel dean as of February 1, 1970. John Hohenberg immediately commended the choice. Pinkham and Kimball objected, the latter asking if Cordier intended to place Abel's name before the trustees regardless of the faculty's opinion. Cordier said he would. Dazed, the faculty drifted back to its own building, having been notified, in effect, that its opinion had counted for nothing. The usually reserved Fred Yu referred to Cordier as "a son of a bitch," and resigned as secretary of the faculty. Kimball, who told the *Spectator* that the meeting had been a "humiliating experience," was at first inclined to resign, as was Pinkham, but both stayed on, and the faculty prepared to greet a dean whom, whatever its illusions, it had long since shown itself to be unable to choose.[20]

# CHAPTER 28

# "Welcome to the Joint"

IN THE FLURRY over the manner of his appointment, it was all but forgotten that Elie Abel brought superior credentials to the deanship. Canadian by birth and forty-nine years old, he was in the class of 1942 at the school when he was called, before graduation, to serve in the Royal Canadian Air Force. His Pulitzer Traveling Scholarship was held until after the war; he used it to cover the Nuremberg war-crimes trials. For the next fifteen years, he was a newspaper correspondent, primarily for the *New York Times*. In 1961, he moved to NBC News, and was a reporter-commentator in London and Washington; he also completed his first book, on the 1962 Cuban missile crisis. In Abel, Columbia was to have its first dean who was still a practicing journalist, and the first with experience in television. If there were any doubts, they centered on whether the soft-spoken, reserved Abel was, in Henry Graff's phrase, "a take-charge guy."[1]

The six weeks between his appointment and his arrival were turbulent. His appointment, in December 1969, was greeted with a negative story in the campus *Spectator*, in which Penn Kimball and Melvin Mencher were quoted as asserting that a majority of the faculty had been opposed to the appointment, because, as Kimball said, it was "outrageous for the president to tell [the faculty] he is appointing a dean that eight out of fourteen professors have not even met." *Time* picked up the story under the heading, "Dean of a School Divided."[2]

The two preceding deans moved forthwith to patching up. Richard Baker gave a reception for Abel in the World Room—where the students waggishly handed the new dean a box, labeled "Welcome to the Joint," which contained a joint—and there was dinner afterward with the faculty. Edward Barrett, still the impresario, staged a gala welcoming luncheon at the Century Association, which included not only faculty but Walter Lippmann, Frank Stanton of CBS, Reuven Frank of NBC, and, seated flanking Abel, McGeorge Bundy of the Ford Foundation and Wes Gallagher of the Associated Press. Gradually many of the discontented became, at least, silent.[3]

There was an opportunity for a further display of unity. All four of the school's deans—Abel, Baker, Barrett, and Carl W. Ackerman—met at Ackerman's apartment to observe the old dean's eightieth birthday, on January 16, 1970. Ackerman also appeared later at the Century luncheon. But over the following summer he suffered heart attacks, and he died on October 9, at the Riverside Drive apartment where he had lived out his retirement years, largely in isolation. The long, respectful obituary in the *Times* depicted his achievement much in terms he would have approved, saying that he had transformed the school "from a literary ivory tower to a hard-nosed practical training ground for newsmen."[4]

Abel must have realized soon enough that he had been dealt a poor hand. Only a day in his new office, he learned that his sponsor in Low Library, Andrew Cordier, would be in Low Library only a few months more and would be succeeded by William J. McGill, chosen in part for his success in dealing with student unrest while chancellor at the University of California at San Diego. In short, any commitments made by Cordier could be annulled. Within the school, Abel soon found the faculty's opposition party—notably Pinkham, Kimball, and Mencher—a headache. And Baker decided he did not want to resume the post of associate dean. Abel had trouble finding a replacement; eventually Fred Yu reluctantly took the job.[5]

Worse, Abel found that he had stepped into the thick of an intensifying struggle with Low Library—specifically, with the new vice president and dean of faculties, Polykarp Kusch. Kusch was a Nobel laureate in physics; as an administrator, he was imperious and outspoken. His correspondence with other members of the administration made clear that the apparently solid reputation that Barrett had built for the school under Grayson Kirk had dissolved during the long search for a dean; both the budget and the faculty were now viewed as impossible. In September 1969, Kusch asked one of his subordinates to prepare a memorandum urging on the president "a major reconsideration of the affairs of the School of Journalism." During the fall, Kusch visited the school and warned the faculty that he meant to take drastic measures, even hinting at merging the school with another small school, such as library services.[6]

Baker had already been dealing with Kusch, which may have been one more reason he showed no enthusiasm for continuing as dean. Kusch, citing Columbia's growing deficits in the wake of the 1968 troubles, contended that the school of journalism was incredibly costly—four times more expensive for each full-time student than the law school—and that the school, with its endowments, should make fewer demands on the university. Kusch also attacked the hard-won gains the school had made in reasserting control of its building, insisting that the school open its classrooms to general university use.[7]

Baker responded robustly to a hint from Kusch that the original Pulitzer agreements might be set aside:

Despite some chuckles we had the other day, I do take very seriously the original agreements covering the legacy of Joseph Pulitzer. The University agreed to the building called Journalism, its erection and its equipment "with all the mechanical and technical apparatus and plant for the demonstration of the physical and mechanical part of the instruction," and the University agreed to use the second million dollars for the expenses of the School "including the care and maintainance [sic] of the building. . . ." I don't want to belabor the point because I know that agreements made in 1904 have to be honored in spirit as much as in fact in the light of new and changing circumstances. Nevertheless, the agreements were made. I would say the same thing about gifts, particularly in view of our Half-Century Fund so lately completed. They were given to the University but were certainly earmarked for the uses of the School of Journalism. . . .

Since you mentioned the quality of our space in the conclusion of your letter, let me say that this is due in large measure to the generosity of a loyal band of alumni and friends of the School. For years we limped along with a broadcast studio that consisted of two small rooms lined with raw fiberglass covered with chicken wire. The print lab was a museum piece. The library space was so abominable that it was cited as such when the accrediting team from the American Council on Education for Journalism visited the School in 1965. The response of such alumni as Max Geffen and Max Schuster and such friends of the School as the Sulzberger family and William Paley to an appeal for funds to renovate these and other areas was made in part because the School had slipped badly in terms of the space in which it had to operate.

This is a professional school preeminent in its field. It may be that ours is the only professional school on the campus that is the acknowledged Number One in the land. A report has just come to me from the American Council for Education in Journalism analyzing a lot of statistical data of the 50 accredited schools and departments of journalism in this country. In table after table Columbia is Number One. The one table in which we are not Number One is in the area of increases of faculty salaries. We are about in the middle. I strongly urge that space problems on this campus not be used as a lever to displace the School from this position it has won.[8]

It was a stiff warning, and Kusch laid off Baker, but he lay in wait for Abel. He chose to pounce on the issue of three new tenure cases the faculty had asked the new dean to forward. On March 19, 1970, Kusch wrote him a "Dear Elie" letter saying that they were agreed on the appointment of Luther Jackson in the slot occupied by John Foster, who was retiring, but warned against making other commitments: "I recognize the problems posed by your faculty and the possibly inappropriate weight, formal or informal, of student opinion." The phrasing suggested that he now regarded the school as the equivalent of the Paris Commune.[9]

On the same day, Kusch wrote to Arthur Ochs Sulzberger, publisher of the *Times* and a Columbia trustee, asking for his evaluation of Abel's two other tenure candidates, Leonard Wallace Robinson, a part-time writing instructor at the school for ten years, and Donald R. Shanor, a veteran foreign correspondent who had earlier been a lecturer at the school. Kusch remarked to Sulzberger, "I really do think the School of Journalism could, with a major change in direction, become an important component of the University." Later, Kusch noted in a memorandum to his files that Sulzberger had responded that Shanor and Robinson were "not as yet men of significant visibility in journalism nor men that have made their mark through the force of their writing, interpretation, etc., etc. [and] made the flat statement that neither of these men would, at this time, be considered for appointment [*sic*] at the New York Times." Kusch notified Abel that he would not authorize budget lines for either Shanor or Robinson.[10]

Further, he set about degrading the school in the eyes of the incoming president, McGill. In a letter on March 27, he wrote: "Unfortunately, there is a lot of money attached to the School of Journalism by way of endowment. What is more, some people are terrified of the vindictiveness of the Fourth Estate. As for the Fourth Estate, I once had a private lunch with Arthur Sulzberger, a Trustee of the University, in his rather elegant quarters at the top of the New York Times Building. His view of the School of Journalism was a rather dim one."[11]

After continuing exchanges of correspondence with Abel—now no longer on a first-name basis—Kusch presented his case against the school to outgoing President Cordier. He argued that the school already had too many tenured faculty members per student in comparison with other professional schools, and that there should be no more tenured appointments until the school underwent reorganization, of a nature that he did not specify.[12]

He won his point. Luther Jackson began the tenure process, but Robinson and Shanor were set aside. After George K. Fraenkel, dean of the Graduate Faculties, reported to Kusch on the proceedings of the ad hoc committee gathered to consider Jackson's qualifications, Kusch responded: "I am not surprised that you were appalled. As far as I am able to make judgments, I think that no other school in the University is quite as dreary as the School of Journalism." He went on: "You may be interested in some correspondence that I had with Dean Abel. There is a thick stack of it, some of it quite offensive. For example, in supporting the tenured appointment for Robinson, he asserted that Robinson would carry on the great tradition of Joseph Wood Krutch, who was at one time a member of the Faculty of Journalism." Why he found the comparison offensive he did not explain.[13]

With the tenure cases in abeyance—Shanor soon won tenure and Jackson was accepted after the ad hoc committee considered further evidence—Abel responded to unremitting pressure from Kusch to cut the school's share of the university's general income in the 1970–71 budget. In the end, the cut amounted to 50 percent of the university's contribution, while the school, under financial pressure to increase tuition income, augmented its enrollment by 25 percent, to more than 150. Several secondary administrative or clerical positions were vacated; the alumni affairs officer, Eileen Grennan Walsh, resigned, and the position was left vacant. A year later, Abel realized that he had given too much. "Chalk it up to my naivete," he wrote to President McGill, and asked for an increase to a total budget of $1.05 million, still short of Baker's last budget, two years before.[14]

Bust of Joseph Pulitzer, a replica of
Rodin's original, often adorned with
laurel wreaths on his birthday, April 10,
in the early days of the school of
journalism.

A 1912 drawing of the schoool of journalism building from the *School of Journalism Announcement,
1912–1913*. The building opened in fall 1913, and "JOURNALISM" was inscribed over the doors.

Portrait of Talcott Williams, painted about the time he became the first director of the School of Journalism, in 1912, at the age of 63. *(Graduate School of Journalism)*

Journalism 43–4: The senior news laboratory—which called itself "The Staff"—of the school's first year, 1912–13, meeting in Hamilton Hall because the journalism building was not finished. Professor Robert E. MacAlarney is in the right background, facing Carl W. Ackerman, destined to be the school's first dean. Hollington K. Tong, fourth from right, was later instrumental in creating the school's Chungking branch during World War II. *(Columbia University Archives)*

The senior news laboratory in 501 Journalism, probably during the Great War, judging from the female majority. Professor MacAlarney and Director Williams are seated in the slot of the copy desk on the left. *(Columbia University Archives)*

Walter B. Pitkin was on the school's original faculty and taught at the school for 31 years. He was famed for dazzling lectures and for writing the best-seller *Life Begins at Forty*. This photograph was taken in the 1930s.
*(Columbia University Archives)*

Charles P. Cooper came to the school from the *Times* in 1919 to head the reporting and editing courses. He was noted for his stentorian voice, his command of profanity, and his award of a symbolic "red apple" to the best story of the week.
*(Graduate School of Journalism)*

John W. Cunliffe, second director of the school, at the dedication of his portrait, about 1931. He is flanked on the left by his successor, Dean Carl W. Ackerman, and on the right by Columbia's president, Nicholas Murray Butler.
*(Columbia University Archives)*

Carl W. Ackerman, class of 1913, who
held the deanship for 25 years, starting
in 1931—by far the longest tenure of any
of the school's administrators—and
converted the school into an exclusively
graduate institution.
*(Columbia University Archives)*

Douglas Southall Freeman, the most distinguished addition to Ackerman's
faculty. Editor of the *Richmond News Leader*, he commuted to Columbia
weekly by train from 1934 to 1941. He won the Pulitzer Prize in biography
in 1935 for his *R. E. Lee*. *(Columbia University Archives)*

Harold L. Cross was associated with the school from 1926 to 1950 as the teacher of libel law, as an associate dean, and as first dean of the Chungking Post-Graduate School of Journalism. Later, he headed a freedom of information campaign for the American Society of Newspaper Editors. *(Columbia University Archives)*

Paul W. White, class of 1923 and one of the founders of CBS News, pioneered in broadcast instruction at the school from 1939 to 1946. *(Columbia University Archives)*

Roscoe B. Ellard, known for his flamboyant classroom style, was recruited by Dean Ackerman in 1940 to supervise the school's educational program, but often disappointed the dean. He was retired in 1959. *(Columbia University Archives)*

Eleanor Carroll, class of 1920 and an experienced magazine editor, worked at the school for ten years (1936–46) as a teacher and an administrator, notably during World War II, when classes had a majority of women. *(Columbia University Archives)*

Class of 1945 at the Columbia-sponsored journalism school in China. Faculty, in front row: Robert V. Ackerman, Steffan Andrews, Rodney Gilbert (the school's second dean), Floyd D. Rodgers, Jr., Anthony F. J. Dralle, and Richard T. Baker. *(Graduate School of Journalism)*

Richard Terrill Baker, class of 1937, taught at the Chungking school during World War II, then joined the permanent faculty in 1948. He was the school's first historian, acting dean in 1968 and 1969, and Pulitzer Prize secretary. He died in 1981. *(Columbia University Archives)*

John Foster, Jr. (left) first served the school as an adviser to the Columbia-sponsored school in Venezuela. He supervised the school's first instruction in television journalism and was the director of the Advanced Science Writing Program. He retired in 1969. *(Columbia University Archives)*

John Hohenberg exemplified the school's tradition of hands-on, high-pressure instruction. He taught at the school from 1950 to 1976, and served as secretary to the Advisory Board on the Pulitzer Prizes for more than twenty years. He died in the year 2000 at the age of 94. *(Columbia University Archives)*

The newsroom that housed the entire class from 1935 to roughly 1965, when enrollment outgrew the space. The desks shown were replaced a year later, thanks to a beer company's sponsorship of the televised *Pulitzer Prize Playhouse*. *(Graduate School of Journalism)*

Edward W. Barrett, dean from 1956 to 1968, escorts former President Truman to an appearance at the school in 1958. Barrett served in the State Department during the Truman administration. *(Columbia University Archives)*

Penn T. Kimball, a veteran newspaper and magazine journalist, was a professor at the school from 1959 to 1986 and a highly independent faculty voice. He was the victor in a struggle with the federal government to open his security files. *(Don Hinkle)*

Melvin Mencher, a demanding teacher at the school from 1962 to 1990, was nationally known for his widely used textbook, *News Reporting and Writing*. He, with Kimball, was one of the "sour apples" who afflicted Dean Elliott. *(Columbia University Archives)*

The school's first substantial full-time faculty, assembled by Dean Barrett. At this 1966 meeting in the World Room, from right around the table: W. Phillips Davison, Frederick T. C. Yu, Robert O. Shipman, Christopher Trump, Theodore Laymon, Lawrence Dana Pinkham, Richard F. Crandell, John Hohenberg, George Barrett, John Foster, Jr., William A. Wood, John Luter, _____, Melvin Mencher, James Boylan, Donald R. Shanor, Penn T. Kimball, Edward W. Barrett, Richard Terrill Baker.
*(Columbia University Archives)*

Fred W. Friendly, a vivid presence at the school, joined the faculty in 1966 after quitting as president of CBS News. He is shown in action here in the school's then-primitive broadcast facility. He retired formally in 1980 but continued to teach and produce his widely known television seminars. He died in 1998.
*(Columbia University Archives)*

The first four deans of the School of Journalism, gathered to observe the eightieth birthday of Carl W. Ackerman in 1970. Left to right: Edward W. Barrett, 1956–68; Ackerman, 1931–56; Elie Abel, 1970–79; Richard T. Baker, acting, 1968–69. *(Columbia University Archives)*

Donald H. Johnston, class of 1950, long-time utility infielder for the school as a teacher, an administrator, and later as president of the alumni association. Among other services, he created the Columbia News Service, a syndicate that distributed student work. *(Alumni Office)*

Osborn Elliott, former editor in chief of *Newsweek*, served as dean from 1979 to 1986 and remained at the school until 1994 as Delacorte Professor. *(Columbia University Archives)*

Frederick T. C. Yu, communications scholar, teacher, and administrator, was at the school from 1962 to 1991 and served as acting dean from 1986 to 1988. *(Graduate School of Journalism)*

Joan Konner, a 1961 graduate of the school and later a Columbia trustee, was named dean after a notable career in public television. She led a revival of the school from 1988 to 1997, recruiting new faculty and rehabilitating the building. As dean emerita, she continued to serve as publisher of the *Columbia Journalism Review*. *(Columbia University Archives)*

Tom Goldstein, class of 1969, became dean in 1997 after heading the Graduate School of Journalism at Berkeley. He left in June 2002 after working to expand the school's curriculum and deal with such long-term financial problems as the *Columbia Journalism Review*. *(Graduate School of Journalism)*

David A. Klatell served as
acting dean in 2002 and 2003 after
Columbia's President Bollinger
declined to name a dean to succeed
Tom Goldstein. In the meantime,
Bollinger named a "task force"
to study the school.
*(Graduate School of Journalism)*

Nicholas Lemann, magazine journalist and author, was named the seventh dean of the
school in 2003. He is shown talking with Ruth Friendly, widow of Fred W. Friendly.
*(Alexandra Boak-Kelly)*

In the meantime, Abel reached a truce with Kusch, who gradually came to tolerate the school or the dean or both. As a consolation prize to the dean, Kusch approved the provisional appointment of Norman E. Isaacs, just then leaving the editorship of the Louisville *Courier-Journal* and the presidency of the American Society of Newspaper Editors. Isaacs, a robust advocate of journalistic accountability, was brought in as a kind of counterpoise to Friendly, to give the school's print instruction an equally strong figure—and one just as outspoken.[15]

When Kusch left his vice-presidential position on June 30, 1971—having resigned abruptly earlier in the year—he wrote a positively cordial letter to Abel, praising him for the deep budget cuts. He added: "I have much higher hopes for the School of Journalism than I had when I first came to my office. I think the trade school aspects of the School will be increasingly muted and that there will be an increasing concern with the very great problem of informing the public of all matters that concern the society in which we live. . . . I do think that the School is under good leadership." So passed the immediate threat, but what an initiation it was![16]

During his first spring at Columbia, Abel was also introduced to campus insurgency. There was an outburst in mid-April, and the journalism building received a glancing blow—broken windows and stink bombs in the elevators. Two weeks later came the American invasion of Cambodia. The administration tried to channel the inevitable by supporting a moratorium—a suspension of classes—starting May 4. President Cordier delivered an antiwar speech, but, as in 1968, the protest was increasingly directed against the the university as the seeming oppressor. As one sign read, "Burn the motherfucker down!"[17]

This time the journalism class joined in, voting, more or less, to strike; that is, those who favored a strike used the old tactic of waiting to vote until the fatigued opposition left. The building became an impromptu strike headquarters—"a pig's pen," Hohenberg remarked in his diary. Pickets stood at the door of the building, and Fred Friendly, after gaining access, led his class outdoors. By the end of May, it was clear that despite losing more than a week Columbia had weathered 1970 much better than 1968, and the journalism class graduated in good order, except for one woman student, who had been tried and acquitted on a disciplinary charge. The dean said he had to threaten to resign on commencement day to get Low Library to release her diploma.[18]

At the end of the year, John Foster, Jr., retired, his departure marked with a quiet luncheon. He was not yet sixty-five, but clearly abhorred the recent turbulence. His management of the Advanced Science Writing Program was unanimously praised by the hundred or so journalists who had passed through it. But the program's financing lapsed not long after Foster left, the first of the Barrett add-ons to fall by the wayside. However, the school retained Kenneth Goldstein, a former science fellow, and he kept science writing alive in the curriculum for the next two decades.[19]

In the summer of 1970, Friendly headed the school's summer minority program for a third year. By now the program had developed a newspaper side to go with the broadcast instruction, and had grown to twenty or so instructors. Among the thirty-seven graduates was Michele Clark of WBBM-TV, Chicago; when she was killed in an airplane crash in 1972, the program was renamed in her honor. Another 1970 graduate was Gerald Rivera of WABC-TV, New York, who became better known with an "o" attached to his first name.[20]

# CHAPTER 29

# Hohenberg and the Prizes

JOHN HOHENBERG worked twenty-six years at the school of journalism. As a teacher, he embodied the practical, get-it-done side of the curriculum, which had been its dominant note since the beginning. He used the hurry-up command he said he first heard from a long-ago deskman: "Go with what you've got"—aimed at what he saw as the chief shortcoming of novices, their inability to produce. When he was in charge of the newsroom in the 1950s, he would peer over a student's shoulder and, if he spotted writer's block, he would edge the student out of his seat and bang out a lead. "Cruel and inconsiderate procedure?" he asked himself later. "Perhaps it was. But I was never a teacher of theoretical writing and the interventions, such as they were, seemed to do the students no harm." If beginning students sometimes wilted, they were buoyed by his excitement and enthusiasm when they won his approval. If female graduates (such as a later dean, Joan Konner) remembered him as less than encouraging to females, at least he never indulged in the kind of derogation of students that Roscoe Ellard had practiced.[1]

As he moved through his fifties and sixties (he was born in 1906), he remained a man of boundless energy, sustained by abstention from drink, devotion to long-distance swimming, and playing the piano. In a span of sixteen years, he completed nine books—a rate of production unmatched since Pitkin's. The first book, *The Pulitzer Prize Story* (1959), collected extracts from prize-winning entries, left the Columbia University Press gasping because it did not know how to deal with a book that sold well. In 1960, he published a textbook, *The Professional Journalist*, which eventually went through four revised editions. It was permeated with his upbeat view of the way that the press did things; one reviewer of a later edition observed that students trying to find their way through the moral dilemmas of journalism probably needed "a Dante and not a Billy Graham." He was deeply annoyed when a reviewer of a later book, *The New Front Page*, called him "journalism's press agent."[2]

He also had a summertime and sabbatical career as a consultant to the military and foreign-policy establishments. Initially, the Air Force tapped him as a speaker at the Air War College, then sent him on a tour to inspect facilities in the Far East. He was being tested, it turned out, for a post as civilian head of Air Force information. He declined, but did other Air Force chores over the years, such as investigating overspending on construction at the new Air Force Academy. In 1963 and 1964, he went on a six-month speaking tour in Asia for the Department of State American Specialist program. The Council on Foreign Relations signed him to do a book on sources of anti-Americanism, and he obliged. The Ford Foundation proposed a book on Asian non-Communists, and he wrote it. The books bore a family resemblance, in their layering of interviews, anecdotes, and statistics, to John Gunther's popular old *Inside* series, and evidently pleased their sponsors.[3]

In the world of American journalism, Hohenberg was best known as the administrator of the Pulitzer Prizes and secretary to the Pulitzer Prize Advisory Board. In this role he was, from the board's point of view, all but faultless. Deferential and supportive to those he viewed as journalism's elite, he remained well beyond the one or two years he was supposed to serve when Dean Ackerman turned the job over to him in 1954; expecting the new dean to take over the position in 1956, he was surprised when President Kirk asked him to continue. He stayed for twenty-two years and also became the authorized historian of the prizes. After the death of the head of the advisory board, the second Joseph Pulitzer, in 1955, he worked with the founder's grandson, Joseph Pulitzer, Jr., and earned the somewhat chilly younger man's confidence, although they never had a friendship that extended beyond prize business.[4]

Inevitably, he faced the spasmodic crises that had always drawn attention to the prizes. One of the first came when the columnist Drew Pearson charged that young Senator John F. Kennedy had not actually written *Profiles in Courage*, the book that won the 1957 biography prize. Hohenberg, who had already investigated the matter, wrote to Kennedy, who took up the matter with Pearson, who withdrew the charge. Hohenberg had already been informed that Kennedy had written the first draft in longhand while recovering from surgery, had dictated the final version, and had had plentiful advice but not ghostwriters.[5]

In 1962, the university trustees, to whom each year's prizes were submitted for pro forma approval, decided to exercise their veto power for the first time in the forty-six years of the prizes. The problem was the biography prize, the subject of which was supposed to be an "eminent example" of "services to the people." In this instance, the board voted for *Citizen Hearst*, by W. A. Swanberg, and the trustees disliked the notion of Hearst as an eminent example; moreover, playing at being more Catholic than the pope, they resisted the idea of a Pulitzer Prize for Joseph Pulitzer's greatest rival. (Hearst's son and namesake had already shared a prize for interviews in 1955 with Soviet leaders.) Lacking authority to substitute another work, the trustees deleted the biography prize. No doubt this planted the idea, later pursued by Hohenberg and Pulitzer, that the trustees should relinquish all authority over the prizes, but matters got worse before they got better.[6]

By contrast, the celebration of the fiftieth anniversary of the prizes in May 1966 was a golden, peaceful moment. Half of the living recipients assembled at the Plaza Hotel for a gala observance. Because journalists received prizes in so many categories, most of the attendees were journalists. But arts and letters had distinguished representation: the historians Samuel Eliot Morison, Richard Hofstadter, and Barbara Tuchman; the novelists Katherine Anne Porter and John Hersey; the old muckraker Upton Sinclair (as a novelist); the playwrights Elmer Rice and Sidney Kingsley.[7]

Five recipients spoke briefly: the poet and playwright Archibald MacLeish, the novelist Robert Penn Warren, the composer Aaron Copland, the journalist James Reston, and the historian Arthur M. Schlesinger, Jr. MacLeish spoke most directly to the occasion: "We are Mr. Pulitzer's dream made flesh." He put the prizes in their best possible light: "No one believes ... that the Pulitzer Prizes will change the art of letters in America; art is not impressed by awards. But there are men and women in this room—among the most intelligent of the time—who will testify that these prizes have warmed the world in which the art of letters must be preserved."[8]

Dean Barrett commented afterward that the evening had had the atmosphere of a "family party." But even in the warmth of the occasion, there were shadows. The advisory board earlier had dispatched Hohenberg, as chief planner of the dinner, to the White House to ask Lyndon B. Johnson to address the gathering. But Hohenberg was stopped short of the Oval Office by the press secretary, Bill Moyers, and informed that the president had no interest in attending. Hohenberg concluded that the president was angry because 1964 prizes had gone to Malcolm Browne of the Associated Press and David Halberstam of the *Times* for their critical reporting from Vietnam. A 1966 prize, also for Vietnam reporting, was to be awarded to Peter Arnett of the AP at the dinner. Afterward, Dean Barrett commented: "On the whole I think we can be grateful that President Johnson did not accept the invitation to speak."[9]

The Pulitzer board had to deal in the years that followed with the increasingly intense confrontations between press and government. Each year, it seemed, there were investigative stories staking out dangerous new territory—reporting from the other side of the war, reporting of American atrocities, reporting on the contents of secret documents, reporting of criminal behavior at the highest levels of government.

Initially the board was cautious. Late in 1966, Harrison Salisbury gained entry to North Vietnam and reported that American claims about the costs of the air war were false; he was attacked, sometimes by other journalists, as a near traitor. (Hohenberg found, curiously, that his reporting class responded coldly to Salisbury's appearance just after his return.)[10]

Salisbury was nominated by the *Times* for a Pulitzer; Joseph Pulitzer, Jr. led the fight for him in the advisory board meeting. A board member, Turner Catledge of the *Times*, following the rule requiring absence during discussion of one's own organization, left the room during the argument. He returned to learn that Salisbury's prize had been turned down, 6–5. He recalled: "I was terribly upset by this vote, because I was convinced that several of my colleagues made their decision on political rather than journalistic grounds; indeed, they made no bones about it. They supported the war, so they voted against Salisbury." A parallel argument at the trustees' meeting later let the result stand; a *Christian Science Monitor* correspondent won the prize. But by 1970, the board no longer concerned itself with defending the war, and unanimously approved Seymour Hersh's exposé of the massacre of Vietnamese civilians at My Lai. The trustees accepted the decision.[11]

The next round was the Pentagon Papers, publication starting in June 1971, of excerpts from a secret government history of the Vietnam war, initially leaked to the *Times* and later given to other newspapers when the Nixon administration halted publication in the *Times*. After weeks of tension, the newspapers won qualified permission from the Supreme Court to resume publishing. The *Times* submission on the papers led to spirited debate in the board, with Pulitzer again in the affirmative. The decision was to give the *Times* the public-service medal (omitting the name of Neil Sheehan, who had played a key role and had to wait nearly thirty years to win a prize).[12]

The trustees rebelled; they initially voted down both the *Times* award and an award to the columnist Jack Anderson for another exposé based on secret documents. President McGill urged them to reconsider, and ultimately the trustees approved the awards, adding a stuffy statement that had it been up to them "certain of the recipients would not have been chosen."[13]

Then came Watergate, the tangle of corruption emanating from the White House. The Pulitzer jurors met to consider the work of the *Washington Post* after Nixon's reelection but before the case blew open in the spring of 1973. The jurors ignored the story; one remarked to Hohenberg: "Watergate is just a pimple on the elephant's ass." By the time the advisory board met in April, the Watergate scandal was in full flower and chairman Pulitzer had good reason to demand the public-service medal for the *Post*. This time the trustees resisted because a small core wanted to prop up the faltering Nixon administration. But they did not dare; they issued another statement noting that they did not have "the authority to substitute their judgment for the judgment of the Advisory Board." That is, they acquiesced.[14]

Again, individual journalists were slighted; there was no mention in the public-service citation of Bob Woodward and Carl Bernstein, the lead Watergate reporters, or of Howard Simons (class of 1952), who organized the coverage. Nonetheless, Woodward and Bernstein became the country's most famous journalists, and were portrayed in film; Simons was played by Martin Balsam, who looked nothing like him.[15]

A legend that has persisted for thirty years insists that journalism school applications spiked upward after the Watergate exposures. No such thing; the rise had begun six years before—Columbia had its first big surge from 1963 to 1965—for reasons still not well explained, and continued through the 1980s, at Columbia and elsewhere.[16]

There was one more crisis before Nixon's departure. In April 1974, the board voted honors for two more exposés—one by Jack White of the *Providence Journal* on the president's income-tax fudging, the other by James R. Polk of the *Washington Star-News* on campaign-financing irregularities. This time the trustees evidently concluded that the advisory board and perhaps journalism in general were out of control. Not only did they attempt to vote down the prizes, but they also—according to what Hohenberg was told afterward—tried to dissolve the prize board through non-reappointment. In the argument, someone even raised the possibility, left open in the original agreements, that the prizes could move to Harvard. In the end, the trustees got over their tantrum.[17]

But the idea of a complete severance of the trustees from the prizes now took on urgency. Earlier, Joseph Pulitzer, Jr. had been reluctant to tamper, envisioning complicated court procedures and years of dealing with lawyers. But, given the serious warning of 1974, he moved ahead. It took a year of maneuvering, but in the spring of 1975, the board adopted what the university counsel had proposed as a "resolution of divorcement." The trustees, perhaps relieved to wash their hands of a source of trouble, promptly adopted the same document, and it was done. The press was so caught up, as usual, in the prizes that it did not notice. The board still had the president as a member, linking it to the university, but otherwise it was on its own.[18]

Within the school, Hohenberg's guardianship of the prizes always gave him a status apart. Erecting an invisible barrier between his colleagues and the workings of the prizes, he and Joseph Pulitzer, Jr. treated Deans Barrett and Abel like interlopers, hangers-on at the fringes of an exclusive men's club. Indeed, when President Kirk told the board he was appointing Barrett as dean, Pulitzer responded irritably that he didn't know the man. Barrett might reasonably have expected a role in the prizes, but found himself shut out; he responded by complaining continually to Hohenberg that he had heard of irregularities at the advisory board meetings, such as late entries that bypassed the jury system. Hohenberg testily denied the allegations.[19]

After a flurry of bad publicity about the awards in 1960, Barrett wrote to the president that they needed to discuss "the now-obvious need for the University to re-assume direction over the Pulitzer Prizes and the process of selecting the Board." He added: "It is clearly unsatisfactory to have prizes going to works that you, I, and a majority of our colleagues do not applaud." He was no doubt referring to the prizes given to the musical *Fiorello!* and Allen Drury's squalid Washington novel, *Advise and Consent*, neither of which had been recommended by the juries. Further, the board brushed aside the jurors' history choices and honored a book by Joseph Pulitzer, Jr.'s aunt, Margaret Leech. Barrett observed, without naming names: "And it is unsatisfactory to have occasional Board members who represent the worst, rather than the best, in journalism." Kirk was usually supportive of Barrett, but in this instance did nothing.[20]

In 1966, Barrett encouraged the *Columbia Journalism Review*, of which he was editorial chairman, to print a decorous editorial questioning the way the prizes were run—particularly what the journalist Robert Bendiner had called the "air of secrecy that on any other front would be intolerable to the very newspaper editors who create it." Specifically, the editorial called for seating others on the board besides journalists, open discussions between jurors and the board, disclosure of jury recommendations, and the end of the rule in which the administrator was required to say stiffly that he did not grant interviews. At Hohenberg's request, the editorial had a note at the end saying that, although he was a member of the *Review*'s advisory board, he had had no role in preparing the editorial. Barry Bingham of the Louisville *Courier-Journal* and other board members wrote to the dean that they agreed, but it was years before the recommended changes came to pass.[21]

In a tenure abounding with frustrations, Dean Abel was furious, according to Hohenberg, at being refused the seat he believed he deserved on the advisory board. In 1974, Hohenberg noted in his diary: "Dean Abel, once an old friend, now was so obsessed with the notion that he should be on the Pulitzer board that he began a tirade against Joe Pulitzer Jr. for blocking his appointment." During discussions about separating the trustees from the prizes, Pulitzer reaffirmed that he would not accept Abel and indeed wanted the prizes to be utterly apart from the school. This position seemed to infuriate the dean anew, for there was another outburst in 1975, when Abel told Hohenberg (who recorded it in his diary) "that he was through with the Pulitzers and that I could run them as long as I wished." In fact, Hohenberg left the next year, and almost immediately Abel was granted a seat on the board, as a nonvoting member.[22]

As a member of the journalism faculty, Hohenberg always did a share of teaching and committee chores. But in faculty meetings he could be thin-skinned and occasionally vindictive. Judging from their absence from his two autobiographical books, he did not count any of his colleagues except Dick Baker as a real friend. In his last years at the school, he was in part preoccupied by the illness of his wife and one-time classmate, Dorothy, afflicted with Alzheimer's disease. He brought her to the office, where she would sit smiling at those who greeted her, although, as Hohenberg noted in his diary, she no longer recognized even him. She died in 1977.[23]

Hohenberg received a full range of honors, including a special citation from the advisory board, when he left in May 1976. But he was by no means in decline. Indeed, the rest of his life stretched almost as long as his quarter-century at Columbia. He was to write six more books, and was a visiting teacher at half a dozen journalism departments, some of them headed by former students. He returned to Columbia in 1979 after his wedding to JoAnn Fogarty, a Tennessee widow, and again in 1982 and 1983 as, of all things, a Pulitzer Prize juror. To the members of the first classes that he taught, he became a kind of icon, a larger-than-life symbol of their nostalgic memories of the school. He died in the summer of 2000, at the age of 94. The alumni staged an elaborate memorial and started a scholarship fund in his name.[24]

CHAPTER 30

# Meeting Fatigue

ELIE ABEL, facing a time of retrenchment at Columbia, could hardly have pursued the expansionism of Dean Barrett. Nor was it his style; he lacked Barrett's public-relations energies. His communications with the alumni were low-key, blending realism and pessimism. Although he did pro bono work—for example, he served as an American member of a UNESCO commission on international communication problems—he did not seek to become a major voice in American journalism, as had his predecessors. At the school, he was usually forced to play the role of protector rather than innovator.[1]

The faculty, having been handed a share of leadership of the school under Baker, was intent on retaining its power and remained contentious, granting Abel little deference. The elders were a volatile mix—Penn Kimball holding out to make a point of principle; Fred Friendly trying to bulldoze opposition; John Hohenberg complaining of personal affronts; Norman Isaacs adding a touch of acid. Mel Mencher was often disenchanted and suspicious; and Larry Pinkham, returning from a sabbatical, was alienated. Abel was appalled at what he heard at meetings, but Mencher tried to persuade him that more might be at stake than personalities. He wrote:

Your shock and dismay at the conflicts within the faculty are understand-
able, but I hope you do not believe the tension is only the consequence of
jealousy, irrational hostility, and the like.

I fear that what we are witnessing is the culmination of a long period of
irritations and friction over legitimate issues: work load, theories
(philosophies) of instruction, quality of teaching, the use of graduate assistants, the proper balance of faculty autonomy and administrative leadership, and responsibility to the students.

Abel was not persuaded; he believed that most of what he heard had little to
do with issues: "What bothered me most, I confess, were the intensely personal thrusts back and forth across that table. . . . I had the impression that at
our last tenured faculty meeting the animosities went far beyond the questions at issue, which never were discussed at all."[2]

Yet Mencher had a point. The years of turbulence had left the faculty
lacking a consensus on much that once was taken for granted, such as the authority of teacher over student, the merits of the kind of hands-on instruction the school had always offered, and the fate of the school in the university. In a sense this was the culmination of a years-long debate as reformers
in the faculty sought to supersede the old "first-job" practical emphasis in favor of what one faculty member called "a more sensitive emphasis on the
substance and ethical consideration involved in writing about the whole of
the New York City community."[3]

In 1972, the spring brought a final campus outbreak, this time part of a national wave of disruption inspired by the resumption of bombing of North
Vietnam. As always, the university, as much as the Nixon administration,
became the target; six buildings were occupied, but were cleared by force,
persuasion, and guile; and the last was vacated by mid-May.[4]

The journalism school was largely untouched, despite persistent rumors
that it would be a target. A volunteer student staff produced an ambitious 28-
page tabloid supplement, titled *Bullhorn*, conceived out of dissatisfaction
with coverage of campus issues in the general news media. Norman Isaacs
advised the editors, and Phill Davison helped the students take a poll and
present the results showing that a heavy majority of students disapproved of
the occupation of buildings.[5]

In a faculty meeting on May 1, Pinkham urged the passage of a resolution
against the bombing, and Shanor and Mencher were assigned to draft it. To
Pinkham's distress, the resolution emerged as a petition to the White House
rather than a resolution, without, as he complained, "the weight of the insti-

tution behind it." But a petition it remained. Mencher rounded up signatures from most of the faculty and saw to it that the document was made available to the campus *Spectator* and the Associated Press, for which "leaking" he was castigated in absentia at the next faculty meeting.[6]

This same month happened to be that chosen for an effort on the part of Abel and Yu to draw the faculty together on long-range goals. Perhaps thinking that moving the retreat—or "smoker," as it was quaintly called at the time—away from the campus would lead to higher contemplation, they summoned the faculty to a Columbia-owned manor in Riverdale, in the Bronx. Part of the strategy was to have no formal agenda. It proved to be a long day, symbolizing the faculty stalemate. Through the morning and afternoon, the participants struggled earnestly with the destiny of the school, focusing particularly on the issue of the generalist vis-à-vis the specialist in journalism. But even before the break for dinner, the old irritations began to emerge, and the discussion degenerated into a quarrel over second-semester turf. Kimball arrived unavoidably late and tried to introduce new questions. Ultimately Abel closed the meeting by stalking out. An "administrative riot," Donald Shanor called it afterward.[7]

Pinkham, a tenured faculty member, left at the end of the 1971–72 year, one of the few tenured professors ever to depart before retirement. Earlier in the year, Pinkham let his reporting class form itself into a "Columbia Journalism Collective," created to investigate the school. In February 1972, it issued a sixty-five-page report. Although it started by dismissing the institution as "little more than a glorified trade school," it went on to offer a variety of mostly worthwhile information on the school's programs and policies. Aside from obligatory references to the "corporate media," the tone was impersonal. But neither faculty nor administration could have welcomed the extensive, and largely accurate, section on faculty factions. Not much later, Pinkham was placed on warning by the dean that he would never again be promoted. Pinkham already had an offer from a budding journalism program at the University of Massachusetts, and left, not to return.[8]

Months after Pinkham's departure, the collective's study leaked into the *Spectator*, the students having failed to sell the material commercially. The story emphasized the report's revelations of what it called the school's "sexist" admissions and hiring policies.[9]

Historically, the charge was true enough, but there had been progress. After the admissions committee resolved in the late 1960s to treat the applications of men and women equally—discarding at last the stricture Ackerman had placed on women applicants in 1935—the percentage of women admitted gradually rose to approximate the proportion of women applicants, which was about 40 percent. A female majority was soon reached—55 percent—with the admission of the class of 1978, approximately at the same time that the same trend reached other journalism schools across the country, and women had an increasing edge thereafter.[10]

As of 1971–72, there was no woman at the school of professorial rank. The adjuncts included two women—the veteran Judith Crist and Soma Golden, class of 1962, associated with *Business Week* before she went on to an extended career at the *Times*. A year later, a woman was hired and placed on tenure track. She was Phyllis T. Garland, then in her mid-thirties, a veteran of the *Pittsburgh Courier* and *Ebony* magazine. No doubt there were some at Columbia who gloated that they had beaten affirmative-action requirements with what was called a "twofer"—hiring a woman who was black. However, Garland's patience and durability made her presence a great deal more than symbolic.[11]

That advance was followed in 1974 with a step backward. After seven years of operation, the summer program for minority journalists abruptly closed. It left hard feelings in its wake, and suspicions that it had not spent its support funds prudently. Its last director was Robert C. Maynard of the *Washington Post*, destined to be the first and only black publisher of the *Oakland Tribune*. Deploring the closing, the *Guild Reporter*, publication of the Newspaper Guild, pointed out that the program's 223 graduates represented 15 to 20 percent of all minority employees in the news media, and that minority journalists still stood decades away from adequate representation and power in newsrooms. Maynard was embittered; he warned that if the program did not continue, "then we go back to the old system." He refounded the program on the West Coast, where it still thrives, based in Oakland, as the Institute for Journalism Education. It was named for Maynard after he died in 1993.[12]

At the last graduation ceremony, Friendly called the program "discriminatory," explaining that minority students in the school's regular program believed that the summer students, fully funded and promised jobs, were unfair competition. He also observed, "It was a crash program, and you can't have a crash program except in a state of war." The war, he implied, was over, or at least he was declaring it over. Indeed, it appeared that he was interested in moving on to a new war, between government and the press; he was just starting his series of televised seminars, in which real journalists and legal celebrities wrestled with hypothetical conflicts between the media and the law.[13]

There was another departure that same summer, 1974, when the American Press Institute held its final seminar at the school. The university had warned API that it wanted to reclaim its space eventually, and API in turn began to search for more spacious quarters, which it found in Reston, Virginia, near Washington. The organization's ancient origins at Columbia are not mentioned on its Web site. For its part, the school moved to reclaim, after nearly thirty years, the ground-floor space API had occupied.[14]

In 1975, Abel made a lasting contribution to the school's program—the establishment of the Walter Bagehot Fellowship. As financing grew tighter in the 1970s, the mid-career progams that Barrett had set up winked out one by one—science reporting; interracial-reporting programs supported by the Russell Sage and Rockefeller foundations; and ultimately the Advanced International Reporting Program. With considerable determination, Abel decided that he would establish a program in economics and business. He had the unusual idea, moreover, of naming the program for a journalist, rather than a donor. Walter Bagehot (baj-et) was editor of *The Economist* in the mid-nineteenth century, and a social and political scientist as well. (Later, the program was renamed the Knight-Bagehot Fellowship, honoring a contribution from the John S. and James L. Knight Foundation.)[15]

The program opened in the fall of 1975 with ten fellows, all journalists. It resembled the Nieman mid-career program at Harvard, except that the fellows concentrated on a single field. Stephen B. Shepard, the first director, returned to *Business Week* after a year, and was succeeded by Soma Golden. In 1977, Chris Welles took over, and the program took a hit when the Mobil Corporation decided, on the basis of Welles's past writings, that he was an enemy of the oil industry. Mobil, then seeking to retaliate against the industry's critics, withdrew its annual contribution of $50,000. But other donors came forward, and both Welles and the program continued. Three other directors followed Welles, the most recent being Terri Thompson. In 2000, the program celebrated its twenty-fifth year by preparing the publication of a substantial volume of essays, *Writing About Business*, and staging an anniversary dinner at which Dean Abel was honored.[16]

Another lasting innovation was Donald Johnston's creation of the Columbia News Service. It was a not-for-profit syndicate, set up to distribute student stories to fifty cooperating newspapers. Initially distributed by mail, the stories were later distributed by the New York Times News Service and InterPress Service, as well as through its own Web site.

For twenty years, the school's print side also published *The Bronx Beat*, a real newspaper replacing the laboratory pages produced by students for the previous seven decades. The *Beat* was a weekly tabloid distributed primarily in the South Bronx. Its mentors in its later years were E. R. Shipp and Robin Reisig. In 2002, only seven students signed up for the staff, and it was dropped temporarily. Tom Goldstein, first dean of the twenty-first century, remarked, "You can't make people do what they don't want to do." The next year, it resumed.[17]

Not since the death of Floyd Taylor of the American Press Institute in 1951 had the school lost an active staff member. But in 1975, John M. Patterson, who had been recruited for the school eight years before by Fred Friendly, died abruptly at the age of fifty. The eulogists at his memorial service—Abel, Friendly, Walter Cronkite, and an alumna, Jennifer A. Siebens—depicted a grimly conscientious, if effective, teacher. His time at Columbia had often been a struggle, and he overcame division in the tenured faculty to win his rank of associate professor. A prize was established in his name.[18]

Even more traumatic was the death of Louis Cowan, and his wife, Polly, in an apartment fire on November 18, 1976. Cowan had come to the school in 1963 as "director of special programs," which meant, in essence, that he made himself useful wherever he was needed. Self-effacing and courteous, he had taught, raised money for and contributed to the *Columbia Journalism Review*, helped with the DuPont awards, and engaged in a wide variety of pro bono work beyond the school. Inevitably, the *Times* obituary bore down on his resignation from CBS after the quiz-show scandals of 1958. The faculty signed a letter of protest asserting that "this good and dedicated man deserves better than to have the final 17 years of his life blotted out by arbitrary editing." The *Times* neither responded nor published the letter.[19]

As the 1970s wore on, the senior faculty—it was quite appropriate that the school played host to a conference on coverage of the aging—failed to mellow. Serious debate was disrupted by discord and distrust. What remained constant was ill temper. Isaacs—aligned with the traditionalists—referred to opponents of his space-reallocation plan in Chinese Communist terms, as "the gang of five." Even Richard Baker, hardly ever known to raise his voice, got into a shouting match over a point of order. On another occasion, Baker said, he went home after a meeting and shook for two hours.[20]

In 1978, Abel decided it was time to leave. In June, he announced that a year thence he would move to Stanford University to become the first occupant of a chair named for Harry and Norman Chandler of the *Los Angeles Times*. He understated his reasons in a letter to the faculty: "You may have sensed a rising restlessness in my attitude toward the business of deaning over the last several years. I cannot see myself in the role of career fund-raiser until age 65; and the psychic rewards of academic administration are, in my view, vastly overrated." When the faculty convened the following fall, he felt it necessary to say that he was not leaving in a huff.[21]

CHAPTER 31

# "It Appears You Have a New Dean"

IN JULY 1978, Richard Baker was tapped by President McGill to head the committee searching for a successor to Dean Abel. The committee had but one carryover: Judith Crist, from the search committee that came up empty in 1969. Senior faculty members were pointedly omitted; the president clearly wanted a committee that would behave itself and get its job done. Penn Kimball nonetheless tried to influence the search by weighing in with a six-page memorandum setting forth his stipulations that a new dean should be an "educational leader" with executive ability. Of fund-raising, he wrote: "The essence of fund-raising . . . is to generate ideas worth funding." He urged selection, finally, of a person still seeking "to make his/her reputation as an institutional leader, not a pasture for honorable retirement."[1]

Even in the preliminary list of candidates, one of Kimball's specifications was ignored; nobody on the list had ever worked in journalism education except Stuart Loory, class of 1958, who had taught for two years at Ohio State during an interval in his distinguished career as a journalist. For the first time, women were mentioned: Charlotte Curtis, editor of the op-ed page at the *Times*, and Flora Lewis, class of 1942, a *Times* foreign-affairs columnist;

as was a black candidate, Robert Maynard, who had headed the summer minority program.[2]

But as early as October, word was spreading that a fix was in. One candidate had presented himself directly to President McGill and was the whispered choice. Osborn Elliott ran counter to most of Kimball's specifications. He had had no contact with journalism schools, and had already had a fulfilling career at *Time* and *Newsweek* (for which he was later elected to the American Society of Magazine Editors hall of fame); he was working on a memoir. He had left *Newsweek* four years before—fired (or perhaps honorably discharged), as he wrote, by the head of the Washington Post Company, Katharine Graham herself—and had been serving as a dollar-a-year deputy mayor in New York City. He was marginally older than any of the three predecessor deans when they took office, yet, at fifty-four, was by no means at retirement age. He had volunteered himself for the deanship.[3]

Reports that Elliott was the choice circulated at the school through the fall. Eventually, the rumor leaked into the city's newspapers when the *Post* gossip page reported that three candidates were in contention—Elliott, Curtis, and Hodding Carter III, then press officer for the secretary of state. Baker remarked, echoing the school's enduring scorn for the rest of journalism education: "We did interview a few academic types, but they didn't impress us."[4]

Three days later, the story of Elliott's selection appeared in the *Times*, although Columbia had not yet taken any official action. President McGill declined to discuss the appointment, saying he had not taken it up with the faculty or the trustees. Indeed, McGill neglected to give the school any formal notification at all, and Michael I. Sovern, the provost, got around to it a month after the fact. Elliott, however, readily confirmed that he had accepted the job and had a commitment from McGill of additional financing, "well into six figures" (one published figure was a mere $150,000), to attract new faculty.[5]

The head of the school of journalism at the University of Wisconsin joshed an acquaintance at Columbia about the appointment: "I see by the Times that you have a new Dean. At least, it appears you have a new Dean. I trust you don't appoint deans before the faculty can vote on them." He was on the mark: McGill had made certain that there would be no negative faculty polls on this candidate.[6]

Before he left, Abel had a last exchange with Mencher, who had come to be a severe critic and adversary, over raises for the faculty: "Thanks to the figures Chris [Trump] and I made available the other day, you now understand, I believe, that the Dean of this School has not had an easy time paying the bills. I continue to hope that Oz Elliott will find the resources to be more generous with the whole of the faculty than it has been possible for me to be in a terribly trying period, which spanned a couple of recessions. I do not ask, or expect, gratitude from my colleagues. But a modicum of fairness in assessing the facts would be most welcome." Abel departed in the middle of the spring semester; his thank-you note to the faculty for his send-off was written from the West Coast.[7]

Elliott proposed to give the school a new and different kind of visibility in New York. He described his family as being "of New York's four hundred, or perhaps four hundred and fifty"—sufficient in any case to warrant reasonably frequent appearances in the *Times*'s society pages. Moreover, he evidently knew everybody who counted in journalism, politics, and the arts. One of his first steps was to create a "Dean's List" of sixty members of the New York establishment who had promised him that they would lecture or participate in seminars. About half came from the media, and the rest ranged from David Rockefeller, chairman of the Chase Manhattan Bank, to the civil rights leader Bayard Rustin. It was a new, gaudier version of the school's use of New York as its laboratory.[8]

But when he checked in for his first full year at Columbia, Elliott faced the same realities that Abel had found so intractable. At the time of his appointment, McGill had sent Elliott a letter expressing his concern about the school and its curriculum. "Neither seems to us to put sufficient stress on the broad base of knowledge and skill necessary for effective reporting on the complex issues confronting America today. The School of Journalism in our view is relatively isolated from the rest of this intellectual community." McGill further remarked to an interviewer that he feared that the school was becoming "a glorified employment agency."[9]

Elliott also faced the reality of an aging faculty. William A. Wood, the first professor hired by the school to give full-time instruction in broadcasting, had retired in 1978. In the spring of 1979, Fred Friendly, after thirteen years as Murrow Professor, was given emeritus status. He was not gone, of course; he resumed teaching under a special arrangement a year later and, in 1982, moved his new series of televised seminars on the media and society to a base at the school. But he no longer ran the broadcast side of the curriculum.[10]

Another elder, Norman Isaacs, was also moving on. He had served ten years at the school in a position called "editor-in-residence," which involved not only teaching but, as it turned out, a fair amount of administration. Just as he had fostered the practice of internal criticism at newspapers—the ombudsman movement—he also became an advocate of the National News

Council, brought into existence in 1974 as a nongovernmental tribunal to judge complaints against the press. In 1977, he became chairman of the News Council, and in 1980, at the age of seventy-one, he left the school and remained with the council.[11]

By this time, Baker was by far the most senior in service on the faculty—his work for the school having begun in Chungking more than thirty-five years before. After he returned from a sabbatical in Malaysia early in 1976, he succeeded John Hohenberg as administrator of the Pulitzer Prizes. It was a task he performed smoothly, facing up to the realities of fund-raising that Hohenberg had avoided. He persuaded the reluctant Joseph Pulitzer, Jr. that it was time to augment his grandfather's endowment. Publishers of newspapers that coveted prizes gave generously—all but the *Times*, which may have calculated that it needed no such enhancement.[12]

Just as important, he dispelled the tone of mystification and exclusion with which Hohenberg had managed the prizes. He broadened the base of jurors, even smuggling in two members of the school faculty, which had been absent from the prize process for decades. He told a student interviewer in 1979 that he abhorred the secrecy surrounding the awards and favored publication of the jurors' recommendations, traditionally kept secret. That first step was reached in the fall of 1979, when the board voted to reveal the two runner-up exhibits in each category. Moreover, the board imposed a term limit of nine years on its members and agreed to add three members who were not journalists.[13]

Even when he took the Pulitzer Prize position, Baker was dealing with uncertain health. In the spring of 1976, he had an episode involving blockage of circulation to the brain. His doctor had told him to quit smoking, he announced to lunch companions, meanwhile still playing the rebellious Methodist preacher's son by puffing on a cigarette and having a martini. In 1981, he contracted a troublesome infection, and a lung blemish, requiring surgery, was discovered in the follow-up. So deeply ingrained were faculty antagonisms by this time that he confessed that he was taken aback at the kindness of colleagues with whom he had quarreled.[14]

Already knowing that he would have to resign, Baker suffered a severe blow on the way out. The feature-story jury, which included Judith Crist from the school's faculty, recommended Teresa Carpenter of the *Village Voice* for the prize. But the advisory board set the recommendation aside in favor of a heart-tugging feature about a child drug addict by Janet Cooke of the *Washington Post*. Crist was furious and confronted Baker, complaining of the "naivete and phoniness" of the Cooke story. Within a day, the winning story was revealed as a fiction, and the prize was returned. Baker took the heat with outward calm, and even appeared before a professional group in May, warning that the board had to take the hard work of the juries more seriously.[15]

Baker had already been given a farewell party in the World Room, and ten days later the trustees approved his appointment as a professor emeritus. He left with his wife, Marjorie Colman Baker, for their house on the St. Lawrence River. He returned to New York and died at home on September 3, 1981, at the age of sixty-eight.[16]

With Baker's death the last active tie to the Ackerman years was severed. Beyond that, Baker had been the keeper of more than forty years of tradition at the school—not only in being the school's first historian but also in a wide-ranging, even intimate sense of familiarity with the school's community—students and teachers present and past, where they were and what had become of them, and sometimes how they had sinned. Moreover, he was regarded as the school's guardian of reason and morals against the forces of journalism rampant.

Yet he was a lost hope—especially the hope, perhaps embodied in his initial appointment, that he would become the leader of the school in fact. At some point, he tacitly rejected that role. Dean Barrett may have glimpsed the inner Baker when he responded to a letter from the trustees of Baker's alma mater, Cornell College in Iowa, asking about Baker's qualifications for president. After the conventional praise, Barrett wrote: "I am by no means sure that Dick's own desires and temperament would make him particularly inclined toward the ceremonial and greeting functions, the fund raising, and the administrative chores that go with any college presidency." Nor with a deanship.[17]

With these losses, Elliott was facing a faculty of two basic components. The first comprised the formidable holdovers from the Barrett years, Melvin Mencher and Penn Kimball, as well as the more suave but equally independent Frederick T. C. Yu and Donald Shanor, both holding named professorships—Shanor the Cabot Professor, a chair initially held by Deans Ackerman, Barrett, and Abel; Yu the CBS Professor of International Journalism, the result of an endowment provided by the network in 1976. In addition, Kenneth Goldstein, the science specialist, was one of the three faculty members (with Shanor and Luther Jackson) who had won tenure during the Abel decade.

The second tier comprised six professors hired in the Abel years and now awaiting the tenure process. Elliott was far from ready for what he faced in tenure politics. He recalled that a law professor presiding over an ad hoc committee—the campuswide group convened to consider a tenure case—demanded of him, "Just why do we have a school of journalism?" He received a memorandum from Low Library warning him that a tenure application had to be accompanied by a vote of the school's tenured faculty and that, moreover, the ad hoc committee would make "mincemeat" of the application then under consideration—Phyllis Garland's—without better documentation. Garland ultimately got through.[18]

But Donald H. Johnston, hired in 1976, was less fortunate. Even the skills of Baker, one of whose last services was to try to shepherd Johnston through his ad hoc committee, failed in this instance. Johnston's professional and teaching credentials—a quarter century of news experience—were as good as or better than the school's norm. But Low Library had now introduced a poison pill into the process: a comparison of the candidate with a list of nationally known practitioners, all at much higher salary levels than Johnston could hope to earn at Columbia. But the underlying problem, perhaps, was the perception in Low that tenuring even a highly regarded practitioner-teacher such as Johnston would not help correct the school's intellectual shortcomings. Eventually, only one other of the six won tenure—Barbara Belford, class of 1962, an industrious magazine editor and freelance writer.[19]

The remaining member of the untenured group was Carolyn Lewis, hired from Boston University in 1978; she served in 1979 on President Carter's commission to investigate the Three Mile Island nuclear accident. At the school, she soon established herself as a tough teacher, and this reputation may have led Elliott to wish to use her as a buffer against the troublesome faculty by naming her as associate dean. She continued with her aggressive style. Within a year, antagonism between her and Christopher Trump, the popular and durable assistant dean and student counselor (recipient of a special alumni award in 1979), led to Trump's departure. She got into a shouting match with Friendly over another instructor's effort to keep him from showing a famous documentary he had made with Edward R. Murrow. She quoted him: "So Johnny Schultz shows 'Harvest of Shame.' Dammit, I AM 'Harvest of Shame.'"[20]

In contrast with Lewis's take-charge style, Elliott developed a reputation for hands-off administration. He conceded in later years that he had never developed a collegial relationship with the faculty. By 1983, the situation was ripe for crisis.

CHAPTER 32

# *CJR*—From New Management to Old

As of fall 1969, the eight-year-old *Columbia Journalism Review* was under new management. Edward Barrett, founding editorial chairman, stepped down when he resigned the deanship in 1968. The first editor, James Boylan, left in mid-1969. His replacement was Alfred Balk, a graduate of Northwestern's Medill School of Journalism, with television, newspaper, and magazine experience. He moved up from acting editor to editor in 1971, at the same time increasing the frequency of the *Review* from four to six times a year. He also collaborated with Boylan in editing an anthology, *Our Troubled Press*, commemorating the *Review*'s first ten years.[1]

Balk put out a *Review* that was grittier, a bit bolder, and denser with prose. In 1971, he produced an ambitious special issue on the Pentagon Papers crisis. With local journalism reviews springing up across the country—the first being the *Chicago Journalism Review*, founded after the turbulent Democratic convention of 1968—Balk publicized them by reprinting their best stories and published as an insert an entire issue of the *Atlanta Journalism Review*, an otherwise stillborn project.[2]

Characteristic of the *Review*'s new toughness was an unsparing examination by Richard Reeves of the closing of New Jersey's leading newspaper, the Newark *Evening News*. The last publisher, Richard Scudder, immediately declared that he had been libeled and filed suit. The case was not resolved until 1977, after Balk had left the editorship, with a settlement requiring the *Review* to publish a dictated statement that it had not intended "to impugn Mr. Scudder's personal integrity" and otherwise to say nothing about the case. No money changed hands, except from clients to lawyers.[3]

Within the school, attitudes toward the *Review* became chilly. Although Elie Abel wrote a generous introduction for the *Review*'s tenth-anniversary anthology, he was otherwise reserved, sometimes unfriendly, toward the magazine. Unlike Barrett, he never wrote for it.[4]

Balk and the faculty advisory board irritated each other. He called on such senior faculty as Fred Friendly and Norman Isaacs for articles, but otherwise sought to distance the *Review* from the school. Ultimately, he proposed that the magazine should sever its Columbia ties altogether. Balk may have been looking over his shoulder at his competition, the New York journalism review *[MORE]*, named for the old "continued" notice typed at the bottom of a page of copy. The new review boasted of being the voice of *real* journalists, and scoffed at its Columbia counterpart as soft, subsidized, and academic.[5]

A senior advisory group chewed on the possibility that the *Review* might maintain a diminished relationship with the school short of sponsorship, somewhat like that of *Public Opinion Quarterly*, an independent scholarly journal then temporarily based at the school. Friendly, speaking on behalf of the Ford Foundation, suggested that the *Review*, with a large infusion of money, might outgrow the school to become a national magazine, a kind of specialized *Atlantic Monthly*.[6]

Before any major expansion could take place, Balk decided to leave, and there was a wide-ranging if informal search for a new editor. It settled on Kenneth M. Pierce, thirty-two years old, one of the pioneers at the *Chicago Journalism Review* and more recently a senior editor of the *Saturday Review* during the disastrous effort to turn that magazine into a big-circulation moneymaker.[7]

On his arrival in mid-1973, Pierce at first kept the *Review* on a familiar track. Well-known bylines—Ben Bagdikian, now listed on the masthead as national correspondent—continued to appear. Stuart Loory contributed a pioneering article on the CIA's efforts to use the press as an intelligence tool, and Roger Morris, who became a regular contributor, fomented a major flap with the *Times* by charging that the newspaper had killed a story on the

Cambodian incursion of 1970 at the request of Henry A. Kissinger. Verdict: not proved.[8]

Like Balk, Pierce wanted to expand the *Review*. Working with a new "publishing director," Harry W. Hochman, he floated a development plan with five major points: tripling the circulation, increasing frequency to ten a year, expanding the contributor base beyond journalists, accepting "ethical" advertising, and creating regional citizens' panels to evaluate communications issues. The funding request was for $993,000 over three years; the Ford Foundation provided $500,000 of that amount.[9]

Pierce began at once to lobby for one key commitment in his proposal—that, for the first time, the *Review* would carry advertising. There was scattered opposition in the faculty, and Edward W. Barrett, in his role as an adviser, doubted that advertising would prove profitable. But in the January–February 1975 issue, the policy of accepting "a limited amount of advertising" was announced, and seven pages of ads appeared. The *Review*'s first advertising director, George C. Wright, made his appearance on the masthead.[10]

Meanwhile, a distinct cloud had appeared on Pierce's horizon. Dean Abel increasingly consulted his predecessor, Barrett, who now worked at the Ford-funded Academy for Educational Development. Barrett, still protective of the magazine, was eager to intervene. Eventually, at Abel's request, he took the title of publisher, returning to the top of the masthead in the May–June 1975 issue. Barrett had already urged reductions in what he believed were unwise expenditures of the Ford grant on circulation promotion. Ultimately, he sounded the alarm that the *Review*, facing annual deficits in six figures, might have to close unless there were further severe cutbacks.[11]

Barrett also continually criticized Pierce's editorial approach, which he regarded as focused less on monitoring press performance than on developing promotable articles. Pierce fought back strongly, contending that during his editorship the *Review* had not "published a single piece that does not meet the editorial criteria followed during the Review's first ten years." Barrett merely bristled and escalated the confrontation. Barrett had long since voiced privately his determination to remove Pierce, a decision that he and Abel reached in mid-March 1976.[12]

The remaining part of Barrett's plan was to reinstall the first editor, Boylan, who found the prospect embarrassing because he had been serving as an adviser to Pierce. But once it became apparent that Pierce would be forced out in any case, Boylan agreed to serve for the time being—a term that eventually stretched to three years. As of summer 1976, the *Review* was under its old management, with Barrett as publisher and Boylan as editor.[13]

Boylan found the *Review* changed from the vest-pocket operation he had left in 1969. Pierce had hired the *Review*'s first true staff. He had dismissed the *Review*'s freelance art director of twelve years' standing, Burton Wenk, in favor of an in-house successor, Christian von Rosenvinge, a design autocrat who butted heads with five successive editors. Jon Swan, a poet who had started as a *New Yorker* apprentice, brought sympathy and skill to *Review* editing for nearly twenty years. Gloria Cooper, who rose to the position of managing editor, became the *Review*'s longest-serving staffer, having logged twenty-eight years by 2002. Robert Smith was managing editor.[14]

Before the air was let out of his balloon, Pierce substantially improved the *Review*'s financial position. After his departure, advertising continued to expand, partly through the magazine's participation in the Leadership Network group of opinion magazines, to a maximum of forty-five pages in a ninety-six-page issue. Pierce's strenuous circulation promotion meanwhile bequeathed a paid circulation that crested at 38,000, an increase of more than 150 percent in three years.[15]

Barrett soon found that he had not entirely restored the *ancien régime*. He and Boylan had a serious fight over the merits of an apparently ghost-written article by Richard Salant, president of CBS News. Barrett demanded that the article appear, and it did, but publisher-editor relations were frayed. Later, Melvin Mencher, as a faculty adviser, proposed a ban on cigarette advertising in the *Review*. The effort ran squarely athwart Barrett's position—that as long as tobacco was a legally sold product it could be advertised. But he went through the motions of soliciting the opinions of both alumni and faculty committees, which split the verdict. Ultimately, Barrett reaffirmed the original acceptance policy on his comment page.[16]

Beyond such disputes was Barrett's unease about the tone of the *Review*, and his fear that it appeared not only critical but too negative or even leftist. He eventually complained to the editor that the magazine might be "inadvertently leaning a bit to one side of the political spectrum."[17]

In the larger world, of course, the *Review* more often had to deal with impressions that it was stodgy and establishmentarian. Such impressions were reinforced in mid-1978 when Barrett agreed to acquire the assets of *[MORE]*, which, after five lively years, had passed out of the hands of the founders to magazine doctors. The *Review* received little in tangible assets beyond unfulfilled subscriptions and unused manuscripts. But the publicity fallout was negative. Anthony Lukas of the *Times*, who had been associated with *[MORE]*, called the transaction "the ultimate obscenity." Commenting after the acquisition, a *Boston Globe* columnist alleged that the *Review*, with ads that made it "a billboard for special interests," was editorially "a fustian compendium of abstract issues of less than riveting attention to the working journalist."[18]

The impression of stuffiness was enhanced by the arrangement, made in 1977, to print the decisions of the National News Council. Its cases were shaped along quasi-judicial lines, with members concurring, dissenting, or abstaining, in full or in part. As it happened, by 1977 the Council was headed by a journalism faculty member, Norman E. Isaacs, and the liaison was close, if sometimes tense. The *Review*'s editors reserved the right to comment on Council actions, and did so on occasion.[19]

The *[MORE]* acquisition gave the *Review* staff a new member: Robert Karl Manoff. With Boylan leaving in 1979, Manoff became the inside candidate in the search for a successor. Manoff held an urban affairs degree from the Massachusetts Institute of Technology and had worked in urban development, with brief experience in journalism. The other leading candidate was Spencer Klaw, a magazine instructor at the school whose record as an editor and journalist stretched back to 1940. Thanks in part to lobbying by the other editors, who were impressed with his energy, Manoff was named editor in March 1979, and the staff broke out champagne.[20]

Although Manoff had impressively projected a magazine of greater intellectual rigor and warmer relations with the school, there were soon murmurs that all was not well. Manoff's management was alienating the other editors; Barrett was alarmed that issues were not being published on time. Once completed, however, the issues were innovative, and more audacious than the old *CJR*. After a series of warnings about the publication schedule, Barrett again entered firing mode, and Manoff was dismissed in February 1980, after serving less than a year.[21]

He did not go quietly. Although there had been nothing overtly political about the action, Manoff asserted that disagreement over policies, not procedures, had led to his dismissal. He had at least a marginal case; Barrett had taken the unprecedented step of recording in his column his disagreement with four articles appearing in the same issue, Manoff's last. The press of the left found the discharge to be fresh meat; Alexander Cockburn in the *Village Voice* hyperbolically called the action "a fusillade in the generation of Cold War II." For weeks, Barrett was writing letters to editors claiming inaccuracies, and eventually got a firm apology in print from Adam Hochschild at *Mother Jones* magazine.[22]

Manoff heaped scorn on the staff as he left. He told the *Spectator*: "Newsroom democracy is not a gift. You earn it." Even so, he left behind one valuable recruit: Michael Massing, executive editor under Manoff, stayed for two years before moving on to become a founder of the Committee to Protect Journalists and, later, a MacArthur Fellow.[23]

Manoff's successor was Spencer Klaw, who forgave being passed over in the previous search. With his arrival, the magazine settled down to steady habits and democratic procedures. If the price turned out to be more sedate content, it was worth it in terms of ending a period of instability that had lasted most of a decade. Klaw obtained a letter from Barrett, with concurrence by Dean Elliott, that the editor "would make final decisions on each individual issue of the *Review*." Barrett subsequently peppered Klaw with hints that he still spotted leftist sentiments in the *Review*, but when he retired the new publisher, Elliott, an editor by trade, observed Klaw's independence scrupulously.[24]

Klaw was faced with a contentious incident early in his tenure. A complaint was filed with the National News Council about an article that had appeared during Manoff's editorship. When the Council upheld the complaint and concluded that the *Review* had departed from "sound journalistic standards," the decision was printed in the *Review*. But in mid-1981, the *Review* stopped printing the Council's reports. Isaacs claimed in his memoir that a 3–2 termination vote of the editors had been retaliatory. Klaw has said that the action came from another cause entirely—the probability that a News Council action in another case exposed the *Review* to a libel action. In any case, the magazine was freed of a tenant that the editors had considered a burden.[25]

Barrett's seven years as publisher ended with his retirement in 1982. They were by no means as happy as his tenure as dean, partly because he undertook the impossible task of shaping the *Review* to his liking by guiding the hands of its editors. The result was that the magazine had four editors in seven years, of whom two were fired. Nonetheless, there was no denying that his tenacity kept the *Review* in existence when faculty and administrative sentiment leaned toward closing it. In a signed editorial, Boylan noted that "it is to that very stubbornness—or, as I might put it in a eulogy, dedication—to which the *Review* owes its existence. The rest of us have come and gone, but Ed Barrett is the single individual who was there at the beginning and is still attending to the *Review*'s needs in 1982."[26]

# CHAPTER 33

## "Sour Apples"

FOR MOST OF its first seventy years of operation, the school of journalism enjoyed a kindly downtown press. The New York newspapers, especially the *Times*, willingly printed the school's news and pseudo-news— anniversaries, ceremonies, prizes, appointments, retirements. What a turn then to open the *Times* on March 20, 1983, to find the headline: "Columbia Journalism School's Future Dividing Administration and Faculty." The article appeared under the byline of Jonathan Friendly, media reporter for the *Times*, no relation to Fred Friendly.

Friendly strongly suggested in his story that even if journalism could be taught, Columbia was not doing it effectively. Most strikingly, he exposed faculty-administration tensions that had been simmering for thirteen years, all sides injudiciously letting everything hang out as if the reporter were their psychiatrist. Penn Kimball was quoted as declaring: "Nothing is going on in the school in terms of leadership." Melvin Mencher said: "Without the impetus and drive of a committed administration, you can't move ahead." The associate dean, Carolyn Lewis, said: "The faculty hate me." Lawrence Pinkham, who had been absent for a decade, was quoted as saying that the school was "intellectually stifling." On his own behalf, the reporter hinted that the faculty was mediocre, remarking that Dean Elliott was the only person at the school who arrived as a well-known journalist, and that faculty efforts to reform or extend the curriculum were at an impasse. Further, the story implied the ambiguity of the faculty position—the desire to lead coupled with the desire to be led.

For his part, Elliott remarked that he had to put up with "two or three sour apples" because they were tenured. The dean defended the advances under his administration—the elimination of the school's continuing deficit, increases in faculty salaries, the acquisition of Fred W. Friendly's seminars on the media and society, and a new ethics course taught by the emeritus Friendly himself.

Finally, the *Times* story quoted damning excerpts from the school's last accreditation visit, by the American Council on Education for Journalism, in 1981. On the widespread impression that the school served primarily as a route to a first job, the accrediting team commented: "The school simply cannot rely on the quality of its students to carry the success of the program." The program, it asserted, was "adrift." (One member of the panel affirmed at the time that even these remarks were considerably softened.)[1]

Although the circumstance could be no particular comfort, the story emerged during a period of reexamination of the worth of journalism schools, as the reputation of journalism itself declined after the ebullience of the Watergate years. The Association for Education in Journalism and Mass Communication undertook a two-year curriculum study mobilized by Everette E. Dennis, dean at the University of Oregon. The problems it examined were as old as journalism education—how to teach relevant substance with training in skills; how to earn respect in the university setting; how to match students with future employers, who often said they preferred pure liberal arts majors and paradoxically demanded schooling in the skills of journalism.[2]

The *Times* story about Columbia had only one apparent immediate consequence, the resignation of Carolyn Lewis, associate dean, after a majority of the faculty petitioned for her to leave. She told the Columbia *Spectator*, "I hand over the school to the faculty. I hope they can run it." Years later, Lewis avenged herself with a stinging article in the *Washington Monthly*, attacking the school as corrupt and lazy.[3]

The tarnish of the *Times* story remained, even as Elliott achieved several fund-raising successes. Saul and Janice Poliak, he a 1926 graduate and already a steady contributor to the school, gave three million dollars for a center to study First Amendment issues. The first result was the establishment of a James Madison visiting professorship, to which Anthony Lewis, the distinguished columnist for the *Times*, was appointed. The gift also helped to support a new Fred Friendly television seminar series on the Constitution.[4]

There was an apparently bigger coup in the spring of 1984, when the Gannett Foundation committed $15 million to Columbia for a center for advanced studies to be housed at the journalism school. It was made clear from the start, however, that the center was not to be part of the school. The school ceded 2,600 square feet on the ground floor. The center's staff, headed by Everette Dennis, and a dozen fellows moved into the comfortable new headquarters. The enterprise was reminiscent of the arrival of the American Press Institute forty years before—prime space given up to a tenant of dubious collegiality.[5]

In 1985, the school received a million dollars to establish the Delacorte Center for Magazine Journalism and, thereafter, two million for the establishment of a Delacorte professorship. The donor was George T. Delacorte, the publisher and philanthropist, whom Dean Barrett had cultivated years before. Now in his nineties, Delacorte had become a beloved figure in the city for such benefactions as the outdoor Delacorte Theatre in Central Park and the park's statue of Lewis Carroll's Alice.[6]

In the meantime, two of the leading "sour apples" on Elliott's tree had become widely known beyond the walls of the school. Melvin Mencher was recognized nationally as the author of a textbook, *News Reporting and Writing*, which to a great degree supplanted John Hohenberg's *The Professional Journalist*. Mencher filled his book with examples from the working lives of journalists, continually freshened as the book and its spin-offs went through eight editions by the end of the century. The text reflected his uncompromising demands in the classroom, which some students regarded as tough—others, as brutal. A poll of the Associated Press Managing Editors association named him one of the country's ten outstanding journalism teachers.[7]

Kimball attracted notice in 1983, when he published a book called *The File*. His career had been afflicted by curious near-misses. After World War II, he had applied to enter the Foreign Service but had not been appointed. In 1962, he was close enough to an appointment to the Federal Communications Commission that he was looking for an apartment in Washington; he was passed over. In 1978, he requested his State Department file under the Freedom of Information Act and was stunned to find that he had been denied his Foreign Service appointment in 1946 for security reasons, somehow relating to his involvement in newspaper union politics before the war. There was evidence of sporadic surveillance thereafter by the FBI and CIA. At the *Times*, an informant insisted, he was part of a Communist cell led by the Sunday editor, Lester Markel. The surveillance ultimately included his wife, Janet, who died not long before the book was published. In the memoir, Kimball was able to write: "There is a classical purity to the case against me in my file. It is 100 percent hearsay."[8]

Kimball became a press hero. Anthony Lewis portrayed him as "Citizen K.," a Kafkaesque victim. But Kimball did not play the role of victim well; those who had faced him in faculty meetings recognized the tenacity with which he sought to call the government to account. In 1984, he filed a suit for $10 million in libel damages and possession of his FBI and CIA files. A decade after he began the effort, he received a degree of satisfaction. His case was settled, without damages paid, when the government acknowledged that it had no information that either Penn or Janet Kimball had ever been disloyal to the United States.[9]

By this time, Kimball had retired at the age of sixty-nine, leaving only three members of the Barrett faculty cohort—Mencher, Fred Yu, and Donald Shanor. Kimball went on to finish his long-deferred Ph.D., remarried (Julie Ellis, class of 1975), adopted a child from China, and adjourned to Martha's Vineyard, where he continued to write and flourish past the end of the century. Meanwhile, Phill Davison, the sociologist who had tried to stimulate communication research at the school, retired in 1986.[10]

After the flap of 1983, there were fewer clashes; Mencher described faculty-dean relations as "quiescent." But in March 1986, Elliott abruptly announced his resignation. There had been no intimation of his plans beyond a press report that he had turned down an offer to become editor of *U.S. News & World Report*. He commented that talks with the owner, Mortimer B. Zuckerman, had "started his juices flowing," stimulating a desire to take on new projects—and, by implication, to give up old ones. He was not leaving the school, but staying on as the first Delacorte professor. He also remained publisher of the *Columbia Journalism Review*, for which he staged a gala twenty-fifth anniversary black-tie dinner in Low Library in November 1986.[11]

As a resignation, this one matched, in suddenness if not in drama, that of Dean Barrett. But the consequences were almost inevitably the same. In mid-1986, the school again had an acting dean and the prospect of another search, during which the school and its reputation would suffer.

In the wake of Elliott's departure, Fred Yu, who with Mencher was the senior faculty member, was named acting dean. Although he had labored faithfully for the school, he remained an anomaly: primarily a scholar and one of the handful of faculty members with a doctorate, he came from the school of international communication scholarship that had allied itself with the social sciences. Besides a major work, *Mass Persuasion in Communist China*, he wrote with Davison and Boylan a textbook not used at the school but at institutions that had communications departments.[12]

Yu developed as an administrative specialty long-term plans that would enhance the school's weight on campus and on the national scene. He worked in vain on a plan to add a second year to the degree program. With Davison, he proposed in the 1970s a "Center for Advanced Study of Public Communication." It had a skeletal existence, and was ultimately outflanked by the creation of the Gannett Center. In 1977, Yu and Davison sought to re-create a body like the Hutchins Commission on Freedom of the Press to be based at the school, but did not find support.[13]

As acting dean, Yu abruptly removed Donald Johnston, who had served as associate dean after Carolyn Lewis left. Johnston, hoping to stay on at the school, was shocked and told Yu that he was being "unfair and unjust." Kenneth Goldstein succeeded Johnston, but the position was his only until a new dean arrived. In the meantime, Johnston went on with a career of service to the school and the university. For years, he edited the *Alumni Journal*, and in 2002 was elected president of the alumni association, while working as director of the international media and communications program at Columbia's School of International and Public Affairs.[14]

It seemed fated that the school, without permanent leadership, would be under attack, as it was during the term of the previous acting dean, Baker, in 1969. This time a commission on the future of the university, created by President Michael I. Sovern, recommended that smaller schools—architecture, the arts, library services, and journalism—pool staff and resources. The administration assured the schools that the plan was for their own good, that schools combined would have a greater voice. With the other threatened deans, Yu condemned the proposal as "a very lousy idea." He said: "I think these recommendations reflect more of a passion—or lust—for organizational neatness than a concern for academic excellence."[15]

The school held a Diamond Jubilee Dinner on May 3, 1988, marking the completion of seventy-five years of operation. But it seemed a dampened celebration, with little of the flair and exuberance that Edward Barrett had brought to the fiftieth anniversary—no honorary degrees, no elaborate honors list, no tributes to the school's excellence. Worst, President Sovern, interviewed by the *Times* for an anniversary story, grumbled about the faculty's lack of research achievement and hinted that a purge of senior tenured professors was in the offing. Mencher responded: "We chose this faculty to train people to go out and practice daily journalism." And the acting dean commented, with perhaps dangerous pride: "Our school is different from 99.9 percent of the journalism schools in the United States."[16]

A month after the anniversary observance, the two-year search for a dean came to an end. The search committee had considered an array of more than a hundred candidates, but only two were given serious offers. The first was Philip S. Meyer, a senior professor at the University of North Carolina at Chapel Hill, and the author of a widely used book on polling and other statistical applications, *Precision Journalism*. But after a briefing from Fred Yu on the school's problems, he promptly withdrew his name, saying that he didn't want to come to a place "where the outcome is hard to predict."[17]

His withdrawal brought to the fore the name of James W. Carey, dean of the College of Communication at the University of Illinois, and a reigning scholar in the new wave of cultural interpretations of journalism. His acceptance would have added immediately to the school's national stature. He declined, believing that he would face steep odds if he came in as an administration choice dumped on an unwilling faculty.[18]

In one of the early news stories on the search, there appeared the name of Joan W. Konner, a member of the class of 1961, president of a television production company associated with Bill Moyers, and a Columbia trustee. Konner was the school's destiny, but it took the university a full year to figure that out.[19]

# CHAPTER 34

# Showdown

THE UNIVERSITY CAME AROUND to appointing Joan Konner dean on June 2, 1988. Like her predecessor Osborn Elliott, she arrived with a rewarding career behind her and trailing awards—Emmys, Peabodys, even the school's own DuPont. Although she lacked experience in journalism education, she knew Columbia, which was probably more important. Not only was she a graduate of the school and a recipient of an alumni award, but she had served as an alumni representative on the university board of trustees since 1978, the first graduate of the school to be elected to the board. (She left the position when she became dean.) She was the first woman, with the exceptions of Eleanor Carroll in the 1940s and Carolyn Lewis, to have a major hand in running the school. And she was the first dean in living memory to be openly welcomed by the faculty, because she ended a long interregnum.[1]

By the time Konner reported for work in the fall of 1988, the school had been under provisional leadership for nearly two and a half years, ever since Elliott announced his resignation in the spring of 1986. It had been dented, as it had during the 1968–1970 interval. Even the story announcing Konner's appointment said that the school's "reputation as the nation's finest has been questioned in recent years."[2]

The phrase was in part an unacknowledged reference to an article that had appeared earlier in 1988 in the *Gannett Center Journal*, published by the Gannett Center for Media Studies, housed in the school's building. In effect, the tenant had chosen to sink its teeth into the leg of the landlord. An article listing eleven "exemplary" journalism schools pointedly omitted Columbia. The writer, Jerrold K. Footlick, a *Newsweek* editor and a fellow at the center the previous year, deplored the school:

> The graduate school of journalism at Columbia is a place of lost opportunities. It should be one of the best schools in the country, but it isn't. As well-sited as it is, the school has relatively little influence on the profession—and none on its university. . . . Columbia's reputation is so strong that people who know only casually about journalism education still think of it as first-rate; people who pay serious attention, however, don't. The best thing about the school is its students—bright graduates of some of the nation's best colleges. To the extent that peer education counts—and it does count—Columbia ranks at the top.[3]

Everette E. Dennis, director of the Gannett Center, weighed in with a comment in the same issue of the journal. He asserted that the school's change to graduate education in 1935 had been a "bait-and-switch" scheme, merely transferring an undergraduate curriculum to the graduate level. Moreover, he added, the switch to graduate status had "unwittingly retarded the intellectual development of the field." He argued that in concentrating on the one-year training model, the school had abandoned any active role in developing new knowledge about journalism and communication, and had left relevant scholarship fragmented among other divisions on campus.[4]

Such opinions—which, whatever their degree of truth, seemed to go out of their way to slight the school—would probably not have been offered, or at least would have been answered at once, in the presence of a strong dean. After a faculty member complained that the Gannett article had caused "much distress and concern" among students, the new dean took up the complaint. Konner wrote to Dennis that the "exemplary" schools listed in his journal were using the article for publicity and recruitment across the country, and that the staff and fellows of the Gannett Center were openly scoffing at Columbia students.[5]

Konner believed that standing behind Dennis was the real source of the harassment, Al Neuharth. Gannett's overbearing chairman was just putting aside his corporate responsibilities, and had turned to wielding power as the head of the Gannett Foundation, in which role he set himself up as the reigning benefactor of journalism education. The school was a beneficiary to a degree, receiving grants in 1988 and 1989 to underwrite visiting professorships and new broadcast equipment.[6]

Neuharth was the author of an autobiography, *Confessions of an S.O.B.*, published in 1989, in which he not only repeatedly demonstrated the merit of the title but also shared his opinions of journalism schools, placing Columbia at the top of a list of most overrated. After an attack by Neuharth along the same lines before a Society of Professional Journalists gathering, Konner wrote to ask him to desist: "I'm here to try to lead an important institution into the future, and I would hope to be given a chance." Neuharth replied, "I recognize what you have inherited at Columbia," tersely wished her good luck, and resumed the attack before a meeting of journalism-school administrators. Konner was there, and challenged him on the floor.[7]

As these exchanges went on, Konner found that she was defending not only the school's reputation but possibly even its institutional independence. She received word from the provost that the Gannett Foundation was planning to establish at Columbia, in addition to the Media Studies Center, an "Institute of Global Communications" that would exclude the school. She protested that such a plan "would be a statement by the University with serious negative implications for the reputation and future of this School." She pointed to the Center for Media Studies as a horrible example: "It penalized the School—in income, and in space it sorely needs. . . . Now it appears there is a new Gannett effort to compete with the School and to use the Gannett Foundation's considerable wealth to overshadow and stunt the growth of our program." The university administration continued to hold its cards close.[8]

Konner saw the threat revived in 1993, when Columbia's contract with the Gannett Foundation—which now bore the grandiose name of Freedom Forum—was up for renegotiation. She stumbled on an alarming development. On June 30, 1992, President Michael Sovern had announced that the following year would be his last, and had let the provost, Jonathan Cole, know that he intended to renew the Gannett agreement, well ahead of its expiration, before he left. Cole told Konner.[9]

Considering the possibilities, Konner believed both her deanship and the school's future were at stake. She had long since come to consider the center a hostile beachhead for a larger entity that would absorb, displace, or super-sede the school if Columbia let Gannett's millions pour onto the campus. Af-ter feverish contemplation, she wrote a fourteen-page memorandum, ad-dressed not to "Mike" but to "President Sovern," presenting the case for the school and against the Neuharth imperium.

She started by noting, of course, that the school wanted to reclaim the space occupied by the Media Studies Center, but her major points of attack were against the ostentatious hostility displayed by the center (for example, it had boycotted the school's observance of the Bill of Rights bicentennial); the disproportionate influence of Freedom Forum money on journalism ed-ucation; and finally, the character of Al Neuharth, based on his own account of his conduct in his *Confessions.*

She voiced her worst fears in her peroration:

> I've said it before to you, and I say it again: Neuharth has made his repu-tation and his money as a master of corporate takeovers. What he is at-tempting at Columbia is no less than an academic takeover of the School. It's the way he operates. With no editorial oversight short of revoking the contract, the University is conspiring in that move, which I have come to believe was the long-range plan that stimulated the relationship with Co-lumbia at the outset—the takeover of the most distinguished School of Journalism in the country as well as a base in the media capital of the world, which Neuharth was never able to accomplish as a publisher. The Columbia Graduate School of Journalism is the only institution standing between Al Neuharth and his wish that he be recognized as the most im-portant force in journalism in this century.[10]

Cannily, she did not count on her fervor to turn Sovern against Neuharth. Sovern soon made it clear that he was a Gannett ally when he accepted a seat on the Media Studies Center board. Just two weeks before her letter to Sovern, George Rupp, president of Rice University, was named Sovern's suc-cessor. Konner promptly won a pledge from Rupp that he would support the journalism school—and he did. Oddly, once the issue was resolved, all par-ties fell silent; Konner did not even mention the crisis in the next issue of her periodic "Dear Alum" letters to graduates beyond saying that she welcomed Rupp's appointment.[11]

When Rupp arrived in the fall, Konner staged a downtown reception for him that was both a welcome and a reminder of the visibility in New York of the journalism school. The graduates on the guest list were among the school's most notable: Louis D. Boccardi, 1959, president and chief executive of the Associated Press; Joseph Lelyveld, 1960, managing editor of the *Times*; Richard Smith, 1970, editor in chief and president of *Newsweek*; Paul Friedman, 1967, executive vice president of ABC News; and Anthony Marro, 1968, editor and senior vice president of *Newsday*.[12]

In the spring of 1995, the Freedom Forum struck its tent at Columbia and departed. The announcement said that the Media Studies Center was moving to midtown to expand its program through an international consortium of universities, of which Columbia would be one. President Rupp said: "While we've greatly appreciated the Center's presence on the Columbia campus, we're also eager to enter into a new partnership in the international consortium of the world's leading universities in media studies."

Konner, with equal cool, said: "This is important for the School, a vote of confidence in the exciting programs we are developing and enlarging. We look forward to continued collaboration with the Freedom Forum, while this change will help relieve what has been a paralyzing lack of space for the School."

And Neuharth too was cool: "This expanded international role will allow us to work with Columbia and a small number of top universities around the world to study the media and their global role for the future."

Then the release listed celebrities among the 133 persons who had held fellowships at the center—none of whom, of course, had been permitted any contact with the school or its students.[13]

# CHAPTER 35

# To the Exits

WHILE SHE WAS KEEPING Gannett at bay, Konner went briskly about her main task, setting the school in order. She started with fresh paint, undertaking the first full-scale cleanup of the building since the fiftieth anniversary, a quarter-century before. But more than paint was needed; she surveyed the condition of the school with a sense of desperation. She wrote to a benefactor after a year: "I feel now I have just reached Ground Zero. That's how far behind we were at the outset of my tenure."[1]

Only months after she arrived, the school faced an accreditation visit from the Accrediting Council on Education for Journalism and Mass Communications. The accrediting team noted obvious shortcomings—the use of manual typewriters rather than computers, the obsolescence of the Friendly-era broadcast facility. But it noted as well the intractable problems—the clumsiness and occasional ineffectiveness of the school's system of faculty governance, and the uncertainty of support from the university.[2]

The dean was able to address some of the glaring problems promptly. Computerization began almost immediately, and with the aid of a grant from the John D. and Catherine T. MacArthur Foundation the broadcast curriculum was revised in anticipation of increasing student demand. Administrative positions—notably in alumni and development—were raised to a professional level. Konner established a board of visitors, designed to play the role that Joseph Pulitzer had envisioned for the original advisory board, and she was able to turn to it for moral and financial support. The board, headed by the chairman and chief executive officer of the Times Company, Arthur Ochs Sulzberger, was composed of executives and editors of a rank comparable to the membership of the Pulitzer board, and strengthened the school's visibility in the corporate media community.[3]

Konner inherited a very senior faculty, among them the last of the Barrett generation. Indeed, she had barely missed being taught by two of its members, Melvin Mencher and Fred Yu, when she had attended the school twenty-seven years before. The transition was symbolically foreshadowed in the death at the age of seventy-nine of Edward W. Barrett in October 1989, five years after he was waylaid by a stroke. There was warm praise for him from the incumbent dean and from two contemporaries. Fred Friendly said that Barrett had taught him how to be a professor. Norman Isaacs called him "one of the great pioneers in trying to lead American journalism into public accountability."[4]

Mencher retired in 1990, early (at the age of sixty-three) and at his own request. He proposed the terms of his own buyout; they were readily, even hastily, accepted. His retirement was greeted by a profile in the *Los Angeles Times* under the headline "Teacher or Tyrant?" Comments by former students were divided between those who found his teaching tough and valuable and those who found it tough and merely humiliating. Women in particular had found him difficult. Konner, the last dean whom Mencher was to bedevil, said coolly: "I think time marches on. Mel will be replaced by somebody very good."[5]

Next to go was Luther Jackson, after years of illness and travail. The National Association of Black Journalists honored him as one of the outstanding black journalists of the century for his work in Newark and Washington.[6]

Others followed in short order. Fred Yu became CBS Professor Emeritus of International Journalism in 1991. Donald Shanor retired in 1992, with praise from the dean: "You have been a steady and solid wheel on this lumbering, sometimes wobbling 20-ton truck." Delacorte Professor Osborn Elliott—who became a supporter and admirer of his successor as dean—left in 1994.[7]

There were other, untenured long-timers, with whom Konner was willing to play hardball. In one instance, a person with the rank of lecturer had been allowed years before to slip past the legal termination date for the non-tenured and had gained permanent employment. After the threat of a salary reduction, the lecturer came to terms and retired. An associate professor without tenure was rebuffed in his desire to continue as "clinical professor"—that is, one of a newly created category of permanent teachers who would not be candidates for tenure.[8]

The net results were dramatic. By 1996, there remained only three of the twenty-two full-time faculty members who had been on hand when Elliott left, the senior being Phyllis Garland, who had arrived in 1973. Meanwhile the full-time faculty expanded under Konner to twenty-nine, paid for in part by cutting back the number of adjunct teachers from almost sixty to thirty-four, with only five, led by the perennial Judith Crist and Bruce Porter, class of 1962, continuing from the Elliott era. The school, with its usual slow-paced academic succession cut short, was quickly swept clean and in effect made a fresh start.[9]

Fred Friendly was still on hand for a time, running his Media and Society seminars at the school and still teaching and lecturing. His productivity remained astounding. By 1994, he and his wife, Ruth, and their team had put together more than six hundred seminars, more than eighty of them on national television, the most notable being his sequences on constitutional issues. In addition, he had written three books dealing with the Constitution.[10]

But even he, ailing at the age of seventy-seven, eventually stepped down and left the seminars to his wife to carry on. When the school honored him on his second retirement, he recalled in a letter to the dean: "I well remember Journalism Day. Twenty-eight years ago—it was 1964—Dean Barrett and the faculty presented the second annual Journalism Award to me. I was an executive producer at CBS and I never dreamed that I would be joining this distinguished faculty in 1966. Now in 1992, twenty-five years since my first journalism class graduated, here I am again being honored with your generous citation. It has a special meaning for Ruth and me."[11]

The last two retirees left in 1996. Kenneth Goldstein, who had initially come to the school as a fellow in the Advanced Science Writing Program in 1966, had taught at the school since 1969, except for an interval as associate dean. Barbara Belford, class of 1962 and the second woman (after Phyllis Garland) to win tenure at the school, also retired. In the meantime, the tenure process deprived the school of an admired and independent teacher, Karen Rothmyer, a gritty investigative reporter and a regular contributor to the *Columbia Journalism Review*. Later, she became managing editor of *The Nation*.[12]

Among the newer faculty, two stood out. Stephen D. Isaacs, son of Norman Isaacs, came to the school in 1988 as a Gannett-supported visiting professor, and remained. He had broad experience in newspapers and television, his longest association being seventeen years with the *Washington Post*. Konner drafted him as an associate dean, and he served as acting dean when she went on leave. At the same time, he became the cochair and steward of the school's Center for New Media.[13]

The other major addition was James W. Carey, who had declined the deanship that Konner now held. He stepped into the slot previously held by Fred Yu, who left as the highest paid member of the faculty. With Carey, for the first time, a mature figure at the center of the academic and scholarly side of journalism and communication education came to Columbia. Most recently, he had served as dean at the University of Illinois College of Communication and as a member of the boards of a plethora of scholarly publications and associations. Unlike many communication scholars, he was not haughty about journalism or about being in a journalism school, and decided to stay on permanently after a year as a visitor.[14]

Carey's first major effort was to offer what once would have been unthinkable—a doctoral program based at the school. He offered his proposal to the committee on instruction late in 1993. It was vintage Carey—literate, eloquent, and more than a little crafty. He took pains to assure the faculty that he was not wrenching the school in a new direction, but stood squarely in the Pulitzer tradition of emphasizing the practice of journalism above all. The details were simple enough: candidates would complete four substantive courses that were also required of master's candidates; a series of courses in other departments; the law school's sequence in constitutional and media law; courses concentrating on the politics, history, language, and literature of a given region; and a dissertation centering on journalism, but not journalism as a business or a social science. The proposal was given unanimous approval and Carey began the long trek toward implementing it.[15]

There were other newcomers. David A. Klatell, with a background in television and teaching, came in 1990 to coordinate the broadcast curriculum, and became the first teacher to bear the title of "professor of professional practice"—that is, occupying a quasi-permanent, "clinical," nontenured position. The school also recruited Samuel G. Freedman, a former *Times* reporter and book journalist who continued to produce while becoming a demanding and respected teacher of writing.[16]

In 1991, Furio Colombo, an Italian journalist and businessman affiliated with Fiat, the Italian automobile manufacturer, arrived with a fully endowed chair worth $2 million. When he left, the school kept income from the money (and, ultimately, the principal) and used it to pay the old China hand and former managing editor of the *Times*, Seymour Topping, who took over administration of the Pulitzer Prizes following the death of Robert Christopher, who had run the prizes since 1981. And upon Spencer Klaw's retirement, Konner brought in the *Columbia Journalism Review*'s first woman editor, Suzanne Braun Levine, for sixteen years a top editor of *Ms.* magazine.[17]

There were further additions later in Konner's term: Sig Gissler, former editor of the *Milwaukee Journal*; E. R. Shipp, class of 1979, of the *Times* and the *Daily News*, and a 1996 Pulitzer Prize winner; Josh Mills, a financial editor at the *Times*; Ari Goldman, a former religion reporter at the *Times*; Lyn-Nell Hancock of the *Daily News* and *Newsweek*; and John Dinges, former editorial director at National Public Radio.[18]

Late in 1991, Konner demonstrated that she could not only fight adverse publicity but generate positive promotion with a flair not seen since Barrett's time. The occasion was the two hundredth anniversary of the ratification of the Bill of Rights, and the First Amendment in particular. Two related books were to be published—a compilation of essays on major free-press battles, titled *Essential Liberty*, and a transcript of the addresses and discussions delivered during what was called Freedom Week. The week centered on a dinner to honor the retired Supreme Court Justice William J. Brennan, Jr., author of much of the century's First Amendment jurisprudence of previous decades, but now too ill to attend.[19]

The moment that turned the arranged program into major news was the sudden appearance, before the diners in Low Library, of Salman Rushdie, the British writer who had been in hiding since 1989, when the Iranian Ayatollah Khomeini had decreed his death for supposed insults to the Muslim religion in his novel, *The Satanic Verses*. The ovation that greeted him was explosive. "Free speech is life itself," he said in a somber address. The applause as he left with armed guards was more subdued and respectful. For the school, the event was a publicity coup that reverberated long enough for President Sovern to recall it as he left office eighteen months later. Nothing else in Konner's tenure matched it for drama.[20]

# CHAPTER 36

## The Conglomerate

ALMOST AS AN ASIDE, in her "Dear Alum" letter for June 1995—just after the Freedom Forum Media Studies Center left for parts downtown—Dean Konner announced that for the first time in its history the school had taken possession of its entire building, top to bottom. The top was the attic, which was being redesigned, at the cost of much noise, dirt, and broken pipes, to accommodate the Delacorte Center for Magazine Journalism; the bottom remained the dank basement, subject to mold and floods. Gaining full custody had taken forty years from the time that Edward W. Barrett had come to a school of only sixty-five students, confined to three of seven floors, and had begun to look for elbow room. Now the building was packed full, and the place was no longer merely a school but a conglomerate humming with variegated activities, as reflected in a bulky catalog that dwarfed the tiny bulletins of the old days.[1]

The strategy that Dean Barrett set in motion had worked. He had wanted to strengthen the school through expansion, thus eventually crowding out all tenants. By 1996, more than two hundred and twenty students—including more than forty from abroad—were enrolled in the basic one-year master's program. The school had also made a dent in the lockstep curriculum by en-rolling "part-time" degree candidates—that is, students permitted to spread their courses over two years. Still others studied in mid-career programs strongly resembling the second year of outside study originally proposed by the faculty in 1935. There were four dual-degree programs—in law, business, international/public affairs, and earth and environmental sciences, estab-lished jointly with Columbia's Lamont-Doherty Earth Observatory. And there was James Carey's impending doctoral program.[2]

Nor was this all. By 1996, there were five fellowship programs sited at the school. The senior program was the Knight-Bagehot Fellowship in econom-ics. A certificate in international reporting had succeeded the old Advanced International Reporting Program. The Prudential Foundation was under-writing a program in children's issues, and the Reuter Foundation support-ed fellowships in medical journalism. Finally, a grant of $3.5 million from the Pew Charitable Trusts created a Columbia segment of the National Arts Journalism Program, for mid-career specialists. In 1997, Michael Janeway, a former editor-in-chief of the *Boston Globe* and dean at Northwestern's Medill journalism school, became director of the program.[3]

There were satellite entities, the most durable being Fred Friendly's Sem-inars on Media and Society, which continued productively after his retire-ment. And there were others:

The Delacorte Center was in charge of the school's magazine curriculum, which had grown in twenty years from a lowly stepchild to equality in the curriculum with the broadcast and newspaper branches. It was first headed by Carey Winfrey, class of 1967, who had diverse experience in magazines and other media; he was succeeded by Victor Navasky, longtime editor and publisher of *The Nation*.[4]

The Poliak Center for the Study of First Amendment Issues, created dur-ing Elliott's term, sponsored two visiting professorships. One, named for James Madison, was first held by Anthony Lewis of the *Times*, author of *Make No Law* (1991), the history of the landmark *Sullivan v. New York Times* libel decision. The other, named for Supreme Court Justice William J. Brennan, Jr., was held by Floyd Abrams, co-counsel for the *Times* in the Pentagon Pa-pers case. The most visible activity of the center was a long-running series of First Amendment breakfasts bringing together lawyers and journalists.[5]

The Center for New Media, a university facility started in 1994 with $5 mil-lion budgeted by the trustees and industry partnerships, set about to convert the school and the campus to the digital age. The center developed swiftly un-der the guidance of John V. Pavlik, a former officer at the Freedom Forum

Media Studies Center, and Josh Schroeter, class of 1991, with Stephen Isaacs and Michael Crow, vice provost, as cochairs. They were later joined by Steven S. Ross, class of 1970, Sreenath Sreenivasan, 1993, and Andrew Lih as director of technology. The center created digital broadcast laboratories and multimedia classrooms, developed a curriculum in new media, put the Pulitzer Prizes and *Columbia Journalism Review* online, and undertook surgery to reconfigure electronically a building that was erected when electric power was new.[6]

Then there was the accumulated awards machinery, which had made the school the greatest distributor of honors in a field overburdened with honors: the Pulitzers, first awarded in 1917; the Maria Moors Cabot prizes for inter-American understanding, dating from 1938; the National Magazine Awards, from 1965, in which the school played an administrative role; and the Alfred I. duPont–Columbia University Awards in broadcasting, which came to Columbia in 1969. As opposed to the simplicity that had always marked the Pulitzers, the duPonts had grown into a two-day event, with panel discussions and a national public television broadcast from Low Library. There were administratively minor awards as well—the Columbia Journalism Award, given to a wide variety of recipients (Mayor Robert F. Wagner got one in 1963 for helping to settle a newspaper strike); the Mike Berger, in honor of Meyer Berger of the *Times*, who died in 1959, for local human-interest reporting; the Paul Tobenkin, started in 1959 to honor a late *Herald Tribune* reporter, for reporting on intolerance. While the Pulitzers were administered separately, the duPonts and others—as well as, for a time, the alumni office—were run by Jonnet Abeles, class of 1967.[7]

For the most part, these subsidiaries hummed along from one year to the next. But one satellite was persistently dysfunctional, financially speaking. That was the *Columbia Journalism Review*. Since the 1970s, the magazine, in appearance and marketing methods, had sought to operate as a commercial periodical in a nonprofit environment. Although its editorial staff remained small, its expenses grew steadily, cracking the million-dollar mark in fiscal year 1991 and running up growing deficits.[8]

Suzanne Braun Levine, editor since 1989, made the magazine more challenging. She was handed an early crisis when Mary Williams Walsh, a *Wall Street Journal* reporter who had covered the guerrilla war against the Soviet Union in Afghanistan, offered to *CJR* a story that she said the *Journal* had rejected—that CBS News coverage of the war had been tainted by employing anti-Soviet propagandists and broadcasting staged film. Inevitably, after *CJR*'s checker called CBS, both the editor and the dean heard complaints. With the editor's permission, the article was shown to Professor Emeritus

Fred Friendly, and the magazine followed his recommendation that it appear, with changes, and it did. The writer, Walsh, then complained to the *Progressive* magazine, which roughed up *CJR* for softening her article and accused the dean of trying to suppress it. The dean responded: "A fact: I did not try to kill the article. As publisher, I could have succeeded if I tried." Nonetheless, the incident demonstrated that the guarantees of independence provided to Spencer Klaw by Dean Elliott were no longer in place.[9]

The more enduring crisis was financial. The recession in the last year of the first President Bush's term all but wiped out *CJR*'s advertising, although its circulation stayed at more than 30,000. The estimated deficit for the fiscal year ending June 30, 1993, came to more than $360,000; in other words, before infusions from other school resources such as Cabot funds, *CJR* was paying only 70 percent of its own way. In August 1993, Dean Konner told the Columbia luncheon at the annual journalism/communication teachers convention that she was contemplating closing the magazine.[10]

That did not happen. Instead, she assembled a group of media executives to create business and editorial plans. The business plan projected making the magazine self-supporting in five years, mostly by substantial increases in advertising. The editorial plan, developed by another board of experts, revived the old dream of finding a general readership outside journalism, of making "a major magazine out of a modest magazine—big in scope and big in audience."[11]

To push these plans forward, Konner tapped Roger Rosenblatt, best known as a magazine essayist. He was given the titles of director of the Delacorte Center for Magazine Journalism and editor-in-chief of the *Review*, thus placing him on the masthead above Levine. With Rosenblatt's arrival, the committee that had developed the new editorial plan appeared on the masthead as the editorial advisory board, thus finally displacing the faculty names that had been almost the last token of a connection between the *Review* and the rest of the school. (Eventually the board included one faculty member, James Carey.) The new board included no one ever previously associated with the *Review*, and only one alumnus of the school, Philip S. Balboni, 1971, creator of the innovative New England News Channel.[12]

Rosenblatt had a brief term. He developed a promotional campaign using a curious T-shirt slogan: "The presses can run but they can't HIDE." He and Konner won help from foundations, many associated with media organizations—notably the *Times*—but that effort eventually stalled. He did not seem comfortable in the job; at a promotional breakfast he wisecracked that the *Review* was not as dull as its reputation. The *New York Observer* got after him for freelancing at magazines that *CJR* was supposed to criticize. He left promptly at the end of an eighteen-month agreement, descended the masthead to become chair of the board of editorial advisers, and disappeared in mid-1996.[13]

In the meantime, Konner continued to focus her attention on the *Review*. As publisher, she revived Barrett's custom of reserving a page in each issue for herself; she customarily used it to publish something not overtly promotional but related to the school. When she announced in March 1996 that she would leave the deanship at the end of the year, she said she intended to remain as *CJR*'s publisher.[14]

In her last month as dean she engineered a change in editors. The relationship between Konner and Levine, it turned out, was a familiar story—an editor wanting to run the magazine as she pleased while fending off a strong-minded publisher/dean. There was an exchange of resignation civilities in December 1996, but Levine commented to a trade magazine: "We've struggled back and forth for eight years. I think journalism is about questions. I think she would say it's about answers. . . . I don't think that she has any understanding of the delicate balance of a magazine—the pacing, the personality." Konner responded that Levine should have quit long before if she disagreed so deeply. Alex Jones, a member of the *CJR* advisory board, summed it up: "I think she just wanted her own editor. It's her prerogative, and she took it."[15]

Konner's designee was Marshall Loeb, a veteran of forty years at Time Inc. and a former managing editor of *Money* and *Fortune* magazines. Loeb immediately bulked up the magazine and used editorial four-color pages and big feature packages to make the *Review* appear more vigorous. Despite the most strenuous efforts, its problems persisted. Circulation barely crept upward, and the deficits grew. *CJR* remained ill, waiting for still another doctor.[16]

CHAPTER 37

# "Deans' Row"

JOAN KONNER announced on March 6, 1996, less than a month after her sixty-fifth birthday, that she would leave the deanship within a year. She intended to remain, she said, as publisher of the *Columbia Journalism Review* and as a professor. The university's announcement printed a compendium of tributes from executives on the board of visitors—Arthur Ochs Sulzberger of the *Times*, Louis D. Boccardi of the Associated Press, Warren Phillips of the *Wall Street Journal*. Perhaps more telling, President Rupp and Provost Jonathan R. Cole affirmed that the school's status on campus was again high.[1]

The problem of finding a successor resembled that of 1968, when another vigorous dean, Edward W. Barrett, left his successor to play Truman after his F.D.R. The president named a search committee, one of its members being James Carey. As its deliberations proceeded, Carey, aided by strong faculty support, emerged as a candidate—as well he might have, considering his stature in the field and his experience at running the School of Communication at Illinois. Curiously, Carey's standing as a scholar worked against him in segments of the Columbia constituency; he became aware of opposition when the search committee heard from graduates urging the appointment of a practitioner.

Tom Goldstein became the competing candidate. Goldstein, of the class of 1969, had worked for the *Wall Street Journal* and the *Times*, and had put in two years as press secretary to New York mayor Edward I. Koch. Most recently, he was the dean of the graduate school at the University of California, Berkeley, one of the few programs that resembled Columbia's. According to Carey, the search committee forwarded his name and Carey's to President Rupp, and Rupp chose Goldstein; Carey was not pleased, viewing the choice as a major reversal and an error on the part of the university, but he decided to stay on.[2]

There was one notable case of sour grapes. One of the school's most widely known alumni, Dick Schaap, class of 1956—sports writer, connoisseur of celebrities, television commentator—listened to the proposition of Steve Conn (class of 1961) that he ought to make himself a candidate for dean. The university was showered with letters from his supporters ranging, as Schaap wrote in his memoir, from "Muhammad Ali to Gloria Steinem to Bill Bradley to Vernon Jordan, and also included the president emeritus of Cornell, the former mayor of New York City, a Minnesota Supreme Court justice, a couple of Pulitzer Prize winners, plus a sampling of my former employers and former students." He wanted, he said, "to have the opportunity to 'give back.'" Passed over, he characterized the new dean as "a former journalist who had become the press secretary to a politician." He added: "Maybe that spoke more eloquently to the state of journalism than I could have." Schaap died four years later.[3]

At the start, Goldstein seemed in danger of being overshadowed by his predecessor. His appointment was noted in a 300-word story in the *Times* on December 14, 1996. Two days later, the newspaper offered an admiring profile of Konner three times as long. She was credited with raising $40 million for the school; with hiring outstanding new faculty; with building new classrooms, electronics laboratories and studios; and with creating (Carey's) new doctoral program.[4]

But the story noted something more basic—that she had defended what now could be seen as the school's core task, preparing journalists for useful careers. Most other university campuses no longer had separate schools of journalism but, under various titles, schools of communication, gathered into a grab bag of scholarly and vocational programs. Public relations, advertising, and telecommunications had outstripped or superseded journalism. Even more than before, the school had become an anomaly, but at least the university now seemed willing for the time being to tolerate its eccentricity.[5]

Konner did not slip from view, despite having yielded the dean's office at the start of 1997 to Associate Dean Sandy Padwe, who served as acting dean. She presided over one of the last stages of the $12 million rehabilitation of the building, the dedication of the "New" World Room, still centered on the stained-glass Liberty window but outfitted with TV-friendly lighting and electronics and new curtains. Most of the burden was borne by the Pulitzer family.[6]

Coincidentally, the acting dean, in 1997, revived the school's long-neglected custom of honoring Joseph Pulitzer on his birthday, April 10. The occasion was Pulitzer's 150th anniversary. The mayor of New York issued a proclamation, and President Rupp declared the date Pulitzer Day at Columbia. A crowd shared a towering cake featuring the Statue of Liberty, and students recited excerpts from Pulitzer's 1904 essay on "The College of Journalism."[7]

The following fall, Konner, as dean emerita, dedicated the refinished vestibule or lobby, featuring a bank of computers mounted on a pair of wooden arcs, to which she and her family had contributed $275,000. Dean Goldstein proposed that it be named for her, and it became the "Dean Joan Konner Alumni/ae Hall." Not only was the space the first to be named for a dean of the school, but the additions somewhat overshadowed the already slight acknowledgment of Pulitzer at the site.[8]

Tom Goldstein, who compared his appointment to managing the Yankees, could not have been blamed if he had been fazed. Rather than having a "murderers' row" of batters he had a "deans' row"—a lineup of offices containing not only Carey and Konner but Michael Janeway, who had been the dean at Northwestern. But Goldstein was too resilient and experienced to flinch. Beyond his practitioner credentials, he held degrees in not only journalism but law; had written or edited three well-received books of press criticism; and was the first dean to arrive fresh from serving as the head of another major journalism school.[9]

As dean, he sought from the start to come to grip with problems that had continued, largely out of sight, during the Konner years. The school was stuffed full: the class of 1998 had a record number of 236 students, 62 percent of them women, chosen from a pool of more than a thousand applicants. Only one junior faculty member, Helen Benedict, had received tenure during Konner's term, so there was an expectant flock to be shepherded through the valley of the shadows. And there was always the *Columbia Journalism Review*.[10]

Just as Konner had faced an accreditation team almost on arrival, Goldstein dealt with a major appraisal of the school in his first year. This was not
an accreditation, but the university's own evaluation, conducted by a team of
outsiders named by the provost. When he discussed the project with the faculty, Goldstein felt that he faced a certain amount of self-satisfaction, but ultimately the long-range planning committee, chaired by David Klatell, produced a critical self-study report. The report, completed in April 1998, listed
fourteen objectives, including a reduction in enrollment, a program of faculty development, a more flexible schedule, greater diversity in the faculty and
student body, and greater collaboration with the rest of the campus and with
peer institutions.[11]

The self-study report was provided to the visiting team, which included
Philip Meyer of the University of North Carolina, who had rejected the
deanship in 1986; and representatives from the S. I. Newhouse School of
Public Communications at Syracuse; the Poynter Institute for Media Studies
in Florida; and the Annenberg School of Communication at the University
of Pennsylvania—none of which had a program resembling Columbia's.
Geneva Overholser, former *Washington Post* ombudsman, represented the
profession, thus excluding the New York media community.

The visitors issued a report that was useful for its detached perspectives.
It granted the school its mission—"to train topflight *journalists*"—and the
worth of the educational experience under a hands-on faculty. It praised the
school's array of fellowship and award programs, and the steady flow of
guest speakers and panelists. Then it reviewed the familiar circumstances of
the school's isolation from the rest of the campus and from other journalism
and communication schools, and added that the faculty showed a lack of curiosity about either. But the committee centered its attention on the jammed
schedule—"the curriculum needs air"—and focused in particular on the
hoariest component, "RW1."[12]

RW1, known more formally as "Advanced Reporting and Writing I," had
existed in more or less the same form since 1969 as the school's boot camp,
when it was put in place to replace the squad teaching in the old single newsroom. Now a student stayed with a single instructor or pair of instructors
through the whole semester. The visiting team believed it saw weaknesses—
variance in the quality of sections, lack of coordination and agreement on
goals, and a feeling by students interviewed that the course was a "mindless
frenzy." The visitors recommended redesign of RW1, expansion of the nine-
month curriculum, and ten other less drastic measures.[13]

The dean received the report calmly and equivocally, but it irked much of the faculty. Professor Stephen Isaacs defended RW1 as "a real-world experience," and others claimed that working lessons in news practices obviated the need for new courses, as recommended, in ethics and theory. Sandy Padwe and Samuel G. Freedman rejected the report as failing to understand the school's mission. James Carey, noting the report's chilly tone, said that it was not "politically astute." Beyond the details, what the report implied was that the rehabilitation of the school in the Konner era had emphasized add-ons and modernization without attacking the quasi-permanent dilemmas of teaching and curriculum.[14]

The school paused twice in the spring of 1998 for memorials. Fred Friendly died on April 3, at the age of eighty-two. The obituaries were followed with reflections on what was seen as the decline of television journalism; in *The New Yorker*, David Remnick wrote that Friendly "left behind a culture of broadcast news which, with rare exceptions, has given way to infotainment." There was a service at Riverdale Temple in the Bronx, and a campus memorial offered jointly by Columbia and CBS News. Mayor Giuliani of New York spoke, as did Supreme Court Justice Antonin Scalia, and former colleagues. Former Dean Konner said: "Fred's presence helped define the school. In fact, no one outside the school knew that Fred wasn't dean."[15]

There were a hundred anecdotes, at the memorial service and later, each trying to describe a combustible, obstinately demanding personality, unlike any other that had passed through the school. Friendly's first teaching assistant, Tom Bettag, who became executive producer of ABC News's *Nightline*, captured it well:

This man did not waste his breath nagging or niggling. This man bellowed, thundered, stormed: "That's unacceptable!" "Is the job too big for you?" "Can't anybody get it right?" "You've got to help me!" Fred was dyslexic. The scrawl he handed you for his next speech took hours to decipher. Fred was clumsy. Fred turned red with frustration at mistakes. Fred always won and not necessarily in the prettiest way. He defined a producer as someone "who wills things into existence." Fred willed so much into existence because he cared so much. He cared more deeply about more things than anyone I have ever known. In an age of cool, Fred was hot. In an age of detachment, Fred said, "What America doesn't know can kill it."[16]

Before Friendly died, a fund drive was started to endow a professorship in his name, and by midsummer 1998 most of the $1.5 million required had been received from many sources, corporate and individual. In 1999, Richard Wald, a Columbia College graduate who had worked at the *Herald Tribune*, NBC News (as president), and ABC News, became the first Fred W. Friendly Professor. In addition, CBS underwrote Friendly scholarships for students electing the broadcast concentration.[17]

A week after Fred Friendly's death, Norman Isaacs died, eighty-nine years old. There was less fuss over Isaacs, and the obituaries were shorter, but there were parallels nonetheless. Alfred Balk, former editor of the *Columbia Journalism Review*, who had worked with Isaacs in creating the National News Council, noted that neither Friendly nor Isaacs had had a university education, that each became a force for ethics in journalism (Isaacs created the first newspaper ombudsman in Louisville), and both had uncompromising, even obnoxious personalities. Isaacs was at the school only in the 1970s, a shorter stay than Friendly's, but his mantle, and his bluntness, were bequeathed to his son, Stephen, who came to the school in the late 1980s.[18]

Reflecting on his first year and the report of the team of visitors, Goldstein offered a redefinition of the school. He wrote that it had a "twin mission" deriving from Pulitzer's injunctions: "that of educating topflight journalists and that of serving as an independent critic and standard-setter for the field of journalism." But criticism, he observed, sometimes made possible donors reluctant. "We are at times obligated," he said, "to bite the hands we count on to feed us. That is the way it has been, that is the way it should be, and that is the way it will be."[19]

# CHAPTER 38

## Trying to Stretch the Year

BEFORE THE END of its first year, the Goldstein deanship moved beyond the Konner penumbra. Although both observed civilities, there was little affinity between them. Konner feared that her successor was jeopardizing her legacy; Goldstein felt on occasion that Konner still wanted to run the show. But he persisted in setting his own direction.

A confessed convert to strategic planning, late in 1998 he issued an ambitious charter humbly titled "Planning Document." It was drafted by Evan Cornog (a historian who had worked with Goldstein in the mayoral press office), whose position—associate dean for policy and development—emphasized a new importance attached to the planning function. The document was in part a response to the report of the visiting team, but went beyond that to attempt the difficult task of articulating the school's goals, which members of the faculty believed the visitors' team had misstated. The plan stated more than forty objectives, many of them easily agreed upon but of course difficult to reach, such as enhancing the quality of the faculty and the student body and improving financial support and placement services.

But other stated goals centered on long-recognized deficiencies, such as a lack of scholarly activity and contact with other journalism educators. The document also urged steps to link students and faculty to the intellectual resources of the university. But the key point, placed in a boldface box, was to "increase the flexibility of school programs"—in other words, to find ways to open up the old cast-iron Ackerman nine-month year.[1]

The boundaries of the Ackerman year had begun to blur at last. The Konner era had brought into existence a part-time degree program, spread over six semesters, and a mid-career master's program, emphasizing theory and use of transcampus resources. These steps, combined with the dual-degree programs in law, business, public/international affairs, and other fields, meant that one-year M.S. candidates were sharing classrooms with students on other tracks. Under Goldstein, the faculty enhanced the flexibility of the part-time program, permitting students to enter at several points during the year.[2]

The first step toward extending the year came in the fall of 1998, when broadcast students were called in four weeks early for technical instruction, to ease the extra burden they carried during the regular year. David Klatell, head of the faculty planning committee, said the change was like "the first section of the Berlin Wall coming down." In 1999, the faculty voted to preface the regular academic year with an additional month, August, starting in 2000.[3]

The chief aim was to loosen the ever more tightly packed curriculum, to permit the class to reach the end of the term, as one instructor put it, without "walking pneumonia." But incorporated in the concept as well was the idea proposed long before by Dean Edward Barrett, of an early opening as a means to give the inexperienced a running start. Secondarily, the school was able to add approximately $3,000 to tuition, adding to an already steep bill of nearly $24,000. Some students of course concluded that the additional month was instituted primarily to raise tuition, but the dean called the step "one of the most fundamental changes" since the change to graduate education in 1935. Fundamental or not, the change merely loosened the old Ackerman year; it did not break it open.[4]

As big a change in its way was the start, in the fall of 1998, of James Carey's Ph.D. program, so long in incubation. Carey was at pains to explain that the doctorate, and its allied master's degrees in communications and philosophy, would not impinge on the professional program; nor, as a multidepartmental program, would it create a turf war in the journalism school. Five candidates were to be admitted for each of the first three years; as of 2002, the school was on the verge of granting its first doctorate.[5]

Even before the planning document was completed, the dean was making progress in attaining his ambitious goal of endowed support for every tenured professorship. A million dollars from the Times Mirror Foundation of Los Angeles created a David Laventhol visiting professorship, honoring the former publisher of the *Los Angeles Times*, and former editor and publisher of *Newsday* of Long Island. Its first occupant was Les Payne of *Newsday*. A pledge of $1.5 million from the John S. and James L. Knight Foundation augmented its support of the Knight-Bagehot fellowship program with a Knight chair in business journalism. The chair was filled by Sylvia Nasar, an economics journalist, nationally known from her biography of the mathematician John Forbes Nash, *A Beautiful Mind*. The Hearst Foundation also underwrote a visiting professorship in new media.[6]

Two more were added later. In 2000, a professorship honoring Henry R. Luce—the media baron once regarded by liberal journalists as a prince of darkness—was established with $2.5 million in gifts from the Henry Luce Foundation and Time Warner Inc. It was the first endowed chair specifically attached to the deanship, and Goldstein became the first occupant. The dean noted that two members of the board of visitors with Time Warner affiliations—N. J. Nicholas, Jr., and Henry Muller—had provided major assistance. In 2001, Bloomberg L.P., the innovative news organization founded by New York's mayor-to-be, Michael Bloomberg, gave $1.5 million to the school for a chair emphasizing business journalism. As of the end of 2001, the school had seven named professorships supported by endowments, not counting the as yet unoccupied Bloomberg chair.[7]

With his experience at Berkeley, Goldstein was prepared to help qualified journalism teachers through the tenure maze at Columbia. His early successes were Samuel Freedman and Michael Shapiro, both in the magazine program, and both named teachers of the year by students, and he added four more before the end of his term, including the eminent media sociologist Todd Gitlin. Meanwhile, the number of adjunct faculty rebounded. The part-timers were no longer the good, gray gang from the *Times*, but were drawn from every type of news organization, including the digital. They were still led in seniority by Judith Crist, whose forty years of teaching were honored at an alumni meeting in 1998.[8]

Among other steps that the planning document proposed was one that was more difficult than it sounded: that all the affiliated programs—the centers, the prizes, the public forums, the publications—be integrated with the school's educational mission. In particular, prize programs, often with their own boards of judges and their own rules, tended to follow the Pulitzer Prizes in distancing themselves from the school.

Nonetheless, new prizes continued to be added to the already ample array. The Alfred Eisenstaedt Awards for Magazine Photography ("Eisies," for short) were named for the enduring photojournalist associated with *Life* magazine, which provided the money. Another was created to honor the memory of J. Anthony Lukas, who died by his own hand after finishing the monumental history of labor revolt in the West, *Big Trouble*. Administered jointly by the school and the Nieman Foundation at Harvard, the project included an award of $10,000 each for a completed nonfiction work and a completed history (named for the historian Mark Lynton) and a grant of $45,000 for a nonfiction work in progress.[9]

Later, there were more. One, sponsored by the Online News Association and backed by a variety of corporations, was the Online Journalism Awards, which gave this emerging spectral medium a place beside traditional print and broadcast media. The first winners for general excellence were *Salon*, an Internet magazine, and MSNBC.com, affiliated with the cable channel. In addition, awards in international journalism were established in memory of the Reuters correspondent Kurt Schork, killed in 2000 in Sierra Leone. The awards, and two scholarships honoring Schork, were set up with the assistance of Reuters.[10]

But much thornier than the prize programs was the planning document's specification: "*Columbia Journalism Review* should be integrated fully into the life of the school." This had not been a fact in perhaps thirty years, nor could it easily become a fact. Instead of supporting or strengthening the school's programs, the magazine continued to be an outsized burden, even with the substantial foundation help it received beyond its circulation and advertising revenue.

Moreover, under the direction of Konner as publisher and Marshall Loeb as editor, its circulation increased only slowly and painfully, reaching 28,000 by mid-1999. The staff was acutely conscious of competitive pressure from *Brill's Content*, a magazine about media that momentarily seemed to be fulfilling the dream of general circulation once projected for *CJR*. But at base the problem seemed to be less promotional than historical, given the magazine's failure to regain its circulation from peaks of the 1970s. With an accumulated operating deficit rising, the dean was urged by Low Library to develop a business plan that would at least assure that the magazine would not become an expensive permanent obligation of the university.[11]

Assisted by Cornog, Goldstein set about to put the magazine on solid ground. In December 1998, he convened four of the former editors and the current editor, and conferred with Suzanne Levine separately. David Laventhol was also there, and was clearly waiting in the wings. In April 1999, Goldstein announced that Laventhol would succeed Joan Konner as publisher when the two and a half years she had promised—in addition to the years she had served while also dean—expired on June 30. Marshall Loeb stepped down as editor, and Goldstein now had his own team in place.[12]

Even before Laventhol first appeared on the masthead in the July/August 1999 issue, he was at work on an overhaul, with a new format and new features. Curiously, the masthead now had no editor as such; the closest thing was Laventhol's added title of "editorial director." Looking to create an instant impression, he published a pseudo-survey titled "America's Best Newspapers" and then a roster of the ten "best" magazine editors. But that was the last of such rankings, and the magazine seemed gradually to settle down to work, especially after the senior editor, Michael Hoyt, whose column had added bite and humor to the magazine, was named executive editor a year later.[13]

In 2001, the *Review* reached its fortieth anniversary and was producing a big commemorative issue when the World Trade Center was attacked. The staff responded by adding a substantial section on coverage of the terrorism and the subsequent Afghanistan war. The result was an issue of 160 pages, the largest in the magazine's history, with a two-page spread devoted to each year since 1961. The effort was worthy of a much larger magazine—as were most issues. But there was no denying that *CJR* itself was still dwindling; the circulation reported in the anniversary issue was less than 23,000. It was clear, as Dean Goldstein pointed out, that the *Review* had survived because of its location—"inside a strong, well-regarded journalism school, part of a great university"—and because sometimes reluctant deans did what they needed to do to keep it going. Yet there was almost a memorial quality to the anniversary issue.[14]

A much overblown flap had taken place early in 2001. A little more than a month after the Supreme Court decided that Al Gore would not become president, the school announced that Gore would teach a course; he planned to teach at two other universities as well. The noncredit course was a hasty improvisation, pasted together in two days after a Gore contact called to signal Gore's willingness. The first class was set for February 6. Because Gore hinted that he would not meet the press beforehand, although this was his first coming-out since his opponent's inauguration, news organizations tried

to sign up students to report what went on in the classroom—whereupon a
school e-mail to registrants warned that the class was "off the record."

That did it. Already annoyed because they knew they would not be admitted to the classroom, reporters now alleged that the students in the class
were gagged. An indignant cluster of press, led by the *Post*'s Steve Dun-
leavy, barked questions at Gore as he entered the building. Afterward, they
had little trouble finding out from students what had happened. Two days
later, the dean tried to explain "off the record" as not gagging students but
merely barring the press from the classroom, and the press interpreted this as
a new policy, created under pressure; the dean correctly pointed out that no
student had been punished or reprimanded for speaking with reporters.
Floyd Abrams, the First Amendment professor, criticized the school, saying
it had fumbled in trying "to transform what is inevitably an event fraught
with public interest into one of purely private or academic interest."[15]

The school was berated for days afterward, but by the time Gore returned
for the next class, two weeks later, the excitement had died down and the New
York media had all but vanished. Gore brought in a batch of celebrity guests,
including Federal Reserve Chairman Alan Greenspan and the media baron
Rupert Murdoch. At the end of the course, Felicity Barringer of the *Times*
termed the episode "a public relations disaster." Goldstein commented: "We
took some lumps in February. We deserved some of them. We also learned a
painful lesson about how the press (or at least some in the press) work."[16]

During the Gore incident, the school was undergoing accreditation, for
the first time since 1995. The evaluation was one of the most enthusiastic the
school had ever received. The chief of the accrediting team, Doug Anderson
of Penn State, commented: "The strengths of the program are almost un-
imaginable." The team praised the faculty, adjuncts and guests, the curriculum, the administration, the outside financial support, the special programs
and prizes, the alumni, placement, and, not least, the student body, which it
described as "driven to be challenged." The negatives were comparatively
mild—bugs in the ten-month curriculum, inconsistencies in the basic RW1,
the need for more emphasis on professional values in the curriculum. On the
whole, it was a "straight A's" report card.[17]

In September 2001, the green class of 2002, having scarcely absorbed its
August basic training, received a baptism like no other. On September 11,
the rest of Columbia shut down, but students and faculty entered days of
wrenching, even dangerous work as they reported the city's fresh wound at
the World Trade Center. Sig Gissler said his students "stayed focused even
with tears streaming down their cheeks." The coordinator of RW1, Bruce

Porter, praised his novices for keeping their heads and remembering that they were reporters. Their work was posted on the school Web site, and read and seen around the world. But as the year progressed, the disaster hung over them; they were a class that was truly touched with fire.[18]

In an affectionate sketch of Goldstein early in 2002, Evan Cornog noted the dean's silent "Harpo Marx" mode. But the dean also had a mode drawn from the Groucho Marx who sang, "Hello, I must be going." As early as the start of his third year, there were hints that he intended to leave. But he stayed the four years he had promised, and at the end of the fourth he issued a statement saying that he would continue for a fifth, more or less. He had strong motivation for going; he had been a dean for most of the previous fourteen years, and his family was waiting for him in California. Discussing his plans with the alumni association's executive committee, he mentioned a further consideration: George Rupp, president since 1993 and a friend of the school, had announced that he was leaving as of mid-2002; Jonathan Cole, the provost with whom he had worked closely, was also scheduled to leave. The new president, Goldstein said, should have the opportunity to appoint the new dean. Rupp's successor, Lee C. Bollinger, president of the University of Michigan, a First Amendment specialist, was named in the fall of 2001.[19]

The search for a successor to Goldstein did not begin until he confirmed his plans in January 2002—that he was resigning effective June 30. It was the shortest term served by any dean of the school. His message to graduates listed nineteen of what he considered the major steps during his deanship, among them: the extension of the school year; the diminution of the over-sized class; the raising of $49 million in grants and gifts; a 64-percent increase in the school's endowment; the tripling of scholarship aid. In addition, the expansion of the school continued with the establishment of a research affiliate, the Project for Excellence in Journalism, in Washington; the transfer of the famed Radcliffe publishing course to the school; and the accommodation of the Columbia Scholastic Press Association under the school's roof.[20]

The new dean, when one was ultimately named, was to find a school that was continuing an expansion that had begun fourteen years before, resulting in an institution that was scarcely recognizable to those who had walked its halls in earlier years. It had reached the bounds of the form it had taken in 1935. Further change would inevitably mean alteration or dismantling of the old program.

CHAPTER 39

# "Clearly Insufficient"

WHEN TOM GOLDSTEIN'S TERM as dean of the school ended on June 30, 2002, there was no new dean in place. As of mid-June, as many as five candidates remained on the active list; before mid-July, it had been narrowed to two. One was Alex S. Jones, head of the Shorenstein Center on the Press, Politics, and Public Policy at Harvard; he had strong ties to the *Times*, where he had covered the press (and occasionally the school); with Susan Tifft, he had written *The Trust*, an epic history of the newspaper's owning family. The other candidate was James Fallows, national correspondent of *The Atlantic Monthly*, who had worked primarily as a magazine editor and journalist; his best-known book was a tough critique of American journalism, *Breaking the News* (1996).[1]

Their names were forwarded to Columbia's new president, Lee C. Bollinger, who had taken office on June 1. The expectation was that a new president and a new dean would work together. But a week or so later, Bollinger shocked the school and its constituencies by declining to appoint either Jones or Fallows. Even more surprising was the statement he issued. He praised the candidates just enough to remove the sting of a rebuff. He went on: "There is a yawning gulf between the various visions of what a modern school of journalism ought to be, and it is unwise for the University to expect a new dean to lead us out of this conflict and into a new direction. There ought to be a greater sense of shared understanding within the University of where we hope to go before we embrace a new dean." Bollinger clearly did not want to try to embrace a new dean who might resist his advances.[2]

To keep the school running while he shaped the future, he named David A. Klatell, associate dean for academic affairs, as the acting dean. The terms of previous acting deans were hardly an encouraging precedent. When Richard Baker served after Edward Barrett's abrupt departure in 1968, the school came under determined attack by the provost. After Osborn Elliott's resignation in 1986, Frederick Yu had to cope with a president's proposals that the school be merged into a larger administrative identity. In both instances, their successors had to deal with the damage. The lack of a sitting dean clearly reduced the school's negotiating power, yet during his year-plus in charge Klatell proved a robust defender of the school's interests.

What was Bollinger after? The sentence that stood out in his statement was: "To teach the craft of journalism is a worthy goal but clearly insufficient in this new world and within the setting of a great university." The statement could be—and was—read as asserting that the school taught only "craft." But there was no way to determine whether the assertion was hyperbolic or misinformed. (Later, Bollinger admitted to an alumni gathering that he had not initially understood the role of skills instruction in journalism instruction.) Graduates were immediately concerned, even angry, both over a possible turn away from the school's hands-on tradition and over a conclusion that appeared to hang the school before a trial.[3]

The "craft" statement opened the gate for hovering critics of the school. Tunku Varadarajan of the *Wall Street Journal*'s editorial page declared that the school was "little more than a vocational workshop," founded by a "charlatan." (A photograph of the wrong Joseph Pulitzer—Joseph Pulitzer II—appeared with the column.) Michael Janeway, director of the National Arts Program at the school, popped up on the op-ed page of the *Times*, characterizing the school's program as an "airless, boot camp-like 10 months." Later, there were other attacks—an odd, bristling article by Michael Wolff of *New York* magazine (which suggested, contrary to fact, that the journalism class had led the campus rebellion in 1968) and a wandering, hostile essay by Jack Shafer in the online magazine *Slate*.[4]

Bollinger blandly observed of this ruckus that he "welcomed the wide, and really quite extraordinary, debate that has been generated on this critically important area of our social and academic life." At the same time, he took pains to portray himself as a good, if newfound, friend of the school. In addressing the incoming class on August 1, he recalled his roots in a West Coast newspaper family, and tossed in a savvy reference to RW1. The effect was soothing, and Klatell wrote reassuringly to alumni that the school was carrying on business as usual.[5]

On September 23, Bollinger announced the formation of a committee, for which he chose the musty term "task force." A roster of thirty-eight was summoned to "examine the issue of what a preeminent school of journalism should look like in the contemporary world." The teaching of future journalists, he added, would be "a critical, but not exclusive question."[6]

The committee was an agglomerate. It had a few celebrities, such as the writer-editor Bob Woodward and the novelist-columnist Anna Quindlen, but many of the names would not have been well known outside journalism. The school's faculty was represented—James Carey, Samuel Freedman (now an acting associate dean), Sig Gissler, Sylvia Nasar, Victor Navasky, and Todd Gitlin, as was faculty from elsewhere on campus. There were a few recent graduates, a current M.S. candidate, and senior alumni from the school's board of visitors—Louis Boccardi of the Associated Press and Richard M. Smith of *Newsweek*. However, newspapers, the basis of the school's instruction for most of the twentieth century, were not well represented, nor was journalism education, beyond Columbia faculty and Charles Eisendrath, who had been an associate of Bollinger's at Michigan. Even so, it was a formidable array, probably the most imposing group summoned to determine the school's future since the first advisory board of 1912.

Over the winter, the task force participated in six long meetings, in which, evidently, participants were urged to avert their eyes from the school as it was and imagine something better. The shape of things to come began to emerge in a story by Felicity Barringer in the *Times* on February 22, 2003. It summarized what she had learned of the debates and the proposals laid before the task force. In a key paragraph, Barringer noted that one task-force member, Nicholas Lemann, had drafted a detailed two-year curriculum for the school that was gaining ground over faculty-based proposals.[7]

Lemann's presence on the task force was no happenstance. Beyond his distinguished record as a writer for *The Atlantic* and *The New Yorker* and his challenging books on dilemmas of American society, he had known Bollinger as president at Michigan. In a story on the Supreme Court affirmative-action cases bearing Bollinger's name, Lemann had written: "If you were called upon to invent a perfect university president, you couldn't do better than Lee Bollinger." Given mutual admiration, it came as no surprise when Lemann was mentioned as the leading candidate for dean. The only question remaining was whether he would turn away from his fruitful writing career to accept the job. He decided that he would, and his selection was announced on April 15.[8]

At the same time, Bollinger issued a document based on the task-force discussions, bearing only his signature so as to avoid dissents and minority reports. For those concerned with the future of the school, it contained expansive promises—that the university would participate (as it had not done previously) in developing the school's curriculum and research capacities; and that students would receive not only craft training but instruction to develop their intellectual rigor, their understanding of the profession's history, and their sense of professional identity. He called for command of "a base of knowledge" developed through means strongly reminiscent of the school's original Pulitzer-prescribed curriculum—courses "crafted specifically for what leading journalists need to know," including statistics, economics, history, and political theory. He suggested a student-based publication, analogous to law reviews. He envisioned, as so many had before him, a second year, facilitated by a financial aid program parallel to those that help subsidize graduate students entering other public-service professions.[9]

He avoided utterly any evaluation of what the school was already doing that might be acceptable or unacceptable in the new era. The strategy was clearly to open the way for reform by hypothesizing that no journalism school already existed. He did not offer even cursory acknowledgment of any current activity at the school beyond skills instruction and the Pulitzer Prizes—not the rest of the curriculum, nor the mid-career and dual-degree programs, nor the doctoral program, nor the other prizes, nor the *Columbia Journalism Review*. In his early interviews, Lemann, the new dean, similarly avoided any reflections on the school now in existence, while reminding his interviewers that most journalists, or so he said, did not go to journalism schools.[10]

As David Klatel prepared to yield the dean's office, the school's future was far from clear, suspended, as ever, between apprehension and hope.

# CHAPTER 40

# Has the Pulitzer Idea Survived?

MORE THAN A CENTURY has passed since Joseph Pulitzer, summering in Bar Harbor in August 1902, set down the "germ of an idea" that became Columbia University's School of Journalism. It is a hundred years since the signing of the patchwork agreement between Pulitzer and Nicholas Murray Butler in the summer of 1903 marked the founding of the institution. In August 2002, with the arrival of the class of 2003, the school reached its ninetieth year of operation. At the same time, the one-year graduate curriculum began its sixty-seventh year.

Time enough, it would appear, for everything to be settled. But it has been a characteristic of Pulitzer's school that nothing is ever settled—philosophy, curriculum, results, reputation. Dean and faculty debate and worry anew every year. Yet, paradoxically, after all the debates over goals and methods, all the attempts at reform, the school has remained much as it has been—a magnet for the energetic and talented, a place that provides intensive short-term training in the skills and folkways of journalism, and promptly pushes its recruits out the door. Although the school now engages in other enterprises that are more visible to the off-campus world, at its heart it remains a workplace, centering always on a newsroom and a teacher who is, at best, a demanding mentor, at worst, a drillmaster in things as they are.

What the school transmits must be measured against Joseph Pulitzer's difficult standard: "to make better journalists, who will make better newspapers, which will better serve the public." Of course, to believe that it has approached this goal requires sharing Pulitzer's faith that good journalism is itself good for democracy—a faith often severely tested by journalism itself. To believe anything less would be to agree that education for journalism is mere training for a traditionally ill-paid, short-term job.

Pulitzer's recommended method, as opposed to his goal, has been difficult to pursue. He saw the road to making better journalists extending through a broad curriculum that emphasized public affairs—an education for polymaths like himself; even the encyclopedia-minded Talcott Williams found it too much. As the school was diminished to a two-year curriculum in the 1920s, the idea of liberal arts tailored for journalists diminished, and was replaced by more technical training, or even by paying (and credit-earning) jobs. Pulitzer's vision, to the extent that it was realized in the school's earliest years, vanished; it was too strenuous and too expensive.

When Dean Carl W. Ackerman and his faculty proposed a graduate school in 1935, they envisioned a true graduate school—a two-year master of arts in journalism, a year of "technical" training followed by a year of targeted general education. But the school's destiny was decided when the university lopped off the second year and insisted on the master of science degree. As a result, its vision became more restricted: general education became the province of the undergraduate institution; the graduate school became an increasingly crowded year of work simulation. The change was consonant with the school's limited resources and the university's reluctance to support the school with faculty or facilities from elsewhere on the campus, which was mirrored by the school's reluctance to engage with the rest of the institution.

Later deans, starting with Edward Barrett, sought to reinstall a general-education component, an equivalent of the vanished second year. Barrett's "Basic Issues in the News" course offered a flash-card look at other disciplines. A more effective innovation was the array of mid-career fellowship programs that he initiated, which was a resumption of education for those who already had their technical training and experience as well. These programs have continued, emphasizing specialties such as science and economics, to this day.

But any evaluation of the school as an educational force must always return to the worth of that foreshortened central curriculum, largely unchanged in boundaries since 1935, even with the addition of a few extra weeks. It is not enough to say of students, as Penn Kimball did: "We don't hurt them at all." Or, as Walter Pitkin put it: "I believe . . . that the School did little for them. They just had what it takes."

Such a position suggests that the admissions process is the only crucial step, and that what happens between admission and the degree is secondary—that the school serves primarily as a credential leading to employment, as has been said by cynics more than once. It should be remembered that Kimball added: "When a student leaves he has two things: a little control over his work and a lot of momentum." These elements are closer to the school's ethic than merely doing no harm. It is agreed by many who have passed through it that the experience—working with demanding teachers, competing with fellow students—can be transformative. One left the school in a different gear, sometimes programmed for life, as are professionals in medicine and law.

The basic master's curriculum has grown steadily denser and more substantial. That substance is sometimes not recognized because it arrives in the form of doing the work of journalism. But, for example, the onerous master's project—an extended essay in a medium of the student's choice—develops skill and rigor. Nor do instructors settle any longer for the stale canned exercises that were once the kindergarten steps to proficiency. Over the years, with the input of talented and demanding teachers, the curriculum has become tough and durable, even indestructible, the best that can be made within its severely limited circumstances.

The school may also be unique in the degree to which it depends on its students. In his otherwise unfriendly article, Jerold Footlick correctly gave the school high marks for the quality and energy of its students. When instruction faltered, as it did in Cunliffe's and in Ackerman's late years, the students carried on, becoming semi-autodidacts. Many students leave the school with a feeling not only of having survived a boot camp but of having participated in a cooperative enterprise.

This pulsing inner life of the school is not as well known beyond the walls of the building as are the school's other enterprises. The Pulitzer Prizes remain the keystone of a unique welter of awards and honors—Pulitzers, Cabots, National Magazine Awards, duPonts, Online Journalism, and a batch of niche awards as well.

Joseph Pulitzer financed his prizes on a scale that indicated that he considered them, if not as important as the school, at least half as important. They started modestly and then gained momentum as the culture of American journalists came to recognize the value, sometimes tangible, of fame and recognition. More than eighty-five years old, the prizes have had infusions of diversity and openness, yet have retained their mysterious potency as symbols of achievement.

Pulitzer could not have envisioned that the school would play host to other major prize programs, which have robbed the Pulitzers of their uniqueness. Ackerman initiated the Cabot Prizes, for inter-American understanding; Barrett acquired the National Magazine Awards and the duPonts, for broadcast journalism; on-line awards have recently been added as well. Each of these enhances the school's reputation as the prizegiver *extraordinaire* in journalism. It is impossible to calculate the influence of the possibility of winning prizes on gaining support for the school, but it cannot have been negligible.

More important is the question of whether the school's plethora of prizes has been, as Pulitzer intended, a force for the improvement of American journalism. If so, the connection has been indirect at best. That some news organizations have come to initiate and shape stories with prizes in mind is, perhaps, a backhanded tribute to their influence. But judges, whatever the state of journalism, can almost always find prizeworthy entries. In the late 1990s, when the Committee of Concerned Journalists perceived a collapse in the standards of journalism, there was no lapse in prizegiving.[1]

The *Columbia Journalism Review* may have a better claim to fulfilling the critical half of what Dean Goldstein called the school's "twin mission." The maintenance of *CJR* has been costly for the school, and not only in the literal sense; it occasionally may have annulled at least minor support. But again, as with the prizes, there can be no direct connection inferred between the existence of the magazine and the condition of American journalism.

Looked at in a larger perspective, however, the elaborate network of prizes, centers, and publications represent the school's interface with the outer world of journalism. Nearly every activity boasts an advisory board or jury, with dozens of practitioners and executives enlisted. A cynic might see a parallel with the ceremonial tasks that Louis XIV devised to render his nobles harmless; the school enhances its reputation by bestowing such relatively innocuous chores on the elite of the news media, thus ensuring that they will think well of the school.

But the network is more than show. Whereas in Ackerman's time the boards for the Pulitzer Prizes and the American Press Institute actively disregarded any connection with the school, later deans have seen to it that the school is seen as the chief source of such patronage. Moreover, these connections have yielded positive assistance; where Dean Abel stood largely by himself in facing administrative attack in the early 1970s, Dean Konner was able to draw on the help of the board of visitors she had created in fighting off the Gannett threat.

The school's least solid relationship has been with its peers. In the field of mass-communication education, the school is considered eccentric and a little snobbish. Although deans attend meetings of the Association for Education in Journalism and Mass Communication, the school's faculty traditionally ignores peer teaching and scholarly organizations, and rarely appears in their publications. The exception is James Carey, who arrived in the 1990s with a long history of such participation and publication.

The only link of substance is that with the American Council on Education in Journalism and Mass Communication, not to be confused with AE-JMC. This is the organization that periodically sends teams to assess the condition of the school and to fix on its brow the stamp of accreditation. Even in the worst of times, the visitors have been gentle; the school has never fallen short of accreditation.

Thus the report by the team dispatched by the university in 1998, freed as it was of the courtesies of accreditation, was of particular importance in evaluating the school. It pointed in particular to rigidities in the structure and culture of the school; it pointed out problems that had been lingering since, at least, the 1960s. To his credit, Dean Goldstein did not follow the instincts of many of his colleagues in brushing off the report as ill-motivated, but attempted to address the problems it discussed.

Yet he left the school, if not as he found it, at least recognizable as the school created in the Ackerman era, much elaborated. Whether it is also the school envisioned by Pulitzer is another question. Judging from the tasks they have borne in journalism and teaching, and from the roles they have played, by and large, in seeking to improve journalism, the school's graduates have been a benign influence. Judging from the loyalty of many of them to the institution, they have found that the school not only did not hurt them but was a guide and support in their careers—well beyond the breaks provided by the old-boy network.

The school's persistence in adhering to its main business has often placed it at hazard in its university setting. Despite Pulitzer's dreams, the school has never been granted a place beside the traditional professional schools of law and medicine. Moreover, given its intense concentration on professional preparation, it has been justifiably perceived as neglecting the university's goal of searching for knowledge. Consequently, the host university at various times has puzzled over the school, and has sought to reform, absorb, or inflate it into something more recognizably academic—and is still doing so.

Whether out of pride or principle, those who have governed the school have refused to countenance the kinds of transformations that have created, on other major campuses, spongelike communications empires. Although Columbia has grown accustomed to the school's presence, academically the school is still as idiosyncratic as when Columbia College men sniffed at and envied the esprit of the upstart on campus.

Although the Pulitzer endowment is now only a minor portion of the school's support, although Pulitzer's words were written in the context of a century ago, and although his concept of the omnididactic school has long since passed into oblivion, it remains by heritage Pulitzer's school, just as surely as if the building or the institution were named for him. He set it on its path, and even in its dullest days it partook of his example and his energy. Where it failed him was in falling short of the expansiveness of his vision.

## ON SOURCES

THIS HISTORY has been constructed primarily from the archives of Columbia University and the Graduate School of Journalism. The assistance of Marilyn Pettit, director of the University Archives and Columbiana Library; Jocelyn Wilk, assistant director; and David Hill, previous assistant director, was invaluable in guiding me into not only the immaculately organized university central files but also the records of the Graduate School of Journalism, which were being processed at the time I was doing my research. Jennifer Ulrich provided assistance in finding photographs in the collections.

In the central files, relating to the subjects' contacts with the university administration, the following files were of particular value: Elie Abel, Carl W. Ackerman, Edward W. Barrett, John William Cunliffe, Graduate School of Journalism, Journalism Building, Polykarp Kusch, Walter B. Pitkin, Joseph Pulitzer, and Talcott Williams. Central files for years after 1971 were not yet open.

I cite under School of Journalism Records several bodies of documents. The largest group was transferred to the archives when the top floor of the

Journalism Building was remodeled in the 1990s. This group covered primarily the years from 1940 to 1985. An overlapping group running into the mid-1990s was stored in the basement of the Journalism Building; these materials have also now been transferred to the archives.

In addition, Assistant Dean Jonnet Abeles made available to me the school's clipping files, dating from 1903. Many citations to newspapers and periodicals are drawn from clippings in these files. There are school documents, covering primarily the years 1950–2002, that I have saved or acquired personally. All documents in my possession will be offered to the archives. Andrew Cooper, the school's alumni officer, made many photographs available.

I have separately cited records that I have saved or acquired relating to the *Columbia Journalism Review*; these too are being donated, as are the relevant extracts from my personal journal, 1969–2002.

In the Rare Book and Manuscript Library, Columbia University, I used the Richard Terrill Baker Papers, relating to his own career and the writing of his 1954 history of the school; the Joseph Pulitzer Papers; and, secondarily, the Nicholas Murray Butler Papers. In the Library of Congress, I spent days with the voluminous Carl W. Ackerman Papers. At the Amherst College Library, I found valuable items in the Talcott Williams Papers, with the assistance of Daria D'Arienzo, head of archives and special collections. In dealing with the Chungking Post-Graduate School of Journalism, I was greatly aided by the papers of Floyd D. Rodgers, Jr., lent by his widow and daughter, and the China diary and correspondence of Harold L. Cross, given by his son Malcolm Cross to the Columbia University Archives.

I was assisted as well by interviews with three recent deans: Joan Konner, on April 4 and 20, 2000, and March 12, 2001; Osborn Elliott, on June 21, 2001; and Tom Goldstein, on February 26, 2002.

Among the published materials cited in the notes, I made extensive use of the following:

On Joseph Pulitzer and the School of Journalism, the founding document is his article, "The College of Journalism," *North American Review* 178 (May 1904): 641–80. The biography by Don C. Seitz, *Joseph Pulitzer: His Life and Letters* (New York: Simon & Schuster, 1924) both records the observations of a close associate and reprints correspondence and documents relating to the school's founding.

On the school itself, Richard Terrill Baker, *A History of the Graduate School of Journalism, Columbia University* (New York: Columbia University Press, 1954) provides a full account of the negotiations that brought the school into being, but is impressionistic on the three decades after its opening. The issues of *The Columbia Journalist*, published by the students from 1923 to 1935, provide glimpses of life at the school. Alumni directories were invaluable, especially the first two: Bernard S. Redmont, ed., *Who's Who / Columbia Journalists* (New York: Graduate School of Journalism, 1939), and *Journalism Alumni Directory 1913–1956*, compiled by Lawrence D. Pinkham (New York: Graduate School of Journalism, 1956). *Journalists in Action*, edited by Edward W. Barrett and Robert Hewes (New York: Channel Press, 1963), recounts experiences of graduates. Of the many later reports on the school, that by George N. Allen, "Changing Times: The Columbia School of Journalism," *Washington Journalism Review* (April–May 1979): 40–45, was the most substantive.

The following were helpful on specific activities of the school: John Hohenberg, *The Pulitzer Prizes: A History of the Awards in Books, Drama, Music, and Journalism, Based on the Private Files over Six Decades* (New York: Columbia University Press, 1974), is a valuable commissioned history; it can be supplemented by extracts from his diaries in *The Pulitzer Diaries: Inside America's Greatest Prize* (Syracuse: Syracuse University Press, 1997). Henry Sweets Ackerman, "A History of the Maria Moors Cabot Prizes: Experiment in Inter-American Journalism, 1938–1956" (master's thesis, University of North Carolina, 1969), based on the Cabot files and interviews with his grandfather, is frank and factual. Don E. Carter and Malcolm F. Mallette, *Seminar: The Story of the American Press Institute* (Reston, Va.: American Press Institute, 1992), explains in detail why the API was an unhappy tenant at the school.

Memoirs and biographies of faculty and administrators supplemented formal records. Among them: Elizabeth Dunbar's jumbled but informative *Talcott Williams: Gentleman of the Fourth Estate* (n.p., 1936); Walter B. Pitkin's voluble *On My Own* (New York: Scribner's, 1944); *John Hohenberg: The Pursuit of Excellence* (Gainesville: University Press of Florida, 1995), a self-regarding memoir; Penn Kimball's *The File* (New York: Harcourt Brace Jovanovich, 1983), incorporating his career at the school; Fred W. Friendly's *Due To Circumstances Beyond Our Control....* (New York: Random House, 1967), written at the start of his association with Columbia; Norman E. Isaacs, *Untended Gates: The Mismanaged Press* (New York: Columbia University Press, 1986), characteristically frank; and Osborn Elliott's *The World of Oz* (New York: Viking, 1980), primarily on his pre-Columbia career.

On Columbia University, I consulted Andrew S. Dolkart's *Morningside Heights: A History of Its Architecture and Development* (New York: Columbia University Press, 1998); Thomas Bender's *New York Intellect: A Histo-*

*ry of Intellectual Life in New York City from 1750 to the Beginnings of Our Own Time* (New York: Knopf, 1987); Horace Coon's *Columbia: Colossus on the Hudson* (New York: Dutton, 1947); and Travis Beal Jacobs, *Eisenhower at Columbia* (New Brunswick: Transaction, 2001). On the 1968 upheavals, I used *Crisis at Columbia: Report of the Fact-Finding Commission Appointed to Investigate the Disturbances at Columbia University in April and May 1968* (New York: Vintage, 1968) and *Up Against the Ivy Wall*, by Jerry L. Avorn and edited by Robert Friedman (New York: Atheneum, 1969).

On origins and aspects of journalism education: *Views and Interviews on Journalism*, edited by Charles F. Wingate (1875; reprint, New York: Arno Press, 1970); Albert Alton Sutton, *Education for Journalism in the United States from Its Beginning to 1940* (Evanston: Northwestern University Studies in the Humanities, No. 10, 1945); Edwin Emery and Joseph P. McKerns, *AEJMC: 75 Years in the Making* (Journalism Monographs 104, November 1987); David Boroff, "A Report on Journalism Education" (New York: Ford Foundation, June 1963) and the short version, "What Ails the Journalism Schools" *Harper's Magazine* (October 1965): 77–85; Everette E. Dennis, "Whatever Happened to Marse Robert's Dream? The Dilemma of American Journalism Education," *Media Studies Journal* 2 (spring 1988): 1–22; and Howard M. Ziff, "The Closing of the Journalistic Mind," *Columbia Journalism Review* (January–February 1992):49–51.

# NOTES

## PREFACE

1. Richard Terrill Baker, *A History of the Graduate School of Journalism, Columbia University* (New York: Columbia University Press, 1954).

2. "Memory": Richard White, "Here Is the Problem," *Journal of American History* 89 (June 2002): 18.

## 1. "I HAVE SELECTED COLUMBIA"

1. "Life of a wanderer": W. A. Swanberg, *Pulitzer* (New York: Scribner's, 1967); Don C. Seitz, *Joseph Pulitzer: His Life and Letters* (New York: Simon & Schuster, 1924).

2. Apologist: Alleyne Ireland, *Joseph Pulitzer: Reminiscences of a Secretary* (New York: Mitchell Kennerley, 1904), pp. 110–16.

3. "Germ": The memorandum is printed in Richard Terrill Baker, *A History of the Graduate School of Journalism, Columbia University* (New York, Columbia University Press, 1954), pp. 23–24. Chair: Pulitzer's will, as it stood in August 1902, provided $250,000 for a chair of journalism at Columbia College. See correspondence, October–December 1902, Joseph Pulitzer Papers, Rare Book and Manuscript Library, Columbia University.

## 2. SCHOOLS FOR JOURNALISTS?

1. "Fit for nothing else": Henry Adams, *The Education of Henry Adams: An Auto-biography* (Boston: Houghton Mifflin, 1918), p. 211. "The New York reporter": Julius Wilcox, "Journalism as a Profession," *Galaxy* 4 (November 1867): 798–99.

2. "Distinct and lofty profession": "Journalism," *United States Magazine and Democratic Review* 10 (January 1842): 52. "Our greatest newspapers": Whitelaw Reid interview in Charles F. Wingate, ed., *Views and Interviews on Journalism* (1875; reprint, New York: Arno Press, 1970), p. 30. "Nauseating trail": James Parton, "*The New York Herald*," *North American Review* 211 (April 1866): 415." "Justice and consideration": Parton, "Falsehood in the Daily Press," *Harper's New Monthly Magazine* 49 (July 1874): 276.

3. "School of Journalism": Reid, "Journalism as a Career," reprint of 1872 lecture in Reid, *American and English Studies*, vol. 2 (New York: Scribner's, 1913), p. 204.

4. "No separate school": Reid, "Journalism as a Career," p. 211. "Only place": Hudson in Wingate, ed., *Views and Interviews*, p. 130. "Swimming school": White in ibid., p. 80. "Professorship of matrimony": quoted in Richard Terrill Baker, *A History of the Graduate School of Journalism, Columbia University* (New York: Columbia University Press, 1954), p. 15.

5. "Broken-down parsons": David G. Croly in Wingate, ed., *Views and Interviews*, p. 326; Jennie C. Croly in ibid., p. 150.

6. Editors in 1900: Jack R. Hart, "Horatio Alger in the Newsroom: Social Origins of American Editors," *Journalism Quarterly* 53:14–20.

7. Camp: Baker, *History*, p. 9.

8. "I have thought seriously": quoted in ibid.

9. Columbia: Horace Coon, *Columbia: Colossus on the Hudson* (New York: Dutton, 1947). "College transforming": Thomas Bender, *New York Intellect: A History of Intellectual Life in New York City from 1750 to the Beginnings of Our Own Time* (New York: Knopf, 1987), pp. 265–93.

10. New campus: Andrew S. Dolkart, *Morningside Heights: A History of Its Architecture and Development* (New York: Columbia University Press, 1998); Low as president: Bender, *New York Intellect*, pp. 279–84.

11. "Fruitful tension": Bender, *New York Intellect*, p. 108. "The city": ibid., p. 282.

12. Scholarships: Baker, *History*, p. 18.

13. Baden Baden meeting: ibid., pp. 18–19.

14. Allen memorandum: Walter Allen, "In Support of a Columbian Lectureship on Journalism," undated, but filed with materials for 1901, Joseph Pulitzer Central File, Columbia University Archives. Baker (*History*, pp. 20–21) dates the memorandum as being written immediately after the 1892 meeting in Baden Baden.

15. "Giving a building": Pulitzer to Low, October 10, November 15, 1895; Low to Pulitzer, March 13, 1896; state of his health: Pulitzer to Low, March 26, 1896, Pulitzer Central File.

16. Lectureship: W. H. Merrill to Low, April 3, 1901, filed with 1899 materials, Pulitzer Central File.

17. Seth Low in politics: Lincoln Steffens, "New York: Good Government in Danger," *McClure's Magazine* 22 (November 1903): 84–92; Gerald W. McFarland, *Mugwumps, Morals, and Politics, 1884–1920* (Amherst: University of Massachusetts Press, 1975), pp. 104–105.

## 3. "DEALING WITH A WILD MAN"

1. Butler and Low: Thomas Bender, *New York Intellect: A History of Intellectual Life in New York City, from 1750 to the Beginnings of Our Own Time* (New York: Knopf, 1987), p. 284. The imperial Butler: Alva Johnston, "Cosmos," in *Profiles from* The New Yorker (New York: Knopf, 1938), pp. 219–46 (originally published November 8, 15, 1930).

2. Contact with Butler: Richard Terrill Baker, *A History of the Graduate School of Journalism, Columbia University* (New York: Columbia University Press, 1954), p. 26. Change in will: October–December 1902 correspondence, Joseph Pulitzer Papers, Rare Book and Manuscript Library, Columbia University, especially telegrams from H. B. Anderson (lawyer) to Pulitzer, October 15, 16, 1902, and from Dumont Clarke (president, The American Exchange National Bank) to Pulitzer, October 18, 1902.

3. Train incident: Don C. Seitz, *Joseph Pulitzer: His Life and Letters* (New York: Simon & Schuster, 1924), p. 435.

4. Hosmer plan: Baker, *History*, pp. 26–27. Eliot contact: Seitz, *Pulitzer*, p. 445.

5. "The gentleman": Baker, *History*, p. 29; Seitz, *Pulitzer*, p. 445.

6. Education committee: Baker, *History*, pp. 29–32.

7. Hosmer letter: printed in ibid., pp. 33–34.

8. "More receptive": ibid., p. 35.

9. Letter from Etretat: text in Seitz, *Pulitzer*, pp. 448–53. Trustee agreement: Baker, *History*, p. 35. The Graduate School of Journalism Central File, Columbia University Archives, contains a handwritten note on the letterhead of The Century Association dated July 20, 1903, the date of the trustees' approval, specifying a schedule of payments to ensure that the school and its building would be ready by June 1904.

10. The text of the agreement is reprinted in Seitz, *Pulitzer*, pp. 445–48.

11. "The *World*'s scheme": Hosmer letter, June 23, 1903. Advisory board: section of Hosmer letter, "verbatim as dictated." "During my life," Seitz, *Pulitzer*, pp. 450–52.

12. "Antagonistic": Butler to Merrill, July 22, 1903, in Seitz, *Pulitzer*, p. 454.

13. White and Eliot: Baker, *History*, p. 38; Seitz, *Pulitzer*, pp. 456–58. "Understand jealousy": ibid., p. 457. "Advertise himself": Butler to John B. Pine, clerk of the trustees, August 13, 1903, Graduate School of Journalism Central File, Columbia University Archives.

14. Instructions to publish: Seitz, *Pulitzer*, p. 458. "Wild man": Butler to Rives, August 15, 1903, Journalism Central File. "Butler is very weak": Pulitzer to Whitelaw Reid, quoted in Baker, *History*, p. 42.

15. "Bales of clippings": Seitz, *Pulitzer*, p. 460.

16. Unhappy letter: Baker, *History*, p. 43. Building plans: McKim, Mead & White to Pine, September 25, 1903, Journalism Central File; Matthews plan: Baker, *History*, p. 41.

17. University Council: Baker, *History*, p. 46; "Report on the Organization . . . ," November 17, 1903, marked confidential, Journalism Central File. "Inchoate": quoted in Baker, *History*, p. 42.

18. Rives–Pulitzer correspondence: January 7–February 27, 1904, Journalism Central File. Cornerstone: Baker, *History*, p. 46. "Mind is unchanged": Pulitzer to Rives, January 26, 1904, Journalism Central File.

19. "Cornerstone": quoted in Baker, *History*, p. 47.

20. "Free to defer": text of agreement, March 19, 1904; new will: "Extracts from the Will of Joseph Pulitzer . . . From the Will dated April 16, 1904," Joseph Pulitzer Central File, Columbia University Archives.

21. Horace White, "The School of Journalism," *North American Review* 176 (June 1904): 25–32; "chair of 'scoops'," 26.

22. Previous article: Pulitzer, "Has Congress Abdicated?" *North American Review* 169 (December 1899): 885–94. "Diffuse and repetitious": Pulitzer, "The College of Journalism," *North American Review* 178 (May 1904): 641–80; quotation is at 641. "Unconvinced": Baker, *History*, p. 48*n*.

23. "Magnum opus": Baker, *History*, p. 50.

24. "Anticommercial" and "mark the distinction": Pulitzer, "College of Journalism," pp. 655, 656–57.

25. "Gallic lucidity": Pulitzer, "College of Journalism," p. 664.

26. "Welfare of the Republic" and "the only great organized force": Pulitzer, "College of Journalism," pp. 678–79.

27. "Our Republic and its press": Pulitzer, "College of Journalism," p. 680. Michael Lewis points out that Pulitzer added the word "corrupt" after "demagogic" in the subsequent pamphlet version of the article. "J-School Confidential," *The New Republic*, April 19, 1993, p. 27.

28. Booklet: Joseph Pulitzer, *The School of Journalism in Columbia University: The Power of Public Opinion* (New York: Columbia University, 1904). "The Power of Public Opinion" was another article by Pulitzer. The revision was also issued by the Press Publishing Company, which published the *World*.

29. "Until his death": "The School of Journalism / It Is Mr. Pulitzer's Wish That It Be Not Established Until After His Death," *New York Times*, February 3, 1905.

### 4. "A POSTHUMOUS AFFAIR"

1. Cordiality: Kate Pulitzer to Butler, November 12, 1907, Graduate School of Journalism Central File, Columbia University Archives.

2. "He had been, he said, an unconscionable time dying; but he hoped that they would excuse it." Charles II, 1685, in Thomas Macaulay, *History of England*, I, ch. 4.

3. "*Chief* man": "Memorandum of message from Mr. Pulitzer delivered to Dr. Butler by Mr. Bates" [May 1907], Journalism Central File.

4. Williams: Lord to Butler, May 24, 1907; Butler to Rives, May 29, 1907, Journalism Central File.

5. Celebration: Ralph Pulitzer invitation to Butler, April 28, 1908; Butler acceptance, April 30, 1908, Nicholas Murray Butler papers, Rare Book and Manuscript Li-

brary, Columbia University. Williams: Elizabeth Dunbar, *Talcott Williams: Gentleman of the Fourth Estate* (n.p., 1936); Baker, *History*, p. 63.

6. University of Washington: Butler to Pulitzer, October 11, 1907, catalogued correspondence, Joseph Pulitzer Papers, Rare Book and Manuscript Library, Columbia University. Missouri school: Butler to Pulitzer, October 5, 1908, Journalism Central File.

7. "Without waiting": Heaton to Keppel, August 17, 1910, Journalism Central File.

8. "What Mr. Pulitzer said to you": Butler to Rives, September 2, 1910, Journalism Central File.

9. "Strictly editorial": Pulitzer to Butler, September 29, 1910; "very good opinion": Pulitzer to Butler, October 3, 1910, Pulitzer Central File.

10. "Delighted": Pulitzer to Butler, October 10, 1911, Pulitzer Central File.

11. *Liberty, Ha! Ha!*: Alleyne Ireland, *Joseph Pulitzer: Reminiscences of a Secretary* (New York: Mitchell Kennerley, 1904), p. 28. "Leise, ganz leise": "Joseph Pulitzer Dies Suddenly," *New York Times*, October 30, 1911; Baker, *History*, p. 54; Don C. Seitz, *Joseph Pulitzer: His Life and Letters* (New York: Simon & Schuster, 1924), p. 415.

## 5. "WE WILL START RIGHT AWAY"

1. "Start right away": "School of Journalism / Now Columbia Obligated to Begin by Mr. Pulitzer's Death," New York *Sun*, October 31, 1911. Rives–Butler meeting: Butler to John B. Pine, November 8, 1911, Journalism Building Central File, Columbia University Archives.

2. "Omniscience": Walter B. Pitkin, *On My Own* (New York: Scribner's, 1944), p. 395.

3. Site selected: Report of the Committee on Buildings and Grounds, November 22, 1911, Journalism Building Central File. Ground broken: "Board Takes Up Plan for School of Journalism," New York *World*, January 16, 1912.

4. Blueprint: "Report of the Sub-Committee on the School of Journalism" [December 12, 1911], Graduate School of Journalism Central File, Columbia University Archives; Richard Terrill Baker, *A History of the Graduate School of Journalism, Columbia University* (New York: Columbia University Press, 1954), pp. 57–58.

5. Beard plan: Beard to Pine, December 12, 1911, Journalism Building Central File.

6. First board meeting: "Board Takes Up Plan for School of Journalism" *World*, January 16, 1912. "Too much of Columbia": Baker, *History*, p. 58.

7. Cunliffe: Baker, *History*, p. 59.

8. Butler strategy: Pitkin, *On My Own*, p. 385; Baker, *History*, p. 59.

9. "More varied experience": advisory board resolution, quoted in Baker, *History*, p. 60.

10. "Felt by every member": Butler to Williams, February 20, 1912, Talcott Williams Central File, Columbia University Archives; Baker, *History*, p. 60.

11. Letter astray: secretary of the university to Williams, February 26, 1912, with hand-delivered copy of February 20 letter, Williams Central File; Baker, *History*, p. 61. "Cuts too deep": Williams to Butler, February 26, 1912; acceptance: Williams to Butler, March 5, 1912, Williams Central File. Pitkin judgment: Pitkin, *On My Own*, pp. 388–90.

12. Photograph: "Talcott Williams for Pulitzer School," *New York Times*, March 11, 1912; "Dr. Williams in Pulitzer School," Philadelphia *Press*, March 11, 1912. "Arduous, unremitting daily pressure": Williams to Butler, March 5, 1912, Williams Central File.

13. Administrative board meeting: Baker, *History*, p. 64; "4-Year Course for Journalism School," *Times*, March 17, 1912.

14. "Girls are not allowed": "Pulitzer School Bars Girls," *Times*, March 16, 1912.

15. Women to study: "Will Admit Women to School of Journalism," Philadelphia *Press*, April 24, 1912. Threat to decline: Elizabeth Dunbar, *Talcott Williams: Gentleman of the Fourth Estate* (n.p., 1936), p. 393, on Williams's recollection in 1927.

16. University Council approval: minutes of April 16, 1912; Baker, *History*, p. 65. "Needs of journalism": "Courses in Journalism," *Columbia University Quarterly* (September 1912): 417–20.

17. "Fresh from the practice": "Courses in Journalism," p. 419. MacAlarney, Slosson: Baker, *History*, p. 73.

18. Matthews: Williams to Butler, February 16, 1914, forwarding credentials, Williams Central File. Faculty on loan: Baker, *History*, p. 70. Pitkin's arrival: Pitkin, *On My Own*, pp. 384–97.

19. *School of Journalism Announcement 1912–1913*, Columbia University *Bulletin of Information*, 12th ser., no. 18, May 18, 1912.

20. Williams trip: Williams to Frank D. Fackenthal, secretary of the university, August 11, 1912, Williams Central File. Encounter with Ackerman: Baker, *History*, p. 62n. Waterbury: ibid., p. 65; *Journalism Alumni Directory 1913–1956* (New York: Graduate School of Journalism, 1956).

21. Journalism teachers: Williams to Fackenthal, August 11, 1912, Williams Central File; Edwin Emery and Joseph P. McKerns, *AEJMC: 75 Years in the Making* [Columbia. S. C.: Association for Education in Journalism and Mass Communication] (Journalism Monographs, No. 104, November 1987), pp. 9–11.

22. "Intestine" and "laboratory": Williams, "The School of Journalism," *Columbia University Quarterly* 14 (June 1912): 235–48.

23. Cornerstone: Baker, *History*, p. 69; *Evening World*, July 2, 1912.

### 6. A BUILDING CALLED "JOURNALISM"

1. Opening: Richard Terrill Baker, *A History of the Graduate School of Journalism. Columbia University* (New York: Columbia University Press, 1954), p. 70. Opening address: Talcott Williams, "Aims and Methods of the School of Journalism," delivered at the opening of the School of Journalism, Earl Hall, September 30, 1912, *Columbia University Quarterly* 15 (December 1912): 52–57; "Pulitzer School of Journalism Publicly Opened," New York *World*, October 1, 1912.

2. Hazing: "Lesson No. 1 . . . Hammond Instructs School of Journalism Student," *New York Tribune*, October 1, 1912.

3. Reporter admitted: "Teaching Cubs to Write / First-Day Work in City Room of School of Journalism," *New York Evening Post*, October 1, 1912.

4. Butler warning: Butler to Williams, October 2, 1912, Talcott Williams Central File, Columbia University Archives.

5. Williams on entering class: "School of Journalism Is Near Its Opening," *World*, September 25, 1912.

6. Roster: "The First Students," typescript, School of Journalism Records.

7. Early assignments: MacAlarney to Williams, October 8, 1912, Box 61, Richard Terrill Baker Papers, Rare Book and Manuscript Library, Columbia University. "Vigilantly 'tiled'": Williams, "The School of Journalism / Technical Training in Journalism," *Publishers' Guide*, January 1913. Criticism: Editorial, "Not the Best," n.p., *Daily News*, February 8, 1913.

8. "The Staff": "Tong Leaves 'The Staff,'" *Evening Post*, January 14, 1913.

9. "Father Hated Inaccuracies": "His Son Explains Pulitzer's Ideals," *New York Times*, December 17, 1912. Reid memorial: "First Duty of the Reporter," Columbia *Spectator*, December 17, 1912. "Valueless": Williams to Butler, January 27, 1913; Butler to Williams, January 31, 1913, Williams Central File.

10. Reading load: Williams, undated memorandum to Butler; Butler to Williams, undated, Williams Central File; Pitkin to Williams, October 29, 1914, Walter B. Pitkin Central File, Columbia University Archives.

11. "The next year's budget": Butler to Williams, January 13, 1913, Williams Central File.

12. First commencement: Baker, *History*, p. 75; Bernard S. Redmont, ed., *Who's Who / Columbia Journalists* (New York: Graduate School of Journalism, 1939) and *The Columbia Journalist 1913–1923* (New York: Alumni Association of the School of Journalism, 1923).

13. "First annual report": *Report of the Director, School of Journalism, for the Academic Year Ending June 30, 1913*; "Journalist School Ends First Year," *Tribune*, December 12, 1913.

14. "Memorandum . . . ,": January 27, 1913, Journalism Building Central File, Columbia University Archives.

15. "Journalism" carving: John B. Pine, clerk of the trustees, to McKim, Mead & White, May 7, 1913, Building Central File.

16. Building names: Andrew S. Dolkart, *Morningside Heights: A History of Its Architecture and Development* (New York: Columbia University Press, 1998); Lewisohn: ibid., pp. 179–80; Schiff: ibid., pp. 221–22.

17. "Hebrew question" and "Jew college": Dolkart, *Morningside Heights*, pp. 159–60. Pulitzer as a Jew: András Csillag, "Joseph Pulitzer's Roots in Europe: A Genealogical History," *American Jewish Archives*, April 1987, pp. 48–68; Daniel W. Pfaff, *Joseph Pulitzer II and the Post-Dispatch: A Newspaperman's Life* (University Park: Pennsylvania State University Press, 1991), pp. 16, 400 (*n7*). Epithets: W. A. Swanberg, *Pulitzer* (New York: Scribner's, 1967), pp. 89, 136.

18. Medallions: Williams to Ralph Pulitzer, January 14, 1913, Box 42, Talcott Williams Papers, Amherst College; John B. Pine to McKim, Mead & White, March 4, 1913, Building Central File; Baker, *History*, p. 69. Rodin bust: Frank D. Fackenthal,

secretary of the university, to Don Seitz, October 18, 1913, reporting installation of bust, Joseph Pulitzer Central File, Columbia University Archives. Female figures: Pine to W. M. Kendall, September 28, 1913, Building Central File.

19. Jefferson statue: Fackenthal to Ralph Pulitzer, February 2, 1914; Ralph Pulitzer to Butler, April 9, 1914, Ralph Pulitzer Central File, Columbia University Archives; Don C. Seitz, *Joseph Pulitzer: His Life and Letters* (New York: Simon & Schuster, 1924), p. 463. Critics: William R. Reynolds, "A Memorial: The School of Journalism," n.d., typescript in Box 61, Baker Papers.

20. Humes plaque: Baker, *History*, p. 77. "Westminster Abbey": Williams to Butler, June 19, 1913; "columbarium": Butler to Williams, June 26, 1913, Williams Central File. Comment in 1935: Isabelle Keating, "Reporters Become of Age," *Harper's Magazine* 70 (April 1935): 603.

21. Williams clipping collection: Baker, *History*, p. 77; "700,000 Items In Clipping Files Of Dr. Williams," *New York Herald Tribune*, February 26, 1928. Disposal: James Boylan, Journal, October 10, 1977, August 30, 1978. The librarians offered the author portions of the morgue dealing with journalism, and they remain in his possession.

22. Building details: "Journalism School Building Plans," New York *Sun*, January 28, 1912; "Pulitzer School of Journalism Well Launched," *The Writer's Magazine*, October 1913, p. 97; Baker, *History*, p. 75.

23. Excess space: Baker, *History*, p. 77.

24. Acceptance: Baker, *History*, p. 80. Cost: Frederick A. Goetze, consulting engineer, to Pine, November 20, 1913, Building Central File. "Corporate union": *Report of the Director, School of Journalism, for the Academic Year Ending June 30, 1914.*

## 7. "WHAT JOURNALISM WILL DO TO COLUMBIA"

1. Williams: Richard Terrill Baker, *A History of the Graduate School of Journalism, Columbia University* (New York: Columbia University Press, 1954), p. 94; "expanses": Walter B. Pitkin, *On My Own* (New York: Scribner's, 1944), p. 389; "Talkalot": Elizabeth Dunbar, *Talcott Williams: Gentleman of the Fourth Estate* (n.p., 1936), p. 321.

2. "Save your money": M. R. Werner, "A New York Adolescence: We Were All Socialists Then," *The New Yorker*, February 11, 1939, pp. 47–57 (50). Snooping: Pitkin, *On My Own*, pp. 390–93.

3. Yalman: "Never Shrink from Sacrifice," in Edward W. Barrett, ed., *Journalists in Action* (New York: Channel, 1963), p. 98.

4. MacAlarney methods: Bronson Batchelor, "Making a Journalist," *Independent*, June 15, 1914, pp. 481–83. Tests: MacAlarney, "Examination in Journalism 42," May 20, 1915, School of Journalism Records.

5. City editor: "Professor MacAlarney to be Tribune's City Editor," Columbia *Spectator*, December 9, 1914, crediting a *Blot* reporter.

6. Omniscience: Pitkin, *On My Own*, p. 396.

7. "Those who failed": *Report of the Director, School of Journalism, for the Academic Year Ending June 30, 1914.*

8. "Punitive way": Dunbar, *Talcott Williams*, p. 326.

9. "My second year": Williams to Reenie (unidentified relative), May 2, 1914, Box 43, Talcott Williams Papers, Amherst College.

10. Graduates: *Journalism Alumni Directory 1913–1956* (New York: Graduate School of Journalism, 1956). McAnney exploit: "Columbia Senior Rescues Girl by Dive Into the Hudson," *New York Herald*, May 18, 1914.

11. No hazing: "1917 Journalism Receive 1918 / Denounce 'Rough' Methods," Columbia *Spectator*, September 26, 1914. Proposed merger: "Communication" [from journalism students], *Spectator*, October 16, 1914.

12. Stretched to the limit: Pitkin to Williams, October 29, 1914, Walter B. Pitkin Central File, Columbia University Archives; "Committee Working for Reforms," Columbia *Spectator*, January 20, 1915; "School Journalists Ask for Less Work," New York *World*, January 24, 1915. Knickerbockers: "Schuster Wins Prize," *Editor & Publisher*, February 19, 1916.

13. Lower attrition: *Report of the Director, School of Journalism, for the Academic Year Ending June 30, 1915.* Ivy Lee: Edwin N. Lewis entry, *The Columbia Journalist, 1913–1923* (New York: Alumni Association of the School of Journalism, 1923), p. 60.

14. End of probation: Baker, *History*, p. 82. First Pulitzer Prizes: John Hohenberg, *The Pulitzer Prizes: A History of the Awards in Books, Drama, Music, and Journalism, Based on the Private Files over Six Decades* (New York: Columbia University Press, 1974), pp. 21–24; "Copy of a Resolution Adopted at a Meeting of November 22, 1915, Executors and Trustees of Estate of Joseph Pulitzer, Decd.," Joseph Pulitzer Central File, Columbia University Archives.

15. "It is plain": Butler to Williams, January 18, 1916, Talcott Williams Central File, Columbia University Archives.

16. "The experience of three years": Williams to Keppel, February 8, 1916, Williams Central File.

17. "Too early a demand": *Report of the Director, School of Journalism, for the Academic Year Ending June 30, 1916.*

18. Geffen: Alfred E. Clark, "Maxwell M. Geffen Is Dead at 84; Publisher of Specialty Magazines," *New York Times*, October 13, 1980. Tolischus: Otto D. Tolischus, "Fiduciary Relationships," in Barrett, ed., *Journalists in Action*, pp. 115–19.

19. "No longer a question": "Columbia School of Journalism Develops Fast," *Christian Science Monitor*, April 26, 1916. Brisbane contest: Columbia *Spectator*, February 15, 1916.

20. "Adventure unparalleled": M. Lincoln Schuster, "Four Historic Years," in Wesley First, ed., *University on the Heights* (Garden City: Doubleday, 1969), pp. 159–65.

21. *Challenge*: April 1916 issue, School of Journalism Records, Columbia University Archives. Seadlers and "crew man": Werner, "We Were All Socialists," pp. 50–51. Intercollegiate Socialist Society: program, eighth annual convention, December 28–30, 1916, School of Journalism Records.

22. Ryskind and "Conning Tower": "S. of J. Students Have Talented Pens," Columbia *Spectator*, February 14, 1916. "Against precedent": "Successful Candidates for

Student Board Resent Lack of Announcement," *New York Tribune*, May 16, 1916; "Journalism Men Lose by Columbia Ruling," *Tribune*, September 29, 1916.

23. Strike: "Rumored that 1916J [1917J] Has Gone on Strike," Columbia *Spectator*, December 13, 1916; "Nip Journalism Strike in Bud," *Tribune*, December 14, 1916.

24. "Lack of memory": Dunbar, *Talcott Williams*, p. 348.

25. "Trouble, trouble": ibid.; Pitkin, *On My Own*, p. 393.

## 8. "IF SEDITION IS TO BE EXCLUDED"

1. "A long war:" Williams to Reenie, August 10, 1914, Box 42, Talcott Williams Papers, Amherst College. "A country sobered": Williams to Butler, August 21, 1914, Nicholas Murray Butler Papers, Rare Book and Manuscript Library, Columbia University.

2. Spingarn: Horace Coon, *Columbia: Colossus on the Hudson* (New York: Dutton, 1947), pp. 122–25. Beard: "A Statement by Charles A. Beard," *The New Republic*, December 29, 1917, pp. 249–51.

3. "Romanticize this era": Richard Terrill Baker, *A History of the Graduate School of Journalism, Columbia University* (New York: Columbia University Press, 1954), p. 84.

4. Emergency Peace Federation: Barbara J. Steinson, *American Women's Activism in World War I* (New York: Garland, 1982). Trip to Washington: M. R. Werner, "A New York Adolescence: We Were All Socialists Then," *New Yorker*, February 11, 1939, pp. 55–57. Butler telegram: "A Social History of Columbia University: The Butler Imperium—A Timeline, 1902–1945," beatl.barnard.columbia.edu/cuhis3057/timelines.htm.

5. Ryskind and *Jester*: "Students Roused by Criticism of Butler / May Oust Editor of 'Jester' for Calling Columbia Head Un-American," New York *Sun*, March 8, 1917; Elizabeth Dunbar, *Talcott Williams: Gentleman of the Fourth Estate* (n.p., 1936), pp. 350–51. Expulsion: *Fourth Estate* (magazine), April 7, 1917.

6. Sokolsky: "Clubbed Leader of I.W.W. Is Freed, Police Censured," New York *World*, April 7, 1914; Werner, "We Were All Socialists Then," p. 50.

7. "Inappropriateness": Butler to Williams, March 5, 1917; "I have the evidence": Williams to Butler, n.d., Talcott Williams Central File, Columbia University Archives.

8. "Duma": *Sun*, March 29, 1917.

9. "Amenities": *Sun*, March 30, 1917.

10. Sokolsky presence: guest list, 1917 Annual Dinner, Pulitzer School of Journalism April 19, 1917; minutes, Committee on Instruction, May 14, 1917, School of Journalism Records. "Withdrawal": Carl W. Ackerman to Frank D. Fackenthal, August 16, 1939, Carl W. Ackerman Central File, Columbia University Archives.

11. "Co-habiting": Baker to Chris [Trump?], March 22, 1968, Box 4, Richard Terrill Baker Papers, Rare Book and Manuscript Library, Columbia University. "Most likely": "Vote World the Best Morning Paper Here," *World*, June 10, 1917.

12. "Courageous editor": Dunbar, *Talcott Williams*, p. 352.

13. Fraser case: summarized in "Statement by Charles A. Beard." Columbia's repressive policies during the Great War are recounted in Richard Hofstadter and Walter P. Metzger, *The Development of Academic Freedom in the United States* (New York: Columbia University Press, 1955), pp. 498–502.

14. "Civic education": Pitkin to Butler, February 10, 1917, enclosing "How Columbia University Can Serve the Country," February 8, 1917; Fackenthal to Pitkin, March 21, 1917, Walter B. Pitkin Central File, Columbia University Archives. "Division of Intelligence": Pitkin to Butler, March 30, 1917, Pitkin Central File; Butler to Williams, April 11, 1917, Williams Central File.

15. War resolutions: minutes, committee on instruction, April 11, 1917; "Journalism Upper Classes Drop Work," Columbia *Spectator*, April 12, 1917; "Meeting the Emergency": editorial, "Journalism's Action," ibid.

16. "War Papers": Pitkin to Butler, April 17, 1917; Butler to Pitkin, May 21, 1917; New Republic News Service: Pitkin to Butler, May 25[?], 1917; Council of National Defense: Pitkin to Butler, July 27, 1917, Pitkin Central File.

17. First Pulitzer Prizes: John Hohenberg, *The Pulitzer Prizes: A History of the Awards in Books, Drama, Music, and Journalism, Based on the Private Files over Six Decades* (New York: Columbia University Press, 1974), pp. 30–32. Scholarships: *The Columbia Journalist 1913–1923* (New York: Alumni Association of the School of Journalism, 1923), p. 17; Baker, *History*, p. 92.

18. Anti-Militarism League: "Partial List of Persons (Furnished by the Secretary of the Meeting) who attended the Meeting held in the rooms of the Columbia Branch of the Anti-Militarism League, at 2875 Broadway, May 8th, 1917," Williams Central File. Danahy: notes on Butler to Williams, May 11, 1917, Box 61, Baker Papers.

19. Danahy defense: resolution reported in Williams to Butler, May 9, 1917, Williams Central File. Ban on opinions: Butler commencement address of June 6, 1917, quoted in Hofstadter and Metzger, *Academic Freedom*, p. 499.

20. Danahy letter: Danahy to Butler, June 7, 1917, enclosed in Butler to Williams, June 8, 1917, Williams Central File.

21. "List": Williams to Butler, June 12, 1917; "clear the skirts": Butler to Williams, June 15, 1917, Williams Central File.

22. Dana and Cattell: dismissed by the trustees October 1, 1917, Butler Imperium, beatl.barnard.columbia.edu/cuhis3057/timelines.htm.; "Statement by Charles A. Beard."

23. Matthews: minutes, committee on instruction, November 26, 1917; Baker, *History*, p. 77. Appointment of younger man: Pitkin to Butler, December 21, 1917, Williams Central File. Brown: Baker, *History*, p. 83.

24. Knitting needles: Dunbar, *Talcott Williams*, p. 357. Enrollment: "Pulitzer School Staff Grows," *Fourth Estate*, n.d. [1919]. Hough: memoir of the school in *Mostly on Martha's Vineyard: A Personal Record* (New York: Harcourt Brace Jovanovich, 1975), pp. 92–143. War casualties: "Journalism Alumni Organize," *Columbia Alumni News*, May 28, 1920, p. 634.

25. Class of 1919: *The Columbia Journalist 1913–1923*, pp. 67–68.

## 9. RED APPLE AND MARASCHINO CHERRY

1. Retirement: "Williams Resigns as Director of Journalism School," *New York Tribune*, May 22, 1919; "Dr. Williams Gives Up Columbia Post," New York *Evening Sun*, May 22, 1919; editorial, "Dr. Williams and Journalism School," *Christian Science Monitor*, June 10, 1919. "Future labors": "School of Journalism Fully Justified Itself, Says Talcott Williams," New York *World*, June 1, 1919.

2. Five-year course: *School of Journalism Announcement 1917–1918*, December 16, 1918, pp. 8–10; minutes, committee on instruction, January 12, 1917, School of Journalism Records. Modification: *School of Journalism Announcement 1920–1921*, pp. 14–18.

3. Disappearance of professors: *School of Journalism Announcement 1918–1919*, December 8, 1917, pp. 5–6. Sackett: *School of Journalism Announcement 1922–1923*, January 28, 1922, pp. 7, 24.

4. Curriculum: for example, *School of Journalism Announcement 1920–1921*, December 20, 1919. Twenty-five percent: The standard is commonly said to have been set by Willard G. Bleyer of the University of Wisconsin; Donald K. Ross, "Willard G. Bleyer and Journalism Education," *Journalism Quarterly* 34 (fall 1957): 466–74.

5. Administrative board: *School of Journalism Announcement 1919–1920*, December 9, 1918, p. 5.

6. Cunliffe's courses: for example, *School of Journalism Announcement 1919–1920*, pp. 20–21. Hohenberg recollection: *John Hohenberg: The Pursuit of Excellence* (Gainesville: University Press of Florida, 1995), p. 152.

7. Cunliffe appointment: "J. W. Cunliffe is Head of Pulitzer School," *World*, May 31, 1920; "Cunliffe Succeeds Talcott Williams as Pulitzer School Head," *Editor & Publisher*, June 3, 1920. "Difficulties of the situation": Cunliffe to Butler, May 25, 1920, John W. Cunliffe Central File, Columbia University Archives. See Richard Terrill Baker, *A History of the Graduate School of Journalism, Columbia University* (New York: Columbia University Press, 1954), p. 96.

8. Pitkin comments: Walter B. Pitkin, *On My Own* (New York: Scribner's, 1944), p. 403.

9. "Fran": *A House Is Not a Home* (New York: Rinehart, 1953; Popular Library, 1954), p. 92. Staff member: Betsy Wade.

10. Students and typewriters: minutes, committee on instruction, September 29, 1919. Cooper: "University Names New Professors," Columbia *Spectator*, October 21, 1919; Baker, *History*, p. 98. Foghorn and Red X's: Herbert Brucker, "A Student Was One Who Studied," in Wesley First, ed., *University on the Heights* (Garden City: Doubleday, 1969), p. 168. Plaque: The Charles M. Lincoln and Charles P. Cooper Red Apple, given by the Society of the Silurians, veterans of the newspaper business; see, e.g., *Graduate School of Journalism Announcement 1960–1961*, April 30, 1960, p. 31.

11. Dickey: "Pulitzer School Staff Grows," *Fourth Estate* [1919]. Hough, Rukeyser, Temple, Levy, Howard: *School of Journalism Announcement 1919–1920*, pp. 6, 7.

12. Class releases: minutes, committee on instruction, January 11, 1920. "Valuable supplement": *School of Journalism Announcement 1926–1927*, January 2, 1926, p. 24.

13. Alumni organization: "Columbia Grads Eat, Think and Are Wary," *Fourth Estate*, February 7, 1920. Founding: "Journalism Alumni Organize," *Columbia Alumni News*, May 28, 1920, p. 634.

14. "Job census": "Journalism Alumni Organize." "Directory Refutes": "Pulitzer School Men Active in Profession," *World*, March 21, 1921.

15. National enrollment: "New Journalism Courses," *New York Times*, October 16, 1921. Drop in city enrollment: Thomas Bender, *New York Intellect: A History of Intellectual Life in New York City, from 1750 to the Beginnings of Our Own Time* (New York: Knopf, 1987), pp. 288–89.

16. "Elite institution": Bender, *New York Intellect*, p. 292.

17. Laurel wreath: "Pulitzer School Honors Founder's Birth Anniversary," *World*, April 12, 1922. Swope and Butler: notes, April 10, 1922, Box 61, Richard Terrill Baker Papers, Rare Book and Manuscript Library, Columbia University.

18. Undersized bust: "Unveil Bust of School's First Director," *Fourth Estate*, June 2, 1923; Elizabeth Dunbar, *Talcott Williams: Gentleman of the Fourth Estate* (n.p., 1936), p. 384. Dinner: "Pulitzer School Holds Annual Dinner To-Night," *World*, May 26, 1923. Yearbook: *The Columbia Journalist 1913–1923* (New York: Alumni Association of the School of Journalism, 1923).

19. Women graduates: Georgette Carneal, "Pulitzer School Graduates 277 in Ten Years of Life," *World*, September 30, 1923; "Pulitzer School Pioneer in Its Class," *Fourth Estate*, October 6, 1923. Hough: "Woman President for Alumni of the School of Journalism," *World*, May 30, 1923. "Extremists": Carneal, "Pulitzer School Graduates 277." Miriam Beard: *The Columbia Journalist 1913–1923* lists her as a holder of a faculty scholarship; see also *Journalism Alumni Directory 1913–1956* (New York: Graduate School of Journalism, 1956).

20. "Hermaphrodite": A. J. Liebling, "How to Learn Nothing," in *The Wayward Pressman* (Garden City: Doubleday, 1947), p. 28. Fischel: Liebling, "Max and the Corpse," in ibid., pp. 34–35. "Maraschino": "The World of Sport," in ibid., p. 43.

21. "Discipline": Brucker, "A Student Was One Who Studied," p. 171.

22. Graduates: *Journalism Alumni Directory 1913–1956*. Hohenberg: *John Hohenberg: The Pursuit of Excellence* (Gainesville: University Press of Florida), pp. 16–22.

23. MacMahon: "Winners of Pulitzer Traveling Fellowships Off for Europe," *Editor & Publisher*, August 14, 1920; "Miss Katherine E. MacMahon," *Times*, November 11, 1924. The obituary attributes her death to "acute indigestion." "Her example": minutes, committee on instruction, November 10, 1924. Scholarship: "Journalism School Scholarship Given," *Christian Science Monitor*, November 21, 1925.

24. Founder's day: "School Decorates Bust of Pulitzer," *World*, April 13, 1927. Death: "Talcott Williams, Press Dean, Dies," *Philadelphia Inquirer*, January 25, 1928; editorial, "Talcott Williams," *World*, January 25, 1928. Service: "Chaplain Conducts Funeral Services for Dean Williams," Columbia *Spectator*, January 27, 1928; Dunbar, *Talcott Williams*, pp. 397–98.

25. MacAlarney: "No Student's Problem Was Ever Too Trivial For Late Dean of School of Journalism," *World*, January 29, 1928.

26. Cunliffe's illness: "Cunliffe Returns After Long Illness," Columbia *Spectator*, February 8, 1928. Reminders: Butler to Cunliffe, January 9, 1930; Cunliffe to Butler, January 16, 1930; Butler to Cunliffe, January 19, 1930 (birthday); Fackenthal to Cunliffe, April 15, 1930, Cunliffe Central File.

## 10. THE FIRST DEAN

1. Graduating classes: tabulated from *The Columbia Journalist 1931* (New York: Students of the School of Journalism, 1931). Study, 1926: C. W. Steffler, *Columbia Journalism Graduates: A Study of Their Employment and Earnings* (New York: Columbia University Press, 1926). Pitkin study: "Columbia Begins Survey of Newspaper Field; To Study Jobs, Ethics and Student Training," *New York Times*, June 9, 1929; Walter B. Pitkin, *On My Own* (New York: Scribner's, 1944), pp. 406–407.

2. Butler and Ackerman: Butler to Cunliffe, June 24, 1930; graduation address: Cunliffe to Fackenthal, May 20, 1930, John W. Cunliffe Central File, Columbia University Archives. "Our friend": Butler to Ackerman, January 22, 1931, 1931 Scrapbook, Carl W. Ackerman Papers, Library of Congress; Butler to Ackerman, January 26, 1931, Ackerman to Butler, January 31, 1931, Carl W. Ackerman Central File, Columbia University Archives.

3. Williams and Ackerman: Robert E. MacAlarney to Ackerman, March 26, 1919, Container 30, Ackerman Papers; Richard Terrill Baker, *A History of the Graduate School of Journalism, Columbia University* (New York: Columbia University Press, 1954), p. 103. Ackerman career: Albin Krebs, "Carl W. Ackerman Is Dead at 80," *Times*, October 10, 1970. Peace negotiations: M. Douglas O'Malley, "Janus-Faced Diplomacy: Anglo-Irish Peace Negotiations, 1920–1921" (bachelor's thesis, Harvard University, 2001); Baker, *History*, p. 104.

4. Advisory board and alumni: Baker, *History*, pp. 103–104. Ralph Pulitzer approval: Ralph Pulitzer to Butler, February 3, 1931; "publicity directors": Ralph Pulitzer to Butler, telegram, February 10, 1931; "brilliant and attractive gentleman": Butler to Ralph Pulitzer, February 11, 1931, Ralph Pulitzer Central File, Columbia University Archives. Appointment: "Carl W. Ackerman Named Director of Pulitzer Journalism School," *Editor & Publisher*, March 7, 1931.

5. Closing of the *World*: Baker, *History*, p. 104. Deficit and sale: James Boylan, ed., *The World and the 20's: The Golden Years of New York's Legendary Newspaper* (New York: Dial, 1973), pp. 328, 341.

6. Advisory board members: listed in Baker, *History*, pp. 134–35. Plaque and medals: Ralph Pulitzer to Butler, May 22, 1931, Ralph Pulitzer Central File.

7. "Reconcile Pulitzer": Bonsal to Ackerman, March 7, 1931; "Dear Teacher": Ackerman to Howard, March 11, 1931, 1931 scrapbook, Ackerman Papers.

8. Welcome by MacAlarney: MacAlarney to Ackerman, "Saturday morning," 1931 scrapbook, Ackerman Papers. "Shock": *The Columbia Journalist 1931* (New York: Students of the School of Journalism, 1931), p. 15. "Personal choice": Columbia *Spectator*, editorial, March 11, 1931, attributed to *Editor & Publisher*, March 14, 1931.

9. Change in status: Baker, *History*, p. 103; Frank D. Fackenthal, secretary of the

university, to Ackerman, April 6, 1931, notifying him of trustee action, Container 90, Ackerman Papers.

10. Master's program: *Announcement of the School of Journalism . . . 1931–1932*, January 10, 1931, pp. 22, 27–28. "Superficiality": Ackerman to Butler, December 21, 1931, Ackerman Central File.

11. Reforms: Ackerman to Butler, January 11, 1932, Ackerman Central File.

12. B. Lit. and B. S.: Butler to Ackerman, January 14, 1932, Ackerman Central File.

13. "Working day" concern: Hawkes to Ackerman, January 19, 1932; "turn in his grave": Ralph Pulitzer to Ackerman, February 8, 1932; Butler response: Butler to Ackerman, February 11, 1932; withdraws objection: Ralph Pulitzer to Ackerman, February 16, 1932, 1932 scrapbook, Ackerman Papers. Faculty response: Charles P. Cooper to Ackerman, January 29, 1932; Walter B. Pitkin to Ackerman, January 29, 1932; F. Fraser Bond to Ackerman, February 1, 1932, 1932 scrapbook, Ackerman Papers. Council approval: Baker, *History*, p. 104.

14. Press reaction: e.g., "Columbia U. Reforms Journalism Teaching, Raises Standards, Limits Enrollment," *Editor & Publisher*, April 9, 1932. ASNE resolution: *Problems of Journalism*, Proceedings of the Tenth Annual Convention, American Society of Newspaper Editors, 1932, p. 26, quoted in Baker, *History*, p. 106.

15. "Virtual complete control": Stanley Walker, *City Editor* (1934; reprint, Baltimore: Johns Hopkins University Press, 1999), pp. 212–13.

16. "Girls' finishing school": "Columbia U. Reforms Journalism Teaching."

17. Brucker hiring: Brucker to Ackerman, March 4, 1931, 1931 scrapbook, Ackerman Papers; Ackerman to Butler, December 21, 1931, Ackerman Central File.

18. Reed Harris: Horace Coon, *Columbia: Colossus on the Hudson* (New York: Dutton, 1947), p. 131. Proposed takeover: Ackerman to Butler, January 10, 1933, Ackerman Central File; "Former Editors Disapprove Ackerman Plan," Columbia *Spectator*, March 6, 1933. "Inaccurate": ibid., April 21, 1933.

19. *Independent Journal*: Ackerman to Butler, March 31, 1932, Ackerman Central File; copy of first issue in Container 91, Ackerman Papers; Baker, *History*, p. 108.

20. Faculty roster: *Announcement of the School of Journalism 1931–1932*, January 10, 1931, pp. 3–4."Dull, handsome old man": Liebling, "Max and the Corpse," in *The Wayward Pressman* (Garden City: Doubleday, 1947), p. 33.

21. Criticism of Pitkin: Ackerman to Butler, March 24, 1933, Ackerman Central File.

22. Terminations: Ackerman to Butler, March 24, 1933, Ackerman Central File. Death of Will: *Bulletin of the Journalism Alumni Association*, April 1934, copy in 1934 scrapbook, Ackerman Papers.

## 11. "ACKERMAN HAILS STAND OF PRESS"

1. Comments on Sinclair: "Defends Journalism," *New York Times*, May 22, 1921.

2. "Tired of hearing": *Quill* (magazine), September 1932, 1932 scrapbook, Carl W. Ackerman Papers, Library of Congress. Nineteen criticisms: *Report of the Dean of the School of Journalism for the Period Ending June 30, 1933*, October 7, 1933, pp. 5–6.

3. NRA origins: Leverett Lyon et al., *The National Recovery Administration: An Analysis and Appraisal* (Washington: Brookings Institution, 1935).

4. "Power to license": American Newspaper Publishers Association, *Bulletin 6130* (June 15, 1933). Code text: "Revised Newspaper Code": *New York Herald Tribune*, August 16, 1933.

5. "Unhealthy state": "Ackerman Asks U.S. Guaranty On Free Press," *Herald Tribune*, August 16, 1933.

6. "Escaping a dictatorship": *Report of the Dean . . . 1933*, p. 11. *Times* headline: *Times*, September 18, 1933.

7. "In balance": "A Statement of Fact," *Independent Journal*, October 16, 1933. "Delicatessen": Broun, "It Seems to Me," *New York World-Telegram*, October 19, 1933. Lindsay Rogers: quoted in "N.R.A. and the Newspapers," *Independent Journal*, November 1, 1933.

8. McCormick at school: Ackerman to McCormick, November 1, 1933, School of Journalism Records. "Fascist government": Phillip Kinsley, "Exempt Press Freedom From U.S. Curb, Plea," *Chicago Tribune*, November 25, 1933. "Tripe": Rogers to Davis, November 26, 1933, quoted in James Boylan, "The Daily Newspaper Business in the National Recovery Administration" (master's essay, Columbia University, 1960).

9. "Nobody waives": NRA, *Code of Fair Competition for the Daily Newspaper Business* (Washington: Government Printing Office, 1934), pp. 69–70.

10. Prize nomination: Bryan to Pulitzer committee, February 26, 1934; Ackerman to Butler, April 14, 1934; Butler to Ackerman, April 16, 1934, 1934 scrapbook, Ackerman Papers. "Homeric laughter": Ralph Pulitzer to Butler, quoting Harris, April 6, 1934, Container 136, Ackerman Papers. ASNE committee: ASNE, *Problems of Journalism*, 1934, p. 143; text of report in *Herald Tribune*, April 21, 1934.

11. "Garbled, suppressed": "Johnson Flays Press Critics": n.p., August 3, 1934. Response: "Columbia Dean of Journalism Assails N.R.A.," clipping, Los Angeles [n.p.], August 3, 1934; "Ackerman Warns Johnson Seeks Control of Press," clipping, Los Angeles [n.p.], August 3, 1934.

12. Skeptics: Ackerman to Butler, April 14, 1934, 1934 scrapbook, Ackerman Papers.

13. Unconstitutional: *Schechter v. United States*, 295 U.S. 495 (1935). "Hails Stand": *Herald Tribune*, May 29, 1935; "Vindication of Press Is Seen in NRA Ruling," *Times*, May 29, 1935.

## 12. THE GRADUATE SCHOOL

1. ASNE proposal: Albert Alton Sutton, *Education for Journalism in the United States from Its Beginning to 1940* (Evanston: Northwestern University Studies in the Humanities, No. 10, 1945), p. 25.

2. "Inexorable logic": Richard Terrill Baker, *A History of the Graduate School of Journalism, Columbia University* (New York: Columbia University Press, 1954), p. 109. Degrees: tabulated from *The Columbia Journalist 1935* (New York: Students of the School of Journalism, 1935).

3. Graduate proposal: Submitted to the University Council, Ackerman to Frank D. Fackenthal, November 7, 1934, Carl W. Ackerman Central File, Columbia University Archives.

4. Rejection: Ackerman to Fackenthal, including minutes of faculty meeting in which he reported on University Council action, December 14, 1934, Ackerman Central File. Fifth undergraduate year: Baker, *History*, p. 111. Acquiescence: "Recommendations for the Establishment of a Graduate School of Journalism," adopted by the Faculty of Journalism, January 18, 1935, Ackerman Central File. Approval: Baker, *History*, p. 110.

5. "Flying professor": "'Flying Professor' Commutes from Richmond Every Week," Columbia *Spectator*, October 8, 1934; his Pulitzer Prize: Baker, *History*, p. 106. "All keyed up": Freeman to Ackerman, February 27, 1935, 1935 scrapbook, Carl W. Ackerman Papers, Library of Congress.

6. "Tussle": Brown to Ackerman, March 12, 1935, 1935 scrapbook, Ackerman Papers.

7. "One year too long": editorial, New York *Daily News*, March 15, 1935, clipping in Container 78, Ackerman Papers.

8. "Journalism as a business": *Announcement of the Graduate School of Journalism . . . 1935–1936*, September 14, 1935, p. 9.

9. "Mass production": Frank L. Perrin, "North . . . South . . . East . . . West," *Christian Science Monitor*, November 7, 1935; "Ackerman Charge Stirs Educators," *Times*, December 1, 1935.

10. "Women of superior ability": *Announcement . . . 1935–1936*, p. 11. "Novel, short story": "Columbia Plans Revised Course In Journalism," *Herald Tribune*, March 10, 1935.

11. "Vindicated itself": Freeman to Brucker, December 28, 1935, Container 67, Ackerman Papers.

12. "Palatial": *The Columbia Journalist 1935* (New York: Students of the School of Journalism, 1935).

## 13. SPEAKING TO CABOTS

1. Cabot meeting: Richard Terrill Baker, *A History of the Graduate School of Journalism, Columbia University* (New York: Columbia University, 1954), p. 113; Henry Sweets Ackerman, "A History of the Maria Moors Cabot Prizes: Experiment in Inter-American Journalism, 1938–1956" (master's thesis, University of North Carolina, 1969), pp. 2–4. Ackerman, grandson of the dean, prepared his thesis with access to Carl W. Ackerman's personal files (now in the Library of Congress) and the Maria Moors Cabot Prize Files, at the school.

2. Disappointment: Henry Ackerman, "Cabot Prizes," p. 5; brief history of the Nieman Program, www.nieman.harvard.edu/about/history.html.

3. "Good Neighbor policy" and gift to Harvard: Henry Ackerman, "Cabot Prizes," p. 26. Skinflint: see the unfriendly biography by Leon A. Harris, *Only to God: The Extraordinary Life of Godfrey Lowell Cabot* (New York: Atheneum, 1967).

4. Creation of program: Henry Ackerman, "Cabot Prizes," pp. 27–32. "Black Plague": "Ackerman Calls for Action To Save Freedom of Press," *Editor & Publisher*, January 8, 1938.

5. Exchanges with Butler: Henry Ackerman, "Cabot Prizes," p. 46; Ackerman to Butler, May 10, 1938; Butler to Ackerman, May 12 1938; Ackerman to Butler, May 16, 1938; Butler to Ackerman, May 17, 1938, Carl W. Ackerman Central File, Columbia University Archives.

6. Agreement: Henry Ackerman, "Cabot Prizes," p. 36; Ackerman to Butler, September 15, 1938, submitting agreement, Ackerman Central File. "Cash on the barrelhead": Henry Ackerman, "Cabot Prizes," p. 37.

7. Cultural Relations: Henry Ackerman, "Cabot Prizes," pp. 47–49. "Covert source": ibid., p. 49.

8. Recommendations and awards: Henry Ackerman, "Cabot Prizes," pp. 51–54; Ackerman to Butler, July 11, 1939, Container 67, Carl W. Ackerman Papers, Library of Congress. Dropouts: Ackerman to Butler, September 18, 22, 1939, Ackerman Central File.

9. Prizewinners' welcome: Henry Ackerman, "Cabot Prizes," pp. 57–62.

10. Braden and Messersmith: ibid., pp. 72, 81–82.

11. "Personally, politically": Dean Ackerman's paraphrase of Messersmith, in ibid., p. 81.

12. Attacks on Rivero: ibid., pp. 82–87; Ackerman to Butler, November 14, 1941, Ackerman Central File.

13. "Over the dam": Henry Ackerman, "Cabot Prizes," p. 84. Regrets from Jews: ibid., p. 85; *Christian Science Monitor* reactions, ibid., pp. 85–87.

14. Cabot stock: Ackerman to Butler, August 4, 1941, Ackerman Central File. Growth in income: Edward W. Barrett to Ellis L. Phillips Jr., n.d. [1961], Edward W. Barrett Central File, Columbia University Archives. Dean Barrett initiated most of the later disbursements from the Cabot income; see Barrett to Grayson Kirk, February 16, 1962, and Barrett to John Moors Cabot, February 16, 1962, Barrett Central File.

15. "Unwritten agreement": Henry Ackerman, "Cabot Prizes," pp. 68–69.

16. Cabot involvement: ibid., p. 89.

17. Expansion: ibid., pp. 70–80.

18. Noble and Beltran: ibid., pp. 90–91.

## 14. "MY DEAR DEAN"

1. Research center: "Foundation Urged for Public Opinion," *New York Times*, November 12, 1936. Radio committee: "Radio Activities at Columbia University," Carl W. Ackerman Central File, Columbia University Archives. School of communication: Ackerman to Frank D. Fackenthal, March 31, 1939; Ackerman to Butler, April 10, 1939; Butler to Ackerman, April 13, 1939, Ackerman Central File. White, Gallup, Roper: Richard Terrill Baker, *A History of the Graduate School of Journalism, Columbia University* (New York: Columbia University Press, 1954), lists White as teaching from 1939 to 1946; Gallup from 1935 to 1938; and Roper from 1939 to 1946, pp. 131–33.

2. "Instrument of the mass": "Ackerman Urges Reforms on Press," *Times*, November 26, 1937.

3. Conversations with Luce: Ackerman to Fackenthal, August 1, 1938; Ackerman to Butler, August 1, 1938 (identical letter); Butler to Ackerman, August 4, 5, 1938; "Have notified Time": Ackerman to Butler, August 9, 1938, Ackerman Central File.

4. Exchange with Sulzberger: Sulzberger to Ackerman, August 15, 1938; Ackerman to Sulzberger, August 18, 1938; "conservative publishers": Ackerman to Butler, September 19, 1938, Ackerman Central File.

5. Hutchins Commission report: Commission on Freedom of the Press, *A Free and Responsible Press: A General Report on Mass Communication* (Chicago: University of Chicago Press, 1947).

6. "Disappointment and injury": "Confidential Memorandum for President Butler From Dean Ackerman, October 2, 1939," Container 67, Carl W. Ackerman Papers, Library of Congress.

7. "Special report": Ackerman to Butler, December 10, 1939, Ackerman Central File. "(Speed) Pitkin": 1934 scrapbook, container 76, Carl W. Ackerman Papers, Library of Congress.

8. "Land of pedestrians": Pitkin, *On My Own* (New York: Scribner's, 1944), p. 449–52.

9. "Sit-down strike": Ackerman, "Special report in regard to present conditions in the Graduate School of Journalism," December 10, 1939, Ackerman Central File.

10. Response: Butler to Ackerman, December 14, 1939, Ackerman Central File.

11. "Similar situation": Ackerman to Butler, December 18, 1939, Ackerman Central File.

12. Brucker raise: Ackerman to Butler, April 9, 1942, Ackerman Central File. Brucker and OWI: Ackerman to Butler, September 23, 1942, Ackerman Central File. Brucker and *Courant*: Ackerman to Fackenthal, April 11, 1944, Ackerman Central File; Ackerman to Dwight Sargent, February 15, 1963, Container 49, Ackerman Papers, saying that he and Butler proposed Brucker for the *Courant* position.

13. Minimum-wage fight: affidavits of Carl W. Ackerman and Kenneth B. Olsen (dean of the Medill School at Northwestern) in federal minimum-wage case against the Easton Publishing Company, ANPA *Federal Laws Bulletin No. 7355*, October 11, 1940, copy in Container 34, Ackerman Papers. "Fifth columnist": Ackerman to Hanson, October 15, 1940, Container 34, Ackerman Papers.

14. "Delays procedure": Ackerman to Butler, December 2, 1940, Ackerman Central File. Retirement: "Cunliffe to Quit Teaching, Give Away Library," *New York Herald Tribune*, May 3, 1942.

15. Cooper retirement: "Cooper's Retirement Recalls Old Days of Newspaper Life," New York *Sun*, June 23, 1940. "High expectations": Ackerman to Fackenthal, December 26, 1939, confidential, Ackerman Central File.

16. Ellard biography: Ackerman to Fackenthal, December 26, 1939. "Stuttered punch line": Mort Stern, "The Lesson," in Edward W. Barrett, ed., *Journalists in Action* (New York: Channel, 1963), p. 105.

17. Ellard appointment: Fackenthal to Ackerman, December 27, 1939; Fackenthal to Ackerman, January 8, 1940, reporting trustee action, Ackerman Central File.

## 15. OUTPOST IN CHUNGKING

1. Higgins: Antoinette May, *Witness to War* (New York: Beaufort, 1983), pp. 49–53. "Open house": Report of Clifford B. Wright to [?] Norris, January 28, 1941; Ackerman to Frank D. Fackenthal, February 10, 1941, Carl W. Ackerman Central File, Columbia University Archives.

2. MacAlarney: Ackerman to Butler, July 13, 1942; Trapp: Ackerman to Fackenthal, June 28, 1943; Ybarra: Ackerman to Butler, May 18, 1943, Ackerman Central File. Blitzkrieg: Kevin McCann, assistant to Eisenhower, to Ackerman, August 11, 1950, container 96, Carl W. Ackerman Papers, Library of Congress.

3. Carroll: "Eleanor Carroll Named Assistant to Ackerman," *New York Herald Tribune*, December 8, 1944. Class of 1943: tabulated from *Journalism Alumni Directory 1913–1956* (New York: Graduate School of Journalism, 1956).

4. Diminished pool: *Report of the Dean of the Graduate School of Journalism . . . 1945–1946*, July 19, 1946. Women graduates: *Journalism Alumni Directory 1913–1956*.

5. Tong and Madame Chiang's tour: Richard Terrill Baker, *A History of the Graduate School of Journalism, Columbia University* (New York: Columbia University Press, 1954), p. 114; W. A. Swanberg, *Luce and His Empire* (New York: Scribner's, 1972), pp. 200–203. Tong proposal: *Report of the Dean of the Graduate School of Journalism on the Chinese Post-Graduate School of Journalism, March, 1943-August, 1945*, October 29, 1945, pp. 3–4. The report was written by Richard T. Baker, F. J. Dralle, and Floyd D. Rodgers Jr., three faculty members at the school established in Chungking.

6. Dean's proposal: Ackerman to Nicholas Murray Butler, February 15, 1943, Container 63, Carl W. Ackerman Papers, Library of Congress.

7. Financing: Harold L. Cross Diary, undated [January 1943], Harold L. Cross Papers, Columbia University Archives. Fellers: Ackerman to Fellers, January 20, 1943 (on OWI); Fellers to Ackerman, January 26, 1943; Fellers to Ackerman, February 18, 1943, Container 27, Ackerman Papers.

8. Formal invitation: Tong to Ackerman, March 18, 1943; Ackerman to Butler, March 19, 1943, Ackerman Central File. Check: Ackerman to Butler, March 29, 1943; Butler to Ackerman, March 30, 1943, Ackerman Central File.

9. Recruits: Baker, *History*, p. 114; Cross Diary, n.d. [May 1943].

10. Travel: Cross Diary, July 17-September 29, 1943; Cross to Elaine Cross (spouse), October 2, 1943, Cross Papers.

11. Opening of school: "New Journalism School for China," press release, October 11, 1943, Ackerman Central File; "Columbia Opens School in China," *New York Times*, October 11, 1943. Living conditions: *Report . . . on the Chinese Post-Graduate School*, pp. 20–21.

12. "Two-fisted": Cross to Elaine Cross, March 30, 1944, Cross Papers. Faculty: *Report . . . on the Chinese Post-Graduate School*, pp. 4–5, 9. "Hill-billy": Rodney Gilbert to spouse, October 10, 1944, forwarded to Ackerman, Container 63, Ackerman Papers.

13. Curriculum: *Report . . . on the Chinese Post-Graduate School*, pp. 17–19.

14. Ministry of Information: *Report . . . on the Chinese Post-Graduate School*, p. 10. Hostility of correspondents: Floyd D. Rodgers Jr. to Jackson Rodgers (spouse), March 31, 1944, Floyd D. Rodgers Jr. Papers, privately held.

15. Audience with Chiang: Cross to Elaine Cross, January 17, 1944, Cross Papers.

16. *Chungking Reporter: Report . . . on the Chinese Graduate School*, pp. 12–15; "Chinese Students Publish Tabloid Paper in English," *Herald Tribune*, January 7, 1944. "Tong liked it": Cross to Elaine Cross, January 25, 1944.

17. "All copy": Cross to Elaine Cross, February 13, 1944; "better than any other": Cross to Elaine Cross, February 17, 1944; uncensored articles: Cross to Elaine Cross, March 26, 1944, Cross Papers.

18. "'Strong' China" incident: Rodgers to Jackson Rodgers, April 14, 1944, Rodgers Papers; Cross to Elaine Cross, April 13, 1944, Cross Papers.

19. "Show-down": Rodgers to Jackson Rodgers, April 14, 1944.

20. "Mothered and coddled": Rodgers to Jackson Rodgers, April 26, 1944, Rodgers Papers.

21. "Thought control" exclusive: *Report . . . on the Chinese Post-Graduate School*, pp. 14–16; press code: ibid., p. 15.

22. Mail pouch: Cross to Elaine Cross, February 17, 1944; Ackerman silence: Cross to Elaine Cross, February 27, 1944; Pulitzer's rest: Cross to Elaine Cross, April 13, 1944, Cross Papers.

23. Study in America: Cross to Elaine Cross, April 30, 1944, Cross Papers. Rice allowance and "ready to pack": Rodgers to Jackson Rodgers, May 22 [?], 1944, Rodgers Papers.

24. Meeting with Gauss: Cross, Baker, Dralle, Rodgers, confidential memorandum, May 25, 1944, Box 4, Richard T. Baker Papers, Rare Book and Manuscript Library, Columbia University. Rodgers on Cross: Rodgers to Jackson Rodgers, May 22 [?], 1944. Travel to Communist area: Cross to Elaine Cross, April 5, 1944, Cross Papers.

25. Cross departure: "Cross Leaving Chungking," *Herald Tribune*, June 30, 1944. Baker travels: Baker to Ackerman, September 4, 1944, Container 63, Ackerman Papers. Rodgers's typhus: Dralle to Cross, September 8, 1944, Container 63, Ackerman Papers; Floyd D. Rodgers. Jr., *Leaves from a China Diary, 1943–45* (New York: Vantage, 1995), pp. 85–87.

## 16. "SWEAT AND TEARS"

1. Cross charges and rebuttal: Carl W. Ackerman to Rodney Gilbert, September 16, 1944, Container 63, Carl W. Ackerman Papers, Library of Congress. "Finger-waggling": Rodgers to Jackson Rodgers, relaying word from Dralle, November 4, 1944, Floyd D. Rodgers Jr. Papers, privately held.

2. Replace faculty: Ackerman to Gilbert, September 16, 1944. "Supreme Educational Command": Rodgers to Jackson Rodgers, November 4, 1944, Rodgers Papers. Cross career: Malcolm A. Cross, "My Dad," private communication, August 9, 2001.

3. New dean: "Rodney Gilbert to Head School of Journalism in Chungking,"

*New York Herald Tribune*, April 19, 1944. "Highbinders": Gilbert to Magruder, April 24, 1944; arrival: Gilbert to Ackerman, August 19, 1944, Container 63, Ackerman Papers.

4. Andrews: Ackerman to Butler, June 19, 1944; Robert V. Ackerman to Carl W. Ackerman, April 8, 1945, Carl W. Ackerman Central File, Columbia University Archives. Robert V. Ackerman: Carl W. Ackerman to Frank D. Fackenthal, April 27, 1944, Ackerman Central File; Rodgers to Jackson Rodgers, December 16, 1944, Rodgers Papers.

5. Graduation: Rodgers to Jackson Rodgers, October 12, 1944, Rodgers Papers.

6. Baker's character: Gilbert to Ackerman, November 14, 1944, Container 63, Ackerman Papers.

7. Faculty continuation: Robert V. Ackerman to parents, November 18, 1944, Container 63, Ackerman Papers; Rodgers to Jackson Rodgers, November 21, 1944, Rodgers Papers.

8. Japanese threat: Ackerman to Fackenthal, December 5, 1944, Ackerman Central File. "End of the road": Rodgers to Jackson Rodgers, December 7, 1944, Rodgers Papers.

9. "Certain statements": Ackerman, "To Whom This May Concern," October 14, 1944, Container 63, Ackerman Papers.

10. "Time has come": Ackerman, "Telephone message to Allman from Lambertville Oct. 15" [1944], Container 63, Ackerman Papers. See also Maochun Yu, *OSS in China: Prelude to Cold War* (New Haven: Yale University Press, 1996).

11. Pay up: Ackerman, notes, October 21, 1944, Container 63, Ackerman Papers. Money released: Ackerman to Fackenthal, September 25, 1945, Ackerman Central File.

12. ASNE mission: a full account of the trip appears in Leonard Ray Teel, *Ralph Emerson McGill: Voice of the Southern Conscience* (Knoxville: University of Tennessee Press, 2001), pp. 185–206.

13. "Emotionally moved": Ackerman to Vandy (Mabel Vander Hoof Ackerman, spouse), April 4, 1945; "liar": Ackerman to Vandy, April 1, 1945, Container 38, Ackerman Papers.

14. "Slumped on the sofa": Ackerman to Vandy, April 1, 1945; "Kan pei's": Chinese Press Review (Mimeograph), April 3, 1945, Container 38, Ackerman Papers.

15. "Disgrace to journalism": Ackerman to John S. Knight, April 4, 1945; future of school: Ackerman to Vandy, April 7, 1945; travel to Philippines: Ackerman to Vandy, April 24, 1945; MacArthur: Ackerman to Vandy, May 4, 1945; San Francisco: Edward Stettinius (secretary of state) to Ackerman, May 12, 1945, Container 38, Ackerman Papers.

16. Roosevelt's death: Floyd D. Rodgers. Jr., *Leaves from a China Diary, 1943–45* (New York: Vantage, 1995), pp. 31–35.

17. Meeting with president: *Editor & Publisher*, June 18, 1945. McGill's frustration: Teel, *McGill*, p. 255.

18. Gilbert departure: Confidential Memorandum, Baker to Ackerman, August 9, 1945, Rodgers Papers.

19. "Earlier than expected": *Report . . . on the Chinese Post-Graduate School*, p. 23.

20. Angry letter: Gilbert to Baker, August 26, 1945, Rodgers Papers.

21. Refund: Ackerman to Fackenthal, September 25, 1945, Ackerman Central File. Personal check: Donald H. Galloway, director, Strategic Services Unit, War Department to Ackerman, April 12, 1948; partial disclosure: Ackerman to president [1945]; Baker alarm: Baker to Ackerman, September 26, 1945, Container 63, Ackerman Papers.

22. "Sweat and tears": *Report . . . on the Chinese Post-Graduate School*, p. 23.

23. Chinese graduates: Eleanor Carroll to Robert V. Ackerman, March 28, 1945, Container 63, Ackerman Papers; *Journalism Alumni Directory 1913–1956.* "Red silk curtain": Richard Terrill Baker, *A History of the Graduate School of Journalism, Columbia University* (New York: Columbia University Press, 1954), p. 114.

24. Later teachers: Glenn Fowler, "James Aronson, Journalism Critic, Editor and Teacher, Is Dead at 73," *Times*, October 22, 1988. He was succeeded by Lawrence D. Pinkham, class of 1952, who returned to Beijing repeatedly; résumé, July 1990, School of Journalism Records.

## 17. POSTWAR VENTURES

1. Butler resignation: "A Social History of Columbia University: The Butler Imperium—A Timeline, 1902–1945," beatl.barnard.columbia.edu/cuhis3057/timelines.htm. Ackerman comment: Ackerman to Vandy (Mabel Vander Hoof Ackerman), April 16, 1945, Container 38, Carl W. Ackerman Papers, Library of Congress.

2. MacAlarney and Cunliffe: *Report of the Dean of the Graduate School of Journalism . . . 1945–1946*, July 19, 1946; MacAlarney died on November 15, 1945; Cunliffe, on March 18, 1946. Loss of faculty members: ibid. Freeman departure: Butler to Ackerman, February 3, 1941; Ackerman to Frank D. Fackenthal, April 22, 1941, Carl W. Ackerman Central Files, Columbia University Archives.

3. Freeman and Brown: Don E. Carter and Malcolm F. Mallette, *Seminar: The Story of the American Press Institute* (Reston, Va.: American Press Institute, 1992), pp. 15–18.

4. Institute proposal: Sevellon Brown, typescript of lecture dated June 1940, Sevellon Brown File, School of Journalism Records. Proposal in 1945: Brown to Carl W. Ackerman, September 13, 1945, Ackerman Central File; Carter and Mallette, *Seminar*, p. 26.

5. Pulitzer opposition: Joseph Pulitzer II to Sevellon Brown, October 4, 1945; Ackerman comment: Ackerman to Fackenthal, October 8, 1945, Ackerman Central File.

6. Financial support: Ackerman to Fackenthal, January 7, 1946, Ackerman Central file. "First time": Ackerman, quoted in Carter and Mallette, *Seminar*, p. 28. Faculty approval: Ackerman to Fackenthal January 15, 1946, Ackerman Central File.

7. Waldorf meeting: Ackerman to Fackenthal, February 16, 1946, Ackerman Central File; Carter and Mallette, *Seminar*, p. 29. Taylor: biographical summary, May 6, 1943, Container 96, Ackerman Papers; Ackerman, memorandum of conference with Fackenthal, January 10, 1946, Ackerman Central File. "For administrative purposes": Ackerman and Brown, background document for news conference, February 14, 1946, enclosed with Ackerman to Fackenthal, February 16, 1946. Ackerman's office: Carter and Mallette, *Seminar*, p. 39.

8. Fackenthal warning: Carter and Mallette, *Seminar*, p. 33.

9. First seminar: Carter and Mallette, *Seminar*, pp. 7, 12–13, 60–61; women: p. 13.

10. Photography seminar: Carter and Mallette, *Seminar*, pp. 62–63. No journalism faculty used: ibid., p. 149. API teachers: *Announcement of the Graduate School of Journalism . . . 1949–1950*, July 23, 1949.

11. Curtis: Carter and Mallette, *Seminar*, pp. 67, 71; Kirchhofer: ibid., pp. 77–84. Curtis nomination: Ackerman to Fackenthal, August 5, 1947, Ackerman Central File.

12. "Formal affiliation": Carter and Mallette, *Seminar*, pp. 152–53; "must remain affiliated": ibid., p. 153. "Dormant": Ackerman to John Godfrey Saxe, March 15, 1948, Ackerman Central File.

13. Aversion to school: Carter and Mallette, *Seminar*, p. 154. Taylor job offer: Ackerman to Fackenthal, January 21, 1948, Container 90, Ackerman Papers. Rockefeller support: Ackerman to Albert C. Jacobs, provost, November 18, 1948, Ackerman Central File; Floyd Taylor to Ackerman, July 26, 1949, Container 65, Ackerman Papers.

14. Overhead: Ackerman to W. Emerson Gentzler, bursar, March 26, 1951; better paid: Ackerman to API advisory board, April 26, 1951; "love feast": Ackerman to Grayson Kirk, acting president, April 26, 1951, Ackerman Central File.

15. Taylor's death: Richard T. Baker, *A History of the Graduate School of Journalism, Columbia University* (New York: Columbia University Press, 1954), p. 120; Carter and Mallette, *Seminar*, p. 148; Brown to Ackerman, August 31, 1951, Ackerman Central File. Curtis and Reese: Brown to Ackerman, September 20, 1951; Ackerman to Kirk, September 21, 26,1951, Ackerman Central File. Bypass: Carter and Mallette, *Seminar*, p. 155.

16. "First home": Carter and Mallette, *Seminar*, p. 152.

17. Venezuela: "To Help Set Up School / Ackerman, Journalism Dean At Columbia, Going to Venezuela" *New York Times*, May 23, 1947. Offers from other countries: Ackerman to Tom Clark, U.S. attorney general, January 17, 1948; Czechoslovakia: Ackerman to Fackenthal, August 1, 1946, Ackerman Central File.

18. Creole support: Bauman to Ackerman, February 26, 1947, Ackerman Central File.

19. "Plan Ackerman": Ackerman to Fackenthal from Caracas, June 27, 1947, Ackerman Central File. John Foster Jr.: Ackerman to Bauman, August 4, 1947, School of Journalism Records. Myrick Land: Ackerman to Dr. Santiago E. Vera, rector of Universidad Central, January 15, 1948, Ackerman Central File.

20. School financing: Ackerman to Bauman, cable, August 24 [1947], School of Journalism Records; Ackerman to Fackenthal, cable, September 16, 1947, Ackerman Central File. Opening: Ackerman to Fackenthal, from Caracas, October 30, 1947, enclosing clippings, Ackerman Central File.

21. "Ability and personality": Ackerman to Jacobs, January 13, 1948, Ackerman Central File. "Stronger and better": Ackerman to Bauman, February 6, 1948, School of Journalism Records.

22. Complaint on visa: Ackerman to Clark, January 17, 1948, Ackerman Central File. Response: "Clark Denies Plan Bars Journalists," *Times*, January 23, 1948.

23. Myrick Land writings: Bauman to Ackerman, May 28, 1948; Ackerman to Bauman, June 1, 14, 1948, School of Journalism Records. Foster's return: Ackerman to Fackenthal, June 16, 1948, Ackerman Central File.

24. New agreement: Ackerman to Lieutenant Colonel Carlos Delgado Chalbaud, December 23, 1948; communists: Bauman to Ackerman, November 18, 1949, School of Journalism Records.

25. Escuela de Comunicacion Social: brief history of school at www.ucv.ve/ftproot/humanidades/organizacion/escuelas/communica/communica2.htm, as of December 8, 2001.

## 18. THE DEAN AND THE PRIZES

1. Early procedures: John Hohenberg, *The Pulitzer Prizes: A History of the Awards in Books, Drama, Music, and Journalism, Based on the Private Files over Six Decades* (New York: Columbia University Press, 1974), pp. 24–32. Reminder from board: ibid., p. 32. O'Neill: ibid., p. 44.

2. Lewis rejection: ibid., pp. 85–87.

3. Grumbling: ibid., pp. 40–41. Executive secretary: ibid., p. 84. "Grave danger": Ralph Pulitzer to Butler, January 4, 1929, Ralph Pulitzer Central File, Columbia University Archives.

4. "Diplomatic questions": Ackerman to John A. Krout, vice president (draft), February 19, 1954, Container 93, Carl W. Ackerman Papers, Library of Congress. "Superior authority": Ackerman to Richard Herpers, secretary of the university, May 23, 1955, Carl W. Ackerman Central File, Columbia University Archives.

5. Abjured authority: Hohenberg, *Pulitzer Prizes*, p. 24. "Took control": ibid., p. 84.

6. Control: Hohenberg, *Pulitzer Prizes*, pp. 138, 171, 181–90. Special citation: to the Edmonton, Alberta, *Journal*, ibid., p. 369. ASNE role: ibid., pp. 172–73. Pulitzer distressed: Joseph Pulitzer II to Ackerman, April 20, 1935, Container 79, Ackerman Papers.

7. "Incompetent": Heywood Broun, "Class Angle It," *The Nation*, May 22, 1935. Hellman and Akins: Hohenberg, *Pulitzer Prizes*, pp. 149–50.

8. Hemingway dispute: Hohenberg, *Pulitzer Prizes*, pp. 143–46. "Reconsider": quoted in Arthur Krock, "Previous Veto of a Pulitzer Board Award," *New York Times*, May 11, 1962.

9. Wolfert incident: Hohenberg, *Pulitzer Prizes*, p. 181.

10. Film prize: minutes of advisory board's reclassification committee, in Ackerman to Fackenthal, January 21, 1947; Joseph Pulitzer II to Ackerman, February 11, 1947; Mathews to Joseph Pulitzer II, February 28, 1947, Ackerman Central File.

11. Veto dispute: Ackerman to John G. Saxe, university counsel, November 19, December 5, 1946, Ackerman Central File.

12. Radio program: minutes of reclassification committee in Ackerman to Fackenthal, January 21, 1947, Ackerman Central File. Hollywood: Ackerman to Fackenthal, February 4, 22, 24, 1947, Ackerman Central File; "Radio Series Set on Pulitzer Prizes," *Christian Science Monitor*, March 11, 1947.

13. "Blistered": Ackerman to Fackenthal, May 8, 1947, Ackerman Central File. ASNE role: Ackerman to Fackenthal, January 21, 1947, Ackerman Central File; "16 Are Named Pulitzer Judges for Journalism," *New York Herald Tribune*, January 25, 1947.

14. Warning: Ackerman to Joseph Pulitzer II, May 22, 1947, Ackerman Central File. Splitting public service: Joseph Pulitzer II to Ackerman, February 11, 1947.

15. "Published criticism": Ackerman to Fackenthal, December 5, 1947, Ackerman Central File.

16. Binder article: Ackerman to Fackenthal, March 23, 1948, Ackerman Central File; Hohenberg, *Pulitzer Prizes*, pp. 173–74. Krock rebuttal: copy of Krock to Binder, March 30, 1948, Ackerman Central File.

17. *Post-Dispatch* prize: tabulation in Hohenberg, *Pulitzer Prizes*, pp. 359–70.

18. Costs of program: Ackerman to advisory board, March 23, 1949; warning to Pulitzer family: Ackerman to Saxe, June 16, 1949, Ackerman Central File.

19. "Storm is brewing": Ackerman to Kirk, January 24, 1950, Ackerman Central File.

20. Change of name: Ackerman to Herpers, May 23, 1955, Ackerman Central File; Hohenberg, *Pulitzer Prizes*, p. 229.

21. "Never agree": Ackerman to Joseph Pulitzer II, March 27, 1950, Ackerman Central File.

22. Television agreement: Ackerman to advisory board, May 8, 1950; Barbara Morse, administrative assistant to the dean, to provost's office, May 11, 1950, Ackerman Central File; "Journalism School Gets Schlitz Grant," *Herald Tribune*, October 7 [?], 1950.

23. WCTU complaint:"Oh, Beer! WCTU Froths At Columbia," *New York World-Telegram*, November 9, 1950. Eisenhower response: Hohenberg, *Pulitzer Prizes*, p. 219.

24. TV sets and desks: Ackerman to Kirk, August 9, 1950, Ackerman Central File.

### 19. "TRAINING GROUND"

1. M. S. degrees: *Report of the Dean of the Graduate School of Journalism . . . 1945–1946*, July 19, 1946.

2. Applications soared: *Report of the Dean . . . 1945–1946.* Admissions policy: "Pulitzer Centennial: Columbia Headlines Progress," *Christian Science Monitor*, April 7, 1947. City graduates: tabulated from *Journalism Alumni Directory 1913–1956* (New York: Graduate School of Journalism, 1956).

3. Class of 1947: *Journalism Alumni Directory 1913–1956.*

4. Ackerman and Ross: "The Joseph Pulitzer Stamp," fact sheet, with first-day cover sent by Ackerman to Nicholas Murray Butler, April 10, 1947, Nicholas Murray Butler Papers, Rare Book and Manuscript Library, Columbia University. Ackerman to Hannegan, August 1, 1946, Carl W. Ackerman Central File, Columbia University Archives.

5. Stamp sales: Albert Goldman, postmaster, to Ackerman, April 15, 1947; Ackerman memorandum, March 1, 1954, Ackerman Central File.

6. "Pulitzer School": "A Pulitzer Centennial," *New York Times*, April 10, 1947.

7. Commission report: The Commission on Freedom of the Press, *A Free and Responsible Press: A General Report on Mass Communication: Newspapers, Radio, Motion Pictures, Magazines, and Books* (Chicago: University of Chicago Press, 1947); press reaction: Margaret A. Blanchard, *The Hutchins Commission, The Press and the Responsibility Concept*, Journalism Monographs 49 (May 1977): 29–50. On schools of journalism: *A Free and Responsible Press*, pp. 77–78.

8. Field trips: Ackerman, identical letters to Butler and to Kent Cooper, Associated Press, April 14, 1942, enclosing the Port Chester *Item* of April 11, 1942. Women's sports page: "Students Operate 8 Papers for Day . . . Girls Issue Sports Page," *Times*, May 9, 1943.

9. "Eminently qualified": Ackerman to Butler, March 29, 1943, Ackerman Central File. Brush with Krock: Ackerman to Butler, May 3, 1943, Ackerman Central File.

10. Associate deanship: Ackerman, notes on conference with Fackenthal, January 10, 1946; Ackerman to Fackenthal, January 16, 1946, Ackerman Central File. "Ellard's plans": *Report of the Dean . . . 1945–1946*. AWOL: Ackerman to Albert C. Jacobs, provost, March 3, 18, April 3, 1947, Ackerman Central File.

11. Foster on faculty: Ackerman to President Dwight D. Eisenhower, June 22, 1948, Ackerman Central File. Facsimile: "15 at Columbia Send 80-Pg. Paper on 3-State Hookup, Called First of Its Kind," *Times*, March 22, 1951. "News-O-Rama": Ackerman to W. Emerson Gentzler, bursar, November 5, 1953, on copyright Ackerman Central File.

12. Baker background: "Richard Baker: the Parish of Print," tearsheet, n.p., October 1956, School of Journalism Records. "Life-time career": Ackerman to Fackenthal, March 24, 1947, Ackerman Central File.

13. Highest salary: Ackerman to George B. Pegram, vice president, May 3, 1950; ad hoc committee: Pegram to Ackerman, June 26, 1950, Ackerman Central File. Lake Success: photographs in *Announcement of the Graduate School of Journalism . . . 1951–1952*, September 29, 1951.

14. Head of instruction: Ackerman to Jacobs, February 21, 1949; Robert Ackerman appointment: Ackerman to Jacobs, June 24, 1948, Ackerman Central File. Adjuncts: listed, e.g., in *Announcement of the Graduate School of Journalism . . . 1949–1950*, July 23, 1949.

15. "Assumption of supremacy": Ackerman to Fackenthal, December 5, 1947, Ackerman Central File.

16. Declining enrollment: Terry Ferrer, "Journalism School Enrollment Down," *New York Herald Tribune*, October 21, 1957. "Young man's salary": Baker, *A History of the Graduate School of Journalism, Columbia University* (New York: Columbia University Press, 1954), p. 128.

17. "The Columbia Journalist": Baker, *History*, pp. 122–25. "Efficiency": ibid., p. 128.

## 20. "THE PULITZER MANDATE"

1. Successor: Ackerman, "The Story of General Eisenhower," typescript, August 5, 1947, Container 89, Carl W. Ackerman Papers, Library of Congress.

2. Eisenhower and Marshall: Ackerman, "The Story of General Eisenhower."

3. Search: Travis Beal Jacobs, *Eisenhower at Columbia* (New Brunswick: Transaction, 2001), pp. 18–47. Ackerman reaction: "The Story of General Eisenhower."

4. Cabot snag: "A Secret Report on the Tenth Annual Maria Moors Cabot Convocation," October [?] 1948, Container 89, Ackerman Papers.

5. Gallegos: Albert C. Jacobs, provost, to Ackerman, June 26, 1948; Ackerman to Jacobs, June 29, 1948; API: Eisenhower to Ackerman, November 6, 1948; "One Hundred Letters on the American Press Institute," 1950 [?]; congratulations: Eisenhower to Ackerman, January 5, 1950, Carl W. Ackerman Central File, Columbia University Archives.

6. "Perfunctory applause": quoted in Jacobs, *Eisenhower at Columbia*, p. 254.

7. Retirement at sixty-five: Jacobs, *Eisenhower at Columbia*, p. 114.

8. Volunteers for Stevenson: "Dean, for Stevenson, Charges Columbia Gag; Kirk Denies It," *New York Times*, October 15, 1952.

9. Telegram: quoted in "Dean, for Stevenson, Charges Columbia Gag"; Jacobs, *Eisenhower at Columbia*, pp. 291–92. Eisenhower and residence: ibid., pp. 279, 283.

10. *New York Mirror* editorial: "As Columbia Goes," October 16, 1952. Congratulations to Kirk: Ackerman to Kirk, January 20, 1953, Ackerman Central File.

11. McCarthy era: Robert Griffith, *The Politics of Fear: Joseph R. McCarthy and the Senate*, 2d ed. (Amherst: University of Massachusetts Press, 1987), pp. 188–220.

12. Asked to withdraw: Harron to Kirk, April 6, 1953; Hoover: Harron to Ackerman, March 18, 1953, Ackerman Central File.

13. Refusal to withdraw: Ackerman to Harron, March 19, 1953, Ackerman Central File.

14. "Dean Closes Files": *Times*, April 4, 1953. College position: George Striker, "College Files Open to Official Investigations," Columbia *Spectator*, April 8, 1953; available at www.english.upenn.edu/afilreis/50s/columbia.html.

15. Wechsler: James A. Wechsler, *The Age of Suspicion* (New York: Random House, 1953). Typing test: the school required a typing test for incoming students at the start of each term; see *School of Journalism Announcement 1925–1926*, February 21, 1925. Priscilla Hobson: Bernard Redmont, ed., *Who's Who / Columbia Journalists* (New York: Graduate School of Journalism, 1939). Her typing test is noted in, e.g., Denise Noe, "The Alger Hiss Case," www.crimelibrary.com/spies/hiss/9.htm; see also "The Alger Hiss Story," homepages.nyu.edu/th15/typedoc.html.

16. Ackerman's stand: noted in David Caute, *The Great Fear: the Anti-Communist Purge Under Truman and Eisenhower* (New York: Simon & Schuster, 1978), p. 429, and cited more recently in Kevin Boyle, "A National Crisis and the Role of the Academy," *Thought & Action: The NEA Higher Education Journal* (winter 2001–02): 9–16. See also an undated recollection by Kent MacDougall, class of 1956, in Box 17, Richard T. Baker Papers, Rare Book and Manuscript Library, Columbia University.

17. API snub, Sheen, and retirement process: memorandum, November 25, 1953, Container 96, Ackerman Papers.

18. "Diplomatic experience": draft letter to John A. Krout, vice president, Febru-

ary 1954, Container 93, Ackerman Papers. Transition: John Hohenberg, *John Hohenberg: The Pursuit of Excellence* (Gainesville: University Press of Florida, 1995), pp. 110–12.

19. *World* window: Ackerman to Kirk, April 29, 1953, Ackerman Central File; "Pulitzer Window Given to Columbia," *Times*, April 21, 1954. Death of Joseph Pulitzer II: Daniel W. Pfaff, *Joseph Pulitzer II and the* Post-Dispatch: *A Newspaperman's Life* (University Park: Pennsylvania State University Press, 1991), pp. 375–77; *Hohenberg: Pursuit of Excellence*, pp. 161–62.

20. Ellard under control: Ackerman to Kirk, March 5, 1955, Ackerman Central File. Joint announcement: "Columbia Fills Two Journalism Posts," *Times*, May 24, 1954.

21. Wife's death: "Mrs. Carl W. Ackerman is Dead at 69; Wife of Columbia's Journalism Dean," *Times*, August 23, 1954. Robert Ackerman: Carl W. Ackerman to Edward W. Barrett, November 12, 1958, School of Journalism Records.

22. Trustee action: Richard Herpers, secretary of the university to Ackerman, April 18, 1955; Ackerman to Herpers, May 10, 1955, Ackerman Central File; Geffen: "Schroeder Gets Geffen Award," *New York Herald Tribune*, October 23, 1955. Adler: "Scholarship Set Up in Honor of Adler," *Times*, October 8, 1955. Franklin: "Ben Franklin Scholarship Established," New York *Daily News*, June 15, 1956. Pinkham: Ackerman to Kirk, November 3, 1955, Ackerman Central File; "U.P. Writer Added To Journalism Staff," *Times*, January 9, 1956.

23. Dean emeritus: Kirk to Ackerman, May 7, 1956; Cabot medal: Kirk to Ackerman, July 7, 1956; Ackerman to Kirk, July 12, 1956, Ackerman Central File. Alumni honor: "Ackerman to Quit Post at Columbia," *Times*, May 9, 1956. "Long remembered": editorial, "Dean Ackerman Retires," *Herald Tribune*, May 10, 1956. "Wasteful": "Ackerman Backs Retirement at 70," *Times*, May 25, 1956.

## 21. FROM DROPOUT TO DEAN

1. Fifty names: Kirk to Pulitzer Prize board and American Press Institute advisory board, January 4, 1955; the file contains more than a dozen responses proposing names, Graduate School of Journalism Central File, Columbia University Archives. Kirk's preference for Curtis: Don E. Carter and Malcolm F. Mallette, *Seminar: The Story of the American Press Institute* (Reston, Va.: American Press Institute, 1992), pp. 156–57.

2. "Formidable name": Catledge to Kirk, June 9, 1955; "tremendously interested": Kirk to Catledge, June 30, 1955, Graduate School of Journalism Central File.

3. Barrett career: Glenn Fowler, "Edward W. Barrett, 79, Ex-Journalism Dean, Dies," *New York Times*, October 25, 1989. Transcript, Oral History Interview with Edward W. Barrett, July 9, 1974, Harry S. Truman Library, Independence, Mo., www.trumanlibrary.org/oralhist/barrette.htm.

4. Barrett's file: Ackerman to Brucker, n.d., Container 96, Carl W. Ackerman Papers, Library of Congress. Bona fide alumnus: Barrett to Kirk, May 10, 1956, Graduate School of Journalism Central File.

5. Opening address: Barrett to Robert C. Harron, enclosing text, September 26, 1956, Edward W. Barrett Central File, Columbia University Archives.

6. "Drawn too little": Kirk to Robert Choate, (*Boston Herald*) January 10, 1955. Broadened curriculum: Barrett to Kirk, April 20, 1956, Graduate School of Journalism Central File.

7. New money: Barrett to John M. Mullins, director of the budget, January 14, 1957, Barrett Central File; "Dean Barrett's Outline of Long-Term Programming," March 1957, Box 17, Richard T. Baker Papers, Rare Book and Manuscript Library, Columbia University. African Americans: minutes, staff conference, January 25, 1957, School of Journalism Records.

8. Visas: "Ban on Press Visits to China Assailed," *Times*, March 5, 1957. Critiques: *Journalism Education Today: Report of the Dean, Graduate School of Journalism, 1956 through 1959*, February 27, 1960.

9. Truman appearance: "Truman Visits Journalism School" (photograph), *Times*, May 2, 1957.

10. Basic Issues: Barrett to Kirk, December 14, 1956, Barrett Central File; "Columbia Course to Explore News," *Times*, October 21, 1957. The first lecturers were John R. Dunning, dean of the Graduate School of Engineering; Philip C. Jessup, Hamilton Fish Professor of International Law and Diplomacy; Robert M. MacIver, Lieber Professor Emeritus of Political Philosophy and Sociology; Wallace S. Sayre, professor of public administration; Herbert Wechsler, Harlan Fiske Stone Professor of Constitutional Law; and Leo Wolman, professor of economics.

11. International Division: *Journalism Education Today*. Journalism history course: "New Foundation to Make Studies," *Editor & Publisher* July 16, 1955. Comparative journalism degree: Herpers to Barrett, December 9, 1958, Barrett Central File.

12. Opinion Reporting Workshop: Barrett to Kirk, November 8, 1957, Barrett Central File; "Columbia Charts Opinion Research Workshop to Be Established in Journalism School," *Times*, November 8, 1957. Project: "Students Find Voters Didn't Rebuke Ike," *Editor & Publisher* (November 30, 1957). Lubell books: *The Future of American Politics* (New York: Harper, 1952); *Revolt of the Moderates* (New York: Harper, 1956).

13. Advanced Science Writing: Barrett to Kirk, July 25, October 21, 1957, Barrett Central File; "Science Writing Aided," *Times*, April 3, 1958. Fellows: "Newsmen Named Science Fellows," *Times*, May 20, 1958; Barrett to Kirk, enclosing report by fellows, June 12, 1959, Barrett Central File.

14. Sokolsky and Columbia: Sokolsky to Butler, March 23, 1943, Nicholas Murray Butler Papers, Rare Book and Manuscript Library, Columbia University. Ackerman opinion: Ackerman to Butler, January 17, 1941, Carl W. Ackerman Central File, Columbia University Archives.

15. Sokolsky resolution: correspondence starts with John A. Krout, vice president, to Barrett, August 23, 1957, and concludes with Kirk's invitation to the Sokolsky luncheon, March 13, 1959; also Barrett to Harron, n.d. [1959], Barrett Central File.

16. Columbia Journalism Award: Barrett to Kirk,, April 29, 1958; Herpers to Barrett, reporting trustee approval, May 7, 1958, Barrett Central File. Heiskell: "Columbia to Hail Arkansas Editor," *Times*, May 29, 1958.

17. Ellard birth date: listed in *Who's Who in America* as March 3, 1896; the correct date was March 3, 1894. Retirement process: Barrett to Herpers, August 27, 1958; Herpers to Barrett, September 10, 1958; Barrett to Krout, January 6, 1959, approving Krout letter informing Ellard of his retirement, Barrett Central File. Silver plate: in "Sulzberger Gets Columbia Award," *Times*, May 30, 1959.

18. Ellard departure: Ellard to Barrett, telegram, May 5, 1961, School of Journalism Records. Field Observation Week: "Students Go To See, Get Jobs to Do," *Editor & Publisher*, n.d. [1962].

19. Kimball résumé: "Journalism Professor Appointed at Columbia," *Times*, June 22, 1959. See also biographical summaries in the annual school handbook and, for details, his memoir, *The File* (New York: Harcourt Brace Jovanovich, 1983).

20. Wood: biography, school of journalism handbook; Herpers to Barrett, October 7, 1957, Barrett Central File. Boylan: Barrett to John M. Mullins, director of the budget, June 27, 1957, Barrett Central File. Alumni: "Journalism Unit Elects Officers / Brucker is Chosen as Head of Alumni Association of School of Journalism," *Times*, May 23, 1957; "Journalism Fund Set at Columbia," *Times*, October 15, 1958.

21. Third-year report: *Journalism Education Today*. "Role of a Graduate School," Barrett to Kirk, January 26, 1959; Salmen to Barrett, February 4, 1959, Barrett Central File.

22. Castro visit: Barrett to Kirk, agreeing to hold Castro news conference at the school, April 15, 1959, Barrett Central File; John Hohenberg, *The Pulitzer Diaries: Inside America's Greatest Prize* (Syracuse, N. Y.: Syracuse University Press, 1997), p. 97; Barrett, Oral History, Truman Library. Truman appearance: Leonard Ingalls, "Truman, in Columbia Lecture, Stresses Political Role of President," *Times*, April 28, 1959; the story notes a separate news conference at the school after his lecture.

23. Kalugin: "A Popular Russian: Oleg Danilovich Kalugin," *Times*, May 11, 1959; Elaine Sciolino, "K.G.B. Telltale Is Tattling, But Is He Telling U.S. All?", *Times*, January 20, 1992; Otto C. Doelling, class of 1959, "Oleg, We Hardly Know You," *Alumni Journal*, winter 1991. Spy game: "Former CIA and KGB Adversaries Are Playing a Different Game Now," February 8, 1996, at. www.spynews.net/formerCi.htm.

## 22. SHORT-CHANGED

1. Small school: "Columbia to Open 205th Year Today," *New York Times*, September 25, 1958.

2. "No credit": Barrett to Salmen, November 18, 1959, Edward W. Barrett Central File, Columbia University Archives.

3. "Alarming": Barrett to Grayson L. Kirk, president, April 1, 1960; Kirk to Barrett, April 19, 1960, Barrett Central File.

4. "By insisting": Barrett to Kirk, June 15, 1960, School of Journalism Records.

5. Revaluation: Kirk to Barrett, July 8, 1960, enclosing carbon of letter to Dallas Townsend, president of the school alumni association; Barrett to Kirk, July 12, 1960; petty thievery: Barrett to William Bloor, treasurer, October 13, 1960; Barrett to "The Cabinet," February [?], 1963, Barrett Central File.

6. "Find another Dean": Barrett to Salmen, September 13, 1960; still waiting: Barrett to Kirk, January 15, 1963; renovation: Barrett to Space Committee, April 30, 1965, complaining that rehabilitation would leave the school with less space than before, Barrett Central File.

7. Curtis and Barrett: Don E. Carter and Malcolm F. Mallette, *Seminar: The Story of the American Press Institute* (Reston, Va.: American Press Institute, 1992), pp. 156–57. Reese warning: ibid., p. 159.

8. Agreement of 1958: Carter and Mallette, *Seminar*, pp. 159–60.

9. Reaccreditation: "Visitors' Accreditation Report," confidential, November 28–29, 1960, School of Journalism Records.

10. World Room dedication: "The World Room at Columbia Is Dedicated to Swope," *Times*, June 1, 1961; "Columbia's World Room Honors Swope," *Editor & Publisher*, June 3, 1961.

11. New appointments: Barrett to Kirk, October 27, 1960, enclosing minutes of faculty meeting of October 13, noting appointments of Lieberman, Horowitz, Leonard Robinson, Dallas Townsend, class of 1941 (substituting for Wood), Shipman, and Hewes, School of Journalism Records. Biographical data and adjuncts: announcement, *Graduate School of Journalism 1961–1962*, February 11, 1961. Luter: "Journalism Aide Picked," *Times*, August 20, 1961.

12. Butler: Dorothy Butler Gilliam oral history interview, Washington Press Club Foundation, 1994, npc.pres.org/wpforal/gillint.htm.

13. Buchanan: *Right from the Beginning* (Boston: Little, Brown, 1988), pp. 232–66.

14. Mencher: "New on Journalism Faculty," *Times*, June 17, 1962; biography in School of Journalism handbook, 1972–73.

15. Yu: biography in school handbook, 1972–73.

16. Motto: used in Graduate School of Journalism, *Fiftieth Anniversary Report of the Dean: "That the People Shall Know"*, n.d. [1963]. Book: Barrett and Hewes, eds., *Journalists in Action* (Manhasset: Channel, 1963).

17. Degrees: "Columbia Journalism School Marks 50th Year," *Times*, April 7, 1963; "Columbia Jubilee Convocation Hails 3 Journalists," *Times*, April 16, 1963. Markel complaint: Barrett to Kirk, April 18, 1963, enclosing draft response to Sulzberger's letter of April 16, 1963, Barrett Central File.

18. Medallions: "3 Editors Honored by Columbia," *Editor & Publisher*, April 25, 1963; "Dean Barrett Given Medal at Columbia," ibid., May 4, 1963; other recipients are listed in *Supplement to the Fiftieth Anniversary Report of the Dean of the Graduate School of Journalism 1913–1963*, n.d. (1963).

19. "Primary value": "'We Don't Hurt Them'," *Newsweek*, April 29, 1963, p. 55.

20. Pulitzer's plan: John Tebbel, "The Pulitzer Idea: Fifty Years Old," *Saturday Review*, March 9, 1963, pp. 52–53.

## 23. "WHY A REVIEW?"

1. "Columbia University Journalism Review": Boylan to Barrett, "A Proposal for a Publication (Preliminary Thoughts)," memorandum, January 26, 1960, *Columbia Journalism Review* (CJR) Records.

2. "Avoid two precipices": Unsigned (Baker), "Memorandum for File," n.d. (spring 1960), CJR Records. API attitude: Don E. Carter and Malcolm F. Mallette, *Seminar: The Story of the American Press Institute* (Reston, Va.: American Press Institute, 1992), p. 152. "Hutchins report" refers to Commission on Freedom of the Press, *A Free and Responsible Press* (Chicago: University of Chicago Press, 1947).

3. Fall 1960 issue: Boylan, memorandum, June 17, 1960; staff: masthead of dummy summer 1961 issue; correspondents: "Confidential Memorandum," to Prospective Correspondents, August 1960, CJR Records.

4. "Why a Review?": *Columbia Journalism Review*, pilot issue (fall 1961): 2–3. Liebling review: "On Looking Into Chapman's News," review of John Chapman, *Tell It to Sweeney: the Informal History of the New York Daily News* (New York: Doubleday, 1961), pp. 32–34.

5. "Parochial, carping": Jack Turcott, quoted in Barrett to Kirk, October 10, 1961, memorandum compiling reactions, CJR Records. "About 99 per cent": "Pilot on Course," *Newsweek*, October 9, 1961, p. 92. Additions to support staff: masthead, *Columbia Journalism Review* (summer 1962). Barrett comment: "Editorial Notes," *Columbia Journalism Review* (fall 1962): 36.

6. Faculty committee: listed for the first time on masthead, *Columbia Journalism Review* (spring 1965).

7. Du Pont article: "Case History: Wilmington's 'Independent' Newspapers," *Columbia Journalism Review* (summer 1964): 13–17; see responses in *Columbia Journalism Review* (fall 1964): 44–46. Conglomerates: "News as a Byproduct," *Columbia Journalism Review* (spring 1967): 5–10.

8. Hohenberg articles: "New Patterns in Public Service," *Columbia Journalism Review* (summer 1962):14–17; "Public Service: A 1964 Honor Roll," *Columbia Journalism Review* (summer 1964): 9–12.

9. Sweeping challenge: Wes Gallagher, "Let's Quit Whipping and Whoop It Up!", text of speech to North Carolina Press Association, August 2, 1963, *Editor & Publisher*, August 24, 1963.

10. Response to Gallagher: "Critics of Press Stand Firm," *Publishers' Auxiliary*, August 31, 1963. AEJ resolution: minutes of 1962 convention, published in *Journalism Quarterly*, tearsheet in CJR Records. Faculty response: Barrett to Baker and others, memorandum, October 9, 1963, CJR Records; minutes, faculty conference, November 7, 1963, School of Journalism Records.

11. Resigning consultancy: Barrett to John Hill, president, Hill & Knowlton, July 30, 1962, Edward W. Barrett Central File, Columbia University Archives. Article: "Smoking and News: Coverage of a Decade of Controversy," *Columbia Journalism Review* (summer 1963): 6–12, Rowse letter to editor and editors' reply: *Columbia Journalism Review* (fall 1963): 44.

12. Critique of Wolfe: Leonard C. Lewin, "Is Fact Necessary? A Sequel to the Herald TribuneNew Yorker Dispute," *Columbia Journalism Review* (winter 1966): 29–34. "Going to a convention": Tom Wolfe, "The New Journalism: A la Recherche des Whichy Thickets," *New York* magazine, February 21, 1972, pp. 47–48.

13. Initial circulation: news release, Columbia University Office of Public Information, March 29, 1962.

14. Endowment and credit: Barrett to Kirk, November 27, 1961, School of Journalism Records; Barrett to Kirk, January 8, 1962, Barrett Central File. Cabot funds: Barrett to Kirk, May 6, 1963; Barrett to John Moors Cabot, November 6, 1963, Barrett Central File.

15. Cowan: "Cowan in Columbia Post," *New York Times*, October 28, 1963; Barrett to Robert C. Harron, November 1, 1963, informing him of a faculty resolution of thanks to Cowan, Barrett Central File. Ford grant: press release, News from the Ford Foundation, August 28, 1967.

## 24. ERA OF EXPANSION

1. "Spectacularly successful": Kirk to Barrett, July 8, 1963, Edward W. Barrett Central File, Columbia University Archives.

2. NASA project: "NASA Pays to Find Out," *New York Times*, July 12, 1963; *Herald Tribune* role: minutes, Faculty of Journalism meeting, September 17, 1963; withdrawal: Barrett to George L. Simpson Jr., NASA, July 16, 1963, School of Journalism Records. Shift to Chicago: "NASA Spends $144,000 To Study Science Impact," *Times*, July 23, 1963. "Fiasco": Barrett to Ralph S. Halford, dean of graduate faculties, September 26, 1963, Barrett Central File; ASNE *Bulletin*, November 1, 1963.

3. Newhouse offer: Boylan and others were consulted on this matter. Barrett to Kirk, January 25, 1960, noting an initial Newhouse gift to Syracuse of $2 million, Barrett Central File.

4. AEJ meeting: Reports in *Journalism Quarterly*, 29 (summer 1952): 379–80; 30 (fall 1952): 494–515.

5. Luncheons: e.g., the convention at the University of Wisconsin in 1977; see *60th Annual Convention . . .* , August 21–24, 1977. Presidency: "AEJ Picks Barrett as Its President-Elect," *Lincoln* (Neb.) *Star*, August 29, 1963, clipping in School of Journalism Records. James Carey was president of the AEJ in 1978, before he joined the Columbia faculty.

6. "Large doubts": Markel, "The Real Sins of the Press," *Harper's Magazine*, December 1962, pp. 85–94. "Shocker": Barrett to Markel, December 14, 1962, Barrett Central File.

7. Boroff study: "A Report on Journalism Education," Ford Foundation, June 1963. Death: noted in published summary of his report, "What Ails the Journalism Schools," *Harper's Magazine*, October 1965, pp. 77–85.

8. Praise for Columbia: Boroff, "Report."

9. "No faith in either": Barrett to Boroff, December 23, 1964, School of Journalism Records.

10. Ford grant: Everett Case, Ford Foundation, to Kirk, March 31, 1965, copy in Barrett Central File; Philip M. Schuyler, "Ford Gift Spurs Changes at Columbia," *Editor & Publisher* (October 2, 1965). Half Century Fund: Barrett to Bell, October 3, 1963, Barrett Central File; "Columbia Journalism School Has Raised Nearly

$3-Million," *Times*, June 25, 1966; Barrett to Eileen Walsh (school alumni and development officer), August 11, 1967, on preparing news release on completion of campaign, Barrett Central File. Cabot gift: "Columbia Journalism Chair Endowed by Cabot Family," *Times*, August 30, 1964.

11. Modernization: Schuyler, "Ford Gift Spurs Changes at Columbia." Sulzberger Library: Murray Schumach, "Columbia Plans Sulzberger Journalism Library," *Times*, June 15, 1967.

12. Fellowships: "Columbia Gets $135,000 For Journalism Program," *Times*, June 28, 1965. Davison: biography in School of Journalism handbook, 1972–73. Far East fellowships: "Columbia to Train Reporters to Work In China and Japan," *Times*, December 4, 1965.

13. Magazine awards: Robert C. Harron to Barrett, September 26, 1956; Barrett to Harron, October 15, 1962, Barrett Central File; "National Magazine Award Established by Columbia," *Times*, November 15, 1965; Barrett to Kirk, March 25, 1966, on first award. *Look* award: *Times*, March 6, 1966. Categories in 2001: Alex Kuczynski, "New Yorker Sets Record at Magazine Awards," *Times*, May 3, 2001.

14. DuPont awards: a brief history is posted at www.dupont.org/intro/history; see also profile of Jessie Ball duPont at www.dupontfund.org/aboutthefund/history.asp. Barrett connection: Barrett to Spencer Klaw, editor, *Columbia Journalism Review*, memorandum, n.d., on the brother of the dean's wife, Mason Daniel Barrett, CJR Records.

15. Agreement: draft, "Agreement . . . between the Florida National Bank of Jacksonville . . . and the Trustees of Columbia University in the City of New York"; administrator: Marvin Barrett to James Boylan, March 1, 1968, enclosing résumé, School of Journalism Records. Startup: "Columbia to Make Review Of Broadcast Journalism," *Editor & Publisher* (April 27, 1968).

16. First awards: Fred Ferretti, "Burch, New F.C.C. Chief, Defends News on TV," *Times*, November 12, 1969. Survey: Marvin Barrett, ed., *The Alfred I. DuPont–Columbia University Survey of Broadcast Journalism 1968–1969* (New York: Grosset & Dunlap, 1969); Ferretti, "Report Deplores Television's Uneven Treatment of News," *Times*, November 11, 1969.

17. Double degrees: Barrett to Kirk, February 8, 1965, Barrett Central File; "Columbia U. Adds Media Manager Graduate Study," *Editor & Publisher* (September 3, 1966). Norman E. Isaacs, *Untended Gates: The Mismanaged Press* (New York: Columbia University Press, 1986), p. 178, notes that graduates of the joint program probably earned more than beginning journalists.

## 25. EDGING TOWARD THE ABYSS

1. ROTC protest: *Crisis at Columbia: Report of the Fact-Finding Commission Appointed to Investigate the Disturbances at Columbia University in April and May 1968* (Cox Commission) (New York: Vintage Books, 1968), pp. 63–64. SDS: ibid., pp. 56–59.

2. Browne: "Viet Nam Reporting: Three Years of Crisis," *Columbia Journalism Re-*

*view* (fall 1964): 4–9. Deepe: William Prochnau, *Once Upon a Distant War* (New York: Times Books, 1995), p. 275. Higgins: "Lady at War," *Time*, January 14, 1966, p. 61. Trotta: see her memoir, *Fighting for Air: In the Trenches with Television News* (New York: Simon & Schuster, 1991).

3. Hohenberg in Vietnam: John Hohenberg, *The Pulitzer Diaries: Inside America's Greatest Prize* (Syracuse: Syracuse University Press, 1997), pp. 137–44. Davison: *User's Guide to the Rand Interviews in Vietnam* (Santa Monica: Rand Corporation, 1972); also *Some Observations on Viet Cong Operations in the Villages* (Santa Monica: Rand Corporation, 1967).

4. Friendly: James Boylan, "TV's Month of Tumult," *Columbia Journalism Review* (spring 1966): 15–20. "Matter of conscience": Friendly's letter of resignation, February 15, 1966, reprinted in ibid., pp. 18–19.

5. Friendly career: *Due To Circumstances Beyond Our Control . . .* (New York: Random House, 1967); Edward R. Murrow and Fred W. Friendly, eds., *See It Now* (New York: Simon & Schuster, 1955). "I'd know": retold in Deirdre Carmody, "Friendly Retiring as Ford Fund's Adviser on News," *New York Times*, December 14, 1980.

6. Journalism Award: text of remarks by Richard T. Baker and Edward W. Barrett, May 29, 1964, School of Journalism Records. Early contact: Barrett, out-of-pocket expense, lunch with Friendly, a "faculty candidate," February 3, 1959; hiring deal: Barrett to Grayson Kirk, March 17, 1966; Barrett, draft letter to Friendly, March 17, 1966; faculty approval: Barrett to Kirk, March 23, 1966, Edward W. Barrett Central File, Columbia University Archives.

7. "Formal education": Barrett to Kirk, March 23, 1966; "dynamic teacher": Barrett to Kirk, October 10, 1966, Barrett Central File.

8. Communications satellites: "Ford Television Plan," editorial, *Columbia Journalism Review* (summer 1966): 2.

9. University Broadcast Laboratory: Jack Gould, "Columbia and Ford Plan TV Laboratory," *Times*, December 22, 1966; Gould, "A Friendly Persuasion," *Times*, December 25, 1966; "Westin Leaves Network," *Times*, January 5, 1967.

10. Trustee actions: Gould, "Columbia Orders Study of Proposal for TV Laboratory," *Times*, January 10, 1967; Gould, "Decision at Columbia U.?", *Times*, February 5, 1967; Gould, "Columbia Broadcast Laboratory To Draw on Colleges' Resources," *Times*, February 8, 1967.

11. Ten-page document: Boylan, notes, March 17, 1967, School of Journalism Records.

12. Alternative solution: Jack Gould, "Columbia News Lab Will Shift to N.E.T.," *Times*, March 17, 1967. Barrett resignation: Robert E. Dallos, "Barrett Quitting as N.E.T. Director," *Times*, April 22, 1968; Barrett to Gould and Dallos, April 22, 1968, challenging quotations in story, School of Journalism Records.

13. Faculty meeting: Boylan notes, March 17, 1967.

14. "Step out of the deanship": Barrett to Kirk, May 6, 1967, Barrett Central File.

15. Curtis departure: "New Press Institute Head Named," *Times*, May 19, 1967. Ackerman comment: Container 65, Carl W. Ackerman Papers, Library of Congress.

16. "Planning disaster": Ada Louise Huxtable, "Expansion at Columbia," *Times*, November 5, 1966.

17. Reorganization: Fred M. Hechinger, "Columbia Names a New Provost in Wide Shake-Up," *Times*, June 10, 1967.

18. Cigarette filter: Barrett to Kirk and Truman, from Santa Barbara, September 11, 1967, Barrett Central File; "name and reputation": Cox Commission report, pp. 52–53.

## 26. FALLOUT

1. Recruiters and demonstrators: *Crisis at Columbia: Report of the Fact-Finding Commission Appointed to Investigate the Disturbances at Columbia University in April and May 1968* (Cox Commission) (New York: Vintage, 1968), pp. 64–69.

2. Baker leave: see correspondence from Taipei, Box 61, Richard T. Baker Papers, Rare Book and Manuscript Library, Columbia University. Demonstrations: Cox Commission, pp. 69–74.

3. Upheaval: Cox Commission, pp. 99–123. See also two contemporary accounts: Jerry L. Avorn (Robert Friedman, ed.), *Up Against the Ivy Wall* (New York: Atheneum, 1969), prepared by the Columbia *Spectator*; and George Keller, "Six Weeks That Shook Morningside," *Columbia College Today* (spring 1968).

4. Cordon: Avorn, *Up Against the Ivy Wall*, pp. 164–66. Barrett grievance: Barrett to Kirk and Truman, May 11, 1968, Edward W. Barrett Central File, Columbia University Archives.

5. Police bust: Cox Commission, pp. 162–67.

6. Journalism student response: resolution, May 1, 1968, minutes, faculty conference, May 2, 1968, School of Journalism Records. *Life* arrangement: "Columbia Quiz," editorial, *The New Republic*, July 22, 1968.

7. "Good conscience": Pinkham to Frederick T. C. Yu, acting associate dean, May 1, 1968, faculty minutes, May 2, 1968.

8. Later turbulence: Avorn, *Up Against the Ivy Wall*, pp. 265–76. Whitehead: noted in Cornelia Marwell, executive secretary, to Baker, June 7, 1968, Box 4, Baker Papers. Restructuring: "A Proposal for the Restructuring of the School of Journalism," May 10, 1968; faculty response, May 23, 1968, School of Journalism Records.

9. Foster motion: minutes, faculty conference, May 24, 1968, School of Journalism Records; reversal: Marwell to Baker, June 7, 1968, Box 4, Baker Papers.

10. Advice letter: Barrett to Kirk and Truman, May 11, 1968, Barrett Central File.

11. "A basis for discontent": Murray Schumach, "Change in Columbia Board Proposed," *New York Times*, June 1, 1968.

12. Resignation: Barrett to Kirk, personal, July 31, 1968; confirmation: Barrett to Kirk, August 3, 1968, Barrett Central File. Statement: Alden Whitman, "Dean Barrett Quits in Columbia Dispute," *Times*, August 3, 1968.

13. Faculty petition: Faculty of Journalism to Kirk, August 1, 1968, Barrett Central File. Alumni action: "Columbia Trustees Asked to Keep Dean," *Times*, August 11, 1968. Affirmation: Barrett to Kirk, August 15, 1968, Barrett Central File.

14. Changeover: faculty minutes, August 7, 1968, School of Journalism Records.

15. Kirk resignation: Avorn, *Up Against the Ivy Wall*, p. 284.

## 27. DESPERATELY SEEKING A DEAN

1. Faculty meeting: conference minutes, Faculty of Journalism, September 16, 1968, School of Journalism Records.

2. Patterson: "John Patterson, 50, Professor of Journalism at Columbia, Dies," *New York Times*, December 10, 1975. Other staff additions: faculty minutes, September 16, 1968. Klauber laboratory: "Radio-TV Laboratory Dedicated At Columbia Journalism School," *Times*, October 16, 1968.

3. Kerner Commission: *Report of the National Advisory Commission on Civil Disorders* (named for Otto Kerner, Governor of Illinois) (New York: Bantam, 1968); see also "Journalism and the Kerner Report," section in *Columbia Journalism Review* (fall 1968):42–65. Minority program: Barrett, "Notes Re: Urban Racial Problems" (draft), April 5, 1968, School of Journalism Records; "Columbia to Train Minorities for TV," *Times*, June 19, 1968. Staff: *Galley 11* (alumni publication) [fall 1968]; students: "20 in Minority Groups Get Radio-TV News Diplomas," *Times*, August 31, 1968. Expansion: news release, Columbia University Office of Public Information, June 23, 1969; cost: Nathaniel Sheppard Jr., "Minority-Journalists' Program Closes," *Times*, August 17, 1974.

4. Minority enrollment: report of scholarship committee, minutes, faculty meeting, September 17, 1968. Jackson: biography in journalism handbook, 1972–73.

5. Tripartite committee: minutes, conference, September 16, 1968.

6. Executive Committee of the Faculty: "To the Students of Columbia University," September 17, 1968, School of Journalism Records. Disciplinary proceedings: Murray Schumach, "Columbia's Battleground Shifting From Campus to Its Senate and Tribunals," *Times*, May 24, 1970.

7. Campus conduct: minutes, Faculty of Journalism, October 22, 1968. Committee on committees: minutes, Faculty of Journalism, November 11, 1968, School of Journalism Records. Senate referendum: "Timeline of the Recent History of Columbia University 1969–2002," beatl.barnard.columbia.edu/cuhis3057/Timelines/Recent1970_1969.htm. First senator: minutes, Faculty of Journalism voting members, May 26, 1969, School of Journalism Records.

8. "Role of the Journalist": Boylan prospectus, n.d.; Boylan, "Statement for Role of the Journalist," December 5, 1968; minutes, Faculty of Journalism, December 20, 1968. "Mutiny": William H. Wilson, Boylan, Journal, May 21, 1997.

9. Disruptions: John Hohenberg, *The Pulitzer Diaries: Inside America's Greatest Prize* (Syracuse, N.Y.: Syracuse University Press, 1997), pp. 189–90. Curriculum: Boylan, memorandums to curriculum review committee, April 7, May 16, 1969; Baker, memorandums, May 5, June 30, 1969, School of Journalism Records.

10. Opposition: Boylan, Journal, May 22, 23, 28, 1969. Backing off: Pinkham to Baker, January 14, 1970, School of Journalism Records.

11. Confidential report: Henry F. Graff, "The Deanship of the School of Journalism," March 6, 1969, Graduate School of Journalism Central File, Columbia University Archives.

12. Baker withdrawal: "Baker Says He's Not a Deanship Candidate," *Editor & Publisher*, April 5, 1969.

13. Search committee: Members were Baker (ex officio), George Barrett (adjunct), Bettag, Boylan, Judith Crist (adjunct), Friendly, William A. Glavin Jr. (student), and Graff. Hohenberg and Cordier: Hohenberg, *John Hohenberg: The Pursuit of Excellence* (Gainesville: University Press of Florida, 1995), p. 99. List of names: Hohenberg to members of committee, summary of meeting of April 28, 1969, School of Journalism Records. Friendly withdrawal: Friendly to Hohenberg, April 28, 1969, Journalism Central File.

14. Four names: Hohenberg to search committee, May 14, 1969, confidential, School of Journalism Records.

15. Report to Cordier: Hohenberg to Cordier, draft, June 3, 1969, noting Boylan dissent; Hohenberg to Cordier, June 7, 1969, noting Glavin dissent, Graduate School of Journalism Central File; Boylan, Journal, June 2, 3, 1969; Hohenberg, *Pulitzer Diaries*, p. 202.

16. Continued search: minutes, Faculty of Journalism, June 3, 1969, School of Journalism Records.

17. Cordier presidency: "Timeline of the Recent History of Columbia," beatl.barnard.columbia.edu/cuhis3057/Timelines/Recent1970_1969.htm. Friendly advice: Friendly to Cordier, October 10, 1969, Journalism Central File.

18. "Lukewarmness": Graff to Cordier, October 15, 1969, Graduate School of Journalism Central File.

19. Baker update: Baker to the faculty, memorandum, November 12, 1969; Yu poll: Yu to faculty, memorandum, November 18, 1969, School of Journalism Records. "Stalling": Graff to Cordier, November 25, 1969, Journalism Central File.

20. Summons: Boylan, "Notes on Meeting Between Faculty of Journalism and President Cordier, December 17, 1969," School of Journalism Records; Joseph B. Treaster, "Cordier Selects Journalism Dean," *Times*, December 18, 1969. "Son of a bitch," Boylan, Journal, January 7, 1970. "Humiliating experience": Martin Flumenbaum, "Cordier Picks Abel As Journalism Dean," Columbia *Spectator*, December 18, 1969.

## 28. "WELCOME TO THE JOINT"

1. Abel credentials: Lawrence Van Gelder, "New Journalism Dean," *New York Times*, December 20, 1969.

2. Negative stories: Martin Flumenbaum, "Cordier Picks Abel As Journalism Dean," Columbia *Spectator*, December 18, 1969; *Time*, December 26, 1969, p. 36; Michael Gerrard, "Elie Abel to Face A Divided Faculty," Columbia *Spectator*, January 7, 1970.

3. Baker reception: Baker, invitation for January 14, 1970, School of Journalism Records; Boylan, Journal, January 27, 1970. Barrett luncheon: Barrett, invitation for January 28, 1970, School of Journalism Records; Boylan, Journal, January 28, 1970.

4. Ackerman's eightieth: Lacey Fosburgh, "Former Dean, 80, Reflects on Time," *Times*, January 18, 1970. Four deans: photograph in *Galley 14*, alumni publication

[January 1970]. Ackerman's death: Albin Krebs, "Carl W. Ackerman Is Dead at 80," *Times*, October 10, 1970.

5. McGill appointment: M. A. Farber, "Columbia Selects McGill, Psychologist, as President"; editorial, "Columbia Finds Its Man," *Times*, February 3, 1970; "McGill, of San Diego, Named President; Will Assume Office by September," *Columbia University Newsletter*, February 2, 1970. Associate deanship: "Yu Named to Columbia Post," *Times*, October 20, 1970.

6. Kusch background: Malcolm W. Browne, "Polykarp Kusch, Nobel Laureate In Physics in 1955, Is Dead at 82," *Times*, March 23, 1993. "Major reconsideration": Kusch to Alexander Stoia, September 10, 1969; Stoia to Kusch, September 12, 1969, Graduate School of Journalism Central File, Columbia University Archives.

7. Journalism costs: Kusch to Baker, November 3, 1969, Journalism Central File.

8. "Chuckles": Baker to Kusch, October 28, 1969, Journalism Central File.

9. Tenure cases: Kusch to Abel, March 19, 1970, Abel Central File.

10. Sulzberger exchange: Kusch to Arthur Ochs Sulzberger, March 19, 1970; Kusch, memorandum for file, April 1, 1970, Journalism Central File. Budget lines: Kusch to Abel, April 22, 1970, Abel Central File.

11. "A lot of money": Kusch to McGill, March 27, 1970, Polykarp Kusch Central File, Columbia University Archives.

12. Case against school: Kusch to Cordier, May 1, 1970, Kusch Central File.

13. Jackson proceedings: Kusch to Fraenkel, June 10, 1970, Graduate School of Journalism Central File; Boylan, Journal, April 27, 1970.

14. Jackson reconsideration: conversation with Jackson, Boylan, Journal, January 26, 1972. Shanor: Cordier to Abel, May 20, 1970; Abel to Shanor, April 5, 1971, reporting on favorable action by ad hoc committee, School of Journalism Records. Budget cuts: Abel to McGill, November 4, 1970; "naivete": Abel to McGill, March 18, 1971, Abel Central File.

15. Isaacs appointment: Abel to Kusch, May 7, 1970; Kusch to Abel, May 14, 1970; "Editors' Group Head Is Joining Columbia," *Times*, May 17, 1970.

16. Kusch departure: Kusch to McGill, January 13, 1971; Kusch to Abel, June 30, 1971, Kusch Central File.

17. Insurgency: "Moratorium: For the Record," *Columbia University Newsletter*, May 11, 1970; Murray Schumach, "Columbia's Battleground Shifting From Campus to Its Senate and Tribunals," *Times*, May 24, 1970. Stink bombs: John Hohenberg, *The Pulitzer Diaries: Inside America's Greatest Prize* (Syracuse, N. Y.: Syracuse University Press, 1997), p. 281; Boylan, Journal, April 16, 27, May 5, 1970.

18. Strike: Hohenberg, *Pulitzer Diaries*, pp. 218–25; Boylan, Journal, May 7, 1970. Commencement: Boylan, Journal, June 8, 1970.

19. Foster luncheon: Boylan, Journal, May 28, 1970. Science Writing Program: Kenneth K. Goldstein, "Training for the Medical Information Complex," www.columbia.edu/cu/21stC/issue—4.2/goldstein.html; and his résumé, www.ldeo.columbia.edu/eesj/CVsEESJKenCV.html.

20. Michele Clark and Rivera: "37 Minorities Graduated Into Jobs," *Editor & Pub-*

*lisher*, September 5, 1970; "Minority Fellowship Plan Named for Black Journalist," *Times*, April 1, 1973; *Galley 15*, alumni publication, fall 1973.

## 29. HOHENBERG AND THE PRIZES

1. "What you've got": John Hohenberg, *John Hohenberg: The Pursuit of Excellence* (Gainesville: University Press of Florida), p. 27; "cruel and inconsiderate": John Hohenberg, *The Pulitzer Diaries: Inside America's Greatest Prize* (Syracuse: Syracuse University Press, 1997), pp. 17–18. Konner recollection: Konner in "Tribute to John Hohenberg, Graduate School of Journalism, New York City," videotape, April 28, 2001.

2. Books: Hohenberg, ed., *The Pulitzer Prize Story, New Stories, Editorials, Cartoons, and Pictures from the Pulitzer Prize Collection at Columbia University* (New York: Columbia University Press, 1959); *The Professional Journalist* (New York, Holt Rinehart & Winston, 1960). "Dante and not Graham": David Waters, "How Best to Define the Professional Journalist?", *Content* (Canadian journalism review), November 1973, p. 13. "Press agent": *Pulitzer Diaries*, p. 157.

3. Air Force assignments: *Hohenberg: Pursuit of Excellence*, pp. 114–15; *Pulitzer Diaries*, pp. 15, 18, 27, 29–37, 42–43, 60. State Department: ibid., pp. 121–23. Council on Foreign Relations: ibid., pp. 145–48. Ford Foundation: ibid., pp. 146–47. Books: *Between Two Worlds: Policy, Press and Public Opinion in Asian-American Relations* (New York: Praeger, 1967); *New Era in the Pacific: An Adventure in Public Diplomacy* (New York: Simon & Schuster, 1972).

4. Asked to stay: *Hohenberg: Pursuit of Excellence*, p. 167; *Pulitzer Diaries*, p. 44. Joseph Pulitzer Jr.: ibid., pp. 21–22.

5. Kennedy incident: Hohenberg, *Pulitzer Prizes*, pp. 271–73; *Pulitzer Diaries*, pp. 49–50.

6. *Citizen Hearst*: *Pulitzer Prizes*, pp. 273–77; *Pulitzer Diaries*, pp. 180–82.

7. Fiftieth anniversary: Paul L. Montgomery, "Dinner Salutes Pulitzer Prizes," *New York Times*, May 11, 1966; Hohenberg, *Pulitzer Prizes*, pp. 290–94.

8. "Dream made flesh": quoted in Hohenberg, *Pulitzer Diaries*, pp. 163–64.

9. "Family party" and "grateful": Barrett to Joseph Pulitzer Jr. and others, May 16, 1966, Edward W. Barrett Central File, Columbia University Archives. White House call: Hohenberg, *Pulitzer Diaries*, pp. 134, 161.

10. Salisbury trip: recounted in James Boylan, "A Salisbury Chronicle," *Columbia Journalism Review* (winter 1966–67):10–14. Student reaction: Hohenberg, *Pulitzer Diaries*, pp. 172–73.

11. Advisory board debate: Hohenberg, *Pulitzer Prizes*, pp. 296–99; *Pulitzer Diaries*, pp. 176–77. "Terribly upset": Turner Catledge, *My Life and The Times* (New York: Harper & Row, 1971), p. 293. Hersh prize: Hohenberg, *Pulitzer Prizes*, pp. 299–300.

12. Pentagon Papers: Hohenberg, *Pulitzer Prizes*, pp. 307–10; *Hohenberg: Pursuit of Excellence*, pp. 195–99.

13. Trustee debate: *Hohenberg: Pursuit of Excellence*, pp. 198–200.

14. "Pimple": Hohenberg, *Pulitzer Diaries*, p. 269, entry of March 9, 1973. "Substitute their judgment": ibid., p. 271.

15. Simons role: Hohenberg, *Pulitzer Diaries*, p. 265; Nat Hentoff, "Woodstein in the Movies," review of *All the President's Men*, *Columbia Journalism Review* (May/June 1976): 46–47.

16. Enrollments: Lee B. Becker and Joseph D. Graf, "Journalism Enrollments in the United States: Disentangling the Trends over the Last Quarter Century," July 1994, at www.grady.uga.edu/annualsurvveys/journEnri.htm; for Columbia, see, e.g., Barrett to Kirk, June 2, 1965, reporting a 50 percent increase in applications over the previous two years, Barrett Central File.

17. Trustee resistance: Hohenberg, *Pulitzer Diaries*, pp. 275–77.

18. "Divorcement": ibid., pp. 286–89.

19. "Didn't know the man": ibid., p. 46; irregularities: ibid., p. 83.

20. "Now-obvious need": Barrett to Kirk, May 18, 1960, Barrett Central File. *Fiorello!* and Drury: Hohenberg, *Pulitzer Prizes*, pp. 257, 264–65; Leech won for *In the Days of McKinley*, ibid., p. 277. "The worst": Barrett to Kirk, May 18, 1960, Barrett Central File.

21. "Air of secrecy": Bendiner quoted in "The Pulitzer Prizes," editorial, *Columbia Journalism Review* (spring 1966): 2; Bingham to Barrett, June 7, 1966; Barrett to Kirk, June 29, 1966, forwarding five letters, Barrett Central File.

22. "Once an old friend": Hohenberg, *Pulitzer Diaries*, pp. 276–77. Pulitzer position: ibid., pp. 284–85. "Through with the Pulitzers": ibid., p. 287. Abel seat on board: Boylan, Journal, July 22, 1976.

23. Dorothy Hohenberg: *Hohenberg: Pursuit of Excellence*, pp. 214–15; "Dorothy L. Hohenberg, Ex-Columnist for the Post," *Times*, September 3, 1977.

24. Hohenberg's later life: *Hohenberg: Pursuit of Excellence*; Hohenberg, *Pulitzer Diaries*. Memorial: "Tribute to John Hohenberg . . . April 28, 2001," videotape; the ceremony was organized by Eve Orlans Mayer, class of 1952.

## 30. MEETING FATIGUE

1. Realism and pessimism: e.g., Abel to "Fellow Alumni," July 1972, School of Journalism Records. UNESCO work: Elie Abel biography, Stanford University Department of Communication, www.stanford.edu/dept/communication/department/faculty.

2. "Shock and dismay": Mencher to Abel, December 31, 1970; "personal thrusts": Abel to Mencher, January 5, 1971, School of Journalism Records.

3. "More sensitive emphasis": Penn T. Kimball, private communication, September 2002.

4. Demonstrations in 1972: John Hohenberg, *The Pulitzer Diaries: Inside America's Greatest Prize* (Syracuse: Syracuse University Press, 1997), pp. 261–62; President William J. McGill to "Alumnus," May 17, 1972, School of Journalism Records.

5. Student publication: Rick Laubscher, ed., *Bullhorn: A Closeup Look at Columbia's 1972 Dilemma*, May 12, 1972, School of Journalism Records.

6. Pinkham initiative: Pinkham to class of 1972, letter explaining petition, May 6, 1972; petition on bombing, May 1, 1972; Mencher to Abel, May 8, 1972; Abel to Mencher, May 10, 1972, School of Journalism Records.

7. "Smoker": Frederick T. C. Yu to "My Colleagues," May 15, 1972; Cowan to "Colleagues," May 18, 1972, enclosing report; Boylan to Yu, May 23, 1972, School of Journalism Records; Boylan, Journal, May 22, 1972. "Administrative riot": Boylan, Journal, May 26, 1972.

8. Report on school: Columbia Journalism Collective, "A Report on the Columbia University Graduate School of Journalism," February 1972, School of Journalism Records. Pinkham departure: George N. Allen, "Changing Times: The Columbia School of Journalism," *Washington Journalism Review* (April/May 1979): 40–45.

9. Study leaked: Fred Schneider, "Journalism Students Charge School is 'Sexist,' Media Tool," Columbia *Spectator*, October 11, 1972. Attempts to sell study: Boylan, Journal, March 6, 1972.

10. Admissions policy: the proportion of women rose from 21 percent in the class of 1965 to 41 percent in 1971; tabulated from *The Alumni Directory* (New York: Graduate School of Journalism, 1972); "Women in Majority This Year At Columbia Journalism School" *New York Times*, September 12, 1977. National trend: Gerald M. Kosicki and Lee B. Becker, "1997 Annual Survey of Journalism and Mass Communication Enrollments," www.grady.uga.edu/annualsurveys.

11. Women teaching: announcement, Graduate School of Journalism, 1971–72, pp. 3–5. Garland: E. R. Shipp, "For a Capital-T Teacher, No More Empty Feeling," *116th & Broadway* (school publication), February 1998.

12. Maynard: "2 Chosen to Direct Journalism Course," *Times*, March 27, 1972; Earl Caldwell of the *Times* served as codirector in 1972. Guild comment: "A Program Crashes," editorial, *Guild Reporter*, October 11, 1974. "Old system": Maynard quoted in Nathaniel Sheppard Jr., "Minority-Journalists' Program Closes," *Times*, August 17, 1974. Maynard Institute: history, www.maynardije.org/about/history/.

13. Friendly remarks: Sheppard, "Minority-Journalists' Program Closes." Seminars: Deirdre Carmody, "Friendly Retiring as Ford Fund's Adviser on News," *Times*, December 14, 1980.

14. API departure: Don E. Carter and Malcolm F. Mallette, *Seminar: the Story of the American Press Institute* (Reston, Va.: American Press Institute, 1992), pp. 239, 251–58. API Web site: www.mediacenter.org.

15. Bagehot program: Stephen B. Shepard, "Founding the Fellowship," in Terri Thompson, ed., *Writing About Business: The New Columbia Knight-Bagehot Guide to Economics and Business Journalism* (New York: Columbia University Press, 2001), pp. 362–63.

16. Bagehot startup: "Columbia Program On Business News To Help Reporters," *Times*, June 22, 1975; Shepard to faculty, "Bagehot Fellowship Program Progress Report," October 31, 1975, School of Journalism Records. Welles problem: "Columbia Says Mobil Oil Will End Aid for Project In Dispute Over Director," *Times*, June 19,

1977; "Believing in Bagehot," *Times*, May 3, 1981. Anniversary dinner: John Henry, "Heading Knight-Bagehot, Seeing the World," *116th & Broadway* (winter 2001).

17. Columbia News Service: Johnston to faculty and class, memorandum, January 23, 1978, School of Journalism Records; Johnston, ed., *New York, New York: Selections from Columbia News Service* (New York: Arno Press, 1981); Graduate School of Journalism announcement, 2000–03. *Bronx Beat*: John Henry, "The Little Newspaper That Could . . . and Does," *116th & Broadway*, April 1999. Suspension: Pete Johnston, "The Beat on Pause," *Alumni Journal* (winter 2002).

18. Patterson: Abel to class, December 9, 1975, School of Journalism Records; "John Patterson, 50, Professor Of Journalism at Columbia, Dies," *Times*, December 10, 1975; memorial service program, December 17, 1975, School of Journalism Records; Boylan, Journal, December 17, 1975.

19. Cowans' death: "Louis Cowan Killed With Wife in a Fire; Created Quiz Shows," *Times*, November 19, 1976; Robert J. Landry, "Louis G. Cowan & Wife Die In Fire / Many-Talented Ex-President of CBS Was Also Book Publisher, Professor, Collector, Host," *Variety*, November 24, 1976.

20. Baker reactions: Boylan, Journal, April 28, 1977, December 19, 1978.

21. Abel departure: "Abel, Dean of Journalism At Columbia U., Resigns To Teach at Stanford," *Times*, June 17, 1978. "Rising restlessness": Abel to faculty, June 16, 1978; huff: faculty minutes, September 7, 1978, School of Journalism Records.

## 31. "IT APPEARS YOU HAVE A NEW DEAN"

1. Search committee: minutes, Faculty of Journalism, September 7, 1978; "educational leader": Kimball to search committee, "Some Notes on the Search for a New Dean of Journalism," memorandum, October 1, 1978, School of Journalism Records.

2. Candidates: Boylan, Journal, December 6, 1978.

3. Elliott career: Osborn Elliott, *The World of Oz* (New York: Viking, 1980); fired: pp. 215–17. Hall of fame: Dinitia Smith, "National Magazine Award to Business Week," *New York Times*, April 24, 1996.

4. Rumors: Boylan, Journal, October 4, 12, 1978. "Academic types": "Three Vie for Top Journalism Job," *New York Post*, December 26, 1978.

5. Announcements: Deirdre Carmody, "Osborn Elliott Selected as the Dean Of Columbia School of Journalism," *Times*, December 29, 1978; Sovern to Abel, January 22, 1979, School of Journalism Records. "Six figures": Carmody, "Osborn Elliott Selected"; $150,000: George N. Allen, "Changing Times: The Columbia School of Journalism," *Washington Journalism Review* (April–May 1979): 40–45.

6. "New Dean": William A. Hachten to James Boylan, January 3, 1979, School of Journalism Records.

7. "Paying the bills": Abel to Mencher, February 8, 1979, confidential; thank-you note: Abel to Harry Arouh and others, April 23, 1979, School of Journalism Records.

8. "Four hundred and fifty": Elliott, *World of Oz*, p. 70. "Dean's List": news release, Columbia Office of Public Information, June 12, 1979.

9. "Sufficient stress": Allen, "Changing Times."

10. Wood retirement: *Galley 25* (alumni publication), fall 1978. Friendly "retirement": Elliott to Friendly, June 28, 1979; Friendly to Elliott, July 3, 1979; Elliott to Friendly, January 5, 1981, School of Journalism Records. Seminars: Wolfgang Saxon, "Columbia Seminars to Study the Press and Society," *Times*, April 27, 1981.

11. News Council: *Galley 22*, alumni publication, winter 1977; Norman E. Isaacs, *Untended Gates: The Mismanaged Press* (New York: Columbia University Press, 1986).

12. Baker and Pulitzers: In John Hohenberg's *John Hohenberg: The Pursuit of Excellence* (Syracuse: Syracuse University Press, 1995), he writes that he asked Baker to succeed him (p. 212); in *The Pulitzer Diaries: Inside America's Greatest Prize* (Gainesville: University Press of Florida, 1997), his diary says that Dean Abel made the nomination (p. 289). Endowment: Boylan, Journal, December 15, 1977.

13. Faculty jurors: James Boylan and Norman Isaacs—news release, Columbia Office of Public Information, March 1, 1978. Secrecy: Richard Hart, "Are the Pulitzers Rigged?", *Broadway* (student laboratory publication), March 1979. Runners-up: Edith Evans Asbury, "Pulitzer Panel to Add 3 Members And to List 2 Runner-Up Entries," *Times*, October 18, 1979.

14. Brain episode: talk with Abel, Boylan, Journal, July 22, 1976; smoking: September 23, 1976; surgery: February 23, 1981.

15. "Naivete and phoniness": Lenora Williamson, "Next Pulitzer Deadlines Set; 1981 Feature Debate Rolls On," *Editor & Publisher*, June 6, 1981, 80. Cooke story: "Exploring 'Jimmy's World,'" special section, *Columbia Journalism Review* (July–August 1981): 28–36, especially Penn Kimball, "A Multiple Embarassment," 33–34, on the sanctimony of the reactions. Baker appearance: Williamson, "Next Pulitzer Deadlines."

16. Farewell party: Boylan, Journal, May 12, 1981; emeritus: Michael I. Sovern to Baker, May 22, 1981, School of Journalism Records; to St. Lawrence River: Boylan, Journal, June 8, 1981; death: Christopher G. Trump, associate dean, to Alumni, September 15, 1981, School of Journalism Records; Peter Kihss, "Richard Baker, 68, Professor Who Held Pulitzer Post, Dies," *Times*, September 4, 1981.

17. "Dick's own desires": Barrett to Trustees, Cornell College, May 18, 1960, Edward W. Barrett Central File, Columbia University Archives.

18. "Why?": Boylan, Journal, July 15, 2000. "Mincemeat": Michael Mooney, deputy provost, to Elliott, March 23, 1981, Box 17, Richard Terrill Baker Papers, Rare Book and Manuscript Library, Columbia University.

19. Johnston process: Boylan, Journal, June 8, 1981. Credentials: résumé, September 15, 1980; comparison list: enclosed with Peter Likins, provost, to Boylan, February 16, 1981; Johnston to Boylan, June 21, 1981, School of Journalism Records. Belford: Boylan to Robert F. Goldberger, provost, April 2, 1985, School of Journalism Records.

20. Lewis: *Galley 25* (alumni publication), fall 1978; "Professor Joins Inquiry Into A-Plant Accident," *Times*, May 16, 1979. Trump leaves: Boylan, Journal, December 3, 1979, June 15, 1981. Trump award: *Galley 27*, fall 1979. Shouting match: Lewis to Elliott, confidential, November 5, 1980, School of Journalism Records.

## 32. CJR—FROM NEW MANAGEMENT TO OLD

1. Barrett and Boylan departures: Barrett, "Adieu," *Columbia Journalism Review* (fall 1968): 25; Boylan: *Columbia Journalism Review* (fall 1969): 2. Balk: news release, Columbia Office of Public Information, August 2, 1971. Bimonthly publication began with the issue of May–June 1971. Anthology: Balk and Boylan, eds., *Our Troubled Press: Ten Years of the Columbia Journalism Review* (Boston: Little, Brown, 1971).

2. Local journalism reviews: "The New Press Critics," *Columbia Journalism Review* (May–June 1971): 29–36; (March–April 1972): 27–38; (November–December 1972): 29–40; (September–October 1973): 29–40; "Atlanta Journalism Review" (July–August 1971): 27–38.

3. Newark article: Richard Reeves, "Newark's Fallen Giant: Euthanasia or Murder?", *Columbia Journalism Review* (November–December 1972): 49–55. Scudder response: "'Newark's Fallen Giant': "Untruths, Distortions, Misrepresentations," (March–April 1973):65–67. Suit and trial: Charles Knapp, "Former Newark Editor Sues Columbia Journalism Review," Columbia *Spectator*, April 25, 1974; settlement: John Consoli, "Scudder Withdraws Suit Agains Columbia J-Review," *Editor & Publisher* (June 11, 1977): 14; "Libel Suit," *Columbia Journalism Review* (July–August 1977): 7.

4. Abel introduction: Balk and Boylan, eds., *Our Troubled Press*, pp. ix–xvi.

5. Balk and faculty: Boylan, Journal, April 27, 1970; May 26, 1970. Friendly: "The Campaign to Politicize Broadcasting," *Columbia Journalism Review* (March–April 1973): 9–18; Isaacs: "Why We Lack a National Press Council" (fall 1970): 16–26. Separation: Boylan, Journal, November 14, 1972 December 5, 1972, notes on meeting of date. *[MORE]*: Thomas Collins, "(More) Competition for Columbia Review," *Newsday*, July 28, 1971; "Press Watchdog Picks a Bone," *New York* magazine, October 14, 1974.

6. *Review* planning: Boylan, Journal, December 5, 1972, March 13, 21, 22, 1973.

7. Pierce selection: Boylan, Journal, March 3, 1973; Pierce to Abel, May 26, 1973, with résumé, CJR Records.

8. Bagdikian: first article for Pierce was "Newspapers: Learning (Too Slowly) to Adapt to TV," *Columbia Journalism Review*, (November–December 1973): 44–51. Loory: "The CIA's Use of the Press: A 'Mighty Wurlitzer,'" *Columbia Journalism Review* (September–October 1974): 9–18. Morris: "Henry Kissinger and the Media: A Separate Peace," *Columbia Journalism Review* (May–June 1974): 14–25; *Times* response: A. M. Rosenthal, "Who Killed What?" (letter to the editor) *Columbia Journalism Review* (July–August 1974): 53–55.

9. Hochman: Balk to Abel and others, August 17, 1973; Pierce plan: "A Brief Overview: Columbia Journalism Review Development Plan," February 26, 1974; Ford grant: Edward W. Barrett, "The C.J.R. in Perspective," memorandum, April 8, 1976, CJR Records.

10. Advertising: Boylan, Journal, May 20, 1974. Hochman, "CJR advertising," memorandum, to Abel and others, April 22, 1974; Isaacs to Hochman, April 23, 1974, approving conditionally; Boylan to Hochman, May 2, 1974, approving conditionally;

Barrett to Hochman, May 15, 1974, approving conditionally; Barrett doubts: Barrett to Isaacs, July 23, 1974, CJR Records. Initial advertising: "Our Policy on Advertising," *Columbia Journalism Review* (January–February 1975): 1; Wright: *Columbia Journalism Review* (March–April 1975): 2.

11. Barrett: Thomas Brady, "Barrett, Ex-Columbia Dean, Named to Communications Post," *New York Times*, January 23, 1969. Cutting back: Barrett, "Notes on Fundamentals of Columbia Journalism Review" [November 20, 1974]; alarm: Barrett, "Status of CJR," memorandum, January 21, 1976, CJR Records.

12. "A single piece": Pierce to Abel, Barrett, Boylan, memorandum, February 16, 1976, CJR Records. Pierce removal: Boylan, Journal, May 19, 1975, February 11, March 16, 1976.

13. Boylan reinstallation: Boylan, Journal, March 26, 27, 1976.

14. Wenk dismissal: Pierce to Wenk, December 6, 1974, CJR Records. Cooper first appeared on the masthead in November–December 1974 as an assistant to the editor; Swan, in January–February 1975, as an associate editor.

15. Advertising record: "Journalism Review Going Strong at Columbia," *Times*, August 8, 1978. Leadership Network: "New Faces Marketing Magazines," *Times*, August 27, 1979. Circulation: from 15,000 (Hochman to Abel and others, memorandum, November 5, 1973) to 38,000, ("Statement of Ownership, Management, and Circulation, September 20, 1976, published in *Columbia Journalism Review* (January–February 1977): 62.

16. Salant dispute: Barrett to Boylan, personal, November 23, 1976, CJR Records; Richard S. Salant, "TV News's Old Days Weren't All That Good," *Columbia Journalism Review* (March-April 1977): 10, 12, 14. Cigarette advertising: Mencher to Boylan, April 30, 1977, School of Journalism Records. Committees: Barrett to six alumni, June 2, 1977, and replies; Boylan, minutes of advisory editors' subcommittee, October 7, 1977, CJR Records; Barrett, "Cigarette Ads," *Columbia Journalism Review* (January–February 1978): 18; Robert C. Smith, "The Magazines' Smoking Habit," ibid., 29–31.

17. "Leaning a bit": Barrett to Boylan, March 9, 1978, CJR Records.

18. *[MORE]* closing: "Chronicle: New York Loses One," *Columbia Journalism Review* (September–October 1978): 12, 18; Barrett, "Publisher's Notes," ibid., 24. "Billboard": Bruce McCabe, "Decline of Journalism's Self-Criticism," *Boston Globe*, September 16, 1978.

19. News Council: Barrett, "Introducing a New Service: National News Council Report," *Columbia Journalism Review* (March–April 1977): 73. Background: "'Monitoring' National News Suppliers: . . . A Unique Proposal," Report of the Twentieth Century Fund Task Force on press councils, *Columbia Journalism Review* (March–April 1973): 43–46. Comment on council: "National News Council v. Panax," editorial, *Columbia Journalism Review* (March–April 1978): 24–25.

20. Search: Manoff background: résumé [1978]; appointment: Barrett to Abel and Yu, memorandum, February 25, 1979, CJR Records; *Columbia University Record*, March 27, 1979. Champagne: Boylan, Journal, February 21, 1979.

21. Manoff plans: Manoff to Barrett, memorandum, February 21, 1979, CJR Records. Staff dissension: Boylan, Journal, June 19, 1979. Warnings: Barrett to Manoff, memorandums, October 16, 1979, January 7, 1980; dismissal: Barrett to Manoff, February 14, 1980, CJR Records; news release, Columbia Office of Public Information, February 21, 1980; Deirdre Carmody, "Columbia Ousts Head of Journalism Review In a Dispute on Policy," Times, February 23, 1980.

22. Manoff speaks: Karl Johnson, "Review Editor's Dismissal: Politics or Procedures?", Columbia Spectator, February 28, 1980. Breach of agreement: charged in joint statement by Elliott and Barrett, February 22, 1980, CJR Records. "Fusillade": Cockburn, "Columbia the Gem," Village Voice, February 25, 1980. Corrections: Barrett to Newsweek, March 17, 1980, responding to "Who'll Watch The Media Watcher?" Newsweek, March 3, 1980; Barrett to New Statesman [n.d.], responding to Claudia Wright, "It's a Free Press in America, Too," New Statesman, February 29, 1980; Barrett to Mother Jones, August 1980, pp. 2, 4, responding to "Hatchet Job in the Pressroom," Mother Jones, June 1980. Apology: Adam Hochschild, Mother Jones, to Barrett, April 3, 1981, enclosing page proof of apology to appear in June 1981 issue, CJR Records.

23. "Newsroom democracy": Karl Johnson, "Review Editor's Dismissal," Columbia Spectator, February 28, 1960. Massing: biographical summary, views.vcu.edu/cpdd/pages/2001_media.html.

24. Klaw appointment: Peter Kihss, "Columbia Journalism Review Names a New Editor," Times, June 30, 1980. Editorial independence: Barrett to Klaw, June 18, 1980, CJR Records. Barrett on political tone: see especially Barrett to Klaw, September 17, 1981, and undated comment on March–April 1981 issue, CJR Records.

25. Complaint: "The Review Slips on 'Banana Republics' Story," Columbia Journalism Review (September–October 1980): 81–83, involving Michael Massing, "Inside the Wires' Banana Republics," Columbia Journalism Review (November–December 1979): 45–49. Isaacs analysis: Norman E. Isaacs, Untended Gates: The Mismanaged Press (New York: Columbia University Press, 1986), p. 129. Klaw rebuttal: interview with author, November 3, 2002. The National News Council was terminated in 1984.

26. Barrett retirement: Barrett to Elliott, February 26, 1982, CJR Records; Albin Krebs and Robert McG. Thomas, "'Family Event' for Columbia Journalism Review," Times, April 20, 1982. "Stubbornness": "Unlikely Event," Columbia Journalism Review (March–April 1982): 22.

## 33. "SOUR APPLES"

1. Remarks softened: James W. Carey, in Boylan, Journal, August 8, 1981.

2. Dennis study: Jonathan Friendly, "Strategies Debated by Journalism Educators," New York Times, January 23, 1984; Friendly, "Education: Plan Urges Broader Scope in Journalism," Times, June 26, 1984.

3. Lewis resignation: Laurie Johnston and Susan Heller Anderson, "Resignation at Columbia," Times, April 26, 1983, quoting the Spectator.

4. Poliak center: Jonathan Friendly, "Columbia to Get Center of Free Press," *Times*, October 14, 1983.

5. Gannett Center: Jonathan Friendly, "Gannett Gives $15 Million for Journalism Center at Columbia," *Times*, April 12, 1984; "Gannett Media Center Dedicated at Columbia," *Times*, March 13, 1985. Size: Michael Mooney, deputy provost, to Dean Joan Konner, August 8, 1988, School of Journalism Records.

6. Delacorte gifts: news releases, Columbia Office of Public Information, March 14, 1985, January 29, 1986; Sara Rimer, "A Philanthropist With a Taste for Whimsy Visits His Gifts," *Times*, March 20, 1985.

7. Mencher textbook: Melvin Mencher, "Travails of a Textbook Author," *Nieman Reports*, fall 1996, pp. 43–47. Outstanding teacher: "Three Professors Are Honored for Their Teaching," *Columbia University Record*, October 28, 1983.

8. "Classical purity": Kimball, *The File* (New York: Harcourt Brace Jovanovich, 1983), p. 4. Surveillance incidents are described in the book.

9. "Citizen K.": Anthony Lewis, "It Did Happen Here," *Times*, November 28, 1983. Libel suit: Paul Desruisseaux, "Columbia U. Professor Files $10-Million Suit Against U.S. Agencies over 'Libelous Files,'" *Chronicle of Higher Education*, June 13, 1984. Settlement: Arnold H. Lubasch, "Professor Wins Battle to Clear Name," *Times*, October 2, 1987.

10. Later career: "A Mellower Kimball? Well . . . Read On," *116th & Broadway* (school publication), July 1998. Davison: "Recollections of Communication Research Done at the School," *Alumni Journal*, spring 1997.

11. "Quiescent": Alex S. Jones, "Elliott Resigns as Journalism Dean at Columbia," *Times*, March 26, 1986. Zuckerman: "There's Only So Much You Can Buy for $164 Mil," *New York Post*, February 25, 1986. Review dinner: "[Thomas] Winship [editor of the *Boston Globe*] Speaks at *CJR*'s Silver Anniversary," *Columbia University Record*, November 21, 1986.

12. Major work: Frederick T. C. Yu, *Mass Persuasion* (New York: Praeger, 1964). Textbook: W. Phillips Davison, James Boylan, and Frederick T. C. Yu, *Mass Media: Systems and Effects* (New York: Praeger, 1976).

13. A second year: Boylan, Journal, September 25, 1973; Center for Advanced Study: proposal, October 1972, School of Journalism Records. Commission: Boylan, Journal, March 21, 1977.

14. "Unfair": Johnston to Yu, June 30, 1987; Yu to faculty, July 1, 1987, announcing change, School of Journalism Records. Johnston's later career: John Henry, "A Quiet Dynamo Doesn't Think of Stopping," *116th & Broadway* (school publication), April 1999.

15. "Very lousy idea": Deirdre Carmody, "Columbia Faculty Faults Plan to Link 4 Schools," *Times*, October 18, 1987; Yu to Sam McKeel, class of 1952, January 6, 1988, School of Journalism Records.

16. Sovern comments with responses: Alex S. Jones, "The Journalism School at Columbia Is 75," *Times*, May 4, 1988.

17. Meyer: "Professor Is Said to Weigh Journalism Post at Columbia," *Times*,

April 29, 1987; Alex S. Jones, "A Setback at Columbia," *Times*, May 4, 1987; Boylan, Journal, April 28, 1987.

18. Carey: Boylan, Journal, March 6, June 16, August 1, September 9, 1987.

19. Konner mentioned: Jones, "A Setback at Columbia."

## 34. SHOWDOWN

1. Konner record: Alex S. Jones, "Columbia Selects Dean for Journalism School," *New York Times*, June 3, 1988.

2. "Reputation questioned": ibid.

3. "Little influence": Jerrold K. Footlick, "Eleven Exemplary Journalism Schools," *Gannett Center Journal* 2 (spring 1988): 68–76; quotation is at p. 75.

4. "Bait-and-switch": Dennis, "Whatever Happened to Marse Robert's Dream? The Dilemma of American Journalism Education," *Media Studies Journal* 2 (spring 1988): 1–22; quotation at p. 12.

5. "Distress and concern": Professor Helen Benedict to Konner, November 4, 1988; Konner to Dennis, January 20, 1989, Dennis to Konner, February 1, 1989, School of Journalism Records.

6. Gannett Foundation role: Jonathan Friendly, "Journalism Schools Are Long on Students, Short on Respect," *Times*, June 3, 1984. Visiting professorships: Yu to Gerald M. Sass, Gannett Foundation, August 12, 1988, notifying him of selection of Stephen D. Isaacs; Konner to Gannett Center Colleagues, August 18, 1989, invitation to meet Gannett Visting Professor Martin Gottlieb; Sass to Konner, November 22, 1989, School of Journalism Records.

7. Overrated: Neuharth, *Confessions of an S.O.B.* (New York: Doubleday, 1989), p. 263. Neuharth attacks: "Gannett Attacks on the Journalism School," attachment, Konner to President Michael I. Sovern and Provost Jonathan Cole, November 20, 1990; Konner to Neuharth, November 29, 1989; Neuharth to Konner, December 3, 1989, School of Journalism Records.

8. "Institute": Konner to Sovern and Cole, memorandum, November 23, 1990; Konner to Arthur Ochs Sulzberger and Warren Phillips, November 29, 1990, reporting on meeting with Sovern and Cole, School of Journalism Records.

9. Sovern retirement: "Timeline of Recent History of Columbia University 1969–2002," beatl.barnard.columbia.edu/cuhis3057/Timelines/Recent1970_02.htm. Contract renewal: Konner to Sovern, February 16, 1993, School of Journalism Records.

10. Takeover threat: Konner to Sovern, February 16, 1993.

11. Rupp named: "Timeline of Recent History," February 1, 1993. Appeal to Rupp: author interview with Konner, April 20, 2000. Failure to mention: Konner, "Dear Alum," letter, June 1993, School of Journalism Records.

12 . Rupp reception: Nadine Brozan, "Chronicle," *Times*, September 20, 1993.

13. Departure: "Freedom Forum to Expand Its Ties in Move to Midtown," *Columbia University Record*, May 12, 1995.

## 35. TO THE EXITS

1. Fresh paint: Alex S. Jones, "Columbia Selects Dean for Journalism School," *New York Times*, June 3, 1988. "Ground Zero": Konner to Peter Malkin, December 28, 1989, School of Journalism Records.

2. Accreditation: reported in "Graduate School of Journalism: 1991 Budget Submission, Part II: Academic Planning Strategy and Three Year Budget Plan," March 8, 1991, School of Journalism Records.

3. Board of visitors: "Seven Media Leaders Join Journalism School's Board," *Columbia University Record*, April 7, 1995.

4. Barrett death: Glenn Fowler, "Edward W. Barrett, 79, Ex-Journalism Dean, Dies," *Times*, October 25, 1989. Friendly and Isaacs: news release, Columbia Office of Public Information, October 24, 1989.

5. Mencher retirement: Konner to faculty, March 21, 1990; "Time marches on": Josh Getlin, "Teacher or Tyrant," *Los Angeles Times*, n.d. [1990], clipping, School of Journalism Records.

6. Jackson: Wayne Dawkins, "Influential Black Journalists of the 20th Century," *NABJ Journal*, fall 1999, www.nabj.org/html/list.html.

7. Yu: Konner to faculty, June 1, 1993, on his emeritus rank; Shanor: Konner to Shanor, May 6, 1992; Elliott: Stephen Isaacs, associate dean, to Jonathan Cole, provost, nominating Elliott for emeritus rank, April 22, 1994; admiration for Konner: Elliott to Konner, May 18, 1993, School of Journalism Records.

8. Hardball: Stephen Rittenberg, associate provost, October 25, 1993, on retirement agreement; rebuffed: subject to Konner, November 20, December 13, 1993; "clinical professor": Stephen Isaacs to Ivan Weissman, May 1, 1991, School of Journalism Records.

9. Faculty changes: announcement, Graduate School of Journalism, 1997–1999, August 30, 1996.

10. Friendly seminars: "Friendly Enters TV Hall of Fame," *Columbia University Record*, October 7, 1994. Books: *The Good Guys, the Bad Guys , and the First Amendment: Free Speech vs. Fairness in Broadcasting* (New York: Random House, 1976); *Minnesota Rag: the Dramatic Story of the Landmark Supreme Court Case That Gave New Meaning to Freedom of the Press* (New York: Random House, 1981); *The Constitution: That Delicate Balance* (New York: Random House, 1984).

11. "I well remember": Friendly to Konner, May 7, 1992, School of Journalism Records.

12. Goldstein and Belford retirements: Konner, "Dear Alum" letter, September 1996, School of Journalism Records. Rothmyer: "Former Faculty—Where Are They Now?", *Alumni Journal*, winter 1999; tenure process: Boylan, Journal, September 25, 1991.

13. Isaacs: Konner to "Gannett Center Colleagues," August 18, 1989, to meet Isaacs as new associate dean for academic affairs; Konner, "Dear Alum" letter, January 1995, School of Journalism Records.

14. Carey appointment: "Media Theorist Carey Promoted at Journalism," *Columbia University Record*, September 23, 1994.

15. Doctoral program: Carey, "A Ph.D. Program for the School of Journalism," memorandum to committee on instruction, December 1, 1993, School of Journalism Records.

16. Klatell: announcement, Graduate School of Journalism, 1997–99. Freedman: "Honoring Teaching at the Highest Level," *116th & Broadway* (school publication), n.d. [1997].

17. Colombo: Susan Heller Anderson, "Chronicle," *Times*, June 10, 1991; departure: Konner to Colombo, December 8, 1993, accepting resignation, School of Journalism Records. Topping appointment: William Glaberson, "Topping Leaves Times Co. to Administer the Pulitzers," *Times*, February 10, 1993. Levine: "New Editor at the Journalism Review," *Times*, February 21, 1989.

18. Anderson, Dinges, Hancock, Mills: "Columbia Journalism Appoints New Faculty," news release, Columbia Office of Public Affairs, September 18, 1996; Konner, "Dear Alum" letters, January 1995, September 1996; see also announcement, Graduate School of Journalism, 1997–99.

19. Bill of Rights: news release, Columbia Office of Public Information, December 6, 1991. Books: *Essential Liberty: First Amendment Battles for a Free Press* (New York: Graduate School of Journalism, 1991); *Freedom Week: A Salute to the First Amendment, December 9–13, 1991* (New York: Graduate School of Journalism, 1991).

20. Rushdie appearance: Esther B. Fein, "Rushdie, Defying Death Threats, Suddenly Appears in New York," *Times*, December 12, 1991; Fein, "Writers See Freedom Come 'Alive,'" *Times*, December 13, 1991. Sovern reference: William H. Honan, "Sovern Era Ends at Columbia," *Times*, June 30, 1993.

## 36. THE CONGLOMERATE

1. Full possession: Konner, "Dear Alum" letter, June 1995, School of Journalism Records.

2. Enrollment: Konner, "Dear Alum," September 1996, School of Journalism Records; announcement, Graduate School of Journalism, 1997–99, August 30, 1996.

3. Fellowship programs: announcement, Graduate School of Journalism, 1997–1999. Janeway: Fred Knubel, "Pew Awards Columbia $3.5M to Run Its National Arts Journalism Program," *Columbia University Record*, October 4, 1996.

4. Winfrey: "Delacorte Center Tops Out at Journalism," *Columbia University Record*, May 10, 1996.

5. Brennan professorship: Nadine Brozan, "Chronicle," *New York Times*, March 2, 1994.

6. New Media: Stephen D. Isaacs, acting dean, "To Alums" letter, July 28, 1994, School of Journalism Records.

7. Awards: announcement, 1997–99, Graduate School of Journalism. Wagner: "Columbia Cites Mayor and Kheel For Work in Ending News Strike," *Times*, May 16, 1963.

8. Expenses: "Actual Operating Expenses and Revenues—FY1990–FY1993," in "The New *Columbia Journalism Review* Business Plan," November 16, 1993, CJR Records.

9. Walsh article: Boylan, Journal, December 4, 1989; Walsh, "Mission: Afghanistan," *Columbia Journalism Review*, January–February 1990; Erwin Knoll, "Afghanistan: Holes in the Coverage of a War," *Progressive*, May 1990; Konner (as publisher) to Knoll, July 27 1990, School of Journalism Records.

10. Advertising: e.g., the issue of March–April 1992 had ten full-page ads in an issue of 52 pages plus covers. Deficit: "Actual Operating Expenses . . . " Threat to close: Boylan, Journal, August 13, 1993.

11. Self-support: "The New *Columbia Journalism Review* Business Plan," November 16, 1993; "major magazine": "The New *Columbia Journalism Review* Editorial Plan," November 29, 1993, CJR Records.

12. Rosenblatt appointment: news release, Columbia Office of Public Information, November 18, 1993; "'CJR' Launches New Promotional, Editorial Campaign," *Columbia University Record*, November 18, 1994. Editorial advisers: Rosenblatt and the editorial advisers appeared in March–April 1994, p. 4; Carey was added in September–October 1994.

13. "Presses can run": "'CJR' Launches New Campaign." New support: Elizabeth Sanger, "CJR's New Vision: More Visibility," *Newsday*, November 21, 1994; Konner, "Dear Alum" letter, June 1995, School of Journalism Records. Not as dull: Boylan, Journal, November 3, 1994; editorial, *New York Observer*, March 15, 1995. Departure: Rosenblatt to Levine and others, June 2, 1995, CJR Records. Chair of advisers: *Columbia Journalism Review*, November–December 1995 to May–June 1996.

14. Konner column: "Publisher's Note" started in *Columbia Journalism Review* in November–December 1994: 4. Stepping down: Nadine Brozan, "Chronicle," *Times*, March 7, 1996.

15. Levine–Konner comments: Jeff Gremillion, "'CJR': Under Review," *Mediaweek*, December 16, 1996.

16. Loeb appointment: Iver Peterson, "Editor Is Named for Columbia Journalism Review," *Times*, December 3, 1996. Editorial four-color appeared in Loeb's first issue, March–April 1997. Circulation statements: 28,736 on October 1, 1996; 28,328 on October 1, 1999, published in *Columbia Journalism Review* (January–February 1997): 62; (January–February 2000): 79.

## 37. "DEANS' ROW"

1. Konner intent: "Joan Konner to Step Down as Dean of Journalism," *Columbia University Record*, March 22, 1996.

2. Carey account: Boylan, Journal, January 16, April 21, 1997.

3. Schaap complaint: Schaap, *Flashing Before My Eyes: 50 Years of Headlines, Deadlines and Punchlines* (New York: William Morrow, 2001), pp. 288–89. Schaap death: Steve Conn, "A Sports Legend," *Alumni Journal*, winter 2002.

4. Goldstein appointment: Iver Peterson, "Ex-Dean at Berkeley to Head Columbia Journalism School," *New York Times*, December 14, 1996. Konner story: Peterson, "Journalism Is Still Columbia's Priority," *Times*, December 16, 1996.

5. Decline of journalism schools: Howard M. Ziff, "The Closing of the Journalistic Mind," *Columbia Journalism Review* (January–February 1992): 49–51. See also seminar papers by Richard Campbell, Betty Medsger, and James Carey sponsored by the John Seigenthaler Chair at Middle Tennessee State University, 1996, www.mtsu.edu/~masscomm/seig96/.

6. World Room: "World Room Rededicated," *Alumni Journal*, fall 1997; Konner, "Publisher's Note," *Columbia Journalism Review* (September–October 1997): 8.

7. Birthday observance: Fred Knubel, "Journalism School Celebrates Columbia's 'Joseph Pulitzer Day,'" *Columbia University Record*, April 18, 1997.

8. "Alumni/ae Hall": "New Dean Konner Lobby Connects Alumni/ae, School," *Alumni Journal*, winter 1998; "Improving, at Last, on McKim, Mead and White," *116th & Broadway* (school publication), February 1998.

9. Managing Yankees: Iver Peterson, "Ex-Dean at Berkeley to Head Columbia Journalism School." Goldstein's books: *The News at Any Cost: How Journalists Compromise their Ethics to Shape the News* (New York: Simon & Schuster, 1985); *A Two-Faced Press?* (New York: Priority, 1986); ed., *Killing the Messenger: 100 Years of Media Criticism* (New York: Columbia University Press, 1989).

10. Enrollment: "In the Biggest Class Yet, More Women (Again)," *116th & Broadway*, n.d. [fall 1997]. Tenure actions: Konner to Boylan, e-mail, April 21, 2000.

11. Report: Graduate School of Journalism, "Self-Study Report," April 1998, School of Journalism Records.

12. Report: "A Critical Evaluation of the Columbia University Graduate School of Journalism, submitted to Provost Jonathan Cole," June 22, 1998. The members of the team, besides Meyer and Overholser, were Russell Neuman of the Annenberg School, Deborah Potter of the Poynter Institute, and David Rubin of the Newhouse School, who served as chair.

13. RW1: Acting Dean (Richard T. Baker) to Incoming Class, memorandum, n.d. [summer 1969], introducing Advanced Reporting and Writing, School of Journalism Records. "Mindless frenzy": "Critical Evaluation."

14. Dean's reaction: Goldstein, "From the Dean," *116th & Broadway*, October 1998. Isaacs, Padwe, Freedman, Carey: "A Critique Gets a Range of Critiques," ibid.

15. Friendly death: Eric Pace, "Fred W. Friendly, CBS Executive and Pioneer in TV News Coverage, Dies at 82," *Times* March 5, 1998. "Infotainment": David Remnick, "Bad News," *The New Yorker*, March 16, 1998. Riverdale service: "Friendly Is Recalled as Loud Voice of Integrity," *Times*, March 7, 1998. Campus memorial: text in *Memorial Service for Fred W. Friendly*, Kathryn Bache Miller Theatre, Columbia University, April 23, 1998.

16. Bettag: quoted in "Remembering Fred Friendly, Who Said, 'You Can Do Better Than This,'" *116th & Broadway*, April 1998.

17. Wald appointment: "Richard Wald named first Fred Friendly Professor," news release, Columbia Office of Public Affairs, April 26, 1999; "At ABC, Bad Time for

Goodbye," *Times*, May 7, 1999. Scholarships: "CBS Gift to Columbia Graduate School of Journalism Honors Memory of Broadcast Giant Fred Friendly," news release, Columbia Office of Public Affairs, December 1, 1998.

18. Isaacs death: Eric Pace, "Norman E. Isaacs, 89, Journalist and Expert on Newspaper Issues," *Times*, March 10, 1998; Balk, "Honoring Norman Isaacs, One of the Giants," *116th & Broadway*, July 1998.

19. "Twin mission": "From the Dean," *116th & Broadway*, October 1998.

## 38. TRYING TO STRETCH THE YEAR

1. "Planning Document": "Journalism School Planning Document: Discussion Draft," December 1, 1998, School of Journalism Records.

2. Other degree programs: announcement, Graduate School of Journalism, 1997–1999, August 30, 1996. Change in part-time program: "And a Landmark in January," *116th & Broadway*, winter 2000.

3. First step: "Some in 98–99 To Start Early; More TK," *116th & Broadway*, April 1998.

4. "Walking pneumonia": LynNell Hancock, quoted in "Historic Step: Full-Time Is 10 Months," *116th & Broadway*, winter 2000; also student and Goldstein comments.

5. Doctoral program: "Treading Carefully, Ph.D.'s Are Coming," *116th & Broadway*, April 1998.

6. Endowed chairs: "Journalism School Planning Document: Discussion Draft," December 1, 1998, School of Journalism Records; "From the Dean," *116th & Broadway*, April 1999. Laventhol chair: news release, Columbia Office of Public Affairs, December 7, 1998; Payne: "Payne Promoted to Associate Managing Editor at *Newsday*," news release, National Association of Black Journalists, October 9, 2000. Knight chair: Kim Brockway, "Author/Economist Sylvia Nasar Named to Knight Chair at Journalism School," news release, Columbia Office of Public Affairs, October 16, 2000.

7. Luce professorship: Kim Brockway, "Time Warner and Henry Luce Foundation Establish Henry R. Luce Professorship . . . ," news release, Columbia Office of Public Affairs, December 4, 2000. Bloomberg professorship: Brockway, "Bloomberg Chair Established at Journalism School," news release, Columbia Office of Public Affairs, May 4, 2001.

8. Freedman and Shapiro: Freedman, "Reminiscences from the Tenure Trek," *116th & Broadway*, summer 2000. Crist: "Former Students Honor Judith Crist For Her 40 Years of 'Tough' Teaching," *Alumni Journal*, winter 1999.

9. Eisenstaedt awards: "First Eisie Photo Awards," *New York Times*, January 13, 1998. Lukas death: Samuel G. Freedman, "A Heart, A Brain and a Good Pair of Shoes," *Salon*, www.salon.com/june97/media/media970612.html; awards: "First Lukas Prizes For Nonfiction Announced by Columbia, Harvard," news release, Columbia Office of Public Affairs, April 5, 1999.

10. On-line awards: Kim Brockway, "Online Journalism Awards Established at Columbia," news release, Columbia Office of Public Affairs, May 8, 2000; Nichole M. Christian, "Columbia Gives Awards For Journalism Done Online," *Times*, December 5, 2000.

11. Circulation: statement, October 1, 1999, *Columbia Journalism Review* (January–February 2000): 77. *Brill's* competition: Robin Pogrebin, "Journalism Review Polishes Look in Light of New Rival," *Times*, June 22, 1998; Boylan, Journal, April 28, May 20, July 8, 1998. Business plan: Boylan, Journal, September 22, 28, 1998.

12. Editors' meeting: Boylan, Journal, November 10, 1998. Laventhol appointment: "David Laventhol, Former Times-Mirror Chief, Named Publisher of *Columbia Journalism Review*," news release, Columbia Office of Public Affairs, April 13, 1999; Alex Kuczynski and Felicity Barringer, "Retooling Columbia Journalism Review," *Times*, April 12, 1999. Loeb departure: "Loeb Moves to the Internet from Columbia Journalism Review," *Columbia University Record*, June 30, 1999.

13. New masthead: *Columbia Journalism Review*, November–December 1999. "America's Best Newspapers": ibid., 14–16; response: David Hall, "'Best' Papers— Trivial Pursuit," *Columbia Journalism Review* (January–February 2000): 8. "The Ten Best Editors," ibid., 14–16. Hoyt appointment: Abigail Beshkin, "Michael Hoyt Named CJR Executive Editor," news release, Columbia Office of Public Affairs, May 31, 2000.

14. Anniversary issue: *Columbia Journalism Review*, November–December 2001. Circulation: cited in James Boylan, "40 Years of CJR," ibid., 148. Goldstein comment: "A Lover's Judgment," ibid., 34.

15. Gore incident: "Former Vice President Al Gore to Teach at Columbia's School of Journalism," news release, Columbia Office of Public Affairs, January 25, 2001; Kevin Sack, "Gore Will Teach at 3 Universities," *Times*, January 25, 2001. "Off the record": Dan Mangan, "Prof. Gore's Class Gagged," *New York Post*, February 7, 2001; Felicity Barringer, "From Gore, an Off-the Record (Kind of) Lecture," *Times*, February 7, 2001; Goldstein, "Nothing Like a Moment in the Winter Sun," *116th & Broadway*, winter 2001. Abrams' and universities' comments: Susan Saulny, "Columbia Takes Wraps Off Seminar With Gore," *Times*, February 9, 2001.

16. Greenspan and Murdoch: Marjorie Olster, "Federal Reserve Chairman Alan Greenspan Gives Journalism Students Fedspeak," Reuters, March 21, 2001; Reuters photo, Murdoch and Gore, *Times*, March 5, 2001. "Disaster": Felicity Barringer, "Student Reviews Mixed After Gore's Final Class," *Times*, May 3, 2001.

17. Accreditation: summarized in "From the Dean," *116th & Broadway*, spring 2001.

18. September 11: John Henry, "The Day the World Changed: Horror, and Journalism to Do," and related articles, *116th & Broadway*, fall 2001; Nick Spangler (class of 2002), "Witness," *Columbia Journalism Review* (November–December 2001): 6–9.

19. "Harpo": Cornog, "The Leadership Secrets of Attila the Dean," *116th & Broadway*, winter 2002. Groucho: Bert Kalmar and Harry Ruby, "Hooray for Captain Spaulding," from *Animal Crackers* (1936), www.math.mit.edu/~bradley/hooray.html. Staying: Goldstein to faculty, e-mail, May 31, 2001; "Dean Is Staying," *Alumni Journal*, fall 2001. Bollinger named: Karen W. Arenson, "University of Michigan President Is Nominated to Lead Columbia," *Times*, October 4, 2001.

20. Plans: Karen W. Arenson, "Dean of Journalism School Is Stepping Down at Columbia," *Times*, January 25, 2002; resignation statement: Goldstein to faculty and staff, e-mail, January 24, 2002. Search: Provost Jonathan Cole to "Fellow Columbians," e-mail, March 26, 2002.

## 39. "CLEARLY INSUFFICIENT"

1. Candidates: "No Secrets in Columbia's Search for J-School Dean," *Chronicle of Higher Education*, June 20, 2002; "Columbia Contest Now Down to Two," New York *Daily News*, Online Hot Copy, July 12, 2002. Biographies: "Faculty Homepage for Alex Jones," http://ksgnotes1.harvard.edu/degreeprog; "James Fallows, National Correspondent," http://www.theatlantic.com/about/people/jfbio.htm.

2. Search suspended: David Klatell, e-mail to alumni, July 24, 2001, enclosing Bollinger to "Dear Colleagues"; Karen W. Arenson, "Columbia President, Rethinking Journalism School's Mission, Suspends Search for New Dean," *Times*, July 24, 2002.

3. Reaction: Felicity Barringer, "Worry Voiced Over Comments on Journalism at Columbia," *Times*, July 25, 2002. See also many statements by graduates filed to the school's alumni online class addresses.

4. Varadarajan: "A Matter of Degree: Which One Makes a Journalist?" *Wall Street Journal*, July 26, 2002. Janeway: "Rethinking the Lessons of Journalism School," *Times*, August 17, 2002. Wolff: "Class Dismissed," *New York* magazine, September 23, 2002 pp. 20, 22. Shafer: "Can J-School Be Saved?" *Slate*, October 7, 2002, http://slate.msn.com.

5. "Wide debate": David Klatell to alumni, September 23, 2002, enclosing Bollinger statement. Address to class: "Opening Day Remarks by President Lee C. Bollinger," www.jrn.columbia.edu/events/news/2002–08/; Klatell to alumni, September 4, 2002, School of Journalism Records.

6. "Task force": Klatell e-mail to alumni, September 23, 2002, enclosing Bollinger statement.

7. Task force meetings: "Bollinger Task Force Will Go On," Alumni Affairs, e-mail to class lists, December 3, 2002. Barringer story: "A Rewrite for a Journalism Curriculum," *Times*, February 22, 2003.

8. "Perfect university president": Lemann, "The Empathy Defense," *The New Yorker*, December 18, 2000, pp. 46–51. Selection of Lemann: Klatell e-mail to alumni, April 15, 2003, enclosing announcement; Karen W. Arenson, "Columbia Names New Dean For Its Journalism School," *Times*, April 16, 2003; Ben Casselman, "Lemann Selected to Be Next Journalism Dean," Columbia *Spectator*, April 16, 2003.

9. Bollinger, "Journalism Task Force Statement," http://www.jrn.columbia.edu/events/news/2003–04/taskforce.asp.

10. Lemann interviews: Karen W. Arenson, "Compelled by What He Didn't Learn, *Times*, May 14, 2003; "Newsweek.com interview with Lemann," April 17, 2003, http:www.msnbc.com/news/901849.asp.

## 40. HAS THE PULITZER IDEA SURVIVED?

1. Committee of Concerned Journalists, "A Statement of Concern" (1997), http://www.journalism.org/resources/guidelines/principles/concern.asp.

# INDEX